DEFEAT IN VICTORY

Jan Ciechanowski

POLISH AMBASSADOR TO THE UNITED STATES DURING THE WAR YEARS

DEFEAT
IN
VICTORY

1947

Doubleday & Company, Inc.

GARDEN CITY, NEW YORK

To Gladys

AUTHOR'S NOTE

THE quotations in my conversations with President Roosevelt and with officials of the American Government are not verbatim minutes. They are reconstructed from comprehensive personal notes of these conversations, as recorded by me immediately after they took place and while they were still fresh in my mind.

*No one will ever be rich enough to buy his enemies
by concessions.*

—BISMARCK

THE AUTHOR wishes to make grateful acknowledgment to Wladyslaw Besterman, former Press Attaché of the Polish Embassy in Washington, for his valuable advice and counsel.

FOREWORD

THIS BOOK is the true picture of events and trends of policy as I saw them developing on the Washington scene during the four and a half years of my last diplomatic mission as Ambassador of Poland in the United States.

It is a personal record of my observations and opinions written in all sincerity.

It is in no sense an official presentation of the Polish problem.

In those crucial years of the world war Washington was the center of fluctuating tendencies and currents of opinion which had a most important bearing on the shaping of the present world situation. They have profoundly affected all nations and all peoples. They belong to the history of our times.

I felt it my duty to place this study of that eventful period before the public.

JAN CIECHANOWSKI

CONTENTS

DEFEAT IN VICTORY

CHAPTER I

Getting Accredited

"COME IN, Mr. Ambassador, I am glad to welcome you. According to my mother, I appear to be the only Roosevelt you have not yet met."

With these friendly words President Roosevelt greeted me on the sunny morning of March 6, 1941, as I was ushered into his study at the White House by the genial George Summerlin, chief of the Diplomatic Protocol Division of the Department of State. I was paying my first official visit to the President for the purpose of presenting my credentials as the newly appointed Ambassador of the Republic of Poland.

Mr. Summerlin had told me that in order to avoid complications resulting from American neutrality in a world torn by Hitler's total war, the President had greatly simplified all protocol procedure. He had done away with formal receptions which had created embarrassing situations at the White House when German and other Axis satellites met and collided bodily with British and Allied envoys. However, I was not prepared to be received on this formal occasion with such human ease and gracious simplicity by President Roosevelt who was regarded by all my compatriots and, indeed, all Europeans, as the Man of Destiny.

As I shook hands with the President and took the chair he waved me to at the side of his desk, he carried on the conversation in an easy and smiling way. He told me that he knew of my former mission in the United States, when from 1925 to 1929 I had represented Poland in Washington. He said he had heard that I had then taken a keen interest in American life and politics.

"Having known America in those times, you will notice many changes," said the President.

I assured him that I had never ceased to observe the trend of

American policies and politics, that I had followed his enunciations, and that I was especially thrilled by the way in which he
appeared to be steering the course of his country since the war
started in Europe.

The President asked what had struck me especially as a European and a student of American politics. I replied that as a European I would venture to say that the United States was physically
neutral but ideologically involved in the war from the very outset. As a student of American politics, I had gained the impression that he was systematically working to prepare the American
people for the great part which the United States would undoubtedly be called upon to play, possibly actively in the war
itself, but certainly after the war, in the establishment of the
peace.

The President became thoughtful and, after a pause, said:
"That is a correct opinion. We are already becoming the arsenal
of the fighting democracies. Britain is doing wonders, but she
needs our help. Your Polish soldiers, airmen, and sailors are
fighting with traditional courage. So are the other Allies of Britain. But the Axis Powers are better prepared and very strong.
They are inflicting heavy losses. As you know, Churchill and I
are increasingly anxious regarding the life line of transport between this country and Britain. It is essential to the Allied effort.
I hope to keep America out of the war. But I keep my fingers
crossed. Germany threatens the whole world, not Europe alone,
and America is next in line should Britain be overpowered." The
President laughed and added: "I see that my informers were
right in saying that you understand our political background. I
am indeed endeavoring to make my fellow citizens world conscious, to lift them out of a home-townish foreign policy into one
of broad world vision. It is no easy matter. Why, even now isolationism still has quite a following."

The President then questioned me on the activities of the
Polish Government. He was interested to hear about the state of
our army and the personality of General Sikorski, then Polish
Prime Minister and Commander in Chief of our armed forces.
He was generous in his praise of the resistance of the Polish people
to ruthless Nazi oppression, and expressed his admiration for the
fact that Poland alone, of all the German-occupied nations, had

not produced a single Quisling. "Poland certainly deserves her independence and must regain it after this war," the President concluded. When I told him that General Sikorski would be happy to have an early opportunity of discussing with him matters concerning Poland's war effort, he replied with charming spontaneity: "I would like him to pay me a visit," and asked me to discuss the date and details with Secretary of State Hull.

Our conversation turned to the Lend-Lease Bill then under debate in Congress. I knew what great importance the President attached to this momentous measure. I expressed my admiration for his genius in devising this novel method of placing American production at the disposal of the fighting democracies without creating heavy and complicated indebtedness.

The President became quite animated when I broached this apparently favorite subject. "You see," he said, "we cannot afford to repeat the mistakes made in the last war. We then created an indebtedness of the Powers to the United States which could not be repaid and which caused a lot of bad feeling and intensified differences and resentment. I am glad you see the advantage of Lend-Lease not only as a help to the fighting democracies but also to the American people. I only wish more Americans realized that aspect and understood that it is not merely another form of aid to Britain, but a wise American investment as well."

My visit was drawing to an end. President Roosevelt leaned toward me and said with engaging earnestness: "Now, my dear Ambassador, I hope you will be happy in Washington. I want you to feel that you may always come to me if you want to talk matters over with me directly, and never hesitate to call upon me if you think I can help you in carrying out your mission. Is there anything now that you would like to touch upon?"

"Mr. President," I replied, "if I may really take advantage of your kind permission, I would like to ask you very frankly to advise me on the scope of my activities. I represent a fighting country overrun by the enemy. I have no economic or other advantages to offer to the United States for the time being. The assets of fighting Poland are exclusively of a military and moral nature at present. Above all, they consist of our Allied loyalty, of our readiness to continue this struggle to the bitter end regardless of sacrifice, and of the fighting spirit of our military and of our civilians. Those being our only assets, I feel it my duty to interpret them to the American people. On the other hand, from some of the conversations I have had with my friends at the State Department, I sensed that too great an activity on my part might be regarded as embarrassing in view of American neutrality, and I felt that I was being discouraged from becoming too active and expected, by some at least, to remain passive. I would be most grateful for your ruling in this matter, Mr. President."

The President replied with emphasis: "I am glad you did not hesitate to bring this matter up. I could not advise you if you had not asked me to do so. I want you to feel free to act as the full-fledged Ambassador of a free country and a great nation. You must not curb your activities. As representative of Poland you have advantages in America which less fortunate Ambassadors of other countries do not have. The millions of Americans of Polish descent are the natural and most responsive group of Poland's American allies in this country. I know that you kept in close touch with them during your previous mission, being a pupil of my old friend Paderewski. Do not neglect them now. I want you to do your utmost for your country here. I want you to re-establish your contacts with these American Poles, to address them frequently. You should enlist the sympathy of all Americans who can assist you in developing the traditionally friendly feeling for Poland in America.

"Do not neglect anything. Build up your contacts. Address American audiences on war problems. Make them realize Poland's war effort. I will go further. You can be very useful to the common cause by explaining the European situation and showing the urgency there is of speeding up American production of war matériel which our communists are trying to prevent.

"I want you to know that personally I have a deep feeling for the Americans of Polish descent, not merely because they voted for me so overwhelmingly in the last three elections," added the President jovially, "but because they are very good citizens, conscious of their duties and always loyal Americans.

"You will have quite a lot to do explaining to the American people that Poland is a democracy. Personally, I know that she is, because I happen to know history. But you will find, if you do not already know, that very few Americans ever bother about history or geography. They are apt to think that because for some time Poland was represented here by an aristocrat, all Poland is feudal and composed of aristocratic landowners. They do not realize that for centuries Poland was the advanced outpost of Western liberalism and culture in eastern Europe. German propaganda has been at work and has inspired the idea that Poland's troubles are due to her own bad politics and reactionary ideas. I know and you know that for centuries Poland has been, above all, the perennial victim of geography. Her role in every war proves it. But the story must be told and often repeated. It is your mission to do so. And I will back your efforts. But please remember, when speaking about the war, when trying to make your American audiences conscious of its implications, do not narrow your scope to Poland alone.

"Make use of all the advantages I have mentioned for the Allied cause. Lend a helping hand to your country's fighting Allies who lack your Polish advantages. Especially to Britain who, unfortunately, still has many critics here.

"As a Pole who witnessed war developments in France and the Battle of Britain in England, you can speak about the British war effort more effectively than Lord Halifax can as an Englishman. Do not forget the smaller Allies, such as gallant little Luxemburg.

"Let no one discourage you from becoming an active ambassador.

"America became actively involved in the last war and yet failed to play her part in the peace. Even now many of our people do not understand how interdependent the modern world has become. They still refer to the Atlantic and Pacific oceans as natural defenses. Above all, they still make the mistake of thinking that giving up the Polish Corridor and Danzig might have averted this war, although it is so evident today that this is a conflict not only for territorial expansion, but one inevitably brought about by the clash of irreconcilable ideologies and aims.

"I feel like you, Mr. Ambassador, that, if democracy is to win, my fellow countrymen will have to understand that this is a war in defense of fundamental democratic principles. And, as we say in this country, 'we Americans will have to buy this war as such.' Let us hope at the price of Lend-Lease only. But who can say what price we may ultimately have to pay to preserve our way of life in a future peaceful world? The threat to America is a direct one, and the sooner the American people realize it, the greater the chance of sparing humanity the prolongation of the tragic plight in which this war has placed it. And now I must say good-by, and I hope to see you soon again."

As I rose to take leave, the President smiled broadly and said: "Oh, by the way, we are forgetting that we had a formality to perform. George Summerlin would never forgive me. I see you have brought the envelopes containing your President's letter accrediting you to me as Ambassador, and your speech, the copy of which I have already read. Let me take them over and hand you in exchange this envelope containing my speech to you. Good luck to you, Mr. Ambassador."

We shook hands very warmly, and I thanked the President for his kindness. He pressed a bell. Mr. Summerlin reappeared in the doorway and escorted me out.

As I recorded in writing that memorable conversation, my memory carried me back to the time when, after nearly four years in Washington, I had informally called to say a final good-by to President Coolidge on February 22, 1929, on the eve of my departure for Europe.

I tried to analyze the contrast between Mr. Coolidge and President Roosevelt as I saw it after my first meeting with Mr. Roosevelt. It was not only the contrast between a Republican and a Democratic leader. It was more profound than that. There was a deep difference from every point of view. There was the difference between Mr. Coolidge's New England temperament and Mr. Roosevelt's more cosmopolitan New York background. There was the difference between the rugged northern farmer strain and that of a more internationally minded statesman with European experience, intensely interested in world history and geography, and endowed with a wide creative vision.

I asked myself to what extent President Roosevelt could be regarded as the embodiment of a new America, more world-minded, more ready to understand and to take part in problems affecting other countries. Was he merely an exception among his fellow Americans, destined to succeed or to fail in his attempt to lead them to the wider horizons which he so clearly embraced?

It would be one of my tasks to study this question on which so much depended as far as the future world was concerned.

I had been a personal admirer of President Coolidge and had always kept a warm feeling for him. Notwithstanding his reputation of being a silent, laconic, and somewhat austere man, he had invariably treated me with great kindness and had conversed with me in a friendly way, perhaps because he knew how sincerely interested I was in America and probably because one of his closest political friends, the late Jimmie C. White, had been such a close and dear friend of mine. I vividly remember my last conversation with Mr. Coolidge who, like myself, in those last days of February 1929 was supervising the packing of his personal belongings prior to leaving Washington. Jimmie White accompanied me on this informal occasion.

When I told President Coolidge that the fact that he also was leaving made me regret my departure less, he asked bluntly: "Why should that make it more easy for you? I regret having to leave Washington."

I asked if in view of the informality of the occasion I might ask him a direct question. He said I could do so. I asked why, if he felt so much regret at leaving his post, he had withdrawn his candidacy by declaring "I do not choose to run." Mr. Coolidge was silent for a moment. He turned to me with a frown and replied: "Very soon America will go through the Goddamnedest financial and economic crash. It will shake the world. American people refuse to see it coming. What they need is a few years of Democratic misrule. That is why I did not care to run and regret that Hoover did."

I remembered some of my other visits to the White House in the Coolidge days and diplomatic receptions at which President Coolidge exchanged a few words with me. I recalled one particular reception when, after shaking hands, he told me he had read reports of a speech I had made in Chicago at a mass meeting of Americans of Polish descent. He said: "I appreciate their qualities. They are good and honest citizens and hard workers. They know where to come for advice. I was their lawyer in Vermont." He paused for a moment, then continued: "They paid promptly."

Those words appeared to me to express Mr. Coolidge's realistic approach to all subjects. In his heart he was intensely human; in fact, truly American, but his New England strain caused him to express himself with a blunt sincerity and a downrightness almost Scotch in its terseness.

During my mission he had in a most tactful way helped me considerably, without outwardly appearing to do so, when in lengthy negotiations I worked for two years on the finally successful monetary stabilization plan and loan for Poland.

What would have been his attitude had he, instead of President Roosevelt, been at the White House during this war? What would have been his relationship with the Britain of Winston Churchill? What would have been his policy in the face of the danger which was so rapidly spreading and threatening the United States and the whole world?

I marveled at the wisdom of Providence who had decreed that in peacetime the rugged and austere Coolidge—an intensely American President who applied in a simple but dignified way the policies of his Republican party, a stickler for economy in government—should lead the United States, while at this time of world conflict, when a new era of imponderables and of unique chances for greatness was opening for America, a broad-minded, creative statesman should hold the steering wheel of this great country—a man capable of devising as bold a plan as the Lend-Lease system, while preserving American neutrality.

After my first conversation with President Roosevelt I felt that the defense of democratic principles, of the freedom of the individual, was safe in his hands. I had the feeling that he fully realized the scope of the menace created by Hitler. I understood that he, and the American people through him, conscious of acute danger, fully appreciated the bulldog qualities of the indomitable Winston Churchill, and that while they were not yet decided when and how to "purchase" the war and how openly and actively to espouse the common cause, their decision was already in the making.

I had the vision of a United States at the head of a future peace table. I saw Mr. Roosevelt dictating, not imperialist demands, but, steering clear of "entangling" alliances, introducing into a new postwar world the law which would serve alike the powerful and the weak. I was impressed by his great simplicity and his proverbial charm of which I had heard so much from American and British friends.

There flashed before my eyes the desperate fight of the Polish Army against Hitler's motorized hordes in September 1939; the activities of our government which I had joined in Paris on September 30, 1939, as Secretary General of our Foreign Office; General Sikorski, who stubbornly pursued one aim: that Poland should fight on against the German onslaught on every available front, regardless of sacrifices, thus holding her place as a fighting ally; I recalled his difficulties in re-forming the Polish Army in France and, later, after the collapse of France, once again in Britain.

I reviewed the evolution of French defeatism as I had seen it unfold on the spot in that winter of 1939; the strategic and moral hopelessness of the Maginot Line; the drama of the collapse of France in June 1940; the unforgettable and tragic June days at Bordeaux where the Polish Government, at the request of the Reynaud Government, had followed it from Angers, the seat of the Polish President and Government during the campaign in France; the last conversations of our Foreign Minister, August Zaleski, with the French Prime Minister, Reynaud, in Bordeaux with the Minister of the Interior, Mandel, with General Weygand and Marshal Pétain; the unhesitating determination of the Polish Government and our military command to stand by Britain and continue the fight, regardless of the attitude of crumbling France, led to defeat by a group of cynical and demoralized politicians.

I thought of the provincial hall of the temporary seat of the French Government in Bordeaux, when Zaleski was ushered into Premier Reynaud's study on June 15, 1940. A cabinet meeting was being held continuously in the adjoining room. The final fight, led by the intrepid Mandel, against the pessimism of the tired Weygand and the cynicism of Reynaud and other members of the Cabinet, was proceeding. It was being decided whether France would fight on, possibly to a glorious defeat, or would ingloriously give up the fight and throw herself on the mercy of Hitler.

Reynaud looked tired and preoccupied as he joined Zaleski, who informed him that the President of Poland would like to know what line of defense the French Government would adopt. He added that General Sikorski was still at the headquarters of the Polish Army directing the action of the divisions fighting on the Maginot Line.

In his reply Reynaud disclosed that the tendency was growing among his colleagues in the French Cabinet to ask Germany for an immediate armistice. Weygand had declared that he could no longer stem the tide. The morale of the French Army was impaired and communism was rife in some parts of France. "We are compelled to face realities," said Reynaud.

Zaleski was shocked. "Such a decision would be catastrophic. Why not fight on even if it means retreating to the Mediterranean, crossing over to North Africa, thus saving the entire French fleet and air force and what can still be saved of the French Army? Why not continue resistance from Africa? There is no possibility of concluding any armistice with Hitler on acceptable terms. It would be a capitulation with all its terrible consequences."

"You are wrong, my dear Zaleski," replied Reynaud. "You think of France in terms applicable to Poland vis-à-vis of the Germans, who persistently regard themselves as a superior race compared to the Polish nation which Germany is determined to enslave and to annex. France is in an entirely different position. The position of France with regard to Germany is that of an attractive and desirable woman persistently courted by a suitor whose advances she has always turned down in the past. When France gives up and asks for an armistice, Germany will be so agreeably surprised and so flattered that we will have no difficulty in obtaining from Hitler—who, after all, is a soldier— honorable conditions as a fighting nation reasonably convinced that it is better to give up than to pursue a hopeless struggle to inevitable defeat."

Zaleski was so taken aback by this surprising statement that for a while he remained silent. Then he said with unusual force: "My dear Prime Minister, it is you who are making a terrible mistake. The Germans know no chivalry. Look at their behavior in Poland, in Belgium, in Holland. Hitler will trample France as he trampled other defeated countries. He gives no quarter. He is ruthless and barbaric, and has none of the finer instincts nor any respect for weakness. . . . And what about France's alliances? The Franco-British, the Franco-Polish alliance? How could France break her pledges by concluding a separate peace? I cannot imagine a France unfaithful to her glorious traditions."

"Unfortunately," replied Reynaud, "it is a case of *force majeure*. Even Churchill understands. He realizes that we cannot hold out. He no longer insists on the terms of the alliance. France, like Poland, has found that the Germans are too well prepared militarily and too strong. We must now bear the consequences."

"But," said Zaleski, "have you considered the situation of the Polish Government in these circumstances? What about our army which has done so much and is now still fighting so gallantly to cover the retreat of the French troops from the east? We are not a nation who capitulates."

"Well," replied Reynaud, "the only thing I can say is that if you will cast your lot with ours and join us in asking for an armistice, we will do all we can in the armistice negotiations to obtain the best possible conditions for your government, your army, and the numerous immigrants and refugees from Poland now in France. What alternative have you? Where could you go? Your army is engaged with the enemy and you have neither enough ships nor planes to evacuate them. But, even if you had, where would you take them? Do you believe that Britain alone can continue to resist Hitler's aggression? She would soon be forced to follow our lead in asking for an armistice. France can hope to obtain better conditions from Germany, being the first of the Allies to give up resistance. That is the opinion of most of my colleagues in the Cabinet.

"But," added Reynaud, "don't rely exclusively on my opinion. Talk to Weygand; he may convince you. He has always been a friend of Poland. Of course you will find that Mandel still holds out for continued resistance. Personally, as Premier, I must face facts. I have decided to adopt an impartial attitude and to let matters follow their course in the cabinet meetings, but, while the Cabinet has not yet taken a final decision, I foresee that the majority will be for an armistice rather than risk prolonging a futile resistance. Pétain may head a new government. With his great military past he might be in a better position to bargain acceptable armistice terms. Apart from that, the venerable defender of Verdun at the head of the Cabinet would make the French people accept the inevitable more easily."

"But," objected Zaleski, "you are making a great mistake. The Germans will admit no negotiations. No bargaining will be possible. They will impose harsh terms, whoever heads your government."

Reynaud's face hardened. "I have told you frankly the position of France. As I see it, the Cabinet's final decision is but a matter of hours. It may vote today. I may succeed in delaying the vote until tomorrow, but probably no longer. And the Polish Government had better come to a prompt decision."

"I will immediately report to our President and General Sikorski," said Zaleski. "I can say now that, whatever the French Government decides to do, the Polish Government and Army will not capitulate. How long have we got to leave France should you decide to sue for an armistice?"

"Three to four days, I should say, at the most," coldly replied Reynaud.

Later that day Zaleski had a conversation with Mandel. He reported to him his conversation with Reynaud. Mandel threw up his hands and said in his terse way: "Reynaud lied to you. The French people can still be roused, and they want to resist the enemy. They have guts, and under suitable leadership would respond to their tradition and continue to fight. Our misfortune lies in the lack of sound and honest leadership. What Reynaud told you about the spread of communism is also untrue. There is no serious menace of communism in France. I have verified this personally. I have proved it to the Cabinet. The evil influences at work to make France surrender are invoking this convenient pretext without foundation."

"But, for goodness sake," said Zaleski, "why don't you, with your courage, take matters in hand? Why don't you and your political friends go to any length, even risking a *coup d'état,* if you know that such is the attitude of the French nation?"

"Ah," replied Mr. Mandel, "I would not hesitate to do so, but you must not forget that I am a Jew. These are different times from those when I served under Clemenceau. Many things have happened since. The Blum cabinets have passed through French history and left their scars. Above all, the forces of moral degradation are too strong. I could not get a sufficient following to oppose them. I am already being closely watched by them, lest I do what you suggest and what I would have no hesitation in doing if among our politicians and military leaders I could rally enough sound and determined men to support me. Unfortunately, it cannot be done. But I do not despair. I am still doing all I can to stem the growing defeatism in the Cabinet. I will prevent the decision being taken today. Maybe I can still hold out and perhaps tomorrow better counsels will prevail. I am getting the prefects of the various provinces to influence the decision. Come and see me tomorrow. . . ."

I vividly remembered the sudden arrival at Bordeaux of General Sikorski on June 17. He had not realized at the front the seriousness of the political situation. He held rapid conferences with President Raczkiewicz and Zaleski and decided immediately to see Churchill.

There followed his dramatic flight to London; his interview with the British Prime Minister about saving what could still be saved of the Polish Army and air force by transporting them to England and re-forming them in Britain so that Poland could continue to fight at the side of her British ally.

I recalled the circumstances of Mr. Churchill's decision to do all that the British Navy could do to save Poland's forces and its government and bring them to England; the silent, efficient, and splendid way in which this was carried out. I relived the voyage of the Polish President and members of the Cabinet, whom I accompanied on the cruiser *Arethusa* to England; the three nights of futile bombing of that cruiser by single German planes as she lay in the port of Le Verdon near Bordeaux before we could put to sea; President Raczkiewicz's arrival at the railroad station in London, to be met by King George in person, the King having considered it his duty to welcome to England the President of the Polish Republic, the only remaining ally of Great Britain.

I reviewed the conversations of General Sikorski and of members of our government and particularly those of Zaleski and myself with Lord Halifax, with Undersecretary Sir Alexander Cadogan and other members of the British Cabinet; the difficulties I had in reorganizing once again the disrupted Polish Foreign

Office. Then the blackout, the Battle of Britain with the blitz and all its horrors.

While our government was still in France in the spring of 1940 and later, when it had installed itself in London, General Sikorski had several times expressed his wish to have me appointed to the post of Ambassador of Poland in Washington.

At that time I was so engrossed by my work as Secretary General of the Polish Foreign Office and so anxious to remain in the center of war events in Europe, that I asked him to delay this appointment. I was convinced that I could be more useful in Washington later, after having gained more direct experience of British and European developments and war policies.

In the beginning of November 1940, as my chief, Foreign Minister Zaleski, and I were walking from the Polish Foreign Office in Queen's Gate to lunch at the St. James's Club in Piccadilly, we met General Sikorski, who was on his way to the Foreign Office to speak with Zaleski and me on what he said was an urgent matter. He walked with us for a few minutes and told us that he had finally made up his mind to ask President Raczkiewicz to appoint me as Ambassador to Washington. The presidential election had just taken place. Mr. Roosevelt had been re-elected by an overwhelming majority. A new phase was opening in America. General Sikorski considered that American neutrality could not be indefinitely maintained. In his opinion, it was important and even urgent that Poland should be represented in Washington by a man who had been in closest contact with European war events in France and in London. He therefore insisted that the necessary formalities of obtaining an *agrément* for me from President Roosevelt be immediately started.

After that conversation I was summoned by the President of Poland who told me that he shared entirely the view of General Sikorski and asked me to accept the nomination. My *agrément* was duly asked for and obtained. After winding up my duties at our Foreign Office, I left London on February 5, 1941, with my wife and my two younger sons (my eldest son, John, was already in the Polish Army in Scotland), and proceeded to Washington via Lisbon.

And now, here I was in the United States, once more given the opportunity of representing Poland. In my first interview with President Roosevelt, he had encouraged me to do my utmost, to be active, to feel free in my work for Poland, for Europe, and the Allied cause.

The President's words of understanding and encouragement evoked in my mind the splendid words of Winston Churchill to Sikorski when the latter appealed to him on June 18, 1940, to transfer the Polish Armed Forces to Britain: "Tell your army in France," Mr. Churchill had said, "that we are their comrades in life and in death. We shall conquer together or we shall die together." The two Prime Ministers, one the leader of a free Britain, the other of a martyred but undying Poland, shook hands. "That handshake," Sikorski told us later, "meant more to me than any signed treaty of alliance or any pledged word." The Polish-British alliance was reaffirmed and cemented.

And now to these words forever engraved in my heart I could add the encouraging words of Mr. Roosevelt. They filled me with new hope.

CHAPTER II

Lend-Lease Points the Way, April 1941

As I STUDIED the Washington political scene in the spring of 1941 and talked at length with Secretary of State Hull, Undersecretary of State Sumner Welles, James C. Dunn, and Loy Henderson of the State Department, as well as with political and press personalities, I gained the impression that the United States was passing through a period of transition from neutrality to increasingly active support of Great Britain and her Allies at war with the Axis.

However, it was still generally hoped that it would be possible to avoid active involvement in the conflict.

A study of President Roosevelt's tactics at that time was in itself a liberal education. He was gradually leading American public opinion to a more complete understanding that the war had become a direct menace to America.

While asserting his leadership, he was doing so in a very subtle and almost imperceptible way, avoiding moves which might be interpreted as an attempt to impose too definite a direction toward active American participation in the war. He was sounding out public opinion and, simultaneously, helping it to crystallize into a state of alertness and preparedness.

The heated debate in Congress on the President's Lend-Lease program deserved special attention. The nature of the attacks against the Lend-Lease plan showed that they were rather what is currently called in French political language *mouvements de mauvaise humeur,* aimed at forcing the President into the open by trying to provoke him into a more direct declaration of policy. At the same time such criticism expressed the growing apprehension that the President was assuming a dictatorial course to the detriment of the jealously guarded rights of Congress. The debate was clearly another round in the duel between the President and his opponents in the legislative body on the issue of congressional rights (allegedly menaced by the tendency toward executive dictatorship).

The Lend-Lease debate was also a final outburst of isolationism on the part of a diehard group, and yet, as soon as the Lend-Lease Bill had been overwhelmingly passed, senators and congressmen vied with one another to prove that they understood the necessity of the Lend-Lease measure. In their enunciations they took pains to explain that, because they so definitely opposed direct American participation in the war, they realized that material support to Britain and her Allies should be as extensive and effective as possible, in order to strengthen the fighting countries and enable them to defeat the Axis without armed support of the United States.

These tendencies fluctuated in direct proportion to the news from the fighting fronts. When the British campaign in North Africa and the magnificent fight of the Greeks appeared to be a promising venture; when Yugoslavia entered the war on the side of the Allies on April 6, 1941, and Turkey's participation appeared probable, approval of the President's policy of support to the Allies increased. When, shortly after a period of undue optimism, news of British setbacks in Africa and in the Balkans began to appear, this optimistic atmosphere gave way to pessimism and the psychosis of Germany's invincibility made its reappearance.

I noted a growing and impatient expectation on the part of public opinion for the President's more definite leadership—an expectation subconsciously accentuated by the increased dangers of the situation created by British military setbacks. The President, however, a past master in timing his moves, continued carefully to allow American opinion to guess the direction in which he would ultimately lead it. I felt that, while his mind was probably made up gradually and methodically to align the United States with the fighting democracies, the President was desirous of creating the impression that his leadership, when he finally assumed it, would be the expression of an already determined American public opinion.

The visit of General Sikorski to the President, which took place at the end of March 1941, helped me to clarify my understanding of American policy in that period.

General Wladyslaw Sikorski, Premier of the Polish Government and Commander in Chief of the Polish Army, had come as the leader of the growing Polish armed forces which had already proved their valor and their importance to Britain in Norway, in France, and in the Battle of Britain, on land, on sea, and in the air.

General Sikorski was eager to follow up President Roosevelt's words to me during our first conversation, that "Lend-Lease material would be available for Poland's war effort." He also felt it was urgent to draw the attention of the President and of American public opinion to the inhuman oppression which the Germans were inflicting upon the Polish nation, and to obtain an official American declaration or intervention which would serve as a warning to Hitler.

In discussing this subject with the President, General Sikorski made an impassioned plea, describing with force and in detail the plight of the European nations oppressed under German occupation. He stressed the inhuman cruelty which Hitler's gangs were imposing on the Jewish populations. He presented a memorandum to the President describing the ghettos and the barbarous humiliations inflicted upon the Jews in Poland, the atrocities of which the Germans were guilty in their methodical destruction of the most patriotic Polish elements, and the particular ferocity with which they were liquidating our intellectuals. This report, couched in the sober language of a soldier, impressed President Roosevelt. He urged Sikorski to take advantage of his press interviews and conversations with American political personalities to arouse public opinion by informing it of "these dastardly acts which should not remain unpunished."

But Sikorski did not come only as a Pole. He came as the spokesman of the smaller European Powers, anxious to ascertain to what degree the future of a civilized and democratically organized Europe could count on the backing of America.

In his conversations with the President, with the heads of the State and War departments, of the Treasury, and of the General Staff, he was the first European since the outbreak of the war boldly to present in Washington the case of postwar Europe. He was the first to initiate the idea of European federation as the best way of creating political and economic security.

I noticed that he made a favorable impression on the President. The handsome, erect soldier, refined of manner and direct of speech, with a ready smile and a twinkle in his blue eyes, approached the subjects which he had come to discuss with soldierly directness. His conversations with the President usually started in French, but both the President and Sikorski appeared to prefer to use their native tongues, and as the talks became more animated I had to undertake the role of interpreter.

The President showed marked interest in Sikorski's plan for a future federated Europe. Sikorski explained to the President his idea of an initial confederation of Poland and Czechoslovakia to which Poland desired to see added the three Baltic States, and, in time, possibly Hungary, Rumania, Greece, and Yugoslavia. He pointed to the advantages of such a system of federation which, among other benefits, would help to ease the friction which for so long had existed between Hungary and Czechoslovakia, and withdraw Hungary from German influences and pressure.

The President repeatedly expressed his approval. He thought it "a great idea." He said he approved it in principle and congratulated Sikorski on what he had already done in laying the foundation with Beneš, for a Polish-Czechoslovak confederation. He admitted having misgivings as to how successful Sikorski might be in bringing the other nations mentioned into such a federation. But he emphatically endorsed the principle as a sound one, because it was the best way of unifying interests and cultures. He called Sikorski's plan one "of great importance not only from the viewpoint of general security, but as a basis of local security and understanding regionally conceived."

"Frontiers," said the President, "must not remain barriers between nations. Real frontiers are those which delimit regions of similar culture and civilization, and they should be regarded as the natural limits of areas inhabited by nations of kindred culture."

"So you do approve of federation, Mr. President?" asked Sikorski.

"I certainly do," replied the President. "How could it be

otherwise? The United States is the best example of the blessings of federation."

When Sikorski tried to ascertain the views of the President regarding the chances of enlarging the Polish-Czechoslovak confederation to include the Baltic States, President Roosevelt laughingly said: "You may be faced with some difficulties on the part of your eastern neighbor who has already declared these small democracies to be part of the Soviet Union."

"Am I to regard this as final, Mr. President?" asked Sikorski.

"I see no reason why you should," replied the President. "I refer you to our strong official declaration on the Baltic States made last year by Sumner Welles, which you probably remember. As far as the United States is concerned, we stand by it. Your Ambassador will tell you that his colleagues, the Ministers of Lithuania, Latvia, and Esthonia, are quite active in Washington. It is one of our basic policies not to recognize unilateral changes brought about by force or threat of force, especially in wartime. We do not contemplate changing this principle. For ten years we have been steadily refusing to recognize the Japanese seizure of Manchuria."

The President confirmed to Sikorski his attitude expressed to me during my first visit at the White House. He said that he was chiefly concerned in preparing American public opinion for a mighty effort of industrial production. He urged Sikorski to go on a speaking tour, to address Americans of Polish descent, and to give press interviews in such centers as Chicago, Detroit, Buffalo, and New York.

This appeared to me all the more characteristic of President Roosevelt's policy, because in my conversations with officials of the Department of State, in discussing the details of the general's visit, it had been repeatedly hinted to me that Sikorski should limit himself to a visit in Washington and possibly a short stop in New York. Again I had been told that, in view of American neutrality, public speeches by a representative of a country at war with the Axis and too much personal publicity should be avoided.

I had reported this attitude of the Department of State to General Sikorski, who asked the President whether he approved of a short visit to Chicago, the center of American-Polish activities.

"My dear General," said the President, "I want to ask you not to neglect this matter during your visit. Even if it means prolonging your stay in America, I ask you to find time to go around addressing American audiences and particularly audiences of Americans of Polish descent. Certainly Chicago is their greatest center. But I want to ask you particularly to go to Detroit. On the effort of that great industrial center of production depends in large measure what Churchill and I are so anxious about at this time, as you well know. In fact, for the time being, at least, on the production of war matériel in Detroit largely depends the success of our great scheme of becoming the arsenal of democracy.

"The Lend-Lease Act has now been passed," the President continued, "but putting it into effect as regards production is not plain sailing. Communist influences inspired from abroad are trying to disrupt our efforts. These elements are especially active in Detroit. We must not neglect any opportunity of counteracting this dangerous work. Your visit there is most timely and can be very useful to our common cause."

"I am glad to hear you say so, Mr. President," said Sikorski.

"I am particularly anxious that you should help us in this way," insisted the President, "because I want you to present to the American people your broad views on problems as you have expressed them to me. It will be most valuable to the common cause at this particular time. Please go to Buffalo as well. That is a personal request I make. I have a special sentiment for that city where, incidentally, you have a very fine group of American Poles. You should get in touch with them, and I hope you will be able to do so."

In Detroit, where I accompanied Sikorski, I had the opportunity of verifying the accuracy of President Roosevelt's reference to the communist propaganda against the war effort. On the day of our arrival a local communist paper came out with this streamer headline: "The warmonger Sikorski, representing capitalism and the Wall Street-Downing Street Axis, comes here."

Undersecretary Sumner Welles, whom Sikorski first met in London in 1940, was the man who, after the President, impressed the general most. Behind the classically cold façade of the diplomat, Mr. Welles showed a profound and informed interest in all the topics we discussed with him.

General Sikorski who, as a soldier, liked to joke about diplomats and diplomacy, said to me smilingly as we were leaving the State Department after one of his conversations with Mr. Welles: "All you diplomats should take example from this man who says so little, knows so much, and appears to understand everything."

To Sikorski's plan for a federated postwar Central-Eastern Europe Sumner Welles seemed to be as sympathetic as the President.

The promise of granting Lend-Lease matériel to the Polish Army was reaffirmed by the President, who told us that he regarded Poland's war effort as a substantial contribution to the Allied cause. Permission was also given to raise volunteer detachments of the Polish Army among Americans of Polish descent. We gained the certainty that there was not the slightest doubt in the minds of any of the military or civilian American officials we met as to Poland's status as a full-fledged partner in the struggle.

The speech of President Roosevelt on the twenty-seventh of May 1941 was another milestone on the road upon which he led the United States to preparedness for eventual participation in the war. He proclaimed the American nation in a state of "national emergency." He definitely placed the United States in the role of "arsenal of democracy."

In his speech he not only alerted the United States but the entire Western Hemisphere. In fact Hitler was told that he had to reckon with the Americas. Moreover, the President defined what the peoples of the Americas would consider as aggression. He stated that America would regard itself as directly menaced if Germany should, through effective weakening of the British Fleet, endanger the line of American defense and communications in the Atlantic, or attempt to establish bases in the Iberian Peninsula or the African continent, or in Greenland, or the Cape Verde Islands.

Thus American policy had gone further than could have been anticipated. And it went further at a time when Hitler's victories made it possible and even probable that he would try to test the sincerity of this declaration by occupying one of the enumerated territories.

It was not only a speech with a definite note of warning to

Hitler. It was in reality a very definite challenge, made at a time when the United States was certainly not prepared for war and when Great Britain was in a precarious situation.

I realized then that President Roosevelt was not only a determined statesman who had made up his mind, but also a great gambler, ready to take considerable risks for mighty stakes.

But the most momentous fact of that period, as I saw it shaping in the shadow of the White House, was that the American people were being slowly but surely roused to the danger of a totalitarian new order being forced upon a world from which they could no longer remain isolated. And the American people were beginning to sit up and take notice.

The President had not yet sounded the trumpet for actual battle. But he was rallying his countrymen to the defense of the fundamental principles of freedom and democracy, and the call was being heeded by a people who for years had been lulled into isolation by the fallacy of the security of oceans, by their love of peace and easy living, by prosperity gained by hard work and efficiency.

America was becoming tensely alert to the rumblings which she had previously mistaken for just another Old World war and was beginning to ask herself if the time to act was coming. Her somewhat aloof interest in a distant conflict was gradually turning into indignation against the tidal wave of totalitarian aggression from which she had felt immune.

The growing realization that it was necessary to be prepared to stand up and fight for the survival of principles which meant life itself for America was opening the way to the next stage of war preparedness in which the unlimited enterprise of a young and free people was once again to be so fully tested and more triumphantly reasserted than it had ever been before.

CHAPTER III

"Change Partners," June 1941

ALTHOUGH in April and May 1941 various indications already pointed to a deterioration in the friendly collaboration of nearly two years' standing between Germany and Soviet Russia, the news of Hitler's sudden attack on Soviet Russia in the early hours of June 22 was unexpected in Washington, to say the least. It was less surprising to the Polish Government which, since March 1941, had been receiving through the Underground organization and passing on to the Allies news of ominous German troop concentrations in Poland.

The news of the German attack reached me in New York. I was anxious to get in touch with American official circles without delay.

I telephoned to Harry Hopkins in Washington and asked if he could spend the evening with me. As he had already accepted an invitation to dine that night with the British Military Attaché, General Beaumont Nesbitt, a very close friend of mine, I flew to Washington and joined them at dinner.

To observe Paddy Nesbitt and Harry Hopkins together was an interesting study in contrasts.

General Frederick Beaumont Nesbitt, tall, exceptionally handsome, and youthful, gracefully combined the upstanding dignity and dapper military perfection of the British Grenadier guardsman with all the human charm of his Irish extraction which had gained him the nickname of "Paddy." Before being appointed to the post of Military Attaché of the British Embassy in the early spring of 1941, he had been for three years D. M. I. (Director of Military Intelligence) at the British War Office.

Harry Hopkins, by general consensus of opinion, was the closest and most mysterious collaborator of President Roosevelt—in fact a power behind the throne of American democracy.

.He appeared to me as a combination of absolute New Deal fidelity to "the great White Chief," of machine-like efficiency and burning energy; of unlimited capacity for work with the most downright, cynical, and witty humor; caustic, ruthless, and untrammeled by any human considerations. He evoked in my mind the famous saying of Clemenceau about Briand: "He knows nothing and understands everything."

I was deeply interested in this mystery man whose frail body, racked by ill-health and overwork, made his unbounded vitality appear even more astounding.

I had met Hopkins before and was most attracted by his exuberant personality. This evening, however, Hopkins's opinions on the German attack on the Soviets, characterized by his usual downrightness, were presented in a more serious vein.

He told us that, in view of the tense situation on the western front and the very difficult position of Britain, the President was inclined to regard the German aggression against Russia as a favorable development. The Germans were undertaking an additional operation on a great scale, which would compel them to throw considerable forces into the fight against their new opponent.

Paddy Nesbitt agreed with Hopkins that Germany had some 150 to 158 divisions on the eastern front. This certainly meant the dispersal of German forces and—though it appeared probable that Germany would be successful in her Russian campaign —it would greatly ease Britain's situation.

We all agreed that by attacking Russia and by conducting a lightning and successful campaign in the east, Germany hoped speedily to liquidate that front and then to turn all her forces against Britain. Therefore it was of the utmost importance not to allow this new war development to become an excuse for any reduction or delay in the American effort of production and transport of war matériel to Britain but, on the contrary, full advantage should be taken of the welcome respite.

Hopkins was clearly apprehensive on this score. "I am afraid," he said, "that the feeling that the respite granted to Britain through the German attack on the Soviets may have bad consequences in the United States. German propaganda will do its best to play it up. The German-Soviet war will supply the isolationists with new arguments and they will play upon American pacifist tendencies, especially on the latent anti-Soviet feelings of the American people. I am sure they will point to the advantage of letting Hitler rout the Soviets and destroy Russian communism which they will present as the greatest menace to the world.

"What I fear most, however," added Hopkins, "is that this further spread of the war will encourage those who, as you know, are now so insistently explaining that the President's duty is to arm America rather than England, and to keep American production on this side of the Atlantic. We will have the devil of a fight against this popular cry to cut down war transports to Great Britain on the plea that she is now running less risk."

Hopkins then turned to me and said that he was also apprehensive of the attitude of the Vatican and the Catholic elements in the United States, predominantly Irish, and, therefore, unfavorable to Britain and to the war. "I am afraid," he said, "that these elements will urge pacifism because they regard Soviet communism as the greatest danger of all."

I replied that, as far as I could see, the Vatican was clearly anti-totalitarian in its enunciations and disliked both nazism and communism as godless teachings.

"Do you think," I asked, "that a peace offensive, cleverly inspired here by German propaganda, could have any effect at this time?"

"I do not exclude it," replied Hopkins. "The isolationist and pro-German elements in this country have made some progress as a reaction to our efforts to raise war production. But I believe American public opinion will instinctively be against any compromise with Hitler. I may be wrong," he added, "but even if isolationist influences in that direction were to gain ground, I am convinced that the last word will be with the President, who always knows how to rally public opinion in the right direction at the right moment."

Hopkins foresaw that the President would undoubtedly make every effort to increase production of war matériel and speed its supply to Great Britain, while observing the development of the campaign in Russia without, for some time at least, too precisely defining the official attitude of the United States to the Soviets.

We discussed the encouragement the British people would draw from the German attack on Russia, but we agreed that in England there were also strong centers of pacifism, inclined toward a compromise peace.

Hopkins threw up his hands and said: "Ah! If only today we could give an answer to Churchill's eternal question: 'When will America finally join us against the common menace?' Of course we must give him the fullest support. There is complete understanding on this subject at the White House, but our public opinion is not yet ripe. The President has to proceed very cautiously and to time his policy step by step."

I was interested to note the contrast between the approach of Hopkins, so representative of the trend of American New Deal mentality, and that of the seasoned career diplomats of the State Department.

On the day after my dinner with Nesbitt and Hopkins I had a conversation on the same subjects with James C. Dunn of the Department of State. While he confirmed some of Hopkins's views, he said that one could now foresee as a first development of the situation that the labor elements in America, hitherto reluctant to speed up war production, would more readily cooperate and redouble their efforts to increase production in order to help Soviet Russia.

He thought the communists who, he said, had been so prominent in promoting strikes and protests, would now be the loudest in calling for an all-out war-production effort.

He told me that preliminary talks with the Soviet Ambassador concerning purchase of war matériel in America were about to begin but that, of course, this was merely theoretical for the time being, considering there was not enough war matériel to supply British needs and it would be a long time before any became available for the Soviets.

"After all," Mr. Dunn continued, "we must not forget that the United States itself is in need of war matériel to insure our state of preparedness. The war is spreading, and who knows how long it will take Germany to deal with Russia, and what the outcome will be."

In discussing the attitude of the communist elements among

American labor, Dunn said that while he was sure that the communists would outwardly strongly support increased war production, he did not believe they would interrupt their communist activities. According to him, the psychosis of the invincibility of the German military machine had become so pronounced as a result of German victories that, even in American pro-Soviet circles, German victory in Russia was regarded as probable.

Dunn said that many Americans foresaw that the German campaign in Russia might even bring about the overthrow of the communist regime. The communists would be concerned by such an eventuality and might work for the transfer of the center of world communist activity from Moscow to the United States. It was therefore necessary to be prepared not only for a welcome increase in war production, but for a less welcome increase of communist propaganda as well. He was of the opinion that the American Government would have to be very vigilant and although, naturally, it viewed Russia's defense favorably and would give it moral support, it would adopt, for the time being at least, a policy of "wait and see."

Winston Churchill, with his proverbial spontaneity, had not delayed a moment to make his historical speech on that fateful Sunday of June 22. Wholeheartedly and unconditionally he welcomed the Soviet Union as the newest victim of German aggression and as Britain's partner into the Allied fold.

The Ribbentrop-Molotov pact of August 1939 had made it possible for Hitler to risk launching a world war.

It had determined the British Government to sign the Treaty of Alliance with Poland on August 25, 1939.

Churchill now drew a curtain over the active collaboration of Nazi Germany and Soviet Russia. He brushed aside all considerations in favor of the greatest and most urgent of all aims—winning the war.

On the Washington scene Churchill could count on increased support from the President. The relationship of these two men had grown into a direct daily contact, so close that one could call it a "personal" alliance. But in America the reaction to the German campaign in Russia was less immediate, less complete than in England, and the United States was still studiously wary.

From the Polish angle, it was regrettable that Churchill had not taken advantage of the Soviet-German war to condition the British attitude on an immediate Soviet declaration re-establishing the *status quo ante* in Soviet-Polish relations by nullifying the Ribbentrop-Molotov pact partitioning Poland.

In my conversations of that period at the State Department and with political friends I sensed a certain apprehension and even regret that Churchill had not seen fit to attach any strings to Britain's declaration of friendship and support for the Soviets.

This feeling found its expression in a statesmanlike letter addressed by Hamilton Fish Armstrong, editor of *Foreign Affairs* and chairman of the Council on Foreign Relations, to Sumner Welles on June 25.

Armstrong referred to the fact that "the report that the Soviet Government had promised to restore the territory seized from Poland seems not to be confirmed." He suggested that "an effort be made to convince the Russian Government of the advisability of its giving the Polish Government such an understanding without delay," and that "a Russian commitment now might be comparatively easy to obtain. Later this might be much more difficult. The United States seems in a particularly favorable position to make this suggestion." Armstrong felt that "the effect of such Russian action would be considerable in all the occupied countries, especially the Slavic ones. Above all, it would provide a moral sugar-coating for the pill which Americans must swallow if our government is to aid Soviet Russia."

I had a conversation with Acting Secretary Sumner Welles on June 27. He started by expressing approval of General Sikorski's radio speech to the Polish people in which our Prime Minister had unequivocally taken the stand that as soon as the Soviet Government decided to renew relations with Poland on the basis of the Riga Treaty, which for almost twenty years had preserved peaceful relations between the Soviets and Poland, the Polish nation would be ready to welcome Soviet Russia into the Allied camp. Mr. Welles rightly considered the enunciation of Sikorski as an indication given to the Soviets by the Polish Government that it was ready to forget the recent past as soon as Russia showed a willingness to wholeheartedly do her part in making this possible.

I asked Mr. Welles whether he thought it would be possible

for the President to make some reservations on behalf of Poland when the time came for defining the American attitude toward the Soviets. I added that if the President agreed to intervene with the Soviet Government on behalf of the readjustment of Soviet-Polish relations in view of the common cause, such an intervention might be very effective.

Mr. Welles was convinced that the re-establishment of Polish-Soviet relations was imperative; moreover, that it would considerably help to popularize the Soviets in American public opinion, and implied that it was regrettable that Mr. Churchill had so unconditionally defined his attitude toward the Soviets. He thought it would have been better for all concerned if some time had been allowed to elapse and the Soviets had applied to the British Government for help and support. However, he thought that at the appropriate moment the President would certainly agree to use his influence on behalf of Poland, and the appropriate time for such a step would be when Moscow applied to the American Government for Lend-Lease aid.

Negotiations sponsored by the British Government between Premier Sikorski and the Soviet Ambassador Maisky had started in London on July 5, and on July 7 I was able to transmit to Mr. Welles a short memorandum of a conversation which had taken place at the British Foreign Office between Sikorski, our Foreign Minister Zaleski, and Ambassador Maisky in the presence of the British Permanent Undersecretary for Foreign Affairs Sir Alexander Cadogan.

The Polish Government had put forward two conditions for the resumption of diplomatic relations, broken off by the Soviet Union when it attacked Poland on September 17, 1939:

(1) The Government of the USSR to declare the Russo-German agreement concerning the partition of Poland as null and void.

(2) The Government of the USSR to agree to free all Polish prisoners of war and all other Polish prisoners and persons deported to Russia.

As soon as these conditions were accepted and carried out, the Polish Government would agree to collaborate with the USSR in the war against Germany and to form units of the Polish Army composed of Poles at present in Russia. This Polish Army would fight alongside the USSR forces. Diplomatic relations between Poland and the USSR to be resumed immediately.

Mr. Welles told me that he had received telegraphic reports on the subject of Polish-Soviet relations from Mr. Winant, the American Ambassador in London, who had discussed them with Foreign Secretary Eden. Ambassador Winant reported that according to Mr. Eden the Soviets were showing some good will toward Poland and that with regard to Czechoslovakia and Yugoslavia, the Soviet Government had also expressed its desire to see the independence of these two countries restored.

However, it was clear from the information obtained by Mr. Winant from Mr. Eden that, particularly in the case of Poland, the Soviets were already making certain reservations. While the Soviet Government expressed its desire to see Poland independent, it had specifically added: "within her ethnographic frontiers."

I referred to Mr. Welles's promise of trying to obtain the President's intervention in support of Poland at this time, either directly in Moscow, or through Ambassador Oumansky in Washington.

"As yet," Mr. Welles replied, "there had been no opportunity which could be effectively used for this purpose. The Soviets have not yet asked for Lend-Lease aid but have only sounded out our government regarding the purchase of certain war matériel and machinery for cash."

He added that in view of the fact that direct conversations between the Polish and Soviet governments had already started, it would be difficult for the American Government to take any steps until the attitude of the Soviets became clearer.

I pointed to the advisability of outspoken clarity in all dealings with the Soviets, especially at this initial stage of the Russian campaign. Mr. Welles agreed with me that the American people were by no means prepared to regard Soviet Russia, whose conduct had been so equivocal until she was attacked by Germany, as a natural ally in the fight of democracy against totalitarianism. He thought that American public opinion would be greatly influenced in defining its attitude to the Soviets by the way in which the Soviet Government acted in the case of Poland. Russia could greatly advance her cause in America by a show of good will in this matter. He regarded it as all the more desirable, because it was clear that in countering anti-Soviet feeling among isolationist and Catholic elements in America, a satisfactory settlement of Polish-Soviet relations would undoubtedly play a considerable part.

Mr. Welles wanted to hear my opinion regarding the possibilities of Russian defense against German aggression. "You probably know," he said, "that some American circles think that this is a conflict between two great totalitarian Powers who have acted hand in hand in recent years and that, therefore, it may be well to let them destroy each other. It will take time and effort to counteract this rather natural but somewhat immature tendency in some circles of our public opinion."

I replied that the United States would probably find it practical to follow a policy which would allow it to remain completely independent at the time when America would be called upon to assume leadership. Undoubtedly totalitarianism was the main enemy, regardless of whether it was nazist or communist. But there appeared to me to be a considerable danger if Germany were to defeat Russia, for then Hitler would certainly proclaim himself the savior of humanity from the undoubtedly genuine danger of bolshevist communism, and the world might be tempted to admit this and to seek a compromise with nazism, which was assuredly the No. 1 enemy of democracy. On the other hand, there was likewise a danger if through a policy of drifting or exaggerated elation at the entry of Russia into the war on the side of the Allies the Soviets were allowed to camouflage themselves as a democracy, fighting in defense of the same ideals as Great Britain and her Allies. A firm course in the prosecution of the war against the Axis and a watchful attitude toward Russian aims seemed to me to be the only sound policies to follow at this time.

From that conversation I gained the impression that Mr. Welles was keenly aware of the difficulties created by the entry of Soviet Russia into the war. It was becoming apparent to me that war-weary Britain, fighting with her back to the wall, would adopt a dangerously hasty course, spurred on by the consideration that, above all, it was by all means urgent to encourage the Soviets to prolong their defense which provided Britain with a very welcome breathing spell.

I deeply regretted that at that time the requirements of what still remained of American neutrality prevented the creation of an openly united policy of the two English-speaking democracies, for I knew that for the time being America was not prepared too easily or unconditionally to unite her democratic destinies with those of totalitarian communist Russia.

It was becoming evident, however, that Mr. Churchill's haste in professing unconditional support of Russia was in no small measure dictated by the then current apprehension that after initial defeats inflicted by Hitler, Stalin might see his advantage in making a separate peace with Germany and turn against the democracies which for twenty-odd years he had so continuously and forcefully denounced as the main capitalist menace.

CHAPTER IV

Poland, the Test Case

THROUGHOUT July 1941 the Germans were making headway in Russia. British anxiety regarding the possibilities of a prolonged Soviet defense was growing.

The Department of State was marking time and appeared to be taking no definite steps to express American policy toward the Soviet Union. However, the British-sponsored conversations between the Polish Government in London and Maisky, the Soviet Ambassador to the Court of St. James's, attracted considerable interest in official American quarters.

Another fact focused American attention on Poland. It was the sudden death of Ignacy J. Paderewski in New York on June 29, 1941. On the twenty-sixth, three days before he died, and only four days after Germany's attack on Russia, the great old man of Poland had issued a strong statement addressed to his compatriots and to Americans of Polish descent. In this last public pronouncement he stressed the importance of Germany's invasion of Russia as a great opportunity for Poland and Russia to resume normal relations and to collaborate against the common enemy. He expressed his faith in United States policy and the hope that, in lending its support to the Soviets in their defense against Hitler's aggression, America would make it clear to the Soviet Union that such support would be conditional on Russia's assurance that she had not only joined the fighting camp of democracies, but that she also realized the necessity of standing for the principles of freedom and justice and applying them in practice.

Paderewski urged that, as a proof of such determination, Russia should be asked to annul in fact the evil results of her collaboration with the Germans and particularly to repudiate the Ribbentrop-Molotov treaty, to free all the Polish people forcibly deported to Russia at the time of her occupation of eastern Poland and to admit Allied missions to ascertain on the spot that she was pursuing such a course. He also urged Russia to bring relief to the starving and dying Polish population in the most remote Asiatic provinces of Soviet Russia.

This parting message of the great musician, patriot, and statesman made a profound impression in Washington. The spontaneous gesture of President Roosevelt and of the United States Congress in offering the Arlington National Cemetery as a resting place until Paderewski's earthly remains could be transported to a free and independent Poland was interpreted as a generous and truly American reaction of friendship to the suffering Polish nation.

My talks with officials of the Department of State confirmed my belief that, as the difficult conversations of General Sikorski and Minister Zaleski with the Soviet Ambassador proceeded in London, the American Government was becoming aware that the haste in which these negotiations were conducted was due to British pressure upon the Polish Government. This did not entirely fit in with the American "wait and see" policy adopted by Washington in that first phase of the German-Soviet war.

Personally, I was disturbed by the telegrams from my Foreign Office showing how urgently the matter was being rushed in London. The question of the relinquishment by Russia of Polish territories invaded and seized by the Soviets in 1939 was, for the time being at least, purely theoretical, considering that her forces of occupation had been thrown out of those territories in the course of the first four days of the lightning German offensive.

In a conversation on July 14 with Undersecretary Sumner Welles I got the clear impression that while he saw the advantages of Polish-Soviet *rapprochement,* he, too, was somewhat perturbed by the British pressure on Sikorski to discourage the Polish Government from insisting on the re-establishment of the prewar territorial status of Poland. Mr. Welles expressed regret that so little was known about the details of the Polish-Soviet conversations. We compared the scanty news we were receiving— he from Ambassador Winant and I from my government—and saw that there was as yet very little to show the actual trend of those talks and to indicate whether a satisfactory settlement could be expected.

He asked me if I had discussed the matter with Ambassador Halifax.

I said that I intended to do so, but feared that Lord Halifax would take the line of least resistance.

I reminded Mr. Welles of Lord Halifax's replies to questions on Poland's eastern boundaries in the House of Lords at the beginning of the war, in October 1939. Halifax's answers indicated that even then, as Secretary for Foreign Affairs, he could not help toying with the idea of leaving open the territorial issue created by the Ribbentrop-Molotov pact on the partition of Poland, possibly as an enticement to the Soviets.

I added that it might be helpful if Mr. Welles could take an early opportunity to discuss this matter with Lord Halifax. It was important for a Polish-Soviet rapprochement and the resumption of diplomatic and possibly friendly relations that no doubt should be allowed to remain that the annulment by Russia of the Ribbentrop-Molotov pact would mean, not merely imply, the restoration of the status of relations governed by the Riga Treaty of 1921.

Mr. Welles promised to bring up the subject with Lord Halifax. He expressed the opinion that the time for discussion with Soviet Russia was appropriate, because the territorial problem was a theoretical one, the Russians having lost that territory to the Germans. It would be a pity, he thought, if this opportunity were not fully utilized for clearing up the matter of Polish-Soviet relations without undue haste, unjustified in the present circumstances.

I learned later that Mr. Welles had taken up the matter with Ambassador Halifax. However, apart from the welcome stressing of America's interest in the matter, his conversation had no effective results so far as British policy was concerned.

I was becoming increasingly uneasy as I continued to receive telegrams from London which made it evident that the British Government was strongly pressing General Sikorski to speed up the conversations with the Soviets, instead of pressing the Soviets to accept the just conditions of Poland.

Through my many years of close association with British diplomacy I knew how difficult it was for British statesmen to understand the Russian mentality and methods of negotiation. Apart from that, in this particular case the Ribbentrop-Molotov line ran uncomfortably close to the famous "Curzon Line" which we Poles had learned to know as the British "sword of Damocles" hung over Poland by Lloyd George in 1920.

Lord Curzon, whom I had known personally when I was Polish Chargé d'Affaires in London, had had little to do with this line, conceived by worthy but now ancient British professors and experts of Chatham House, who elaborated and launched it. They had done so, urged by the overanxious British Government of Lloyd George, to find a temporary means of stopping the Russian advance through Poland and of preventing the Soviet tide from sweeping into Germany and destroying the Versailles settlement.

I felt that it was not only opportunism which made the British try to coerce Sikorski into an agreement based on territorial concessions to Russia, or at least on non-insistence on the return to the prewar status. Churchill's pressure on Sikorski appeared to me to express the British tendency of propitiating a new and powerful partner rather than insist on persuading the Soviets to change their attitude toward Poland.

From personal sources of information I learned that Sir Stafford Cripps, British Ambassador in Moscow, was not pressing the Soviets unduly to make a friendly gesture toward Poland and had given them the impression that a superficial gesture would satisfy the British Government. I was convinced that our British ally was less anxious to insure the respect of legality and the triumph of principles of justice, than to build the closest relationship with Russia in view of all-absorbing war necessities, coupled with the fear that Stalin might conclude a separate peace with Hitler.

What made me even more anxious was the rift which was being created within the Polish Government itself. General Sikorski, primarily a military leader, was convinced that Poland's greatest asset consisted in fighting on all fronts, including the Soviet front. He harbored the illusion that nothing could bring the Soviets and Poland closer than brotherhood in arms which would allow them both to share in a future victory over Germany. He would certainly work for the return of the prewar status of relations and territorial settlements, but he hopefully believed that the mere annulment by the Soviets of the Ribbentrop-Molotov agreement could only be interpreted as automatically restoring the status of the Riga Treaty. He was also inclined to believe that a gentleman's agreement or a tacit understanding between a gallantly fighting Poland and a gallantly fighting Russia, concluded in the course of an unprecedented war, would be a sufficient safeguard of mutual loyalty. He seemed to favor the view of his great friend Winston Churchill in adopting this somewhat romantic attitude with regard to a bluntly "realistic" Russia. He had the excuse that, having been born and brought up in Galicia (the part of Poland which after the partitions of the eighteenth century had become part of the Austrian Empire until 1918), he, like British statesmen, also did not sufficiently understand Russian mentality.

On the other hand, the President of the Polish Republic, Mr. Raczkiewicz, born and brought up under Russian domination, and Foreign Minister Zaleski, whose family came from the Polish Ukraine, had a profound knowledge of Russia and of her very specific methods. They likewise considered it of paramount importance to restore Polish-Soviet relations and to conclude a treaty of friendship and collaboration with the Soviets, but realized that it was of equal importance to Poland and Russia and to the peace of the world that a Polish-Soviet pact be founded not merely on an equivocal tacit gentleman's agreement, but on a treaty in which all the "i's" were dotted and all the "t's" crossed in order to exclude any misinterpretation and doubts in the future.

These differences in viewpoints within the Polish Government, added to British pressure which helped to accentuate them, created a major crisis in our government and resulted in the resignation of Minister Zaleski from his post of Foreign Secretary when Sikorski signed the Polish-Soviet pact on July 30, 1941.

The contrast between the British and the American approach to the Soviet war and the problems which it had opened was at that time quite evident. To war-weary Britain, Russian defense, so long as it lasted, was a Godsend, and it made her conveniently forget that major Soviet and British aims were mostly irreconcilable. As I understood it, the United States was still sitting back as an observer, still partly neutral, still disposed to build its policies on fundamental democratic principles and to study critically the conduct of Soviet Russia, forced into a war against her will by her former partner in the crime of aggression. America could still afford to hesitate before defining her new relationship to a Stalinist totalitarian Russia whom circumstances had forcibly landed in the democratic camp.

From the very wording of the Polish-Soviet agreement it was evident that any precise definition of the return to the *status quo ante* preceding the Molotov-Ribbentrop pact had been studiously avoided, and this lack of precision regarding territorial matters was to be supplemented by the British Government in a note or statement to the Polish Government.

I asked Mr. Sumner Welles immediately if he could obtain a declaration from the President once more reasserting non-recognition of territorial changes brought about by use of force. I found him fully aware of the necessity for the United States Government to make some such declaration. He assured me that he would take up the matter with the President, and if the President did not see his way to make a definite personal statement at this time, he would obtain his authority to issue such a statement on behalf of the Department of State.

The British official note was couched in the following terms:

On the occasion of the signature of the Polish-Soviet Agreement of today, I desire to take this opportunity of informing you that in conformity with the provision of the agreement of mutual assistance between the United Kingdom and Poland of the 25th of August 1939, His Majesty's Government in the United Kingdom have entered into no undertaking towards the Union of Socialist Soviet Republics which affect the relations between that country and Poland. I also desire to assure you that His Majesty's Government do not recognize any territorial changes which have been effected in Poland since August 1939.

The American pronouncement took the form of a statement to the press, reading as follows:

Mr. Welles described as gratifying to this government the Russian-Polish agreement signed in London yesterday. He made clear, in commenting on it at his press conference, however, that he was discussing only general policy, not details.

The United States position toward Poland, he pointed out, was made clear immediately after that country was invaded. It was one of not recognizing any change in her status as a free, sovereign, and independent nation. That position, he added, is maintained and continued.

His understanding of the Russian-Polish agreement was that it was in line with the United States policy of non-recognition of territory taken by conquest.

But something else happened which greatly weakened the meaning of the British note. After Mr. Eden made his very clear statement of policy on behalf of the British Government in the House of Commons, he was asked by Captain McEwen, Member of Parliament for Berwick and Haddington, whether it was right to assume that as a result of this Polish-Soviet agreement a guarantee of frontiers in eastern Europe would be undertaken by His Majesty's Government. Mr. Eden replied that the exchange of notes between the British and the Polish governments "does not involve any guarantee of frontiers by His Majesty's Government."

Finally, when Mr. Mander, Member of Parliament for Wolverhampton East, asked Mr. Eden whether this pertinent question of the guarantee of frontiers "held good," Mr. Eden said: "There is, as I have said, no guarantee of frontiers."

The perusal of that brief and pointed debate in the House of Commons deserved special attention because, quite apart from its bearing on the Polish question, it was so characteristic of British foreign policy.

To all intents and purposes the British note to the Polish Government, supplementing the lack of precision in the wording of the Polish-Soviet agreement concerning territorial matters, was undoubtedly meant as an assurance that the British Government did not approve and did not recognize the changes of Poland's territorial status. But, after having made this clear statement to the House and read the note to Sikorski, in which the British Government had once more expressly stated that it did not recognize these changes, Mr. Eden bluntly declared that this attitude of the British Government was not to be interpreted as a guarantee of any territorial status.

This answer given by the British Secretary for Foreign Affairs could be interpreted by the Soviet Government only in one way; namely, as the first swallow on the rising dawn of a new British policy of appeasement.

In Washington, those aware of the behind-the-scene story of the Polish-Soviet negotiations were asking questions: Is Russia, the new partner, so warmly welcomed and so readily admitted as a new ally by Churchill, to be but a short-lived asset, or to become a liability? How far could the Russians be relied on if Hitler made peace proposals after considerably weakening or smashing Soviet resistance? How sincerely had Stalin espoused the democratic common cause?

Nobody appeared to have the answers, but one thing was becoming increasingly evident. A new member had been haled into a highly respectable club of nations, a club whose statutes professed certain fundamental principles. Could this new member be regarded as having qualified for membership? Was he going to abide by the rules? Or would he use his membership rights to suggest amendments to the club's bylaws? Would he become a constructive or a disruptive force?

These unanswered questions reflected the concern increasingly felt at the White House and the Department of State regarding the nature of Russia as a partner in a world war against totalitarian aggression. If Russia was too mysterious to be fully understood by the British, then one could frankly say that Russia for the American people was an even more unknown problem child who had to be carefully observed before being fully adopted.

Harry Hopkins was once more selected by President Roosevelt personally to investigate Moscow tendencies. He was to try to gain the confidence of Stalin and to report directly to the President on the burning question: What did Russia now stand for in reality, and what were her intentions, policies, and aims?

The instinct of self-preservation caused Roosevelt and Churchill to seek closer personal contact, to review the situation, and to redefine British and American aims in view of Russia's entry into the war. It was in an atmosphere of dramatic tenseness, shrouded in secrecy, that Roosevelt and Churchill met for the first time on the Atlantic.

There would have been no necessity for the President of the United States personally to meet the Prime Minister of the British

Empire at that time. The war was still young and uncertain as to its outcome, and Anglo-American unity of views on fundamental aims was instinctive and complete. But a new force had entered into the reckoning—a force powerful in resources and unpredictable in policy. It was necessary and even indispensable to review the new situation, to redefine viewpoints, to restate fundamental principles, in view of the ominous entry of Stalin's Russia on the Allied side. The very nature of Russia's participation on the democratic side of the world conflict, after having been forcibly switched away from the Axis camp, had created a formidable paradox requiring clarification.

The Atlantic Charter was to be the answer. It was intended as a declaration which would solidify around its principles all the elements of freedom and democracy, not only in America, but in the whole of Europe. It was necessary as a statement which would break through Nazi German propaganda indefatigably working upon the tired populations of countries dominated by Germany, aiming to frighten them by the specter of a communist Russia. It was indispensable because in the first two years of the war Soviet conduct toward the Baltic States, Finland, Rumania, and Poland had not helped the Soviets to gain the confidence of Europe or of America. Circumstances made it urgent to reassure the nations of Europe that an Allied victory even now, when Russia was participating, would not bring them enslavement.

Out of these considerations and instinctive fears was born the Charter of Principles, in defense of which, henceforth, the soldiers and civilian fighters for the cause of freedom would sacrifice their lives.

But Russia had not been asked to participate in the Atlantic meeting. Perhaps it was feared that she would refuse to attend.

The Atlantic Charter appeared to me to be the first step toward the firm establishment of a welcome, widely conceived international community of aims. On reading it and carefully analyzing its wording I asked myself whether the new element which had been added to the coalition of forces of good against the forces of evil could ever be coerced, cajoled, or persuaded wholeheartedly to endorse the gospel of the Atlantic Charter, so fundamentally alien to the concepts of a totalitarian communist state.

CHAPTER V

Collaboration

AFTER the signing of the Soviet-Polish agreement in London re-establishing diplomatic relations between the Soviets and Poland, I asked the Soviet Ambassador, with whom hitherto I had had no contact, to receive me on my first formal call. Ambassador Oumansky responded immediately that he would receive me on August 16.

I duly called on him at the Soviet Embassy on Sixteenth Street. I was met at the door by one of the Secretaries of the embassy who escorted me upstairs to the Ambassador's study.

Oumansky received me with a great show of welcome. For the first time I had the opportunity of meeting this young, smiling, dynamic, and enigmatic man. We conversed in French which he spoke fluently with a slight Russian accent.

"I am indeed delighted to make Your Excellency's acquaintance and very grateful to you for calling on me," said Oumansky.

"It gives me great pleasure," I replied, "to be able to call upon Your Excellency and to assure you that I will be most happy if our contact serves to further good relations between Poland and Soviet Russia."

"I understand our new contact in the same way as you do, Mr. Ambassador," replied Oumansky with emphasis. "I also promise myself considerable advantages from it for our two countries and for the cause of the peace for which the world is now fighting."

After this exchange of diplomatic courtesies, I inquired about the situation on the Russian front and expressed anxiety concerning the latest news of the reported retreat of General Budienny's forces in the Ukrainian sector.

Oumansky led me to the map where the line of the front was

marked. He explained the latest phase of the Ukrainian campaign and added: "The press always exaggerates and has a tendency to take a pessimistic view of our defense."

"I have been told," I said, "that your civilian population is suffering great hardships on account of the German advance and that there is a shortage of food. I am sure you have found that all American relief agencies and organizations are anxious to help your people."

"Our people do not need outside help. The Soviet Government looks after them and, of course," he added, "it also looks after the Poles at present in Russia."

He then asked me whether I had any news about the formation of the Polish Army in Russia. When I replied that our government was optimistic regarding this matter, he said: "I am afraid that there are fewer officers and soldiers in our war prisoner camps than your government imagines."

"But, Mr. Ambassador," I replied, "I think that we have good reason to know that there are quite considerable numbers which will enable us greatly to strengthen our army. We have official Soviet figures of our officers and men detained in Russia which numerically are quite encouraging on that score. Surely you know that among the prisoners taken by the Soviet Army in Poland during the regrettable incidents of 1939 we have many professional officers, technicians, and airmen who will prove of considerable use in supporting the valiant effort of the Soviet armed forces."

"I am delighted to hear it, Mr. Ambassador," said Oumansky, "and I am sure that every facility will be granted by my government to speed up the formation of such an army."

We then spoke of war matériel to be supplied to Russia by Britain and the United States. "That is a very interesting subject," said Oumansky, "I am glad you mentioned it. Both the United States and Britain must understand that the supply of matériel to Russia is the most important of all problems, and that the wonderful defense of the Soviets against the Germans makes it imperative that this should be recognized because the entire issue of the war may depend upon it."

I switched the conversation to the problem of relief for Poles deported to Russia.

"I am not aware that there are any great numbers of Poles now in Russia," said Oumansky. "What is your opinion, Mr. Ambassador?"

I replied that there were over a million and a half Polish deportees in the Soviet Union and that it would certainly be very helpful to Polish-Soviet relations if these people could now benefit by a system of relief, and if a friendly American-Polish delegation could report publicly how they were treated and disprove current reports that they were being badly treated in Russia.

"That would be a very difficult matter," answered Oumansky. "I do not even see how I could suggest such a move to my government. Could you think of any other way of helping to solve this problem?" he asked.

I replied that the Polish-American Council of Chicago was the leading organization which had undertaken Polish war-relief activities in the United States. I said that I thought it would be a very fine gesture on the part of the Soviet Government if it would allow, or even invite, the representatives of the Polish-American Council to go to Russia.

"It would be," I said, smiling, "a great feather in the Soviet cap in America if this were done with a show of spontaneity on the part of your government. It would help to allay certain doubts and misgivings concerning Soviet Russia in this country. Apart from these advantages it would also bring welcome assistance to the Polish people in Russia."

"I do not know how my government would take such a suggestion," said Oumansky, "but personally I share your view that it would help the Soviet cause in America, and I certainly will do my best to sound my government on this proposal."

Seeing his readiness to take up the matter, I decided to take advantage of his attitude. "My dear Ambassador," I said, "I see that you realize that your government will have to expend some efforts in this country to make public opinion more favorable to Soviet Russia. I think that there could hardly be a better opportunity of doing so than to make all facilities available for direct contact, and I take the liberty of urging you to use the problem of relief to the Poles, at present in Russia, as a test case. You see, there is such a difference between the American and the Soviet viewpoints. The American people are accustomed to regard the

American Red Cross and their social-welfare institutions as entirely non-political bodies, anxious only to do their duty to suffering people. They could hardly believe in your sincerity if you told them that you see any danger in their attempts to help the Russians or the Poles in your country. So please do not underestimate the importance of such a gesture."

"Personally, I entirely agree with you," answered Oumansky. "I know that it would greatly facilitate my task if I could break through the traditional prejudices of my government. But you know us well enough to know our specific viewpoints. You realize how doubtful it is that I could ever obtain such permission. Up till now all requests on the part of foreign-welfare institutions have always been flatly refused by our government because, unfortunately, we suspect them of wanting to investigate internal problems, to control our politics, and to pry into our affairs."

"Don't you think, Mr. Ambassador," I replied, "that this attitude should now be modified in view of the great advantages it would give your country? I know that the American Red Cross is anxious to help the Russian people, and that the Polish-American Council is ready and willing to spend considerable sums and to send their delegations to distribute relief supplies to our Polish population at present in Russia. If you, Mr. Ambassador, could succeed in making your government change its attitude and allow these institutions to work among the needy Soviet and Polish people in Russia, if only partly to unburden the Soviet Government at a time when it must be so exclusively concerned with military matters of national defense, you would indeed have done a very great thing."

Oumansky became thoughtful, and, after some hesitation, said that he had never heard the matter put in this way. "I believe," he said, "that I might possibly use such a formula in making this suggestion to my government. It might certainly help matters, and, between ourselves," he added, "you certainly know what difficulties I encounter here. I am looked upon with the utmost suspicion by the majority of the American people. But, on the other hand," continued Oumansky, "the American Red Cross has never made a gesture in my direction. They have not suggested helping the Russian people at all. We only hear constantly about the misery of the Poles in Russia. Why, even the Methodists and the Quakers, the Y.M.C.A. and others, have most insistently raised the subject of help to the Poles in Russia. But our poor Russian people seem to have been forgotten."

"But, Mr. Ambassador," I said, "if you have been telling people, as you just told me, that the Soviet Government was in a position to cope with the relief needs of your country, then they certainly must have concluded that their services were either unnecessary or unwelcome."

Oumansky appeared to be somewhat perplexed by my remarks. "Yes," he said, "I admit you may be right. I remember that when the State Department inquired about the situation and asked us to facilitate relief activities by American institutions, we rather categorically told them that they could not hope to obtain our permission for the work of foreign-welfare organizations in Russia."

"Well, Mr. Ambassador," I replied, "I believe that this is a matter of great importance not only from the relief point of view, but also from the viewpoint of good diplomacy and of helping the cause of Russia in America."

Oumansky replied that personally he agreed with my views. I was about to leave. He showed me the reception rooms of the embassy and then accompanied me downstairs, saying that he would have great pleasure in returning my visit very shortly.

Scrupulously observant of diplomatic protocol, he telephoned the following day, asking when I could receive him at the Polish Embassy. I replied that I would be delighted to see him two days later, on August 18.

I received Oumansky in the big drawing room of the embassy. I noticed from the outset that he was out to charm and to inspire confidence. After expressing his admiration for the way in which our embassy was furnished and for our fine Polish pictures, he opened up by asking about his former Polish friends of our diplomatic service. He soon returned, however, to the matter of relief.

I told him that since our last meeting I had had an opportunity of seeing Mr. Norman Davis, chairman of the American Red Cross.

"I am glad to tell you that Mr. Davis confirmed all I told you," I said. "I found him most anxious to be helpful to the Russian people. But if I may be quite frank, Mr. Ambassador,"

I added, "he did not conceal that the three rebuffs which the American Red Cross had suffered when they approached your government through their embassy in Moscow, on the possibility of obtaining permission to help the Polish people, have greatly discouraged him. 'What more can I do?' Mr. Davis had said. 'I can but offer the services of the American Red Cross. I cannot force locked doors and unresponsive governments.' You see, Mr. Ambassador," I continued, "that it is up to you to use your diplomacy in order to bring about an understanding on this subject."

"But how can I," said Oumansky, "as Ambassador of the Soviet Union, take the first step and go begging for relief? After all, my government rightly assumes that the fact of our powerful defense against the Germans is invaluable to the Allied cause. The least the American Red Cross can do is to show some interest in our suffering population and take the first step in offering relief. How can an Ambassador ask for favors of a foreign-relief institution?"

"My dear Ambassador," I replied, laughing, "you remind me of an old Polish saying which you probably know, about the peasant girl who is wooed but cannot make up her mind and admits: 'I long to, but I fear me.' Believe me, no question of prestige need be involved in this simple gesture of taking the first step. How could you face the accusation that, when your people and mine in your country needed help, the Soviet Government was stopped from trying to alleviate their plight by old-fashioned methods of diplomatic protocol? In talking to Mr. Davis I took it upon myself to tell him what you said to me about the difficulties arising out of your traditional methods of not admitting foreign institutions to work inside Russia for relief or any other purposes. Davis then asked me: 'Do you think that the Soviets could persist in this curious method if their population really needs our help?' I admit that I did not know what answer to give him."

"I will think it over," replied Oumansky, "and see what can be done. There may be a way out. But I wish you would realize that our methods are very different from the informal methods of America, and that I would have more difficulty in convincing my government to change their views than in persuading foreign governments to change theirs."

We both laughed at this remark.

In telling Oumansky about the initiative I had taken in discussing this matter with Norman Davis, I had not told him all. As a matter of fact I had explained to Mr. Davis the curious misgivings which Oumansky mentioned to me during our first talk. With his usual kindliness, Norman Davis admitted that he was worried by Oumansky's attitude which prevented the American Red Cross from doing what he considered was its duty. He would gladly help the Russian people.

"My dear Chairman," I said, "if I may make a suggestion, why not take advantage of the Department of State and use its intermediacy? Surely Mr. Hull, with his direct American approach, might just mention to the Soviet Ambassador that he would gladly put him in touch with the chairman of the American Red Cross."

"That," said Davis, "is an excellent idea. I will go to Hull and put the matter before him. I am sure it is the best solution."

We walked over to the Department of State where I had left my car, and Norman Davis promised to telephone me the result of his conversation with Mr. Hull. That same evening he telephoned that the Secretary was very pleased with the suggestion and in the course of the next few days would either suggest to the Soviet Ambassador that he get in touch with the American Red Cross, or even simplify the matter by having Mr. Norman Davis meet Oumansky in his room at the State Department to help break the ice between them.

After my last conversation with Oumansky I informed Norman Davis that I thought the Soviet Ambassador was quite prepared and receptive.

Contact between Davis and Oumansky was established a few days later, entirely in accordance with our scheme. Thus a friendly personal Polish-American conspiracy for Russian relief was satisfactorily launched.

The absence of Soviet Russia at the Atlantic meeting had made it necessary and indeed urgent to draw this formidable new partner into the Allied camp by stressing the Soviet acceptance of the principles of the charter.

That concern was clearly reflected in the energetic and definite way in which the follow-up period of the Atlantic meeting was dealt with by the British Government in the fall of 1941.

Mr. Churchill and Mr. Eden, with great diplomatic subtlety, adopted a line of procedure which, for the time being at least, proved to be well chosen and successful.

An Inter-Allied meeting was held in London at St. James's Palace on September 24, 1941. Mr. Eden presided, and representatives of all the Allies took part in it. For the first time the Soviet Union was represented by Mr. Maisky, its Ambassador to the Court of St. James's, and by Mr. Bogomolov, Soviet Ambassador to Poland and to the other Allied governments-in-exile in London.

Mr. Eden opened the meeting, speaking highly of the tenacity of the Soviet people in their defense against German aggression. He welcomed the Soviet Ambassador who, for the first time, could now represent his government at an Allied meeting. He then referred to the Atlantic Charter, inviting "its acceptance by the Allied governments."

Ambassador Maisky in an inspiring speech declared, on behalf of the Soviet Union, that it "was, and is, guided in its foreign policy by the principle of self-determination of nations.

"Accordingly," he continued, "the Soviet Union defends the right of every nation to the independence and territorial integrity of its country, and its right to establish such a social order and to choose such a form of government as it deems opportune and necessary for the better promotion of its economic and cultural prosperity."

Maisky went on denouncing "all and any attempts of aggressive Powers to impose their will upon other peoples," and stressed the fact that the Soviet Union has been and still is "striving for a radical solution of the problem of safeguarding freedom-loving peoples against all the dangers they encounter from aggressors."

After which Maisky solemnly declared the acceptance of, and adherence to, the Atlantic Charter in the following words:

"In accordance with a policy inspired by the above principles . . . the Soviet Government proclaims its agreement with the fundamental principles of the declaration of Mr. Roosevelt, Presi-

*dent of the United States, and of Mr. Churchill, Prime Minister
of Great Britain—principles which are so important in the present international circumstances."*

Mr. Eden then put the following resolution to the representatives of the Allied nations which was unanimously accepted by
them:

*The Governments of Belgium, Czechoslovakia, Greece, Lux-
emburg, the Netherlands, Norway, Poland, Union of Soviet Socialist Republics, and Yugoslavia, and the representatives of General de Gaulle, leader of free Frenchmen,*

*Having taken note of the Declaration recently drawn up by
the President of the United States and by the Prime Minister,
Mr. Churchill, on behalf of His Majesty's Government in the
United Kingdom,*

*Now make known their adherence to the common principles
of policy set forth in that Declaration and their intention to co-
operate to the best of their ability in giving effect to them.*

Through this conveniently forgotten document and the solem-
nity which surrounded its inception at that meeting at St. James's
Palace, Soviet Russia's formal adherence to the Atlantic Charter was officially declared.

CHAPTER VI

Storm Signals Up

THE AUTUMN OF 1941 was closing down upon the vast territory of Russia.

As the mechanized German divisions steadily advanced on Leningrad and Moscow and invaded the fertile lands of the Ukraine, an endless trek of emaciated, half-clad Polish deportees and prisoners from the farthest reaches of Siberia started on the move toward the centers of enlistment for the new Polish Army to be formed in southern Russia.

Three successive documents had opened the way to these Polish civilians and military men, to our women and children, eager to regain freedom.

First and foremost was the basic agreement re-establishing Polish-Soviet relations, signed in London on July 30, 1941, next, the decree signed by President M. Kalinin, on August 12, 1941, in which it was said that

amnesty is granted to all Polish citizens on Soviet territory at present deprived of their freedom as prisoners of war or on other adequate grounds. . . .

The third document was the Polish-Soviet military agreement signed in Moscow on August 14, 1941, in which it was stipulated that:

. . . a Polish army will be organized in the shortest possible time on the territory of the USSR. . . .
. . . it will form part of the armed forces of the sovereign Republic of Poland. . . .
. . . it will be destined with the armed forces of the USSR and other Allied Powers for the common fight against Germany. . . .

. . . the pay, rations, and maintenance will be in accordance
with the regulations of the USSR army. . . .
. . . armament, equipment, uniforms, motor transport, et cetera,
will be provided as far as possible by
    a) the government of the USSR from their own resources,
    b) the Polish Government from their own supplies granted
       on the basis of the Lend-Lease Act.

In the permanent Soviet blackout it had never been possible to
establish the exact number of the Poles forcibly deported from
Poland in 1939 and 1940, concentrated in prisons and forced
labor camps in Soviet Russia.

As far as it was possible to ascertain a conservative estimate
fixed their total somewhat above a million and a half men,
women, and children. On September 17, 1940, the official Soviet Army paper *Red Star* declared that in addition to civilians,
181,000 Polish prisoners of war were held in Soviet camps and
that this included twelve generals, fifty-eight colonels, seventy-
two lieutenant colonels, and 9,227 officers of lower ranks.

The liberation of these Polish people was a slow process. Soviet Russia, engaged in a most courageous and self-sacrificing
defense against the German onslaught, could do little to speed
up this march of Poles through the almost infinite open spaces
of its vast territory. However, our Polish Embassy was already
functioning in Moscow and its delegates were handling this new
migration. Polish prisoners released from Russian concentration
and prison camps were doing their best to obtain the necessary
means of transport to reach the new Polish camps for military
training.

General Wladyslaw Anders, just released from the Lubianka
prison in Moscow, a splendid officer and a personal friend of
General Sikorski, was appointed to the post of Commander in
Chief of the Polish Army in Russia. With untiring energy this
Polish soldier was performing miracles of efficiency to help speed
up the transport and the first stages of physical reconditioning
so necessary to these starved people, who had to regain sufficient
strength before they could start their training.

I noted with gratification the sincere interest and solicitude
which this problem of the miraculous resurrection of a new

fighting force of Poles in Russia was arousing in America. With their natural simplicity and logic, the American people rightly regarded the way in which this unprecedented development would be carried out, as a test case of Soviet good will.

I was continuously asked for details of how the Russian Government was carrying out its new obligations toward Poland. I knew that President Roosevelt, with his subtle sense for probing American public opinion, was anxious to know every detail of the developments in Polish-Soviet relations at that time. Conscious of the importance of the influence of the churches on American public opinion, he watched with special interest any indication showing that Soviet Russia was turning a new leaf in the matter of religious tolerance.

In September 1941 I was receiving reports from our embassy in Russia which showed that the Soviet Government had yielded to the wish expressed by the Polish Government and had agreed to grant permission for Polish Catholic and Jewish chaplains to take up their assignments with the Polish Army being formed in Soviet Russia.

When I conveyed this information to the State Department, I noted that it created the greatest interest. On September 27 my old friend Colonel Bill Donovan called on me at the embassy and told me that he had been asked personally by President Roosevelt to discuss with me all the aspects of Soviet-Polish relations, especially as regards the carrying out of the military agreement of the fourteenth of August, and quite particularly to note all that I knew about religious liberalism on the part of the Soviet Government.

I showed Bill Donovan all my information on that subject and we discussed the matter at length. He told me that the President thought it was of such importance from the viewpoint of American public opinion to stress this new departure on the part of the Soviet Government, that the President wanted me to give some public expression to these welcome new facts.

Donovan suggested I write a letter to him which he would submit to the President and which could later be used in the press. I agreed to do so, being especially anxious to stress the fact that the Polish Government, sincerely pursuing a policy of collaboration with Soviet Russia, welcomed every proof of Russian good will.

On that same day I wrote a letter along the lines suggested by Donovan, and on the next day Bill told me over the telephone that the President would be grateful if I would make the matter more official by communicating a similar report to the Secretary of State. I did so immediately.

The State Department saw to it that my letter was publicized in the American press, and President Roosevelt made a reference to it at his press conference on September 30.

Soviet Russia's "religious tolerance" was in this way given a clean bill of health.

At this time I was particularly concerned with the problem of speeding up the delivery of Lend-Lease war matériel to the Polish forces. I had been helped in the most friendly way by the Lend-Lease Administration, where Oscar Cox and his colleagues always did their best to back my efforts.

However, the matter was not so easy as it first appeared, when the President declared that the Polish war effort was of direct interest to the United States and that Lend-Lease would be granted our army. There was not enough war matériel to go around to satisfy the increasing demands of Britain and Russia on Lend-Lease supplies. The British were quite openly anxious to delay the supply of Lend-Lease matériel to their Allies and to insure priority for the British fighting forces.

On September 4 the President signed the long-awaited declaration making Poland eligible for Lend-Lease aid. He said in his declaration that "the gallant resistance of the forces of the Government of Poland is vital to the defense of the United States," and added that "this action demonstrated our intention to give material support to the fighting determination of the Polish people to establish once again the independence of which they were so inhumanly deprived."

Two days later, on September 6, the American Government also informed me that American volunteers joining the Polish Army would be granted the same status and privileges as Americans who joined the British Army.

Fully conscious of the importance of speeding up the formation of the Polish Army in Russia, I was doing my utmost to urge that the Lend-Lease equipment indispensable for this purpose should be supplied to the training camps which our High Command was then setting up on Russian territory. I knew how anxious General Sikorski was for a Polish-Soviet brotherhood-in-arms, which he regarded as the best basis for friendly relations between the two peoples.

President Roosevelt shared this opinion and decided to send special instructions to W. Averell Harriman, who headed the American Lend-Lease mission to Moscow. The decision to give American Lend-Lease supplies to the Polish troops in Russia was to be stressed in Harriman's conversations with the Soviets in Moscow, as well as the importance of the Polish Army, not only to the Soviet Government, but also to America and Britain.

At the request of the President I was invited to the State Department on September 23, and the text of the instructions which he had prepared for Mr. Harriman was read to me by Mr. Sumner Welles.

However, in the second half of October 1941 the information reaching me from Moscow and London became somewhat disturbing. The freeing of our deportees in Russia was apparently not proceeding so smoothly as we had been led to hope. The Polish Embassy in Moscow had to intervene repeatedly by means of notes and verbally with the Soviet Government, and to point to the desperate situation of Poles still deprived of freedom in the Arctic regions of Russia.

General Anders was likewise becoming uneasy when he found an unusually small percentage of officers among the 46,000 soldiers who had succeeded in reaching the Polish training camps. He rightly feared that the forming of the Army might be greatly delayed or even become impossible for lack of officers.

General Sikorski, alarmed, addressed a note on October 15 to Soviet Ambassador Bogomolov in London, expressing concern over the fate of the Polish officers detained in Russia as prisoners of war who had not yet appeared at the Polish training camps. He mentioned that "the fate of several thousand Polish officers who have not returned to Poland and who have not been found in Soviet military camps continues to remain uncertain."

Ambassador Bogomolov replied bluntly on November 14 that "all Polish officers on the territory of the USSR had been set free."

But the fact that the missing Polish officers failed to report in the camps was causing increasing concern to my government. Our Ambassador in Moscow took up this subject with Marshal Stalin on November 14 in the office of Foreign Commissar Molotov at the Kremlin. He stressed the delay in freeing our citizens from the Soviet camps and went on to complain about the lack of food, shelter, and equipment for our army. Finally, he touched upon the mystery of our missing officers.

"You are, Mr. Prime Minister," said the Polish Ambassador, "the author of the amnesty for the Polish citizens detained in the USSR. It was your gesture, Mr. Prime Minister, and I would be very grateful if you would exert all your influence to have it carried out in full."

"Are there still Poles who have not been liberated?" Stalin raised his brows.

"In this connection I addressed a note to Mr. Vishinsky on October 6." Here our Ambassador turned to Mr. Molotov, and after his affirmative nod, continued: "But I want to mention, Mr. Prime Minister, that we have not yet heard from even one of the officers, prisoners of war, detained in the three camps of Starobielsk, Kozielsk, and Ostashkov, who were transferred to an unknown destination in the spring of 1940."

"I shall look into this matter," said Stalin. "Our amnesty knows no exceptions."

"We have lists of names of a great number of these officers," added the Ambassador, "and we know that they were removed from these three camps in April and May 1940. May I most urgently request that you issue orders for the release of these officers whom we need very badly for the Army."

Stalin got up and started to pace the room, puffing at his cigarette.

"Have you any detailed lists of names of those officers?" he asked.

"We have," answered the Ambassador, "and all the names in our possession have been registered with your camp commanders and with the NKVD."

Stalin turned around briskly and approached the telephone on Molotov's writing desk. Molotov followed him quickly.

"That is not the way to get connected." He smiled to Stalin, switched the telephone over, and resumed his seat at the conference table.

Stalin dialed a number and said: "Here Stalin. Have all the Poles been released from prisons?"

After listening to the reply, he continued: "I have here with me the Polish Ambassador, who tells me that not all have reached the Polish camps." And after another moment of listening: "Well, call me back later. . . ."

He replaced the receiver and returned to the conference table. "May I also ask you a question, Mr. Ambassador? When and where do the Polish troops intend to fight against the Germans?"

"I am not a military man," replied the Ambassador, "but I want to make it clear that we Poles take war seriously. We don't want only to make a show of our participation in the battles on the Russian front. We want to be equipped and armed and sent to the front immediately. General Sikorski and General Anders want an important sector of your front entrusted to the Polish troops so that they can give their reply to Hitler. We desire to have our army fighting right here on the eastern front, so that the Polish-Soviet agreement may be sealed by this brotherhood of arms."

"I understand," said Stalin.

"I would like to stress," continued the Ambassador, "that the news of every new Polish division being formed in Russia, when it reaches Poland, has a tremendous importance for the shaping of friendly feeling toward Russia among our people over there. That is why we are so anxious to have more of those divisions formed here."

Stalin nodded vigorously. "Naturally. naturally, I understand this."

The telephone rang. Stalin rose, picked up the receiver, muttered a short, "Yes, Stalin here," and for a long while listened without making any remarks. After hanging up the receiver he resumed his place at the conference table and changed the subject of conversation.

In view of the stalemate reached at Moscow, of which I was immediately informed, I decided to ask to be received by President Roosevelt. On November 5 the President received me with Mr. Sumner Welles. I noted that he was looking tired. The strain of work had left deep marks on his expressive features.

As soon as Mr. Welles and I were seated he started by saying that he was greatly concerned by what he had been told by Mr. Welles about the deterioration in Polish-Soviet relations, and particularly about the difficulties our government was encountering in the formation of our army in Russia.

The President said that the situation appeared to him to be unfortunate. "I regard this matter as one of great importance not only for Poland and the Allied cause, but especially for Soviet Russia," he added.

He said that, according to him, General Sikorski's conditions were very reasonable and should be met.

The President expressed the opinion that the Soviets had a specific way of complicating matters rather than of simplifying them. To them, simplification was a novelty. However, he added that one had to be fair in appraising the situation. Russia was facing great difficulties. She might really be lacking food. Her system of transport was disorganized. Equipment might not be available. But the President stressed that one could not agree to such a delay. He agreed with General Sikorski that "to use splendid fighting men" as he regarded the Poles as workmen in camps, rather than as soldiers, would be contrary to Allied interests. It would be squandering very valuable fighting material.

The President paused for a moment and appeared to concentrate on the problem. He then referred to my request for diplomatic intervention in Moscow. He said that he would willingly intervene but did not think it would be the best way to deal with this matter. He said that Mr. Harriman had gained the confidence of Stalin. It would therefore be advisable and more effective if he addressed a personal telegram to Stalin on this subject. He asked Mr. Welles what he thought of this.

When Mr. Welles signified his approval, the President explained that Mr. Harriman ought to tell Stalin in a telegram, in a very friendly way, that considerable importance was attached in America to the formation of as big a Polish Army as possible, and that he should at the same time emphasize how valuable to Russia would be an army of such high fighting qualities.

"But," added the President, "I want him also to stress in his message that if for any reason the Russian Government should find it difficult to undertake the feeding and equipment of that Polish Army, then the Soviets should do all they can to facilitate the speedy transfer of these Polish troops from Russia to another country, where they would be more accessible to the United States and Britain, who could then insure their equipment, training, and armament, and put them in the line of battle as soon as possible." The President went on to say that Harriman should point out that wherever the Polish Army fought it would engage German forces and, therefore, detract them from pressing on Russia. "This is an urgent matter," said the President to Mr. Welles, "and I want to have such a telegram drafted without delay."

The President then asked me for details regarding the spirit of our deportees in Russia. I told him that according to reports from our Moscow Embassy, these people, regardless of their state of health and of their emaciation, were most enthusiastic to join in the fight against Germany. I gave him several details from reports describing the despair of these men when they were told that they were not to be enlisted but would have to return to work in industries or on state farms.

The President was very moved. He said: "Your people are indomitable. They are really extraordinary. We must do all we can to give them the chance to fight. I can assure you that I will do all I can." He asked me to keep him informed through Sumner Welles, or directly, on all further developments. "This is a matter of deep concern to me," he ended as we said good-by.

Two hours later I received an invitation from Mr. Welles to call on him the next morning, November 6, in order to discuss these matters at his office with Mr. Edward R. Stettinius, Jr., Lend-Lease administrator, General James H. Burns, chief of the Munitions Assignment Board who, as military expert on Lend-Lease war matériel, had accompanied Mr. Harriman on his mission to Moscow, and other high State Department officials.

At this meeting I explained that there were two distinct problems: One, of obtaining the acceptance of the Soviet Government for the speedy formation, equipment, and armament of the Polish armed forces in Russia. Should that, however, be impossible in view of the great demands which the war was making upon the Soviet Government, I suggested Mr. Harriman should, according to the President's directives, propose to Stalin that the Polish soldiers be allowed to leave Russia for some determined destination in the Middle East where they could be more easily supplied with war equipment and matériel from the United States.

The second problem was that of the actual supply of war matériel and equipment from Britain and America for these men.

General Burns told us that he fully supported the idea of getting the Polish troops out of Russia. He said that from a military point of view he considered that a Polish soldier was "worth six soldiers of almost any fighting force except perhaps the Australians, whose fighting qualities and indomitable spirit were on a level with those of the Poles."

Mr. Stettinius, with his usual precision, explained that at this time the problem of munitions was the most difficult of all. There were not enough weapons and munitions anywhere for a war so lavish of war matériel. He also foresaw difficulties, the British being so anxious to obtain priority for their Indian formations.

On November 10 I called on Assistant Secretary of State Ray Atherton to tell him that since our meeting in Mr. Sumner Welles's office I had received telegrams from General Sikorski and from our Ambassador in Russia from which it appeared that the situation was becoming increasingly difficult, both regarding our deportees and the formation of our army. I expressed the hope that Mr. Harriman's telegram to Stalin would not long remain without effect.

Finally, I had a long conversation with Mr. Harriman in his rooms at the Mayflower Hotel on November 14. He was sorry that he had not got the text of the telegram which he had sent to Marshal Stalin after our consultations with the President and Mr. Welles. From the text which he summarized for me, I saw that he had raised practically all the points under discussion. He expected a reply at any moment.

Mr. Harriman told me how pleased he had been with the

results of his first mission to Moscow and appeared surprised that the Polish Government was having difficulties in the formation of our army in Russia. He asked me what I thought was the reason for this.

I replied frankly that I thought that this might have resulted from the fact that, when Mr. Harriman and Lord Beaverbrook first visited Moscow in September and, in accordance with the President's decision, Mr. Harriman was directed to declare America's interest in Polish-Soviet relations, he had refrained from doing so.

Mr. Harriman readily admitted this. He asked me to realize that when Lord Beaverbrook and he reached Moscow and started their conversations with Stalin, which continued for four nights, Mr. Harriman was impressed by the British anxiety that overwhelming German power might break Russian resistance. They came to the conclusion that it was above all important to gain Stalin's confidence by promising him the fullest material and moral support. He admitted that he certainly could have made an issue of the Polish military problem, but the situation, as he and Lord Beaverbrook saw it, made them decide not to do so.

Mr. Harriman said that on the part of Stalin he had met with a friendly attitude toward the United States, but Stalin did not appear to regard Britain with the same degree of confidence. Harriman reminded me of "the regrettable things said in England by irresponsible people." This, naturally, had aroused Soviet suspicion. The Soviet Government appeared to attach importance, for instance, to sayings that "it would be a good thing if Russia and Germany should weaken each other," or that "the Soviet-German war should finish in a stalemate rather than become a definite Soviet victory over Hitler."

He told me that he had had to use his influence to correct this unfortunate impression and to concentrate exclusively on finding arguments which might satisfactorily prove to Stalin that British and American help was not going to be doled out with any such ridiculous idea in view, but wholeheartedly and to the fullest extent. He went to Moscow to encourage Russia to resist, and all other matters had to be subordinated to this one aim. In fact, he could not afford to give the impression that there were any strings attached to American support of the Soviet war effort.

However, he admitted I might be correct in assuming that the absence of a more definite show of interest in the Polish question could have contributed to the way in which the Soviets were now dealing with our government.

I told Mr. Harriman that I understood his difficulty. I expressed the fear, however, that it would be much more difficult to obtain a satisfactory result as time went on, and I thought it would have been advisable to lay the cards on the table in his first conversation with Stalin.

We then dropped this subject and went on discussing his impressions of Moscow.

He told me that not once in his conversations with Stalin did he feel that the old Lenin policy of world revolution was still an aim of Stalinist Russia. On the contrary, Stalin appeared to him to be not a revolutionary communist, but, above all, a Russian nationalist. He spoke to Mr. Harriman about Russia's aims and her war effort as a nationalist leader.

I told him that such opportune nationalism might not necessarily prevent a later return to the old basic policy of world communism. And nationalism easily tended to develop into imperialism. I asked him whether he had read and analyzed Marshal Stalin's last speech in which he said that it was Russia's aim to restore her frontiers of June 21, 1941. That certainly was not reassuring, either for the three Baltic countries or for Poland, and, in my opinion, it sounded an ominous warning regarding Stalin's policies. It certainly did not appear to fit in with the Atlantic Charter.

Mr. Harriman admitted that he had heard of these passages in the Russian version of Stalin's speech. He was inclined to think, however, that these enunciations might have been necessary for domestic consumption.

As I rose to leave I told Harriman that I was sure he would in due time find that, in view of their mentality, it was advisable to speak to the Soviets frankly and definitely. I regretted that circumstances had prevented him from raising the Polish issue in his first conversations with Stalin and I felt sure that very soon he would find it necessary—I hoped before it was too late—to stress the importance attached by the United States to the war aims and principles declared in the Atlantic Charter and accepted by all the Allies, including Russia. Mr. Harriman admitted that I might be right.

We parted amicably but I went out pondering over the great responsibility which President Roosevelt appeared to have entrusted to two men, both of whom acted as his personal envoys to Moscow: Harry L. Hopkins and W. Averell Harriman.

I asked myself: What chance had these men, regardless of their devotion to the President, and of their prodigious American efficiency, in a duel of statesmanship with a master mind like that of Stalin?

CHAPTER VII

Sikorski and Stalin, December 1941

THE mighty Russian war effort was beginning to slow down Hitler's rapid advance.

From the lively exchange of correspondence between General Sikorski and myself I noted his anxiety that all should be done in Washington to help in speeding up the formation of our armed forces in Russia to enable them to go into battle on the Soviet front.

With his characteristic spontaneity General Sikorski, being so sincerely determined to do all in his power to solve the difficulties which the Soviet Government was placing in the way of a cordial Polish-Soviet understanding, felt that it was ultimately up to him to try a direct approach.

"I am certain," he wrote to me, "that I cannot fail to impress upon Stalin how sincerely I desire collaboration. I have therefore decided to go to Moscow and to put the whole matter up to him. My policy is a simple one. I want to do all I can to make these relations normal, frank, and friendly, and if this proves impossible, I want to have my conscience clear that the responsibility does not rest upon me or upon my government."

Therefore I was not surprised when I received news that General Sikorski had arrived at Kuibyshev, the temporary seat of the Soviet Government, on his way to Moscow on December 1, 1941.

Marshal Stalin and his military staff were in Moscow.

Shortly after his trip to Russia General Sikorski came to Washington on his second visit. I asked him to supplement the laconic reports of his Moscow visit by giving me his personal impressions of his meetings with Stalin.

"Stalin received me rather coldly at first," replied General Sikorski. "He seemed to suspect me of being a sort of agent of Churchill. However, when I convinced him that this was not the case, the atmosphere quickly changed and became more favorable."

Sikorski traveled to Russia from London via Cairo and Teheran, arriving in Kuibyshev on the cold and dreary evening of December 1. He was given a full-dress state reception at the airport where he was met by the diplomatic corps and by the Soviet Vice-Commissar, Vishinsky, representing the Soviet Government. As a typically Russian expression of welcome, vodka and special hors d'oeuvres were served in the wooden shack used as a waiting room at the airport.

The general took up his quarters at the temporary Polish Embassy in Kuibyshev.

After one day in Kuibyshev, Sikorski flew to Moscow to visit Stalin. His plane was escorted by Soviet fighter machines—a precaution taken not merely out of courtesy, but for reasons of safety, considering that the Germans were then fighting in the streets of Rostov and the Soviet front was barely twenty miles distant from Moscow.

General Sikorski described to me the sunny, frosty, snow-covered Moscow, where the thunder of guns was clearly audible. The population of that city accepted the menacing closeness of the front with commendable stoicism, undoubtedly based on the confidence it gained from the knowledge that Marshal Stalin was directing the defense from behind the red walls of the Kremlin.

On the evening of December 3 Sikorski, accompanied by our Ambassador and General Anders, had his first conversation with Stalin in the presence of Commissar Molotov and one of his aides.

Outside the Kremlin, in the complete blackout of Moscow, the thermometer showed thirty-two degrees below freezing. In Stalin's brightly lit study the temperature of this first meeting of the two neighbors rose and fell in the course of the conversation, sometimes descending to zero, but at times warming up considerably.

With his usual serenity and optimism Sikorski began by expressing his admiration for the heroism of the Red Army and for the outstanding talent which Stalin was showing as a military strategist. He then adopted a more serious but very friendly tone.

"From the full and loyal carrying out of our agreement depends whether we actually are at the turning point of history," said Sikorski, "and," he continued, "that depends on you, Mr. Prime Minister, since your decisions in this country are final. Our agreement must be fulfilled and the continuous abuse of our people must cease. I realize your difficulties. I know that the German Reich has attacked you with four fifths of all its armed might. I am an ardent advocate of your cause in London. I submitted to Churchill some time ago military facts and figures proving the necessity of the speedy creation of a second front."

"That is good. I thank you, Mr. Prime Minister," nodded Stalin.

"But establishing a second front is no easy problem," elaborated Sikorski, "and you know the difficulties, Mr. Prime Minister. The invasion of Europe must be very carefully planned and very large contingents of troops and matériel must be assembled before it can be successfully undertaken."

"You are right," interjected Molotov. "If the invasion were unsuccessful, the moral effect would be detrimental."

"I return, however, to our business," said Sikorski. "I regret to say that the amnesty granted by you to our people is not being carried out. Many of our most valuable men are still in labor camps or in prisons."

Stalin jotted down a few notes and turned to Molotov. "That cannot be correct, since the amnesty was to embrace all, and all the Poles are liberated by now."

Molotov nodded his assent, but General Anders unfolded several sheets of paper and read depositions by liberated Poles testifying to the fact that many of their former camp colleagues were still being detained.

"You see," said Anders, lifting his head from the papers and looking at Molotov, "many camp commanders who have to carry out a production plan do not wish to deprive themselves of workmen, without whom the execution of their plan may be impossible."

Molotov smiled broadly. "I think that may be so."

"Those camp commanders do not appreciate the full importance of our common cause which suffers greatly by their reluctance to free the detained Poles," said General Anders.

"Such commanders should be punished," remarked Stalin grimly.

"It is not our business to submit to the Soviet authorities lists of our people," Sikorski said, joining in at this point, "since we were never informed who, for what, and how many were deported to Russia. But I have with me a list of about 4,000 Polish officers, taken prisoner in Poland, who have not appeared at General Anders' military camps. This list is far from complete, since it contains only those names which could be remembered by soldiers commanded by these officers. Not one of these officers—and their number is probably at least twice as large as the 4,000 shown on my list—has turned up as yet."

"That is impossible," snapped Stalin. "They must have escaped somewhere."

"But, Mr. Prime Minister," said General Anders, "where could they have escaped?"

"Well, to Manchuria, maybe," answered Stalin.

"It is out of the question that all of them could have escaped," remarked General Anders. "Moreover, all correspondence with their families in Poland ceased abruptly in April and May 1940 when they were transferred from their three former prison camps to an unknown destination. I want to stress, Mr. Prime Minister, that the majority of officers whose names appear on the list just handed to you by General Sikorski are known to me personally. There are among them high-ranking staff officers, excellent fighters, many army doctors and surgeons. Believe me, I need them very badly."

"Unquestionably they were liberated," insisted Stalin, "but they have not yet reached your quarters."

"I know that Russia is enormous," interjected Sikorski, "but is it possible that several thousand officers could escape or disappear without even one of them being accounted for? And, moreover, if they reached some foreign country, it does not appear possible that not one of them should report to me. Every Pole who is able to make his way abroad joins the ranks of our army in England or Canada. But let us not dwell at present on this problem, Mr. Prime Minister. What we really need is your order to bring about a basic change of the Soviet attitude toward the Poles now in Soviet Russia. After all, they did not come here as tourists, or of their own free will. They were forcibly driven from their homes, deported, and have gone through horrible suffering in your prison and labor camps."

"The population of the Soviet Union is well disposed toward the Poles. Errors may be committed only by individual officials," replied Stalin calmly.

"If so," remarked Sikorski, "it should be easy to correct the situation. I saw in Kuibyshev a transport of our people which made a horrible impression on me. It is very necessary to give them speedy aid. I should divide our people into two categories: able-bodied men who should join the Army, and older persons who should obtain work under possibly good conditions."

"Under the same conditions under which Soviet citizens are working?" asked Stalin.

"Certainly," agreed Sikorski. "Even if it cannot be under the same conditions, it must be at least under tolerable ones. It is obviously in our mutual interest. I am sure you realize, Mr. Prime Minister, that it is not fitting to use a mechanical engineer or a specialist in tank construction for cutting trees in a Siberian forest, or to have a prominent chemist spreading manure on a farm."

Stalin nodded.

The conversation went on, touching upon details of resettlement of Poles in some provinces of Russia with a better climate, of giving them modest but livable quarters, and allowing them to get relief from America to be distributed to them by delegates of the Polish Embassy.

"I am sorry, Mr. Prime Minister," said Sikorski, "that I have to bother you with such details, but at a time when you are so busy conducting a war so magnificently they are important."

"Magnificently?" smiled Stalin. "Not quite. Let's say moderately well."

"Now I want to turn to military matters," Sikorski went on in a serious vein. "We Poles are not fighting merely as a symbolic force, but as a genuine active fighting force."

"And we want to fight here, on the continent, for the independence of Poland," emphatically added General Anders.

"In Poland," continued Sikorski, "we have a strong underground military organization. For obvious reasons I have forbidden any publicity about this organization, since German reprisals are terrible."

"I know, I know," assented Stalin.

"Our troops are fighting everywhere," continued Sikorski. "We have an army corps in Great Britian, we have a navy and a merchant marine which work perfectly, and we have seventeen air squadrons in action. You probably know that nearly 20 per cent of all German losses in the air in the Battle of Britain were accounted for by Polish pilots."

"I know that the Poles are courageous," remarked Stalin.

"Particularly when they are well commanded," said Sikorski, "and I am especially happy that we have here General Anders, under whose command the Polish Army will fight alongside of your army, Mr. Prime Minister. I don't have to praise Anders; you know his courage, you know that he was wounded eight times. As a matter of fact, you imprisoned him because he wished to join me in 1939." Sikorski smiled.

"How long were you in prison?" Stalin asked General Anders.

"Twenty months."

"And how did they treat you?"

"Exceptionally badly in Lwow. In Moscow," answered Anders, "slightly better. But you understand yourself, Mr. Prime Minister, what is meant by 'better' in a prison when one is held for twenty months."

"Oh, well"—Stalin raised his hands—"such were the conditions."

Sikorski told Stalin about the Polish brigade fighting in Tobruk and said that if Stalin desired, this brigade, reorganized as a motorized division, could be sent to the Soviet front.

"Poland is in Hitler's hands," pointed out Sikorski, "and our only human reserves are over here. I would like to form seven divisions in Russia and send about 25,000 men from here as reinforcements to Scotland, particularly picking men for the air force and the Navy. Our forces now in Scotland will be used in the invasion of Europe or transferred here, to Russia, to join the seven divisions we are planning to create. In that case I would personally assume command over these forces and come to Russia myself."

"But, Mr. Prime Minister," Sikorski added with fervor, "the present conditions as regards feeding, equipping, and training of our men here fill me with anxiety. They don't get food. They live in flimsy tents without stoves. They wake up in the morning with frostbitten noses and ears. They are literally starving. Under such conditions one cannot form an army. You would not call that even a miserable existence. You know that the British have sent them some uniforms and boots, but until recently over 60 per cent of our men here were actually barefoot. They do not receive the food rations due a soldier."

"What do you suggest?" asked Stalin.

"I fully realize the difficulties of transport and supply in which Russia is now fighting the war, and therefore I propose the transfer of all our manpower fit for military duty to Iran, where the climate is milder and where American and British aid could reach them. There they could regain strength and form an army which would return to Russia, to the front where you would assign to them a sector to defend.

"Our Ambassador in Washington," continued Sikorski, "studied this possibility with the American Government and the Lend-Lease Administration. They think that it would be easier to supply our army if it were transferred to Iran. I also have Churchill's approval of this scheme. I am willing to give you a declaration that this army will return to the Russian front, reinforced by several divisions. It is my sincere desire that the Soviet Government should treat my proposal with full confidence. I am a man who means what he says."

"And I am an experienced man and an old man," replied Stalin, raising his voice, plainly dissatisfied and irritated. "I know that, once your men leave for Iran, they will never return here."

After a few seconds' silence Stalin added with a grin: "I now see that England has her hands full and needs more Polish soldiers badly."

"You hurt me greatly, Mr. Prime Minister," said Sikorski indignantly. "Not words, but facts prove that we want to fight. Moreover, we want to fight right here. According to my calculations, I can have 150,000 soldiers in Russia, which is the equivalent of over eight divisions with all auxiliary services. But we have only just begun the formation of two divisions, and the possibilities offered here are less than limited. General Anders has brought all the records with him. We do not receive the food rations due, no clothing, no barracks, let alone armament."

"If the Poles do not want to fight, then let them go," insisted Stalin irritably. "Be it as you wish. We cannot detain them. If they want to—let them go."

"I do not want you to put the matter in such a way," replied Sikorski. "Perhaps you can suggest a new formula. I am ready to accept any fair solution."

"Shall we call in General Panfilov?" asked Molotov.

Stalin agreed and turned to Sikorski with a grin. "I see that the British are badly in need of a good army."

"Mr. Prime Minister," said Sikorski, "you are wrong. I know Churchill and I know the British people. They appreciate us in England, but they do not exploit us. And I also know, Mr. Prime Minister, that Churchill wants to do all he can to help Russia."

"I know I am crude," said Stalin, smiling. "Maybe I am rude, too, but I want to know plainly whether you want to fight or not. If I allow your army to go because I am unable to give you all you need, the world would say that the Russians can only squeeze the Poles but will do nothing for them. They will say again that we are savages."

"Mr. Prime Minister, I cannot regard this as a reply to my proposal," replied Sikorski. "Can I have your support to organize our army here so that it can participate in the war, or must our people die here in appalling conditions? Please give me a concrete counterproposal. Once more I most emphatically declare that we want to fight for Poland at your side on the Russian front."

"If you go to Iran," said Stalin, "you will probably have to fight soon against the Germans in Turkey. Tomorrow Japan will attack, and then you will have to fight against Japan. You will have to do just what the British order you to do—maybe in Singapore."

"We want to fight against the Germans, for Poland, on the European continent. And from here it is nearest to Poland. But

I still have not heard any comprehensive counterproposal from you."

"If you absolutely insist, all right," answered Stalin. "Two or three of your divisions may leave. I see the British need Polish soldiers. I have already received requests from Harriman and Churchill to evacuate the Polish Army. But I will give you the place and the means to organize an additional seven divisions here."

"The British are not in such bad shape that they have to rely on the Polish Army for their salvation," said Sikorski. "In fact it was I who asked the British and American governments to intervene for the evacuation of those of our people who cannot be looked after in Russia. However, I am willing to leave the entire force in Russia if you will assign a fitting region for its concentration, assure the necessary food, equipment, and living quarters as well as conditions which would make its training possible. We will then have to find ways of bringing American Lend-Lease matériel to them here."

Just then a secretary announced the arrival of General Panfilov, Deputy Chief of Staff of the Red Army, summoned to join in the conversation.

All present listened to a detailed conversation between General Anders and General Panfilov concerning the conditions indispensable to the formation of the Polish forces in Russia. Records were studied, lists of supplies verified, and the sites of camps discussed.

When General Anders drew the attention of General Panfilov to the fact that food for the Polish soldiers had been abruptly decreased to 30,000 rations, in spite of Stalin's promise to our Ambassador regarding the reinstatement of previously fixed numbers of food rations, and that some of the Polish camps were receiving no food whatsoever for upward of a week—Stalin turned to Panfilov and asked severely: "Who is to blame for this?"

"The instructions have been issued," reported Panfilov, looking scared.

"When did I give the order to increase the quantity of food rations for the Poles?" pressed Stalin while Panfilov was turning red and pale.

"Two and a half weeks ago," replied Panfilov.

"Why was my order not carried out? Do you expect them to eat your instructions?" Stalin asked fiercely.

General Panfilov retired soon after this outburst and Sikorski resumed the conversation, repeating once more that he had asked the British and the American governments to help evacuate the Polish soldiers from Russia but only in view of the insurmountable obstacles encountered by Anders in the formation of our army in Russia.

"And I was convinced that it was the British who were insisting to get your army," Stalin said again.

"Once more, Mr. Prime Minister, I assure you that you are mistaken," said Sikorski. "Should the conversation just held between General Anders and General Panfilov favorably change the situation, I am absolutely willing to leave our people here and I will then ask you to allow me to evacuate only about 25,000 men as replacements for our aviation and our navy."

"How many airplanes does your squadron have?" asked Stalin.

"Twenty-seven, out of which eighteen are in the first and nine in the second line," replied Sikorski.

"Well," said Stalin, "this is the equivalent of our air regiment."

"I would like to send several of our air squadrons from England to serve with our army in Russia," said Sikorski. "Some of our fliers are very anxious to come here. They are good fliers, very brave, quick, and have excellent eyesight."

"The best and bravest airmen are the Slavs," said Stalin with finality. "Their reflexes are very rapid because they belong to a young race which has not yet been worn out."

Sikorski got up to leave. "I thank you very much, Mr. Prime Minister," he said, "and I would suggest that at the close of my visit in Moscow tomorrow we should both sign a joint declaration. Although I cannot insist on it, I have brought this draft, Mr. Prime Minister, and I leave it with you to look over."

"I agree in principle and I will read it over. I want you to come with your party to dinner tomorrow night and we can attend to that business then."

Sikorski, with his hand outstretched, added: "I consider the military question settled. I understand you will issue the necessary orders so that appropriate areas for camps and training are assigned to our forces and that the supply problem will be more efficiently looked after by your officials. On my part, I will do all in my power to obtain speedier and greater shipments of war matériel from London and Washington. General Anders will represent me here, and I understand that we will create a mixed Polish-Soviet Commission to watch over the process of freeing of our deportees and the formation of our army."

"I fully agree," said Stalin, and warmly clasped Sikorski's hand. Then he turned to General Anders. "I would like you to stay with me a few minutes longer."

Sikorski was escorted back to his hotel. General Anders stayed with Stalin, who inquired insistently whether General Panfilov was co-operating in the task of getting supplies to the Polish forces. General Anders replied frankly that the co-operation was harmonious but that General Panfilov appeared unable to do very much.

"But now, Mr. Prime Minister," Anders added, "after your promise to remove all difficulties, I firmly believe that the formation of the army will go ahead."

"Yes," said Stalin, "and I very much regret that I did not see you before."

"I am not to blame for that, Mr. Prime Minister," replied Anders. "I was not called by you."

"Come again," said Stalin, taking leave of Anders. "I will always be very pleased to see you."

The conversation had lasted two and a half hours.[1]

[1] Conversation quoted from a report, personally revised by General Sikorski.

CHAPTER VIII

Tactics versus Policy

ON THE following evening, December 4, General Sikorski with his staff and the Polish Ambassador were entertained by Stalin at a banquet at the Kremlin. Stalin was in excellent form, and the characteristic richness and variety of the menu, as well as the atmosphere at the table, bore out his friendly and hospitable mood.

After the banquet Stalin invited Sikorski to see some motion pictures of the battles on the Soviet front and, as a special attraction, movies of Sikorski's arrival in Kuibyshev and Moscow.

When describing this General Sikorski smilingly told me that even his morning walk in Moscow on the same day was shown on the Russian newsreel, which led Stalin to ask him whether he admitted that Moscow newsreel efficiency equaled that of Hollywood.

After the movie and a friendly exchange of views between Sikorski and Stalin they both signed the joint Polish-Soviet Declaration of Friendship.

For the first time Stalin had put his signature to a document of postwar collaboration between Soviet Russia and one of the Allies—Poland. For the first time in history Stalin signed a document in which he spoke of a "new organization of international relations . . . after a victorious war . . ." one in which he promised that "in peacetime . . . mutual relations will be based on good neighborly collaboration, friendship, and reciprocal honest fulfillment of . . . obligations." For the first time he also assured for the postwar period "respect for international law, backed by the collective armed force of the Allied States."

Sikorski told me later that he was greatly elated by this result. The ice appeared to have been definitely broken between himself and Stalin.

Sikorski believed in Stalin's sincerity. He was sure that, as a dictator, Stalin undoubtedly could redirect Soviet policy and make it friendly to Poland. He could check the tendencies of some of his followers, who still appeared to be hostile to Soviet-Polish friendship.

In the reports on the Sikorski-Stalin conversations received by me in Washington one thing had struck me. The discussions at the Kremlin covered almost all aspects of military and peaceful collaboration between Poland and the USSR. Progress appeared to have been effectively made. However, it was obvious from these reports that the territorial issue, previously so brutally raised by the Soviets, had not been mentioned at all in the conversations.

This appeared to me to be a reassuring sign of Soviet sincerity. It seemed that Moscow was now placing the same interpretation as the Polish Government and the rest of the Western world on the first paragraph of the Polish-Soviet agreement of July 30, 1941, which stated that the USSR henceforth regarded the Ribbentrop-Molotov pact on the partition of Poland as null and void.

If that were the case, then a welcome change indeed had come over Moscow. In the early days of August Sikorski had interpreted that paragraph in a radio broadcast. He explained that the nullification of the Ribbentrop-Molotov pact automatically restored the recognition by the Soviets of Poland's western territorial status as fixed by the Polish-Soviet Treaty of Riga in March 1921.

This interpretation had been immediately challenged in the official Soviet press which said that the Polish-Soviet agreement did not necessarily mean what General Sikorski had said.

However, the fact remained that all other details of our collaboration with Soviet Russia had been thrashed out in a direct exchange of views between Sikorski and Stalin, partly friendly, partly pointed, and yet the Soviet dictator appeared not to have insisted on discussing the territorial issue.

I was soon to learn that this was not the case. In the course of General Sikorski's second visit to America in March 1942, when we discussed the details of his Moscow visit, I asked him if Stalin had made any reference to Poland's eastern frontiers.

"I had the feeling," replied Sikorski, "that Stalin would raise the issue regardless of our agreement of July 30, 1941. And I was right, for he finally did raise it. But I refused to discuss the subject. How could I agree to discuss it? Constitutionally I had no right to do so, and I regarded this question as definitely eliminated by our agreement."

General Sikorski told me that after the Kremlin banquet Stalin suddenly turned to him with a smile and asked: "Should we not now talk about the frontier between Poland and Russia?"

"I replied," said General Sikorski, "that I did not see any reason to discuss a matter finally settled since 1921."

"Nevertheless I would like to see some alterations in these frontiers," countered Stalin.

"I told him," said Sikorski, "that he was surely aware that I could not discuss this matter because under our constitution I had no right to do so without having a definite mandate from the Polish parliament. Moreover, it was not a matter for discussion during a war and in view of its imponderables.

"I added jokingly," said Sikorski, "that on this subject I had to adopt the same attitude Stalin had adopted when I asked him to allow our army to leave Russia if he could not feed, equip, and arm it. I reminded him that he had said then: 'The whole world would laugh at me if I allowed your good fighting men to leave Russia when they can be so useful to us here.' Well, I told him that the whole world would laugh at me if I were to agree to reopen a territorial issue so satisfactorily and finally settled between our two countries.

"However, Stalin continued to insist: 'I think it would be useful if we discussed it,' he said. 'After all, the alterations I want to suggest are very slight. You seem to think, General, that I really want you to agree to some great territorial sacrifices. What I want is only a very slight alteration of your prewar frontier—one which would hardly change your territorial status and would in no way seriously affect it. In fact, a *chut, chut,* which in Russian means a hardly perceptible alteration.'

"Even a chut, chut alteration is more than I have the right to discuss," replied Sikorski. "You must realize that it is not only the territory of my country which I must regard as inviolable, but especially the principle which I cannot compromise with. So please let us not spoil the harmony we have achieved by insisting on raising this matter."

The subject, Sikorski told me, was then dropped.

The general must have noticed that I looked depressed. "Tell me," he said, "would you have acted differently? You diplomats are apt to discuss any subject and to risk being drawn into conversations on any issue. We soldiers have to guard against such talks. What would you have done in my place? If you were the responsible Prime Minister of Poland, fenced in by the limits of your responsibility to our constitution and unable to retract or to qualify your statements . . ."

"Having been born under Russian domination, I think I know Russian mentality better than you do, General," I replied. "I know how dearly the Russians love debate. I admit I probably would have yielded to the temptation of discussing this legally tabooed question with Stalin.

"For one thing, my curiosity would not have resisted such a test. I would have been tempted to know exactly what Stalin's chut, chut meant in terms of square miles, especially at that time, when your conversation was punctuated by the thud of Hitler's guns pounding practically at the gates of Moscow. I would certainly have made all necessary reservations by telling him that it was only my personal curiosity which made me accept such a discussion, which would be purely theoretical."

Sikorski was silent for a moment. "You may be right. However, I still persist in thinking that I had no right to discuss this subject even on the plea of curiosity. Some things are sacred, and may not be discussed. Moreover, if I had accepted such a discussion, I would have appeared to admit that after having signed the agreement with Poland of July 30, Stalin could try to qualify its only correct interpretation. It was my duty, as Poland's Prime Minister, to refuse to reopen the subject and thus to insist on the mutual respect of the terms of our agreement."

It was characteristic of Sikorski to take this lofty attitude.

And yet, while he and Stalin were discussing Polish-Soviet relations and collaboration, Sikorski had an official note in his pocket handed to our Ambassador in Russia by the People's Commissariat for Foreign Affairs on December 1—the very day of Sikorski's arrival in Kuibyshev—in which for the first time the Soviet Government had officially notified our embassy in Kuibyshev that Soviet Russia interpreted the meaning of the annulment of the Ribbentrop-Molotov pact quite differently from the rest of the world.

In this note, in reply to one from the Polish Ambassador of November 10, in which he complained that Polish citizens "of Ukrainian, White Ruthenian, and Jewish origin" were not being liberated from Soviet camps and prisons and thus prevented from joining the Polish armed forces, the Soviet Government had advanced an entirely new interpretation of the text of the existing Polish-Soviet agreement.

The Soviet note stated that ". . . in accordance with the decree of the Presidium of the Supreme Council of the USSR . . . all citizens of the western districts of the Ukrainian and White Ruthenian SSR . . . acquired the citizenship of the USSR. . . . The Soviet Government's readiness to recognize as Polish citizens persons of Polish origin . . . gives evidence of good will and compliance on the part of the Soviet Government, but can in no case serve as a basis for an analogous recognition of the Polish citizenship of persons of other origin, in particular those of Ukrainian, White Ruthenian, or Jewish origin, since the question of the frontiers between the USSR and Poland has not been settled and is subject to settlement in the future. . . ."

In this way the specific Soviet interpretation of the clauses of the Atlantic Charter, in which it was clearly stated that the United Nations would seek no territorial aggrandizement, had been officially defined.

In the light of this note the personal attempt made by Stalin to discuss territorial issues with Sikorski was, to my mind, a typical Russian method of following up the matter and of hammering in a wedge previously placed in position.

Outwardly, Soviet Russia had agreed to abide by the terms of the Atlantic Charter. She had signified this decision in Ambassador Maisky's speech at the meeting at St. James's Palace on September 24, 1941. Stalin had just signed a treaty of friendship with Sikorski. But in diplomatic documents, which were not destined to see the light of day for some time to come, an entirely different interpretation was stressed by the Soviets—an interpretation which once more reopened the territorial issue.

In line with Soviet diplomacy, tactics were flexible and directed by opportunism. Policy was inexorable, continuous, and inflexible.

CHAPTER IX

Launching the United Nations, January 1, 1942

In the fall of 1941 events were gradually leading up to the active participation of the United States in the war. American-Japanese negotiations were beginning to cause grave concern in Washington.

I learned that during his Atlantic meeting with President Roosevelt, Mr. Churchill had insistently urged a more direct and firmer policy toward Japan. The President, however, carefully timing his moves, was still tending to give Japan the chance of avoiding the folly of launching into a war. In fact, the President still felt compelled to do his utmost, by means of economic and other concessions, to "buy out" Japan from the Axis.

However, the proposals made by Japan's Prime Minister Prince Konoye showed that there was little chance of appeasing Japan. While expressing his readiness to declare Japanese neutrality in regard to the European war, Konoye indicated that this could be done only at the price of considerable British and American concessions, affecting their loyalty to China, and including the immediate unfreezing of all Japanese state and private assets in Britain and the United States.

Such conditions could hardly be accepted by the Western Powers. And yet President Roosevelt continued for some time his attempts to reach a peaceful solution.

I learned that the President was receiving strongly worded telegrams from Generalissimo Chiang Kai-shek, who feared that some of China's vital interests might finally be sacrificed in an attempt to appease Japan.

The situation was becoming tense.

Through our embassy in Tokyo I learned that Ambassador Joseph C. Grew was reporting the difficulties he encountered in his conversations with the Japanese Government. One thing was becoming certain. The last attempt on the part of President Roosevelt and Secretary Hull to reason Japan out of the Axis and in a "horse trade" to purchase Japanese good will, was a final one which, if it failed, would be replaced by a more definite American policy even if it led to armed conflict. In fact it was America's final bid for peace.

Japanese-American conversations were rather suddenly transferred from Tokyo to Washington, with the arrival in Washington of Japan's special envoy, Kurusu. For a short while his arrival gave rise to the wishful hope that open conflict might still be avoided.

Personally, I had few illusions concerning the attitude of Japan at that time. I felt sure that Japan meant business. From information received from the Polish Embassy in Japan I had followed the situation from another angle—that of the gradually growing involvement of the Japanese Government with Hitler and indications that Soviet Russia intended to remain neutral in the war in the Far East.

In a conversation with President Roosevelt on November 5, 1941, I informed him that the Japanese Government had suddenly decided to break diplomatic relations with the Polish Government on November 1 and that our embassy in Japan, headed by Ambassador Tadeusz Romer, a close friend of Ambassador Grew, was forced to leave Tokyo.

"In view of all that I hear about American-Japanese relations," I said, "I think, Mr. President, that this move on the part of Japan may be of special interest to you, coming, as it does, at this time."

"It certainly is a very interesting development," replied the President. "What, in your opinion, decided Japan to take this unexpected step?"

"I think, Mr. President," I answered, "that it is an ominous sign of the weather. In itself it appears a futile move on the part of Japan to sever relations with Poland. But from a broader aspect, this sudden decision may be a definite sign of a new and closer relationship between Berlin and Tokyo. It may even mark a definite turning point in Japanese-German collaboration. It may be a move exacted by Hitler as an indispensable show of

good will, and possibly of allegiance to Axis policy, on the part
of Japan. What other meaning could it have, Mr. President?"

"You may be right, Mr. Ambassador," responded President
Roosevelt. "I will bear this in mind."

On the fateful and surprisingly warm and sunny Sunday of
December 7 I stayed at the embassy. I knew that Secretary Hull
was to receive the Japanese envoys that morning. I realized how
much depended on the way in which these conversations turned.
I had tuned in my radio. And suddenly, instead of the expected
State Department release about Kurusu's visit, I heard the radio
announcer telling the American people of the treacherous attack
on Pearl Harbor.

The inevitable had happened.

It meant the entry of America into the war with all the Axis
Powers—a war which had become world-wide in one short in-
stant.

The arrival of Mr. Churchill on December 22 was a natural
outcome of these stirring events. He came surrounded by a staff
of some eighty military and civilian experts, and was greeted in
Washington with enthusiasm as the welcome outward confirmation of Anglo-American collaboration.

To me it was gratifying to note that the long-hoped-for pool-
ing of interests and war efforts of the two English-speaking
democracies was finally taking shape under my very eyes. It was
no longer merely a personal friendship between Roosevelt and
Churchill. England had come to Washington, no longer as a
client of the American arsenal of democracy, to ask for "more
tools to finish the job," but as the most powerful naval ally of
America upon whom the United States would have to rely while
faced by Japanese aggression before it was ready actively to join
in the war in Europe.

This final stage of American-British discussions on the definition of the now over-all alliance of nations necessitated by the
entry of the United States into the war closely affected all European countries.

It was a problem which aroused the keenest interest in the
diplomatic corps. We all knew the traditional line of American
policy. We remembered that, while actively participating in
World War I, America had painstakingly maintained the posi-

tion of an associated Power, steadfastly avoiding alliances, in line with George Washington's precepts.

Would the United States define its position differently this time?

I remembered what President Roosevelt had told me about preparing the American people to take their part more permanently in world affairs, and I must say that I was not surprised by the announcement that, after lengthy discussions with Churchill, the President had invented the formula of The United Nations which, in the early morning, he triumphantly personally carried to one of the White House bathrooms, where Mr. Churchill spluttered his soapy approval.

I firmly believed that President Roosevelt intended his newly born concept of the United Nations to be the expression of a great and entirely novel program of world unity in war and peace. As such, it appeared to me a stroke of his genius.

Any alliance or association of nations was but a temporary partnership for limited purposes. A union of nations meant something more tangible and durable, and was unlimited in its scope. It might be interpreted as less than an alliance, but in fact it was more than an alliance, inasmuch as it was conceived on the noble principles of the Atlantic Charter, which might even allow it to develop, in time, into a world federation.

In my opinion the greatness and boldness of this Roosevelt initiative would be proved if in its application the new United Nations concept really broke through the old traditional differentiation between Powers and lesser States, if it admitted all nations belonging to the new association to discussions of world problems on an equal footing, mindful of human and national equality of their respective rights, obligations, and responsibilities.

I watched tensely to see how the actual establishment of this new United Nations concept would be carried out.

On Saturday, December 27, the accredited representatives of all the States fighting in the Allied camp were invited to the White House by the President.

On receiving this invitation, I immediately communicated with the dean of the Diplomatic Corps, Ambassador van der Straaten of Belgium.

He had been in Washington for many years. He was a most delightful companion, reflecting all the great qualities of heart and mind so characteristic of the Belgian people.

I asked him whether, as senior Ambassador, he had any special wishes to express regarding details of this collective official visit of Allied Ambassadors at the White House. He replied that he had just received a similar invitation and had asked the Protocol Division of the Department of State for details. He had been told that we were all expected to meet at the White House and would be taken to see the President, who would probably receive us in company with Mr. Winston Churchill.

We understood that we were invited to see the President in connection with the founding of the United Nations, probably to discuss with him the further developments of that momentous event.

We arrived at the White House promptly and almost simultaneously. As we gathered in the reception room to which we were shown by George Summerlin, I was somewhat surprised to see that we were by no means the complete group of the fighting Allies.

Only the Ambassador of Belgium, myself, the Ministers of Yugoslavia, Greece, Luxemburg, Norway, Czechoslovakia, and Iceland were present. After waiting a few minutes we were escorted upstairs to President Roosevelt's study.

The President received us sitting at his desk, with Mr. Churchill at his side, as usual puffing on a long cigar, while Lord Halifax occupied an armchair on Mr. Churchill's left.

President Roosevelt, with his ever-charming manner of the gracious host, shook hands with us, greeting each one of us with a few words of personal welcome. We shook hands with Mr. Churchill and our colleague, Lord Halifax, after which we were asked by the President to occupy chairs facing these three men.

The President addressed us. He said how pleased he was that Mr. Churchill could be in Washington on this occasion. He told us that he was anxious to create a united front of all the co-belligerent Allies fighting against the Axis Powers. A declaration emanating from all the United Nations was being prepared by Mr. Churchill and the President and would be communicated to us in the early days of the following week and simultaneously submitted to our respective governments for their approval.

The President then said that he was very desirous that the Axis Powers should realize that they had against them an indomitable and closely knit coalition of nations with virtually unlimited resources, fully determined to fight to final victory. He assured us that the restoration of independence of the countries occupied by Germany and suffering under the Axis yoke was his greatest concern which, of course, was shared in like degree by Mr. Churchill. He promised that all would be done to insure the independence of our countries.

Mr. Churchill silently nodded his acquiescence.

The President then explained that, at this stage of his conferences with Mr. Churchill, they were both especially occupied in working out a plan which would divide the fighting world into theaters of war, grouping in each of these theaters the nations most directly involved and interested in each given sector.

"That is why," he said, "you notice the absence of the Netherlands at this meeting, although Holland is a European nation. But for practical purposes at this stage of the war we have to regard the Netherlands as a Power of the Pacific Ocean, mainly fighting in the Dutch East Indies against Japan, and, therefore, belonging to a group formed by Great Britain, the United States, Australia, China, and the Netherlands."

The President expressed the hope that to this group he might shortly add Soviet Russia, for he hoped that she would eventually join in the war against Japan.

"The defense of the United States on the Atlantic and the defense of Great Britain are, of course, concentrated in the hands of these two nations and, naturally," he added, "also in the hands of the Allies of Great Britain, whom you, gentlemen, represent."

The President then stressed the effective part played by the armies and navies of the European countries, and mentioned especially the heroic resistance and underground activities of the populations of our countries, which he said were conducting "with such magnificent and untiring valor" effective resistance and sabotage against the enemy forces.

He said that he attached great importance to the fact that all the United Nations, regardless of their territorial size and importance in this war, should solemnly sign the joint declaration as "a document of Allied unity in this conflict for human freedom."

"And now," said Mr. Roosevelt, turning to Churchill, "I hope you will say a few words."

Mr. Churchill said that he had little to add to what the President had said, but wanted to assure that in all matters hitherto discussed between Britain and the United States he had gained the certainty that full understanding would be easy to reach and that closest collaboration was assured.

"There still remain many details to be worked out," he added, "but these are rather of a technical nature. The main aim of all of us is to win this war. And to do this we need the collaboration of all of you."

And then, in his inimitable way, Mr. Churchill turned to us and said: "Britain is keenly aware of what your nations are doing to support her fight in this war."

He turned to me first, and said: "We shall never forget what glorious Poland has done and is doing, nor what heroic Greece, Norway, and Holland have contributed in this war. All your countries' contributions are important to our common cause. I hope I need not add," Mr. Churchill went on, "having so repeatedly made these assurances in my speeches and in conversations with your governments, that Great Britain has set for herself the aim of restoring full freedom and independence to your nations overrun by Hitler. That is, and will remain, our foremost concern. I can assure you all that Great Britain will never tarry in the fight until that aim is achieved."

By stretching his hand to Ambassador van der Straaten the President signified that the meeting had come to a close.

I expected Van der Straaten to make some reply in our behalf, but he did not do so.

We shook hands with the President, Mr. Churchill, and Lord Halifax, and were ushered downstairs, where we took leave of Mr. Summerlin.

Before leaving, we asked him why the representatives of some of the other co-belligerent Allies, for instance, Ambassador Litvinov of Russia, and the Ministers of the British Dominions, were not present on this occasion.

Mr. Summerlin, with his usual suavity, explained that this was due to a certain classification made by the President and Mr. Churchill: the representatives of Latin-American countries had been asked to visit the President earlier that morning; immediately afterward the Ambassador of China was received separately, and was shortly followed by Minister Loudon of the Netherlands. Then came Ambassador Litvinov, who stayed to lunch with the President, Mr. Churchill, and Harry Hopkins. In the early afternoon the British Dominions, represented by the Ministers of Canada, Australia, New Zealand, and South Africa, as well as the recently arrived representative of India, had called at the White House. Then our turn had come. . . .

As our group of representatives of eight European countries, overrun by Hitler and Mussolini, minus the Netherlands, strolled out of the White House, we stopped for a moment on the historic porch waiting for our cars to drive up, and instinctively got together to compare our impressions.

"This," said the Belgian Ambassador, "is a somewhat novel way of organizing an international association. I was not sure whether I was expected to respond to the President's address. I refrained because no discussion appeared to be possible. And how new and original is this grouping of States and receiving them separately, when all of us are about to sign the same document and to participate in carrying out its clauses."

We all agreed that it was indeed a novel way of being graciously invited "to sign on the dotted line."

My Greek colleague, Diamantopoulos, who always puts a kindly and favorable interpretation on every situation, said that the circumstances of war and the dispersal of war fronts over the whole globe might have dictated this new form of grouping of nations.

"Well," said Fotitch, my dear friend and colleague of Yugoslavia, as usual hitting the nail on the head, "if we are being grouped according to respective theaters of war, why is Russia not grouped with us in the European theater? She is certainly not fighting Japan, only Hitler, and, for the time being at least, in Europe."

"I am afraid," I said, "that this novel way of grouping, initiated by President Roosevelt, may not be entirely geographical.

We are shortly to sign a declaration, which the President has just told us would be all-important because it would declare the unity of all the great and small United Nations and become the joint responsibility of all of us. And yet we are not invited to participate in working out its wording, we are not even shown the draft."

"Well," said Ambassador van der Straaten turning to me, "what do you make of this meeting we have just attended?"

"While I am convinced of the sincerity of the President's and Mr. Churchill's praise for the war effort of our nations, and while I have noted how insistently they ask us for ever greater efforts, I cannot help feeling that we have been invited here today as 'poor relations,' whom rich and powerful uncles have to see from time to time."

My colleagues did not even smile.

The drafting of the declaration went on in secret. On January 1, 1942, I learned at the State Department that the declaration was finally drawn up and that Soviet Ambassador Litvinov and the Chinese Foreign Minister, T. V. Soong, were invited to the White House "to get acquainted with its terms." But I happened to know that the Soviet Ambassador and Minister Soong had already received the text on Tuesday, December 30, 1941, to enable them to submit it to their governments in distant Moscow and Chungking respectively.

In reply to my question as to when I would finally be informed of the text of the declaration, I was told by Loy Henderson, chief of the Eastern European Division of the Department of State, that for reasons of urgency the text of the declaration was being communicated directly to the governments of the European countries in London and that I would probably hear from my government concerning its acceptance.

On the same Thursday, January 1, 1942, I learned that Minister Soong and Ambassador Litvinov were invited to the White House to sign the declaration on behalf of their governments. This was to take place in the presence of President Roosevelt and Mr. Churchill, who were simultaneously to sign on behalf of the United States and Great Britain.

When the Chinese Foreign Minister and Mr. Litvinov arrived at the White House it appeared that Minister Soong had received his instructions to sign on behalf of the Chinese Government, but

Mr. Litvinov had not yet received his instructions, therefore on that first of January the declaration was actually signed by only three Powers: the United States, Great Britain, and China.

Mr. Litvinov returned next morning and signed on behalf of Russia.

All the representatives of the remaining United Nations were informed by the State Department that the declaration would be held for their signature at the office of Assistant Secretary of State Adolf A. Berle, Jr., from ten o'clock in the morning of January 2, 1942, and that we could "drop in at our convenience at any time" to sign it on behalf of our governments.

On January 1 I received instructions from my government to sign on their behalf, and the next morning I arrived at the State Department.

In Mr. Berle's office I met my colleagues, the Ministers of the Netherlands, Yugoslavia, Greece, Luxemburg, and Norway, who had come to sign on behalf of their governments. The declaration was waiting for us on Mr. Berle's desk. We signed it without any formality.

Thus was born the momentous Declaration of the United Nations.

CHAPTER X

Russia Demands a Second Front

IN THE course of Mr. Churchill's Christmas visit, which ended on January 10, 1942, the personal Roosevelt-Churchill collaboration became an active partnership of the two Western Powers.

However, the British partner, who for nearly two and a half years had been wholly involved in the war, pressed on the President to shelve for the time being all the political international problems and to subordinate them to the all-important aim of winning the war.

At a time when the Atlantic Charter and the United Nations concept were in their early childhood and required careful nursing, Churchill's influence and the American setback in the Pacific caused them to be set aside and sacrificed to more urgent, purely military considerations.

The enthusiasm created by the hope of a Russian counter-offensive against Germany swept America, and Washington wishfully hoped that Russia would soon join America and Britain in the war against Japan.

At the close of Mr. Churchill's visit it became clear to me that wide circles of American public opinion were worked upon and propagandized into adopting the British viewpoint of unconditional support of Russia and of avoiding any questions of principle. The British in Washington were busily spreading the fear that a Soviet-German partnership might be re-created if the Soviet Union saw any advantage in concluding a separate peace.

From information I gathered, I knew that Mr. Churchill was keenly apprehensive of such a possibility. He lost no opportunity to impress his fears upon the President.

Very naturally the successes of the Soviet armed forces on the

Moscow front were being most effectively sold to the American and British public. This unexpectedly good news was absorbed with enthusiasm in London and Washington. And already in that initial stage of the slow and laborious Russian advance westward Soviet propaganda started to demand the rapid opening of a second front.

The increasing number of admirers of the Soviet Union in America worked assiduously in support of this ever more insistent Russian demand, appearing to ignore the circumstances which at that time made it utterly impossible to open a second front with any hope of success.

In an "order of the day" Stalin personally came out with a strong indictment of the Western Allies for what he called their "inactivity." This was immediately followed up by Soviet Ambassador Litvinov speaking at the Overseas Press Club in New York on February 26.

To those conversant with Soviet methods it was clear that this was but a preparatory barrage for building up the thesis that Soviet Russia was exclusively bearing the entire burden of military operations against the common enemy.

Simultaneously, inspired by Moscow, a score of American writers started a well-timed campaign supporting the "ethnographic rights of Soviet Russia to certain territories," openly referring to the defunct Curzon Line, and going into elaborate analyses of the rights of Russia to the Baltic ports of the three small Baltic republics: Lithuania, Latvia, and Esthonia.

This propaganda was a cleverly timed accompaniment to the great diplomatic Soviet offensive launched at Secretary Eden during his New Year visit in Moscow.

Mr. Eden's visit coincided with the first definite successes of the Soviet winter counteroffensive. I was informed that at the very moment when, in Washington, Mr. Churchill was signing the Declaration of the United Nations embodying the Atlantic Charter, Mr. Eden in Moscow was faced with the proposal of signing a Soviet-British-American treaty which, among other items, was to grant to Soviet Russia the territories of Finland acquired by force in the Russo-Finnish war of 1940, the entire territories of the three Baltic States, almost half of Poland, and the Rumanian provinces of Bukowina and Bessarabia.

The Soviet Government maintained the view that Russia alone was fighting Germany. Apart from this, Soviet propaganda launched hints and rumors in Washington and London that Russia might have to interrupt her offensive and possibly even be forced to conclude some arrangement with Germany.

In the middle of February 1942 the Acting Minister of Foreign Affairs of Poland, Edward Raczynski, since November 1934 Poland's Ambassador to the Court of St. James's, arrived in Washington on a short visit.

On February 16 I invited Ambassador Litvinov to luncheon to meet Raczynski. These two men had come to know each other during the years when they represented their respective governments at the League of Nations in Geneva.

In the very friendly atmosphere of that luncheon Litvinov took the opportunity to express his conviction that a German offensive on an enormous scale would take place in the spring and that the only hope of stopping it lay in the immediate opening of a second front by Britain and America in western Europe. It was characteristic that in this conversation Litvinov also hinted that as soon as this German offensive started, Japan would most probably attack the Soviets.

I had once more the opportunity of watching the great diplomatic talent of Litvinov, who suddenly asked Raczynski how the Polish-Czechoslovak conversations about the contemplated federation of the two countries were progressing. When Raczynski answered that they were progressing very favorably, Mr. Litvinov said: "That is very interesting. But has your government consulted the Soviet Government on this matter?"

Raczynski replied that he really did not see the necessity for such a consultation. We let the matter drop.

When I visited Assistant Secretary Berle with Raczynski on the twenty-fourth of February, we had the opportunity of realizing how effective Soviet pressure was at that time and how strongly it appeared to impress American official circles.

In the course of the conversation Raczynski mentioned that he had heard that Eden had been faced in Moscow by definite territorial demands on the part of the Soviets, especially on the Baltic. Berle most unexpectedly expressed the prophetic view that Russia would emerge from this war as one of the few greatest world

Powers, and added that he thought that the granting of special demands of so great a Power would probably be inevitable. He added that it was difficult to conceive that unlimited sovereignty of smaller States in the prewar sense of the word could stand in the way of the natural and inevitable political and economic expansionism of a great Power.

It was then, for the first time, that I heard such an opinion from a high American official.

When Raczynski criticized Soviet expansionism as akin to the German Haushofer "Grossraum geopolitical theory," Berle expressed the view that it should be possible to secure the development of smaller States while simultaneously taking into account the defensive requirements of great Powers directly interested. As an example he pointed to Costa Rica, which, as he said, the United States could have occupied if it had ever wished to do so, but which permitted and appeared quite satisfied to have American defensive bases on her territory and showed no concern for her own safety.

I reminded Mr. Berle of the unhappy situation of the three Baltic States, resulting from the establishment of Soviet "defensive bases" on their territory, and added that, soon after the first Soviet garrisons had occupied them, the entire countries found themselves incorporated in the Soviet Union.

Berle admitted that the Baltic States were deeply attached to their independence and added, as if withdrawing from his former argument, that the ideas he had outlined were still quite unprepared and would need to be carefully thought out.

Nevertheless, this conversation gave us much food for thought. We could not help wondering whether these remarks were the prelude to a possible change of fundamental American views repeatedly declared by the President and the American Government.

On the following day, however, when I introduced Raczynski to President Roosevelt at the White House, the conversation did much to allay our fears.

The President opened the conversation by defining his attitude toward the Soviet claims to the Baltic States.

He said he was glad that, although Eden had listened carefully to Stalin's demands on the subject, he had refrained from giving any binding reply. He added that the British Government, through Churchill, had entirely co-ordinated its views with the American Government on the fundamental principle that the two governments would not agree to any territorial or political changes during the war.

The President admitted, however, that, about two weeks before, the British Government had once more approached the American Government on the subject of the Baltic States.

The President was frankly critical of this wavering attitude of the British Government, which he called "provincial." He assured us that he had not changed his views and persisted in believing that there could be no question of solving fundamental issues during the war and especially in a spirit contrary to the Atlantic Charter.

In the special case of Soviet claims, the President was of the opinion that they were all the more unjustified because, after the war was won and Germany was deprived of the possibility of endangering world security, under what pretext could Russia demand the extension of her territorial bases?

The President said that the Russian demands were causing general anxiety and mentioned a personal letter he had just received from Crown Prince Olaf of Norway in which the latter asked the President whether it was true that the Soviets had demanded the cession of northern Finland, northern Sweden, and northern Norway, with a port on the Atlantic Ocean.

"I was glad," the President said with a smile, "that I could answer Prince Olaf that I had not heard of any such fantastic claims."

Our apprehensions, somewhat allayed by the conversation with the President, were again revived when we were informed that the demands which Stalin had presented to Mr. Eden had not been finally rejected by the British Government. On the contrary, London was trying to persuade Washington to agree to participate in the conclusion of a tripartite agreement which would recognize Soviet territorial demands.

It was obvious that a complex of fear was growing in Britain and that intensive Soviet pressure was making more headway in London than in Washington.

Harry Hopkins lunched with us at the Polish Embassy on

March 6, and the conversation naturally centered on the Soviet demands and on Soviet pressure exercised in Washington and London.

With his customary bluntness Hopkins expressed the view that Stalin was pursuing "a game of nerves" by implying a veiled threat of a possible arrangement with Hitler.

"In reality," he said, "Russia has no choice in the matter of selecting her Allies even if she would prefer to cast her lot with Hitler rather than with the Western democracies. Stalin cannot get out of the war. Soviet tactics should be regarded as a means of pressure. Stalin's main aim is to obtain the fullest material aid from us rather than to get territorial or other concessions. However," he added with a broad smile, "it is possible that Britain, unable to invade western Europe for the time being, hopes to placate Russia by paying her at other people's expense."

"If Soviet claims were merely a bluff," remarked Raczynski, "and Russia was so much in need of help from her Allies, would it not be advisable to put things on a clear footing and frankly to stress America's determination to abide by her policy repeatedly stated by the President, thus putting an end to further pressures?"

Hopkins raised his hands and said that he thought this might be a good time to do so, but that we must realize that he could not interfere in such matters. "I never encroach upon matters within the competence of the Department of State," he said, laughing at his own joke.

The atmosphere prevailing in British circles was somewhat different. We noticed this on the following day, March 7, when Raczynski and I had a talk with Lord Halifax.

Raczynski informed the British Ambassador of the pending visit of General Sikorski in Washington, and very frankly told him that the main reason for this visit was the apprehension of our government concerning the British-Soviet conversations. Ambassador Winant was on his way to Washington with a letter from Churchill to President Roosevelt, explaining the necessity of accepting the Soviet claims and insistently asking Mr. Roosevelt to agree to United States participation in a tripartite agreement.

It was true, Raczynski admitted, that the Soviet territorial claims on Poland were not being stressed for the moment and that Stalin was most insistent in pressing his claims to the Baltic

States, Bukowina, and Bessarabia. This, however, did not re-assure the Polish Government. One look at the map would convince anyone that the grant of such demands would result in the almost complete encirclement of Poland by the Soviets.

Contrary to Hopkins, Lord Halifax did not think that the Soviets were bluffing. He brought forth a series of arguments in favor of acceptance of Moscow's claims. He explained that in Russia one had to deal not with public opinion but with one man —the dictator, Stalin. In countering any of his demands one would merely be strengthening his already considerable distrust of his Western Allies, thus increasing the risk that Russia "might get out of the war."

On March 13 we had a talk at our embassy with Ambassador Winant, who had just arrived from London. It showed us that the tendency of British official circles to yield to Soviet demands had influenced him to some extent.

According to Winant, the most important thing at this stage was to convince Stalin of the good will of the Western Allies.

"After all," he said, "one should not forget that the Baltic States had been given their independence contrary to the will of Russia. Tsarist Russia had held these territories. As regards Poland, Stalin claimed territories only up to the Curzon Line, and his leading concern was Russia's security."

Considering how deeply such arguments appeared to have permeated the mind of Mr. Winant, Raczynski replied by making a full exposé of the realities of the situation.

He reminded Winant that the Baltic States had primarily fought out their own independence. He expressed the opinion that the Russian attack on Finland in 1940 was hardly the best method of insuring Finland's friendly neutrality toward Russia. He went on to analyze Stalin's policy, and to show that it was characteristically and very openly deprived of any moral or legal consideration and merely expressed a crude imperialist dynamism. He said that he had regretfully come to the conclusion that Stalin would understand only counterarguments as downright as his own.

"Small territorial gifts," said Raczynski, "or other concessions made to please Stalin, could in no way alter or even influence him in his drive for the realization of fundamental Soviet aims.

On the other hand, any show of weakness and of readiness to compromise with the principles laid down as the war aims of the United Nations, any readiness to sacrifice weaker States to the rule of the mighty, would be a decision fraught with incalculable consequences, particularly for the British Empire."

Winant, impressed by these arguments, referred to recent Soviet enunciations and especially to the "order of the day" of Stalin to the Army, and to Litvinov's New York speech on February 26. He wondered how far these speeches should be taken as attempts at pressure on the Allies or as trial balloons intended to encourage Hitler to open discussions for a separate peace with Russia. Personally, he thought that they were mostly intended as a means of pressure on Britain and the United States, but he did not exclude that the second version might also be correct.

Sikorski arrived in Washington the latter part of March.

His two conversations with President Roosevelt—on March 24 and March 26, at which I was present—confirmed me in the opinion that at that stage President Roosevelt was entirely engrossed in matters of war strategy, and that he had relegated international problems to a later date. From his opening sentences we noted how anxious he was to obtain the opinion of General Sikorski on various aspects of military problems. He even wanted to ascertain Sikorski's opinion on the Japanese war.

Sikorski was plainly optimistic in his analysis of the military situation. According to him, Japan's first strong attack was not in proportion to her military resources, which he estimated as much smaller than had been supposed at the beginning. Japan could maintain her temporary advantage only so long as she could hold the initiative.

President Roosevelt agreed with this view and told us that in the first months of the American-Japanese war Japan had already lost 1,500 planes, which was serious, considering that her production was only about 300 planes monthly. The President added that it was most important to continue to inflict such losses on the Japanese air force.

In discussing the Mediterranean front, the President wished to know the possibilities of getting the Polish trainees out of Russia and forming a unit of the Polish Army in the Middle East. He considered it of the utmost importance to get as many Poles out of Russia as possible, adding that, "to say the least, they would be treated in Russia like stepchildren."

President Roosevelt also asked Sikorski's views on the Soviet front. The general gave him the latest information received from the Underground organization in Poland. In summing up the situation Sikorski said that in his opinion the Germans had suffered a defeat in 1941. They had lost a great number of their very best forces in the Russian campaign and it was doubtful whether, in the course of the summer of 1942, they would be capable of developing any considerable offensive on the entire front from the Arctic Ocean to the Black Sea. He thought one could rather foresee a strong German attack on the southern sector from Kharkov to the Sea of Azov in the direction of the Caucasus. However, the Soviet forces had not yet regained the key positions, with the exception of Mozajsk.

"You, Mr. President," said Sikorski forcefully, "will have to do your utmost to help Russia at this time by means of war matériel and the opening of a second front as soon as the shipping and technical difficulties are overcome."

Then Sikorski pointed out on the map what he considered to be the most vulnerable points of attack on the western part of the European continent.

President Roosevelt showed keen interest in this analysis of the military situation and asked Sikorski to discuss his views with the Combined Chiefs of Staff during his stay in Washington.

He then asked General Sikorski about the state of British-Soviet discussions on the recently advanced Soviet demands.

The general told the President that he had talked these matters over with Churchill and Eden in the course of the last few days. He feared that the British Government was on the point of giving in to Soviet pressure and of agreeing to their territorial demands on the Baltic States and the Rumanian provinces bordering on Poland.

Eden had assured him that the territory of Poland was to be excluded from these concessions.

However, this did not make matters any better, considering the concessions made on the Baltic and in Rumania would virtually result in the encirclement of Poland from the north and the south. The Polish Government could not accept such an arrangement, and Sikorski had definitely made its position known. Moreover, he considered that this would be a direct abandonment of fundamental principles. He emphasized the special interest of Poland in the independence of the Baltic republics. He expressed the hope that the British and American governments would not continue discussions on these subjects with Soviet Russia, but, if they did, he added that Poland would insist on taking part as a directly interested Power.

President Roosevelt replied emphatically that the United States Government was determined not to depart from its declared position of not admitting the settlement of any territorial issues in time of war. He said that at present the Soviet Government limited its demands to Esthonia, Lithuania, and Latvia. However, should the Allies yield to pressure on this issue, it was certain that Russia would put forward further demands for territory of other countries: of Bukowina, Bessarabia, and Finland, possibly even Norway.

"I want you to understand, General," said the President, "that the American Government has not forgotten the Atlantic Charter. As soon as Germany is defeated and disarmed, any threat to Russia from the Baltic will have vanished and the Soviet argument, based on anxiety for Russia's security, will become futile. I want you to know that I made this position quite clear to Stalin through Litvinov, and told him that it was too early to sit down to enjoy a cake before it was baked. I have received no answer from Stalin."

When Sikorski drew the President's attention to the fact that it would not be sufficient for the United States to refuse its agreement to Moscow's claims because one had to reckon with the pressure of Moscow on London for an Anglo-Soviet treaty embodying these claims, President Roosevelt assured Sikorski that he was very strongly opposing the conclusion of any such treaty and that he intended to use all his influence to persuade the British Government to refrain from concluding a treaty on these lines.

He felt confident that he would succeed in preventing the signing of such a treaty. In the President's opinion, Britain's conciliatory attitude was based on the fear that Russia might make some arrangement with the Germans, as she had in 1939. He considered this fear as absolutely groundless and said that he regarded it his duty to stiffen the attitude of the British Government.

In a conversation on March 25 Sikorski informed Mr. Sumner Welles of his recent conversations with members of the British War Cabinet and said that he had definitely gained the impression that some of the members of the Cabinet, especially Ernest Bevin, had personal misgivings about making any concessions to Russian territorial demands. The British Cabinet would probably welcome such American arguments.

Mr. Welles replied that he was preparing for the President the text of a declaration stressing once more the decision of the United States Government to enter into no secret treaties on the solution of any postwar problems during the course of the war.

He added that American policy was clearly defined in the Atlantic Charter. The solution of international relations and especially frontier matters and territorial issues would have to await the end of the war.

A considerable part of this conversation with Mr. Welles bore on the subject of the growth of German terror and inhuman treatment of the Polish population, especially of the Polish Jews.

The general reminded the Undersecretary that during his first visit he had already brought up this subject. He once more urged the necessity of direct declarations on the part of the United States Government, warning Hitler of reprisals if he continued his present policy leading to the virtual extermination of whole groups of the Polish population.

He frankly admitted that, while he had met with understanding when he had broached this subject, he was greatly concerned because no steps had been taken by the United States which would make Hitler understand that he would be made responsible for these numerous breaches of international law, and especially for the barbarity perpetrated by the German forces of occupation.

Mr. Welles promised once more to go into the matter with the President and to urge that some action be taken.

General Sikorski was emphatic in his plea for definite action in this urgent matter and said that the population of Poland was clamoring for reprisals against the Germans as the only possible way of effectively stopping this intolerable situation.

He then returned to the subject of Polish policy tending to create a system of federations in eastern Central Europe between the Baltic, the Black Sea, the Aegean, and the Adriatic.

He expressed regret that the Soviets did not seem to approve this policy, which was by no means aimed against them, but, on the contrary, tended toward the establishment of a security bloc of friendly nations which would be very useful to Russia.

However, he thought the critical attitude of the Soviets toward European federation, coupled with recent Soviet territorial demands, might be proof of Soviet imperialist designs aimed not alone at the Baltic States and Poland, but which might later develop in the direction of the Balkans.

In my talks with General Sikorski and Edward Raczynski, before their departure from Washington, we analyzed the situation on the basis of the general's recent talks with Churchill, Eden, and other members of the British Government in London, in the light of his visit to Stalin, and of his Washington conversations with the President and the Combined Chiefs of Staff.

We came to the conclusion that 1942 would be a decisive year in shaping the policies of our great Allies—Britain and America. We noted with regret the differences of approach to the subject of collaboration with the Soviets between London and Washington, as we had observed them. We feared that, if the British desire to accept Soviet territorial and other demands materialized, appeasement of Russia would replace the sound policy of good partnership.

Appeasement could lead only to incalculable and dangerous consequences. We came to the conclusion that only a firm and unswerving determination on the part of President Roosevelt could prevent Britain from making concessions in a bilateral agreement with Soviet Russia and save the world from this regrettable eventuality.

Sikorski was keenly aware of the British readiness to make concessions, and our anxiety was further increased by another new factor.

On the basis of information from Russia, we realized that

Stalin's plans with regard to Poland were not limited to territorial demands, but went much further.

We had been greatly shocked by the news that on December 1, 1941, the day Sikorski was being so ceremoniously received in Kuibyshev by the representatives of the Soviet Government as the chief of an Allied Government and the Allied commander of a fighting nation, only 200 miles away, in the town of Saratov, a secret meeting of Polish communists was organized by the Soviet Government.

This meeting had laid the foundations for the creation on Russian territory of a political group of communist Poles groomed by the "allied" Soviet Government to become the future government of Poland. That group was then headed by Wanda Wasilewska, a Polish communist writer. The Soviet Government had made her the editor of a newspaper in Moscow, entitled *Free Poland,* which from its very first publication started a rabid campaign against the legal Polish Government in London.

General Sikorski and Raczynski told me that they took a very serious view of the creation of this group sponsored by the Soviets. It had recently been transferred from Saratov to Moscow and established there under the name of "Union of Polish Patriots."

We saw in this Soviet move that Stalin's territorial claims, at first launched unofficially in the Soviet press, later made more official in notes to our Ambassador in Moscow, and now finally quite officially stressed to Mr. Eden during his visit to the Kremlin and in Stalin's "order of the day" of February 23, 1942, were imperious demands, couched in words which clearly implied that the Soviets wanted their flag to wave over all territory given to Russia by Hitler. We realized that these demands by no means exhausted Soviet imperialist claims on Poland.

Apart from territorial imperialism, political expansionism was appearing on the Soviet horizon and shaping into a policy of grab and control, which could be summed up in one word— *domination.*

CHAPTER XI

America Checks British Appeasement, May 1942

IN APRIL 1942 it was becoming evident that the difference of views between the American and British governments on the matter of the British tendency to conclude a treaty with Russia was causing some tension between Washington and London. The British continued to harbor the illusion that it was necessary to humor Stalin "to gain his confidence" and to buy his further participation in the war.

In London, Sikorski and Raczynski had discussed the matter with Mr. Eden and had gained the impression that the President's warning to Mr. Churchill that the United States Government was opposed to the conclusion of any treaty at that time had not succeeded in changing the British attitude.

On this side of the Atlantic Mr. Welles assured me on April 15 that the President had very definitely stated his position directly to Mr. Churchill. It had been confirmed by Mr. Welles to Ambassador Litvinov, who had communicated it to Moscow.

It stated clearly and unequivocally that the United States excluded pacts between the United Nations pertaining to the future postwar territorial settlements during the war; that the United States Government considered that any such treaty with Soviet Russia at this time would in fact weaken or possibly even disrupt Allied unity; that apart from this it would have regrettable consequences in neutral States, and might call forth serious reactions in countries occupied by the enemy.

Mr. Welles was most emphatic on the subject. He added that in communicating this opinion to the British Government the President had with the utmost finality informed it that he desired this attitude of the American Government to be regarded as its definite policy for the duration of the war—a policy from which he was determined to make no departure.

President Roosevelt also warned Mr. Churchill that, should the British Government insist on concluding a treaty with Soviet Russia, the President would not permit silence on his part to be interpreted later as tacit approval of such an agreement.

When, on April 18, we compared with Mr. Welles the latest information we had received from London, we came to the conclusion, however, that the British were still under the wrong impression that the President's warnings to Mr. Churchill might not preclude a later acquiescence of the United States to a British-Soviet treaty, once it had become an accomplished fact.

Mr. Welles told me that he was pleased to say that this illusion had now been finally dispelled in a conversation between Ambassador Winant and Mr. Churchill.

Winant, just returned from Washington, had spent a day with Churchill and Eden at Checkers. Not only had the American Ambassador very forcefully stressed the President's warning, but he went even further. He declared to Mr. Churchill that should a British-Russian treaty be concluded, admitting Soviet territorial demands, the President would be forced to make a public statement dissociating the United States very definitely from any part in such an agreement. Such a statement certainly would adversely affect harmonious Allied collaboration and would most unfortunately give encouragement to the enemy.

I agreed with Mr. Welles that this was the strongest of arguments and would certainly make the British Government realize the importance President Roosevelt and his government attached to the maintenance of the common war aims and principles linking the United Nations.

But Mr. Welles had some misgivings that, having advanced so far on the way to meet Soviet pressure for a treaty, the British Government might not deem it possible entirely to reverse its attitude. He hoped, however, that it would still be possible to prevail upon the British Government to avoid making any definite commitments on Soviet territorial demands on the Baltic States, Poland, Bessarabia, and Bukowina.

From conversations I had at this time with friends at the British Embassy I was aware that American pressure was finally having some effect in London. I was told that negotiations between London and Moscow had been slowed down. It was becoming evident that Churchill was applying the brakes and, while perhaps not in a position entirely to abandon the negotiations, was trying at least to direct them in a way which ultimately would be acceptable to his American partner.

This uncertain situation continued to prevail until the British-Soviet treaty of alliance was signed on May 26.

Until the last days before its final signature the treaty had embodied British acceptance of Soviet territorial claims, but at the very last moment the text of the agreement had been altered and all territorial clauses had been eliminated.

The British Government had yielded to American determination.

On June 4 I called on Sumner Welles to congratulate the United States Government on the result achieved. I asked him if there was any likelihood of the United States acceding to the pact.

Mr. Welles answered emphatically that the United States Government had no intention whatever of participating in the treaty. He smiled as he added that this decision was greatly facilitated by the fact that the Soviet-British treaty was a bilateral alliance between Britain and the Soviets for a period of twenty years. The traditional policy of the United States prevented the conclusion of alliances, and this had been made very clear both to the British and to the Soviet governments.

I noticed that Mr. Welles was in an exceptionally good mood and carried away the impression that he was relieved and pleased that American diplomacy had succeeded in persuading the British Government to alter its decision of appeasing the Soviets by granting their territorial demands.

Indeed the President appeared to have won a considerable victory, not merely because he had succeeded in making Mr. Churchill refrain from adopting a course fraught with danger to British interests and those of other United Nations, but also because it was the first victory for the principles of the Atlantic Charter.

This American diplomatic victory had been laboriously won,

but it seemed to me a definite step in the direction of asserting American moral leadership in the United Nations camp.

In that period of 1942, however, powerful elements in American opinion were beginning to exercise a dangerous pressure, tending to influence the government to a course of compromise with the fundamental principles upon which the war aims of the United Nations were founded.

There still was a difference between the respective trends of the British and American governments at that time in their relationship to Soviet Russia. While in England it already appeared to have evolved into a policy of appeasement, in the United States, at least superficially, it was still a policy of adherence to principles and avoidance of commitments which might prejudice the status of the future postwar world.

It was becoming apparent, though, that various factors were already working out a pattern of pro-Soviet propaganda which was destined in time to direct the course of American policy, also to one of appeasement of Stalin.

Radical New Deal politicians, and especially Vice-President Henry A. Wallace, as well as the increasingly active political elements of the CIO, were gradually becoming more and more vocal in their unstinted praise of Soviet Russia. The process of overselling the Soviets to the American people had become fashionable. A press campaign lauding the achievements of the Soviet winter campaign was rapidly developing under the obvious inspiration of Soviet propaganda, which took full advantage of every opening.

Washington was experiencing an uncanny period of self-accusation for the lack of a second front, and we read and heard outright criticism of the government for its allegedly inadequate aid to the Soviets.

These tendencies and the growing active enthusiasm for Soviet Russia displayed among New Dealers of the group surrounding the President gradually merged with the British pro-Soviet tendencies, which, as Mr. Churchill had admitted to the President, were exercising such pressure on his government.

However, fundamental official American policy was still sufficiently true to its principles and traditions and it showed no outward signs of weakness.

On June 13 I called on Secretary of State Hull. He stressed the fact that it had been no easy matter to obtain the final elimination of the territorial clauses which the President considered "absolutely unacceptable."

He greatly praised Ambassador Winant for the way in which he had fulfilled his mission in the course of the last days preceding the signature of the treaty, and especially during the London visit of Commissar Molotov.

Mr. Hull told me that two days before the actual signing of the treaty the draft still contained the territorial clauses. He understood that England still refused to believe that the United States would actually be forced to make a public statement dissociating itself from such a treaty.

"We certainly had to give them hell," said Mr. Hull, "before we could make them realize it."

CHAPTER XII

Moscow Obstructs Formation of Polish Forces

THE improvement of Polish-Soviet relations brought about by the visit of General Sikorski to Premier Stalin had been but superficial and short-lived. Very soon afterward, on all matters agreed upon by Sikorski and Stalin, a new hostile Soviet policy was developing, tending to make it practically impossible to carry out these agreements.

Contrary to the established figure of 96,000 soldiers to be trained, jointly fixed by Stalin and Sikorski, the Polish High Command in Russia was informed that only 44,000 could be recruited on the pretext that the Soviets could not supply food or equipment for more.

Contrary to the Sikorski-Stalin arrangement, a considerable number of Poles were being forcibly conscripted into Soviet labor battalions instead of being allowed to join the Polish Army.

As a climax, Stalin suddenly gave orders for the immediate transfer to the Middle East of all Polish soldiers already in training camps in Russia, simultaneously ordering all further recruiting to be stopped.

At the same time the Soviet authorities, undoubtedly encouraged by the conclusion of their pact of alliance with Britain, denied Polish citizenship to Polish deportees of Ukrainian or Jewish extraction, and abruptly stopped the distribution of relief supplies from Britain and the United States among the Polish deportees in camps all over Russia. Polish representatives entrusted with the distribution of relief in the various camps were arrested, regardless of their diplomatic immunity, and accused of spying.

I kept the President and the State Department fully informed of these developments. All the facts were presented by me in the form of detailed memoranda, and several times I asked for direct intervention in Moscow.

But it was becoming increasingly clear that American diplomatic interventions in the Soviet capital were of little avail. They were either entirely ignored or dealt with in a curt and discouraging way. The President frankly admitted in one of our conversations that it was evidently hopeless to get Soviet Russia to change her methods.

Mr. Sumner Welles told me also, very frankly, that Admiral Standley, the energetic American Ambassador in Moscow, had repeatedly reported difficulties encountered every time he intervened in Polish-Soviet matters.

However, in view of the increasing instances of Soviet hostility in its dealings with the Polish Government, and of the grave situation reached in Polish-Soviet relations, Mr. Welles was of the opinion that Ambassador Standley would have to intervene again in order to impress upon the Soviets the concern of the American Government and its interest in this matter.

When, on July 31, 1942, I called on Mr. Hull, I found him fully informed of the facts by Mr. Welles and Ray Atherton, whom I had been seeing frequently. He told me that he was greatly disturbed. He regarded the tactics of the Soviets as fraught with grave consequences. He said that while he considered it absolutely necessary for the United States Government to intervene, he feared such intervention would not bring any result. He added that during his conversations with Molotov in Washington, when expressing his concern he had alluded to the various incidents created by the Soviet Government in its dealings with the Poles, Molotov had very curtly changed the subject without any discussion.

When the Secretary insisted on the importance for the Allies of obtaining fresh Polish military contingents, Molotov replied that he regarded these matters as purely Soviet-Polish problems, and wished to assure the Secretary that the Soviets were carrying out their obligations.

We discussed what could be done if normal diplomatic intervention was unavailing. In view of the importance of maintaining good Polish-Soviet relations and of preserving the united front of the Allies, Mr. Hull considered that only joint diplomatic action of the United States and Britain could succeed in prevailing upon Soviet Russia to change the course of her policy toward Poland. Russia was obtaining considerable Lend-Lease aid from Britain and the United States. Hull was of the opinion that this advantage should be made use of to save the situation from deteriorating beyond remedy.

We agreed that only such an intervention on the highest level, by the President, together with Prime Minister Churchill, might still convince the Soviets of the importance which the two Western Allies attached to this problem. This interest would have to be forcefully stressed if any result was to be achieved. The Secretary promised me to take the matter up immediately with the President and to arrange for me to see him in the near future.

I was received by the President on the fifth of August. He appeared to be keenly interested and, as he said, "bewildered by the state of Soviet-Polish relations." He reviewed the facts, thus showing me he was fully informed of every stage in the deterioration of those relations.

He said that the matter deserved careful thought and rapid action. He confirmed what Mr. Hull, Mr. Welles, and Mr. Atherton had already told me concerning the negative and unfriendly attitude of the Soviets on all occasions when Admiral Standley intervened in Polish affairs.

He added that actually Ambassador Standley had difficulties in seeing Molotov, let alone Stalin.

Mr. Roosevelt asked me to tell General Sikorski that he was aware the Polish Government had been doing its utmost in steering a friendly course in its policy toward the Soviet Union, and that he was "greatly concerned" to find that the Soviets were adopting an entirely negative attitude to all Sikorski's "sincere and statesmanlike advances."

The President then said that he had made up his mind once more to intervene. In a few days he would send Harriman to Moscow to take part in discussions on war supplies. He thought it would be well to take advantage of Harriman's visit, "whom Stalin cannot refuse to see," and to try direct intervention with the Soviet dictator on Polish matters.

He explained that he would tell Harriman to ask for the immediate release of the 120 arrested Polish relief officials and to request that all further investigations in this matter be dropped in the name of the unity of the United Nations at this crucial phase of the war.

He said that as one has to reckon with "Stalin's realism," he would tell Harriman to add that after their release the Polish officials would be sent out of Russia and replaced by others. He would also instruct Harriman to present the human aspect of the question to Stalin and ask for immediate resumption of the distribution of relief to our deportees.

The President showed great interest in another aspect of Polish-Soviet relations; namely, the refusal of the Soviet authorities to recognize the Polish citizenship of Ukrainians and Polish Jews. He regarded it from the legal point of view as "a curious decision," and said he wondered what Americans would think if traveling, say, in Portugal, they were suddenly told that their citizenship had been changed and that henceforth they were to consider themselves Portuguese citizens. He added that according to his understanding this was by no means a simple matter. It confirmed General Sikorski's apprehensions regarding Russian territorial ambitions.

At the end of our conversation the President said he was pleased General Sikorski now shared his opinion that it was better to evacuate the entire Polish contingent from Russia than to pursue the forlorn hope that the Soviets would allow the formation of a strong Polish army on Soviet territory.

I reminded the President of Sikorski's main aim in forming a strong Polish force to fight shoulder to shoulder with the Russian armies. The President admitted the idea had strongly appealed to him.

"In any normal relationship this would have been accepted as the best proof of Sikorski's sincerity. But the Russians think on different lines, and it was perhaps too much to hope that they would take a normal Western view in the matter," he added sadly.

I explained that General Anders especially had been most insistent in persuading General Sikorski and our General Staff in London that the Russian front was closer to Poland than a problematic western front, and urged that the Soviets would surely interpret favorably our government's desire to share Soviet difficulties in their fight against the Germans on Russian soil and later on in Poland. This common fight might lay the foundations for future friendship.

I told the President that this problem had been very thoroughly discussed by our government in London and between the Polish and British General Staffs.

The British view that the second Allied front in Europe would lead through the Mediterranean and the Balkans finally decided our staff not to insist on leaving our army in Russia, but to try to transfer it to the Middle East.

The President agreed with the logic of this attitude and thought that a Polish army abroad might be more useful to the Soviets, especially if the line of attack through the Balkans was decided upon.

There was yet another consideration, of which I reminded the President. It had also contributed in determining the Polish Government to evacuate our forces to the Middle East. It was the fact that we could not trace the Polish officers taken prisoner by the Russians during the Polish campaign in 1939 and, therefore, General Anders was very short of officers. We had, however, officers at our disposal in greater numbers in the Polish Carpathian Brigade in North Africa and in Scotland.

The President said he had not forgotten Sikorski's request for intervention in the matter of the missing officers. The President had ordered such intervention, and had asked the Soviets to free our officers. He even remembered that General Sikorski had said that some 9,000 officers could not be found or traced. He knew I had repeatedly discussed the matter with Mr. Hull and Mr. Sumner Welles and was interested to know what stage this problem had now reached.

I explained that our embassy in Moscow and General Anders had continuously stressed this matter to the Soviet Government. They always got vague answers.

Sometimes they were told that the officers had escaped in an unknown direction. At others, that some were probably in Arctic regions of Russia where they could not be reached. Their fate was causing us deep concern. Our government had communicated lists of these officers to the British and American embassies in Moscow. Most of the officers had been concentrated in Russian prisoner-of-war camps at Starobielsk, Ostashkov, and Kozielsk. None had appeared in our training camps when the call for all able-bodied Poles in Russia was published and broadcast.

The President agreed that there appeared to be serious ground for anxiety. He remembered Ambassador Standley's interventions on this subject and admitted that he had likewise been put off by the Soviet authorities. He added that it was unthinkable that Polish officers, if alive, should not rally to Sikorski's call.

"Whatever our views have been in the past on the way of utilizing your Polish troops in Russia," the President concluded, "circumstances appear to have decided for us, because obviously Russia does not want them." He said that it was now the duty of the Polish Government and of the Allies to get "these excellent fighting men" out of Russia as soon as possible and to give them the opportunity of fighting for Poland's independence and for the liberation of the world from the totalitarian menace.

General Anders's army was being gradually evacuated from Russia and re-formed in the Middle East.

Exhausted youths and older men were recovering surprisingly rapidly after their ordeal in Russia. They were being armed and equipped, and their fighting spirit aroused high praise from British and American officers who had occasion to observe their training under Anders's diligent command.

This contingent was emerging into an army, later to be known as the Polish Second Corps. It was joined by the Polish Carpathian Brigade, under General Kopanski's command, which had already proved its fighting valor in the North African campaign, and together, later, were to render valuable service in the Italian campaign from the southernmost point of Italy, through allegedly impregnable Monte Cassino up to Ancona and Bologna.

CHAPTER XIII

Fear of Russia Grows

My CONVERSATIONS with the President, the Secretary of State, Mr. Sumner Welles, Ray Atherton, and others at the State Department, and the reactions I gathered in my talks with American political and press friends, made me realize the unfortunate trend of American psychology as it was shaping at that time under the pressure of war events, and of the new line of policy now definitely adopted by Soviet Russia. There seemed to be no doubt that Stalin wanted to impose his will at that phase of the war when Russia certainly was the main actively fighting force on whose resistance so much depended.

In the summer of 1942, after checking the Soviet winter counteroffensive, the German forces in Russia were once again on the march southeastward. Japan was pressing her advantages and occupying islands in the Pacific, adding new successes to her attack on Pearl Harbor.

Allied lack of preparedness and the stupendous task of war production on a colossal scale required not only energy which certainly was forthcoming, but also time, which was short. The opening of a second front, so desirable from all viewpoints, had to be delayed until it could be launched with greater prospects of success.

Russia was naturally looked upon as the only active partner in that period. Politically, the Soviets were pressing their advantages, profiting by their dominant military situation. In this they were supported and encouraged by a large part of the American press and the growing number of admirers of Russia among the New Deal politicians close to the White House.

Of all the United States Government agencies, the Office of

War Information, under its new director Mr. Elmer Davis, had very definitely adopted a line of unqualified praise of Soviet Russia and appeared to support its shrewd and increasingly aggressive propaganda in the United States. The OWI broadcasts to European countries had become characteristic of this trend.

As a high light of this pro-Soviet psychosis, which was being actively instilled in the minds of American public opinion from official quarters, I should mention the refusal I got from the OWI when I asked this agency to help me in obtaining the rectification of maps of Poland which then appeared in the current issue of the Encyclopaedia Britannica Atlas.

While agreeing with me that a rectification was desirable, considering that these maps showed a final incorporation into Russia of the territories given by Hitler to the Soviets during the Russo-German honeymoon in 1939 and 1940, the OWI officials contended that any rectification might annoy the Soviets and this they were not prepared to risk.

The matter was taken out of official hands and finally settled satisfactorily, after the spontaneous intervention of Americans of Polish descent who obtained from the editors of the Encyclopaedia Britannica Atlas the publication of a corrected issue.

I was aware that, while the President and the high officials of the State Department always showed genuine concern and tried to find a way to bring Moscow to its senses, their attitude was one of helplessness similar to that encountered in London. To me, who never had the slightest doubt concerning the power and tenacity of the United States, it was hard to understand that an attitude almost of defeatism was gaining ground in Washington.

Psychologically, it was a mixed complex in which one could discern an unjustified sense of guilt for the inability to open a second front in response to Soviet insistence, coupled with a growing fear, possibly inspired from London, that the Soviets might suddenly give up the fight and come to terms with Hitler.

The principles of the Atlantic Charter were still being half-heartedly upheld. The speeches of Secretary of State Hull and of Sumner Welles still showed that American traditional sense of justice required their restatement from time to time.

But already in Mr. Hull's speech of July 23, 1942, the main

accent was placed on the "unity of the Allies," on their international collaboration, in a very definite and positive way, while the Atlantic Charter, although mentioned, was referred to much less emphatically.

A new pattern, which later was to govern American world policy and which can be expressed in the formula "Allied unity at any price," was already then in the making.

It was heartbreaking to observe that, parallel with the growth of Soviet imperialism and British-American political inactivity, an alarming wave of German oppression in occupied countries was growing.

The incredible details of the system of human extermination started by Hitler's gang were as yet unknown to Americans at large. But the Polish Government was being fully informed about all these happenings owing to the perfect system of daily contact which it had successfully set up with the Polish Underground.

From information I was receiving and constantly communicating to the American Government and to the press, and describing in my numerous speeches in many American cities, the monstrous pattern of Hitler's mass extermination of Polish Jews and of Jews brought to Poland from other countries was becoming clearly evident. The Polish Underground insistently demanded that our government present these facts to our Allies and especially to the American Government.

General Sikorski was working on it overtime in London and I was following up his requests to the President, the State Department, and the Combined Chiefs of Staff in two directions:

First, to obtain a few modern planes of the Liberator type which would facilitate and speed up contacts between London and the Underground in Poland which, both as a fighting and sabotaging force of resistance and as an Allied center of military intelligence, was rendering great services to the Allied cause.

It was important also to drop Polish parachutists into Poland, chosen from among our officers and men in Scotland, to carry messages and to instruct the Underground forces of resistance in the art of modern guerrilla warfare.

Also arms, munitions, and explosives necessary to the Underground army were being sent by air and, therefore, more and better planes were urgently needed.

President Roosevelt had promised these planes to General Sikorski. But, notwithstanding continuous reminders and the fact that the President and the American General Staff appeared fully to appreciate the importance of giving our High Command in England these modern means of transport, we never succeeded in obtaining them.

General Sikorski's second great concern was to try once more to persuade the President of the increasingly urgent necessity of direct repressive Allied action against the Germans, such as bombing of German cities in open retaliation for the barbarous extermination of Polish citizens, and especially of the Polish-Jewish population.

I had many conversations on this subject, and constantly stressed this urgent necessity in my official contacts at the State Department and with the Combined Chiefs of Staff.

While my representations were sympathetically received, no action followed, and I found it most difficult even to get a strongly worded enunciation from the President warning Hitler of the consequences which inhumanly oppressive Nazi methods in Poland would bring upon Germany.

I returned once more to this subject with President Roosevelt on August 5, 1942, and explained that a collective note, initiated by General Sikorski, had been presented by the representatives of the nine occupied European States on behalf of their countries.

The President said he was aware of the situation and greatly deplored it. He had been informed by the Secretary of State of the collective *démarche* of the European countries. He said, however, that he had refrained from making any public declaration because Secretary of State Hull was of the opinion that such a declaration would bring no result. He did not think it advisable to start actual reprisals or bombing of German cities at a time when the Allies had not yet reached their full air power, and Germany might use this as a pretext for increased bombing and terrorism.

I pointed out to the President that he might possibly have overlooked one very important aspect of the matter; namely, that hitherto all protests against German acts of oppression and terrorism had been voiced exclusively by the victims of these acts, while the Great Powers, the United States and Great Britain, had never directly participated in any such protests and remained mere spectators and witnesses.

"This might have been defensible," I concluded, "while the United States was not at war. At present such an attitude on the part of America, whose moral leadership had been spontaneously acclaimed by all freedom-loving nations, might be misinterpreted as a lack of solidarity and support for nations suffering from the acts of the barbaric enemy against whom the United States had entered the war."

The President immediately saw the importance of this point and told me he had not realized this aspect of the question. He promised to take the first opportunity to broadcast a declaration, categorical in its wording along the lines suggested, which, as I was gratified to note, he did a little later.

The general lack of understanding of German barbarity and a certain basic kindheartedness toward the Germans were most striking at that time. They appeared suddenly in some of my contacts with American officials and representatives of American public opinion. A sort of natural sympathy for Germany, for her music and art, her touristic charm, and her business opportunities, which for so long had impressed America, was slow to die even in the face of the grim reality of ruthless German war methods. The average American, and even officials who had every means of being fully informed, practically refused to believe the Germans capable of the horrors which they were committing.

But apart from such pro-German sympathies, this passive attitude—just as the one adopted toward Russia's growing expansionism—might also have been the result of a complex which somehow prevented American statesmen from realizing the great weight of every word publicly spoken on behalf of the United States as a decisive power in the world conflict.

In a different field, the Jewish tragedy which was being staged in Europe brought another terrible episode which took place in Russia and which stunned and surprised American public opinion for a moment.

Two of the most prominent Polish-Jewish socialist leaders—Henryk Ehrlich and Victor Alter—found themselves among the population deported from Poland by the Soviets in 1939. They were arrested and kept in prison and were only liberated on the repeated insistence of the Polish Government. As soon as they had been freed these exceptionally fine and noble men started social and political activities inside Russia in a spirit most friendly to Russia and in keeping with our efforts for Polish-Russian understanding. This work could in no way be regarded as suspicious by the Soviet authorities. They organized relief aid for over 250,-000 Jews deported from Poland and concentrated in the farthest reaches of Siberia, in Kazakstan, and on the borders of Tibet and China. Their political activity was distinctly anti-German and anti-fascist.

Ehrlich and Alter worked in the closest understanding with our embassy in Kuibyshev and with our Military High Command in Russia. Although they were no longer young and had experienced terrible hardships, they did not spare their efforts, and the results they achieved were outstanding.

In December 1941, shortly after they had started to establish a Jewish anti-fascist committee in Russia, which they openly organized, in full understanding with the Soviet authorities, our embassy in Kuibyshev was alarmed by the news that they had suddenly been arrested.

The embassy intervened almost daily in their behalf, doing its utmost to obtain information which might at least help to locate them. However, the Soviet authorities ignored all these interventions and answered invariably that they regarded these two prominent Jewish-Polish leaders as spies.

The anxiety about their fate quickly spread in America.

Ambassador Litvinov received many letters and telegrams questioning him about the fate of Ehrlich and Alter and asking for his immediate intervention. Among these letters some were signed by such prominent personalities as Mrs. Franklin Delano Roosevelt, Wendell L. Willkie, William Green, and many other leading social workers and liberals.

The Soviet Embassy in Washington did not react to these pleas.

Finally, in December 1942, almost exactly a year after their arrest at the Grand Hotel in Kuibyshev, Ambassador Litvinov, in a short letter to William Green, president of the American Federation of Labor, wrote that both these Jewish leaders had been shot under sentence of a Soviet tribunal.

The Soviet Ambassador did not hesitate to add that "they had been judged and executed for collaboration with the Nazis and for their work among the Red Army and among the Soviet population on behalf of Hitler."

To all those who knew how indomitably anti-fascist and anti-Hitlerite Ehrlich and Alter had been, how strong were their radically liberal convictions, proved by their long and fruitful work for the cause of humanity and justice in Poland, and, lately, in Russia—to those who realized, moreover, how impossible it would be for any foreigner or, in fact, even for any Soviet civilian to conduct any sort of propaganda within the Red Army—Litvinov's crudely untrue statement could be regarded only as a tragic farce.

His letter was a heavy blow to all radical circles in America. For a time it appeared to shake their determination of giving unqualified support to all that the Soviets did or said. But it soon became apparent that even this incredible act of Soviet totalitarian brutality would not affect the pro-Soviet sympathies steadily gaining ground in radical American circles.

CHAPTER XIV

"Soviet Enigma" Puzzles Washington

On December 1, 1942, General Sikorski arrived in Washington on his third and last visit to the President. His arrival had been scheduled for November 30. He was to come from Montreal in a special plane which was placed at his disposal by Mr. Churchill. The usual wartime secrecy marked his trip.

Just before noon on November 30 I was called on the long-distance telephone from Montreal. Sikorski's aide-de-camp was at the end of the wire and announced that the general's plane had just landed after a somewhat jumpy flight and that he wished to speak with me.

General Sikorski asked me what arrangements I had made for the first days of his visit. I said I had just heard from Mr. Summerlin that the President wished me to bring him to tea at the White House straight from the airport on that very day.

"I am not even shaved," said Sikorski, "and as I am to leave for Washington immediately, I will not even have time for a bath and change of uniform. Could you not explain this to the President and ask him to agree to receive me tomorrow? I will then be better prepared to meet him."

I laughed as I assured the general that the President certainly would not hold it against him if he appeared unshaved and travel-stained.

The general's plane was due in Washington around four o'clock. About twenty minutes after our conversation I was called away from lunch to the telephone. In a voice tense with emotion Sikorski's aide-de-camp reported that the plane had hardly left the ground when all four engines stalled and, owing only to the exceptional skill of the pilot, a fatal accident had been avoided. The plane fell in a field outside the airport sustaining considerable damage. Sikorski and his staff escaped injury virtually by a miracle.

I asked how the general was feeling and if he was capable of continuing his journey. Just then Sikorski came to the telephone. He said that he was neither hurt nor even shaken, but that no other plane being ready for him, he could not arrive in time to be with the President that afternoon. He asked me to inform the President and to present his excuses. To my question as to whether he thought the failure of the engines was accidental, the general replied that an investigation was under way and withheld his opinion.

I immediately reported the accident to the White House. A few minutes later Mr. Summerlin telephoned, expressing President Roosevelt's concern, and saying that the President was having inquiries made directly in Montreal, as he wished to be posted on all details of the accident.

General Sikorski arrived next day in an American military bomber. I met him at the airport together with Mr. Sumner Welles, Mr. Summerlin, and the diplomatic representatives of the United Nations, accompanied by their military attachés.

On December 2, at the White House lunch hour, the President greeted General Sikorski with exceptional warmth. He inquired with great solicitude about his plane accident in Montreal. The general treated the matter lightly and said that it was just an accident. He said he only regretted that it had delayed his meeting the President by twenty-four hours.

The President turned to Mr. Welles and asked what information was available at that time on the nature of the accident. Mr. Welles replied that experts were inclined to suspect foul play. The President asked to be informed of the results of the investigation. He then turned to General Sikorski and said it was evident that Providence watched over him and Poland. It was a good thing because, as the President put it, "we all need you so much."

Luncheon was brought in, and the conversation turned on military and political matters.

The President said he wanted to have several long talks with Sikorski on both war and postwar problems, and that this first contact was but a preliminary survey of the general situation. He then dwelt at some length on Polish-Soviet relations, which were becoming difficult, and asked what he could do to help Sikorski in his attempts to reach a better understanding with Stalin.

The President and General Sikorski agreed to discuss this matter at length.

Sikorski's visit coincided with the great Allied military successes on the North African and on the Far Eastern fronts which were definitely turning the tide in favor of the United Nations. The successful American and British operations in North Africa had changed the somewhat gloomy atmosphere which Sikorski had encountered in Washington during his previous visits. The mighty American war effort was no longer in its first infancy. Washington was beginning to plan for the invasion of Europe.

The African front and the planned offensive in Italy were opening vast possibilities for the co-operation of Polish armed forces, some of which had already fought in Africa.

London and Washington were beginning to understand that the Polish troops might also become an important moral factor in the European offensive. It was rightly considered that their appearance spearheading the Allied forces in their planned advance through the Balkan countries, Hungary, and Austria, would help to rally the peoples of these countries to the Allied cause.

Poland and Rumania had been allies. Close ties of friendship linked Poland and Yugoslavia. The Polish people had always had a traditional friendship with Hungary also. A feeling of natural sympathy existed between Catholic Austria and Poland. The appearance of Polish troops in the vanguard of an allied army of liberation fighting the Nazi menace would undoubtedly exercise an important influence on the minds of these people, and help to obtain their active participation against Germany, thus swelling the Allied armed forces.

It was clear that such a move would speed up the European campaign and relieve the Soviets by tying considerable German forces in the south and southeast of Europe.

Poland's increasingly efficient Underground organization and Underground Home Army could then lend their full support to the Russian forces when these advanced westward through Poland.

The Polish Underground organization was not limited to Poland alone.

In the midst of the millions of Polish slave laborers, forcibly deported to Germany, the Polish Underground had managed to organize a secret intelligence and the nucleus of another secret army, which were already becoming useful to the Allies.

These men and women were organized in small secret underground detachments, ready to carry out mass sabotage in Germany at the right moment, at a given signal from London. They were prepared to disrupt the German system of communications between the eastern and the eventual western fronts, paralyzing German mobility.

Only one most unfavorable factor appeared to threaten this promising picture of Polish-Allied collaboration and to endanger its full success. It was the growing tension in Soviet-Polish relations.

As Sikorski straightforwardly put it to President Roosevelt, the concern which this matter caused him was one of the main reasons for his visit.

However, he was still hopeful. In his opinion the successful African operations and the more heartening news from the Pacific front allowed the Allies to develop an offensive action against the Axis Powers, unburdening Soviet Russia, and assuming a greater part of leadership in military operations in Europe. This would soon allow the United States and Britain to assert their moral leadership in their political relations with Soviet Russia.

I pointed out to General Sikorski that in his reasoning he was being too exclusively a soldier. We differed in our respective appraisals of American and British psychology. I attached greater importance than Sikorski to the difficulties already encountered by the Western Allies in their diplomatic relations with Moscow.

I was acutely aware of the lack of a common dictionary between Russia and the Western Powers. I had watched with growing apprehension the shaping of American opinion and the growth of influence of men in official and semi-official positions around the White House, whose natural enthusiasm for the Russian war effort appeared to have steadily developed into a pro-

Soviet psychosis blinding them to the deep differences between American and Russian mentality, and to the very different meaning of words in the Soviet and American vocabularies. They appeared to have conveniently accepted the false idea that the Russians were very akin to Americans in their way of thinking, and regarded Russia as a near democracy, somewhat more radical than the American democracy. They believed that by stressing Soviet-American friendship, and in every way humoring Soviet whims, Stalin's Russia could be persuaded to accept American principles and might adopt the American way of life.

I warned Sikorski, that in view of this rising uncritical pro-Soviet enthusiasm, the American Government might not find it possible to lend him support to the degree which he rightly considered indispensable to impress upon Stalin the necessity of changing his hostile policy toward Poland.

There could be no doubt about the sincerity of President Roosevelt's very favorable response to Sikorski's appeal for support, but I was afraid his friendly intentions might not be carried out. As the war progressed and Allied successes increased, Soviet propaganda intensified its efforts to impress upon receptive American minds the belief that the war was being won primarily by Russia, who was consequently entitled to privileged treatment and an unconditional granting of her growing demands.

My conversations, particularly with my friends at the State and War Departments, had convinced me that American policy was indeed becoming paradoxical.

Increasing confidence in victory, based on actual military successes, had helped to develop a feeling of self-assurance. This tendency, however, did not produce a consequent consciousness of American power and a bold assumption by the United States of the leadership expected of America by world opinion.

Russia's predominant part in the war against Germany, at a time when the United States and Britain were still incapable of opening a second front, had greatly impressed the honest American people. American policy and peace planning appeared to be remarkably timid and still governed rather by wishful thinking than by the certainty that the United States would ultimately become the leading world Power after playing a major part in achieving inevitable victory in the war.

The congressional elections had just been held in November, 1942. They brought considerable gains to the Republican party, expressed by forty-four additional mandates in the House of Representatives and nine in the Senate.

I had discussed the reasons and implications of these election results with some politicians of the New Deal group closest to the President. While all agreed that the headway made by the Republicans was an event deserving their close attention, they did not consider it as an expression of adverse criticism of Mr. Roosevelt's war leadership and foreign policy. As a leading New Dealer pointed out to me, there was no ground for serious alarm concerning the Administration's policy. It was true that some isolationists had been re-elected, but they had been forced to adopt a novel platform; namely, to declare themselves for an all-out war effort and align themselves with the President's war policy.

It was interesting to hear from leading New Dealers that now, after the elections, the numerically increased Republican minority in the House and Senate would have to shoulder some of the responsibility in matters of war leadership.

Thus the President's course in his foreign policy could gradually become a bi-partisan or non-partisan one. The question was: What would that course be?

I regretfully noted that my apprehensions concerning the official attitude to the United Nations concept, which I had regarded as one of the President's strokes of genius, had been well founded.

In theory the United Nations, as conceived by the President, was to be a permanent association of nations, linked by a common determination to fight for the highest principles of freedom, justice, international security, and for the respect of law, before which all nations were to be equals.

In practice, however, these ideals were gradually being shelved. The tendency was growing to revert to less modern concepts. The classification of the United Nations, according to the old and insecure formula into big and small powers, was being applied. The threat of a precarious Four-Power alliance was emerging. What was even worse, there appeared a tendency to segregate

even the smaller nations into those who, owing to their more secure geographical position or their greater economic importance,
would be reckoned with, and others, whose very independence
was becoming doubtful because they did not possess the natural
geographical advantages of security.

In a report I wrote for General Sikorski, summing up my
views on the situation he would find on his arrival in Washington at the end of 1942, I said that if the concept of the United
Nations could still be regarded as an international family concern, it was one definitely composed of rich and poor relations.

The establishment of the United Nations had not even led to
their more intimate collaboration on war problems.

The Office of the Combined Chiefs of Staff was an exclusively British-American institution in which Russia, China, the
Netherlands, Australia, and New Zealand were only sporadically
consulted.

The Pacific War Council which met twice monthly at the
White House under the President's personal direction and con-
sisted of Lord Halifax, the Chinese Foreign Minister T. V. Soong,
Ambassador Loudon of the Netherlands, and the Ministers of
Australia and New Zealand, could at best be defined as a con-
genial gathering and never became a really active war council.

A pattern was being set up which was gradually excluding
other actively fighting nations from all discussions on postwar
planning. This alignment was adversely affecting the true unity
of the United Nations.

Postwar planning in America presented a rather curious spec-
tacle at the time. Every institution or individual who had had
anything to do in the past with the study of world affairs or international relations now took up postwar planning. At the beginning of 1943 there were some 150 organizations and groups
assiduously working out, and mostly duplicating, postwar plans,
without visible co-ordination even among the various departments and government agencies. A sort of fervent zeal to give
birth to new conceptions for a better future world appeared to
have got hold of American study groups. For the most part this
work was kept highly secret. The President had instructed the
government departments cautiously to avoid open discussions on
postwar planning. I was authoritatively told that he was not un-

mindful of the situation which had finally brought down President Woodrow Wilson after the last war, and was determined to avoid giving any outward signs of premature involvement in world planning which might encourage isolationist attacks on his world policy. Mr. Roosevelt also kept a watchful eye on Congress, which was becoming increasingly alert and critical of New Deal postwar plans.

Thus, while a considerable number of more or less comprehensive postwar plans emerged at intervals sponsored by semi-official or private-study groups, the United States Government did not appear to have worked out any definite program to implement the Atlantic Charter and the Four Freedoms which, in the wake of war events, seemed gradually to recede into growing dimness.

The greatest damage was done in this respect when hesitancy on the part of President Roosevelt prevented the United States from making any headway in working out a joint United Nations policy for dealing with a defeated Germany after the war. There was, however, an additional reason which caused the American Government to be hesitant in too actively furthering postwar planning and in admitting representatives of other United Nations to participate in it or at least to submit their views. It was the growing fear of Soviet Russia.

Soviet demands and apparent lack of compliance with the war aims of the Atlantic Charter and the Declaration of the United Nations made the American Government hesitant and passive.

I considered this attitude as a serious tactical error at that time and said so frankly.

In my opinion, when Soviet Russia was largely dependent on the aid of her Western Allies, when, in discussions with Stalin on the fundamentals of postwar planning, full advantage could be taken of bargaining points such as Lend-Lease, food supplies, the timing and location of the second front, it probably would have been easier to convince or to coerce the great eastern totalitarian dictatorship that it could not hope simultaneously to benefit by the advantages of its alliance with the United Nations, and to retain the advantages gained by its association with Hitler in the first two years of the war.

Washington had already lived through a first phase of pro-

Soviet psychosis when Russia fascinated American officials and was sold by them to the American public as a savior and possibly the only hope of defeating Hitler.

It had already gone through the second phase—that of the second front which, on account of Soviet pressure and Soviet accusations, had called forth feelings of guilt.

It had also passed through a third phase resulting from the first two—a phase which evolved into the tendency of avoiding anything which might create Soviet-American friction or in any way displease Stalin and increase his deep distrust of Western democracy.

This phase prevailed at the end of 1942 and looked as if it had come to stay. It gave birth to a sort of tacit determination to allow and even encourage pro-Soviet propaganda, to pretend not to notice communist infiltration, and allow and even encourage the development of such un-American activities as those of the "American Slav Congress."

The seasoned officials of the Department of State were undoubtedly aware of the danger of these tendencies. I noted the same understanding among some of my friends of the War Department and among the Joint and Combined Chiefs of Staff. Many members of the press, and especially those who had lived and worked in Europe, were aware that the time was ripe for the adoption of a different attitude by the United States in its dealings with the Soviets.

But, curiously enough, while some government departments realized the danger of unduly encouraging Soviet-Russian appetite, some of the new war agencies actively conducted what could only be termed pro-Soviet propaganda.

So-called American propaganda broadcasts to occupied Poland were outstanding proofs of this tendency. Notorious pro-Soviet propagandists and obscure foreign communists and fellow travelers were entrusted with these broadcasts.

I protested repeatedly against the pro-Soviet character of such propaganda. I explained to those responsible for it in the OWI that the Polish nation, suffering untold oppression from Hitler's hordes, was thirsting for plain news about America and especially about her war effort, her postwar plans, and her moral leadership, that Soviet propaganda was being continuously broadcast anyway to Poland directly from Moscow, and there seemed no reason additionally to broadcast it from the United States.

When I finally appealed to the Secretary of State and to divisional heads of the State Department, protesting against the character of the OWI broadcasts to Poland, I was told that the State Department was aware of these facts but could not control this agency, which boasted that it received its directives straight from the White House.

In the conversations General Sikorski and I had with official and unofficial American personalities during his visit, we noted that apart from military war problems the subject which appeared especially to interest American statesmen and politicians was the so-called "Russian enigma," as the already then very unenigmatic Soviet moves were frequently indulgently called by our American friends.

CHAPTER XV

Stalemate at Casablanca, January 1943

GENERAL SIKORSKI told the President that he was contemplating a second visit to Stalin to discuss all the accumulated difficulties with the Soviet dictator. He planned to visit Moscow after his projected trip to the Polish Army in the Middle East, but added that he regarded one condition as essential to the success of this venture; namely, that he should have the full support of the President and that Stalin should be made aware of it.

While agreeing that such support was necessary, the President did not think he could express it in any too definite a way at the time. He agreed, however, to give a letter to Sikorski assuring him of the President's support. Sikorski could make use of the letter when talking with Stalin.

The general, naturally, was anxious that the wording of the letter should be as clear and unequivocal as possible and that the respect of Poland's territorial status should be specifically mentioned. The President pointed out that he could not go into "such detail, on account of the declared American policy of not discussing territorial issues during the war."

In his conversations with General Sikorski the President kept on returning to the subject of France which appeared then to be on his mind.

Since November 8, 1942, diplomatic relations between Vichy France and the United States had been severed by Marshal Pétain. The whole of France was now occupied by Germany. Vichy's Admiral Darlan in Algiers had come out on the side of the Allies, how sincerely was very questionable. The African campaign had brought the French problem to the front.

The President explained that he was faced with having to steer a course which would allow the Allies to avail themselves of the support, or at least friendly neutrality, of the representatives of the Vichy regime in Africa while continuing to support the Free French headed by General de Gaulle.

Sikorski stressed the fact that, for the time being, de Gaulle alone was the symbol of the traditionally indomitable France.

The President's questions to General Sikorski on this subject showed how difficult he found it to shape a policy consistent with American principles and yet flexible enough to meet the requirements of military considerations.

Sikorski, always closely connected with France throughout his career, was very definite in his opinions on this subject. He admitted that from the point of view of military considerations the Allies were compelled to deal with Darlan, but he reminded the President that already, during his previous visits, he had warned him of the dangers of continuing diplomatic relations with the Vichy Government, especially on account of the sinister figure of Laval, who appeared to dominate it.

The general advocated the rupture of diplomatic relations between the United States and France as soon as Laval's influence became more pronounced. He now emphasized to the President that while the utilization of Darlan was a temporary military expediency, great caution should be applied to prevent this relationship from becoming too close or too prolonged. It would, he said, raise difficulties for the United States and for all the European United Nations if thereby even a semblance of collaboration with the Vichy Government were to exist.

While agreeing with the President that General de Gaulle was not always easy to deal with, Sikorski repeated that however difficult the President might find it at times to humor de Gaulle, he was the only real symbol of the true France; that in fact he was not only a symbol of fighting France, but of her national conscience after she had been betrayed by a gang of defeatist and corrupt politicians. Hence, he urged that such men as Darlan should be dispensed with as soon as possible, and a more definite policy should then be followed toward de Gaulle by granting his movement full recognition. Sikorski added that so far as Poland was concerned, he intended immediately to accredit Polish diplomatic representatives to de Gaulle's Fighting French in the French colonial territories liberated by de Gaulle.

The President, referring to de Gaulle as a prima donna, agreed that such a course would in time be justified, but thought it was still premature.

In my last conversation with General Sikorski on the afternoon of January 10 in New York, we reviewed his visit.

Having observed so closely in London, Moscow, and Washington the increasing difficulties of harmonizing the differing views of the Powers on postwar problems, Sikorski regretfully admitted that he was leaving America still confident in President Roosevelt's statesmanship, but that, for the first time, he was beset by the fear that American policy was beginning to drift in the direction of appeasement of Soviet Russia. This passive drifting of American policy, if unduly prolonged, would lead to compromises on fundamental principles of the Atlantic Charter and the Declaration of the United Nations. He felt that if this happened, there would be no possibility of return to the basic elements of justice upon which the declared aims of the United Nations had been founded. He then took stock of the high lights of his conversations in the five weeks of his stay in America.

"We shall win the war because of the indomitable courage of our soldiers in the United Nations camp and of American determination and British doggedness to overcome all difficulties.

"But we can win the peace only if the same qualities of boldness, courage, and determination inspire the leading statesmen of our camp—especially Roosevelt and Churchill."

He added that he did not at this time see such indomitable determination either in American or British statesmanship.

He hoped that President Roosevelt would soon succeed in persuading Stalin to meet him. The President had told him how anxious he was for such a meeting. But he doubted if Stalin would risk seeing the President while he was still uncertain of maintaining his initiative and his advantages in such a meeting.

The piling up of accomplished facts by Soviet Russia appeared to confirm his apprehensions. He feared that it might be too late radically to alter situations unilaterally created under the veiled threat that the mighty Russian partner could change sides in the conflict.

In taking leave of Sikorski, the President had assured him in his most winning manner that "he valued his opinions and his constructive advice, and regarded him not only as the leader of Poland, but as the natural spokesman of democratic European interests."

Sikorski was very gratified by this gracious remark. "But," he told me, "the President has honored me by discussing with me practically all war and peace problems. He has taken me into his confidence. And yet he has not discussed with me the subjects he intends to raise at his pending meeting with Churchill, and possibly with Soviet representatives.

"Our powerful Allies," said Sikorski, "do not appear to realize the necessity of strengthening their hand in their dealings with the Soviets by drawing the governments of other European nations into the discussions. They appear to be afraid of Soviet Russia's unfavorable reaction. And that in itself is characteristic of appeasement by which a realist like Stalin will never be taken in."

As I sat listening to Sikorski's comments I noted the expression of grave concern on his handsome, virile, and still youthful face. Suddenly the plane accident in Montreal flashed through my mind. It was Sikorski's third narrow escape since the beginning of the war. I was filled with a premonition that this Polish soldier-statesman, so typical of our people, was a man exposed to great personal danger and that I might perhaps never see him again.

Before we said good-by I asked him to take more care of himself and to avoid taking unnecessary risks. Sikorski smiled as he answered that he had never known how to look after his personal safety and could not promise to do so. He thanked me for my collaboration during his visit and, suddenly, his eyes aflame, he said:

"I shall live, because I have still one thing to do. I shall lead our troops in a victorious offensive into Germany, and through Germany back to Poland."

Those were his parting words.

The Allied leaders' meeting Sikorski referred to was the conference held at Casablanca at the end of January 1942.

News of the sudden secret departure of President Roosevelt and the subsequent information published on the evening of

January 26 of the results of the Casablanca meeting turned the attention of official, political, and press circles on that event.

The first reaction was one of disappointment that Stalin, or at least Molotov, had not taken part in this conference. The official announcement of the results of the conference came as an anticlimax, after the tension caused by high expectations aroused by the mystery surrounding the President's absence and the entire proceedings.

I had been confidentially informed on January 14 of the departure of President Roosevelt for a conference with Mr. Churchill. The very comprehensive program of the Casablanca conference embraced such important items as the choice of an Allied Commander in Chief, the conciliation of the two French groups respectively headed by General de Gaulle and General Giraud, and the establishment of a Supreme War Council of the United Nations, composed of President Roosevelt, Prime Minister Churchill, Premier Stalin, and Marshal Chiang Kai-shek.

The drafting of a declaration as a follow up to the Atlantic Charter was also planned, one in which the bases of United Nations collaboration and Allied war aims were to be more definitely stated.

Before leaving for Casablanca the President apparently had the intention of embodying in such a restatement of principles and aims to be made on behalf of the four principal Powers a passage reassuring the smaller European nations that their future was not menaced by any imperialist designs on the part of the Powers, and that all attempts at aggrandizement would be severely put down.

However, these laudable intentions were not carried out at Casablanca, and American official and public opinion, as well as a part of the press, reflected in comments and conversations the regret felt generally.

Admittedly, the absence of Russia at the conference had prevented the taking of any far-reaching decisions of a political nature. Considerable difficulties cropped up in the way of the half-hearted attempt to reconcile the two French generals, which had been only partly successful. The question of the appointment of a Supreme Allied Commander in Chief was left unsettled. Numerous comments gathered in my conversations showed the sincere disappointment on that score, especially because there had been a general hope in Washington that General George C. Marshall would be selected to fill this most responsible post.

No declaration had been prepared or issued as a reaffirmation of the principles of the Atlantic Charter. The impression ripened that at this time, when Soviet Russia was beginning to have considerable success in its military operations, Stalin would not agree to be bound by any conditions which might in any way limit his aspirations or cramp his initiative in his relations with the Western democracies.

After all the hopeful anticipation with which informed Washington circles awaited the results of the Casablanca conference, it was the general consensus of opinion that "a mountain had given birth to a mouse."

CHAPTER XVI

Trifling with Principles . . .

ON JANUARY 29, 1943, I was informed by my government that on January 16 the Soviet Government had notified our embassy in Moscow that it had decided to regard all Polish deportees still remaining in Russia as Soviet citizens, on the pretext that they originated from the Polish eastern confines which, as the note bluntly stated, had become part of the USSR.

The Polish Government protested vigorously in a note dated January 26, stating that it could not accept any such illegal decision of the Soviet Government. It pointed out that there could be no compromise on this issue, that it would refuse to yield to pressure, and demanded that this unilateral Soviet decision be revoked.

On January 30 I communicated with Mr. Sumner Welles and informed him of the proceedings in detail. He was deeply concerned by this sudden and dramatic turn of events which threatened completely to disrupt Soviet-Polish relations.

I went over the unusually brutal text of the Soviet note with Mr. Welles. We came to the conclusion that in all our diplomatic experience we could not remember an instance of such disregard for international law and usage.

What struck us in particular was the form adopted by the Soviets and the tone of the Soviet note. The Soviets had not only taken the decision to withdraw the Polish citizenship of all the Poles at that time in Russia, but they had done this as a sort of reprisal for the refusal, as they put it, of the Polish Government to recognize "the sovereignty of the USSR" over the Polish territories, which the note referred to as Western Byelorussia and Western Ukraine.

Mr. Welles told me that, for the time being, he was expressing only his personal opinion. He then said that he considered that a very grave situation had arisen, that the Soviets had brought their relations with Poland to a dangerous climax, and that immediate and very definite action was indeed necessary on the part of the United States and Great Britian.

On my part I made it quite clear that this was a matter of fundamental principle, involving the most basic concepts of international law, and that the Polish Government would, under no circumstances, agree to make concessions or to compromise with these principles.

Mr. Welles agreed on the impossibility of giving in to this Soviet decision. Referring to the President's and his own conversations with General Sikorski, and to the visit planned by Sikorski to Moscow, he asked me whether I knew if such a visit was contemplated. He thought, if circumstances permitted, Sikorski's visit might still open the way to an understanding.

I reminded him that General Sikorski had made it very clear that he was willing and ready to go to Moscow to discuss the difficulties which the Soviets had been creating with a view to their clarification and to the re-establishment of normal and possibly friendly relations. However, I added that the general had explained that he could only hope to succeed in such an enterprise if he received the fullest measure of support from the President on behalf of the United States Government.

Mr. Welles replied that the President had given General Sikorski the assurance that he could count on his support and asked me, after a moment's hesitation, whether the Polish Government was of the opinion that American support would have explicitly to include the entire territory of prewar Poland, and if it meant that the Polish Government rejected the possibility of making any territorial concessions whatsoever to Soviet demands.

"Am I to understand," said Sumner Welles, "that the Polish Government is determined not to sacrifice even an inch of its eastern territory?"

I was somewhat taken aback by this question.

I replied that in effect he had correctly interpreted the attitude of our government. I said I was sure he would agree that no government, forced to function outside of its territory as a result of war, could hope to maintain its authority and keep the support of its nation if, contrary to that nation's will, and without having the possibility of consulting its parliament in the course of a war in which that country was directly and actively engaged, it were to agree to make any territorial concessions.

Mr. Welles agreed that this was indeed a matter of principle and that I had correctly stated the case. He shared my opinion that the situation was further complicated by the fact that territorial demands had been made, not by an enemy, but by Poland's partner in a war fought for a common cause.

He doubted, however, my apprehension that the Soviets desired to cause a break in diplomatic relations with Poland. The Soviet counteroffensive was making good headway westward. Russia had every reason to hope that she would succeed in throwing the Germans out of Poland, of occupying that country, and she was apparently preparing the way for the fulfillment of her imperialist designs on Polish territory. In these circumstances he thought, somewhat paradoxically, that it was in the interest of the Soviets to maintain diplomatic relations with the Polish Government. For one thing, it would make them too unpopular with their British and American Allies if they made these relations impossible. According to him, General Sikorski's federative plans for Europe were the main reason for Soviet irritation. The Soviets were afraid of the creation of what they regarded as an Eastern European *cordon sanitaire*.

I reminded Mr. Welles that in our conversation and those of General Sikorski with the President this point had been discussed, and both the President and Mr. Welles appeared to favor the idea of European federation. Both had agreed that, far from being a menace to Soviet security, such a federation would become a stabilizing factor of peace of special value to the Soviets. While admitting that this was true, Mr. Welles expressed the conviction that Russia could not easily be persuaded to change her view on the subject.

I left Sumner Welles with mixed feelings after this conversation. He had shown full understanding of the gravity of the situation created by the Soviets, of its illegality and brutality, and of all its implications. I had no doubt that he would present the case forcibly to the President as soon as he returned to Washington from Casablanca. I knew that he would suggest American intervention, and that he realized how urgent it had become to give support to General Sikorski's sincere policy of pursuing good relations with the Soviets.

But his words, "Am I to understand that the Polish Government is decided not to sacrifice even an inch of its eastern territory?" were rather unexpected.

For the first time since my arrival in Washington one of the highest officials of the American Government, a very close collaborator of President Roosevelt, had hinted that allied Poland —the first of the United Nations actively to oppose Nazi Germany, the only European country without a Quisling, with an unstained record of active resistance—was to make territorial concessions to an allegedly allied Power as the price of "friendly relations."

I fully realized the importance of Sumner Welles's question which reflected, in my understanding, the helplessness of the American Government to assert its moral leadership in the United Nations concept, established on American initiative.

Contrary to all principles, and legal conceptions for centuries in existence, and flagrantly contrary to all basic principles of American policy of non-recognition of territorial changes by force or threat of force, his words showed me that American policy in relation to the USSR had reached a turning point. He had disclosed to me that appeasement was becoming the keynote of American policy toward the Soviets.

Stalin had shrewdly chosen his moment for imposing Soviet citizenship upon some million and a half Polish deportees in Russia. Thereby he was forcing a showdown. He appeared fully to understand the psychological trend of opinion in the Western democracies. His armies were now successful. The victory at Stalingrad had definitely turned the scales. He could afford to persist in refusing to meet President Roosevelt, and thus avoid discussion of matters of principle and co-ordination of war aims and of postwar plans. Like a great gambler, he knew when he held a good hand.

American and British opinion believed that soon Germany might be sufficiently weakened to allow Stalin to play his ulti-

mate trump card of a separate peace and use it as a decisive bargaining point.

The African offensive of the Allies was proceeding slowly and
could not replace Stalin's version of a second front. American
public opinion had wholeheartedly "bought" Russia as a providential ally. Stalin knew that the psychosis of avoiding anything
that might irritate Russia had already settled on Washington and
London. He undoubtedly knew that the meeting at Casablanca
had not resulted in establishing complete unity between America
and Britain. It had bared certain differences of opinion on the
conduct of war.

Now was Stalin's chance to advance a step further and to use
the Polish test case in a more definite move.

Mr. Welles called me up on February 5 and asked me to see
him that afternoon. The President had returned and he wanted
to tell me the result of their talk. Since my last visit Mr. Welles
had been receiving telegraphic reports from London and Moscow
and he knew that the Russians were in deadly earnest in their
determination.

They had gone even further, because, on the basis of their
withdrawal of Polish citizenship, they had refused to grant any
more exit permits for the evacuation of the families of already
evacuated Polish soldiers. These had become virtual hostages in
Russia.

The Soviets had also decreed that relief activities among Poles
in Russia were to cease entirely. Mr. Welles was aware of the new
and tragic human problem created by this measure for multi-
tudes of Polish men, women, and children in Russia, who were
to be deprived of all outside aid, of food and clothing.

Sumner Welles told me that he had made a very detailed report to the President. The President considered the situation
"so delicate and difficult" that he had asked Mr. Welles to impress upon me that, in the circumstances, the Polish Government
should not press him for immediate intervention. For various
reasons connected with the war situation he did not think he
could effectively act at once, but hoped to be able to do so in the
very near future.

In the meantime he told Mr. Welles to request me to tell General Sikorski and the Polish Government to "keep their shirt on."

On February 16 I had a conversation with the President. I found him much graver than usual as I entered his study at the executive office. He opened the conversation by saying that he was much concerned by this unforeseen development because he realized what a blow it must be to his "good friend Sikorski." He knew all the facts and regarded the situation as very serious. He deeply regretted that he could not personally see Stalin. He said he was convinced that he could have made him understand all the serious implications of the situation he had created and influence him in the right direction.

The President stressed once again that the moment was unfavorable for any effective diplomatic intervention in Moscow. Very frankly he told me that the Soviets were in a phase of considerable military successes at a time when the American armed forces were meeting difficulties in their African campaign.

He said he had thought of summoning Ambassador Litvinov and starting an intervention through him. But he had come to the conclusion that this was not a good way of proceeding. He doubted whether Litvinov had any influence with Stalin. Therefore he had contacted Mr. Churchill in view of a joint American-British intervention and he thought it should be opened by Mr. Churchill preparing the way through conversations with Ambassador Maisky, whose words carried more weight in Moscow than those of Litvinov.

In discussing the details of the situation the President agreed with me that owing to the piling up of accomplished facts the problem had become one of great urgency. It was of considerable importance that it should be favorably settled, if only on account of the morale of the Polish Army of 100,000 men, upon which the Allies were counting and which could not fail to be seriously affected by the forcible retention and imposition of Soviet citizenship on their kin in Russia.

The President fully realized the importance of these factors but explained that the matter was too serious to risk an intervention which might not succeed. According to the President, Stalin's realism required a realistic approach. He would have to work out a method of intervention accordingly, and this demanded some preparation.

He admitted that he did not understand the curious workings

of Soviet mentality. He said that the Soviets obviously did not realize that no Western mind could understand or accept the sudden imposition of Soviet citizenship upon nationals of a foreign country. "But," he added, "we have to face facts and try to meet these curious workings of the Soviet brain with arguments which impress them."

I took advantage of this opening and asked the President if he would allow me to be quite frank with him on this very serious occasion. He encouraged me to do so. I told him that I believed American diplomacy had hitherto only superficially admitted the deep difference between Western and Soviet mentality which he had just alluded to. It struck me that it had always been waiting for Stalin's further demands, and only then tried to find a way out, finally giving in to him in most matters. That very realism of Stalin, so frequently stressed by Americans, surely required a more realistic approach than had been used hitherto.

Did not the President think, I asked, that Stalin would continue to avoid meeting him as long as he felt he could have his way without embarrassing discussions on fundamental principles and issues?

Being a realist, he would surely react more directly if he realized that he had to ask for something *before* he could get it. This required the erection of a solid moral wall—a wall of American principles between the United States and Soviet Russia, a wall built of the principles which the President had so frequently declared in his speeches, and had embodied in the Atlantic Charter and the Declaration of the United Nations.

I told the President that from my previous conversations I knew that personally he had no illusions about the territorial appetites of Russia, and that he did not believe that they would be satisfied even if the Western Powers were to agree to the annexation of the Baltic States, of part of Poland, of Bessarabia, and Bukowina.

We were living through a time of Russian trial balloons, I went on, which floated to Britain and America with ever-increasing demands. If they were not immediately pricked, more would follow. If no definitely negative attitude were encountered by Soviet Russia at this time, when her need of Allied assistance was so great and she was still so dependent on Allied support in war matériel and on a second front, what could one later interpose to stop that *Drang Nach Westen* which might replace the German *Drang Nach Osten* and disrupt world security and peace?

The President listened attentively, at times nodding approval. He asked me whether I had definite suggestions to make.

I replied that I would like to take the liberty of making two definite suggestions:

First, that for once an energetic joint American-British intervention be attempted in support of Poland, that it should be both insistent and sufficiently clear to convince Stalin that this time the United States and Britain were solemnly warning him that they would never agree to any violation of the fundamental principles on which the concept of the United Nations was based, and which the Soviets had accepted when they signed the Declaration of the United Nations.

Second, that I thought it had become urgent for the President, and possibly also for Mr. Churchill, publicly to restate the principles of the Atlantic Charter and their unswerving determination to refuse to recognize any territorial changes brought about by force or threat of force during the war.

The President readily replied that he thought this a very good idea and that my suggestions appealed to him. He would certainly consider them and would like me to discuss them in greater detail with Sumner Welles.

I talked the matter over on the following day with Mr. Welles and gained the impression that he also approved of my suggestions. He promised to work on them and asked me what kind of statement I had in mind.

I drew his attention to statements on United States Government policy regarding non-recognition of unilaterally imposed territorial changes. I suggested that a declaration by the President should refer to the statement of policy by Secretary of State Henry L. Stimson relating to the annexation of Manchuria by Japan in 1931, which, so far as I knew, had become a basic axiom of American policy. I reminded Mr. Welles of his own statement on the independence of the Baltic republics and suggested finally that it might be possible to link the passage on Manchuria to the presence in Washington of Madame Chiang Kai-shek, then a guest of the President.

As I saw it, the President's public statement might say that the United States Government had never deviated from its policy, that it did not intend to do so, and was determined not to recognize any territorial changes brought about by unilateral act on the part of any Power and (further quoting Mr. Welles's own words) would be "opposed to any form of intervention on the part of one State, however powerful, in the domestic concerns of any other sovereign State, however weak."

I referred repeatedly to these suggestions in subsequent conversations with Mr. Welles, but soon realized that President Roosevelt would not make use of them, notwithstanding his first spontaneously favorable reaction.

Some time later the President told me that, though he deeply regretted it, his advisers—as he put it—had persuaded him "that the moment was ill chosen for such a declaration which might be resented by Stalin."

From conversations I had with New Deal friends close to the President I learned that he was so intent on meeting Stalin that he did not wish in any way "to lessen his chances (as Harry Hopkins put it) by making a statement which Stalin might regard as unfriendly."

I admit I was shocked when I heard this. I felt sure that, far from diminishing the chances of a Stalin-Roosevelt meeting, a specific statement made by the President would place the initiative in his hands and might induce Stalin to ask to see him in order to ascertain in what degree he was determined actually to defend his principles.

It was all very well for the President to tell us to "keep your shirt on."

On the other hand, it was no less necessary to give some support to the morale of the Polish people, so sorely tried by German and Soviet pressures.

It was obviously imperative to show Stalin the natural reactions of American and British public opinion to his imperialist designs on Poland and other neighboring countries, and to demonstrate to the Soviet Government that democracy was not prepared to sacrifice its principles to totalitarian imperialism while fighting a war against Hitler's totalitarianism.

I had been asked by the President to impress upon my government the necessity of keeping the whole matter strictly secret.

I felt this was a mistake. I was convinced that the mere publication of the brutal Soviet note to Poland and of Poland's determined but courteous answer would provoke unanimous support for Poland on the part of the American people.

The Polish Government was in a most embarrassing situation. Our only hope lay in American and British intervention. That support was indispensable to our cause. On the other hand, we could not disregard the President's wishes. And yet every day of delay was weakening our position with regard to the Soviets.

The cautious way in which previous American interventions on Polish matters were made in Moscow had naturally been interpreted by Stalin as proof of American lack of interest which he could ignore. To be effective at this advanced stage of the problem, intervention would have to be immediate, strong, and publicly known. And we were asked to keep everything secret.

We were deprived of the possibility of obtaining the support of public opinion. Our lips were sealed.

It was obvious that a delayed and secret intervention would have no effect in Moscow. I had told the President and Mr. Welles that General Sikorski was apprehensive that this grave incident created by the Soviets was probably only one of a series intended by Stalin to force a rupture of relations between the Soviet and the Polish governments. The very wording of the Soviet note appeared to confirm these fears.

One thing became clear in my mind, and I warned General Sikorski accordingly. We could not expect substantial support on the part of an American government which was pursuing a policy of appeasement of Russia and could ill afford to stand up and restate its own principles as conditions of future harmonious American-Soviet co-operation. We might get some support, but it was likely that it would come too late and be of a nature which Moscow could disregard.

To me, who considered American leadership in the war, and especially in the shaping of postwar peace, as indispensable to security and the rule of decency in international relations, it was becoming painfully evident that there was little chance that this moral leadership would ever materialize.

I still believed in the sincerity of President Roosevelt's intentions, of his vision of a united world, re-created on American principles of justice and democracy. But I was beginning to be beset by doubts, and I feared that considerations of a political nature, rather than perseverance in his bold initiative in world statesmanship, would finally influence his policy and direct it into channels of deals and compromise.

CHAPTER XVII

. . . *at Poland's Expense*

IN FEBRUARY and March 1943
the decoding clerks at my embassy worked overtime. A flow of
telegrams kept arriving from London and Moscow bringing me
information on the daily incidents which marked a steady deterioration in Soviet-Polish relations. It was apparent that a Soviet-
Polish crisis was approaching.

The Soviet forces were pushing the German armies westward and had launched simultaneously a political offensive syn-
chronized with their military advance. Moscow was creating a
series of accomplished facts, calculated to pave the way to ultimate mastery of Poland.

The accelerated pace of this activity made it look like a virtual
barrage of hostile incidents in preparation for Soviet military
occupation of Poland. The Soviet note of January 16, bluntly
communicating the fact that the Soviets had decided to withdraw the Polish citizenship of all the Poles forcibly deported by
them from the parts of Poland they had invaded in the autumn of
1939, had been but a prelude to further unilateral acts. Having
rejected all our protests, the Soviet authorities started a phase of
direct action.

The Polish deportees in Russia were now prohibited from
leaving the localities where they had been settled, and were being
forced, under duress, to accept new identification papers proving
their Soviet citizenship.

Simultaneously, on February 4 the communist Polish language
paper *New Horizons,* printed at Kuibyshev by order of the Soviet
Government, published an appeal to all Poles in Russia to enter
the ranks of a Soviet-sponsored "Polish Army" to be formed in
the Soviet Union.

At the same time activities of the group of Polish communists, founded in the winter of 1941 under the leadership of Wanda Wasilewska, were greatly increased. That group had now changed its name to "Union of Polish Patriots."

The Soviet press and the bulletins of the Soviet Embassy in Washington began to publish numerous articles tending to show that the only just and fair boundary between Poland and the Soviet Union was the so-called Curzon Line.

Thus, Soviet Russia was getting ready to carry out the annexation of nearly half of Poland. At the same time the Soviet Government was laying the foundations for the imposition upon Poland of a puppet government, completely subservient to Moscow, supported by an allegedly Polish armed force commanded by Red Army officers.

Our Ambassador in Kuibyshev, Tadeusz Romer, anxious to save the situation and patiently refusing to be provoked by the Soviet moves, carried on endless conversations with Molotov. His reports showed that he was faced by an impenetrable wall, only thinly whitewashed with diplomatic courtesy, which was wearing down as time went on. He was becoming aware that, whatever arguments he used, the Soviet determination to overpower Poland militarily and politically was grimly set in the minds of the men controlling Russia's policies.

Polish citizens were being summoned daily to Soviet police stations where their Polish passports were confiscated. Terrorism was being applied by use of threats of imprisonment, and our people were detained for long periods of time in police stations without food or water. Instances of physical brutality were recorded even in the temporary capital of Kuibyshev. In many localities Polish citizens were beaten. They were required to produce Soviet visas proving their legal entry into Soviet Russia. As they had been forcibly deported from Poland to Russia, they naturally had no such documents. They were prosecuted and sentenced to two years' imprisonment "for illegally residing in Russia without proper documents."

Information was piling up on my desk proving that Soviet diplomacy and propaganda were also greatly increasing their activities in Great Britain while conducting this brutal campaign.

In England, the news of ever-greater Soviet victories called for the almost hysterical admiration for Soviet military achievements while, at the same time, the Soviet advance westward raised new fears regarding future Soviet conduct.

A year ago London had been apprehensive of the conclusion of a separate Russian-German peace under pressure of the German advance eastward, now Soviet victories were arousing the fear in London that Germany might surrender to Soviet Russia, suddenly ending the war in Europe before British and American forces invaded the continent. This strengthened the British tendency to appease the Soviets.

Stalin was obviously aware of this favorable situation and insistently pressed his claim that the Curzon Line be recognized as Russia's permanent frontier with Poland.

In the United States, where ex-Ambassador Joseph E. Davies came out with a comprehensive pro-Soviet drive culminating in the publication in 1942 of his book *Mission to Moscow,* the adoption of a distinctly pro-Soviet attitude was less pronounced and more gradual than in Britain. Nevertheless, I was becoming aware that official American policy, gradually but surely evolving into appeasement of Russia, had the support of White House circles and, at intervals, appeared to be directly inspired by them.

My diplomatic activity in Washington at that time consisted mostly in impressing upon the President directly and through the State Department the necessity of speedy and decisive intervention in Moscow in time to prevent a rupture of Soviet-Polish relations, which Moscow appeared anxious to provoke.

In my conversations and numerous memoranda submitted to the State Department, I used all the arguments at my disposal, as well as my knowledge of Russian methods and psychology, to prove that this matter of Polish-Soviet relations had long ceased to be a regional problem and had become, in the fullest sense of the word, a test case of the relationship between the Western Powers and Russia.

I kept the State Department informed about the measures applied by the Soviet Government to Polish citizens in the USSR to force upon them Soviet citizenship by means of intimidation, beatings, starvation, and imprisonment. I pointed out that these measures were intended to bring pressure upon the Polish Government with a view to obtaining its recognition of Soviet sovereign rights over the territories of Poland, which they had invaded and occupied by virtue of their agreements with Germany. I drew the attention of Mr. Hull and of Mr. Welles to the fact that lack of American and British intervention in support of Poland's rights in Moscow was encouraging Stalin to believe that Poland was at his mercy, and that his territorial claims on Poland were already tacitly approved by Great Britain and the United States.

All I could obtain was the promise that, "pending the President's personal intervention with Stalin, Ambassador Standley would be instructed to stress United States interest in the situation."

In a conversation with Mr. Welles on March 26 he told me that he had found it possible only to give very general instructions to Ambassador Standley, because the President had not yet decided when and how he would undertake his promised intervention.

Mr. Welles explained that, important though this problem had become, there were other weighty circumstances which required the United States to apply the greatest caution in its conduct toward Soviet Russia. This did not mean, he assured me, that the United States would remain passive on Polish matters or would not support us, but other important considerations delayed the President's intervention and forced him to await a more favorable moment before undertaking it.

In the first days of April Mr. Welles asked me again to impress upon my government the necessity of remaining calm and continuing negotiations between Ambassador Romer and Mr. Molotov, so as to prevent the Russian Government from "provoking the Polish Government to a rupture of relations which would make matters so much more serious."

I reassured Mr. Welles, and asked him to assure the President, that our government was doing its utmost to prevent a rupture of relations. At the same time I pointed out that the Soviets had intensified their propaganda of vilification of the Polish Government in their press and radio broadcasts and by influencing their American and British "fellow travelers," who had now joined in giving their open support to the Russian claims on Poland.

I warned the Undersecretary, and asked him to warn the President, that in this situation the Polish Government could not long continue to remain silent. As a matter of fact, it might greatly assist our just cause if at this stage public opinion were informed about the true details of the case. I told him I was sure that the Soviets were watchfully observing all public reactions in America and Britain as indications which would show them whether they could, with impunity, pursue their ruthless imperialist policy toward Poland or if they had to reckon with any criticism on the part of the Western democracies.

Mr. Welles agreed with me in principle. However, in view of the President's promise to intervene, he once more insistently requested that the Polish Government remain patient and refrain from making public statements which would disclose the impasse reached in Soviet-Polish relations. He believed that publicity might embarrass the American Government and make it more difficult for the President to intervene.

I was informed that Ambassador Standley had been complaining at that time of his difficulties of getting even a hearing from Stalin or Molotov. On the other hand, the President continuously hoped to bring about a meeting between himself and Stalin, and was confident that he would be able to convince the Soviet dictator that harmonious collaboration of the United Nations required a definite change in Russia's policies. In a moment of frankness the President admitted to me that he was greatly disappointed that Stalin, under the pretext that he was too busy with military matters, had declined the invitation to Casablanca.

"I have made five attempts to see this man," exclaimed the President, "but he has always eluded me."

The President added that Stalin and even Molotov sometimes greatly delayed seeing Ambassador Standley, who had to wait for weeks to be received by them even on urgent war matters.

The President asked me how I could explain this attitude on the part of Stalin. I replied that if the President would allow me to be as frank as he had been with me, I would say that it was rather his own attitude than that of Stalin which appeared to me difficult to understand. Stalin was avoiding meeting the President because he had gained the conviction that he could achieve his aims without having to risk a discussion which might prevent him from carrying them out. He was using the Polish test case as an opening wedge in the same way Hitler had used the Austrian Anschluss and Czechoslovakia. After having been allowed by the appeasing Powers to grab these two countries, Hitler had concluded that appeasement had come to stay and that he could continue his policy of grab without fear of resistance.

I added that I honestly believed, even quite apart from its purely Polish aspect, that a strong intervention by the President on the Polish test case in Moscow would certainly contribute toward altering Stalin's reluctance to meet the President.

Concerning the difficulties encountered by Ambassador Standley in Moscow, I ventured the opinion that this was another instance of Soviet methods. I admitted I was surprised that the President had not taken a more definite stand on the matter.

The President asked me what I had in mind. I replied that when any Ambassador in Washington, including myself, asked to be received by him, even at times when he was very busy with war problems, he always showed the utmost graciousness and courtesy by granting the interview. I expressed my conviction that if the President would make it quite clear that unless similar reciprocal treatment were granted to the United States Ambassador in Moscow, he would recall him, leaving but a Chargé d'Affaires. I added that I felt sure that if such a line was adopted, Ambassador Standley would have no further difficulties in being received by Stalin and his functionaries.

The President said he would think it over and might possibly follow my suggestions if he "found that circumstances permitted him to do so."

Information reaching me from my government showed that at that time, in London, the policy of appeasing Soviet Russia was even more pronounced than in America. I had proof of this in conversations I had had in the early days of March with Lord Halifax, the British Ambassador in Washington.

Lord Halifax was anxious to learn from me all the details of Polish-Soviet relations. I told him of my conversations with the President and the State Department on this subject and the latest developments reported from Moscow. I stressed the necessity of an urgent and strong joint intervention of the English-speaking Powers, and dwelt on the fact that Poland was but a test case of Russian policy which, I was sure, would be followed by further territorial and political demands in the Balkans, the Straits, and the Persian Gulf, directly involving British interests.

Lord Halifax appeared inclined to share my views. He asked what arguments could be used to stop Russia from pursuing her aims. I told him what I had suggested to the President, and stressed how urgent it was to adopt a more realistic method of dealing with Russia.

Lord Halifax doubted if such a change of tactics could be effective, and then suddenly asked me whether I did not think that, in our difficult negotiations in Moscow, our government "should make some concessions to Soviet demands which might ease the situation." He asked me whether the acceptance by Poland of the Curzon Line as a border between Poland and the Soviets would really be such a hardship. He admitted that our cause was a just one, but said that he did not see how the Soviets could be stopped. There was always the fear that Stalin might conclude a separate peace with Hitler. This fear was a serious deterrent for energetic intervention and, therefore, Lord Halifax did not think that any decisive steps could be taken to prevent Russia from pursuing her present policy.

When Mr. Eden arrived in Washington on the eleventh of March he brought with him two of my old friends of the British Foreign Office: Sir William Strang and Oliver Harvey. Several appointments were made for me to see Mr. Eden, but I soon realized that he was determined to avoid me. These tentative appointments were all canceled later, under pretext of other important official duties.

However, I had several talks with Strang and Oliver Harvey. Strang, who at the British Foreign Office headed the department which dealt with Polish and Soviet affairs, appeared to be as convinced as I was that a joint British and American intervention should be attempted, but felt it was for the United States rather than Britain to take the initiative. I arranged for him to meet Loy Henderson from the State Department and General Bill Donovan at our embassy for lunch. We discussed the Polish-Soviet problems and Soviet policies at length. This conversation certainly showed Strang how firm was the attitude of these two fine Americans on the necessity of giving support to Poland. He told me later that he was all the more surprised by the fact that the American Government had not shown more initiative in pressing London for a joint intervention in Moscow. He admitted that in Britain the pro-Soviet feeling made it particularly difficult for the British Government to adopt a more active course in its dealings with the Soviets. But he felt sure that Mr. Churchill and Mr. Eden understood the gravity of the situation and would ultimately intervene.

Shortly before Mr. Eden's departure for England I had the occasion of speaking to him briefly at a large reception at the British Embassy. He told me how sorry he was that he "had been too busy to see me" and assured me that "the impasse reached in Polish-Soviet relations was a matter of deep concern to the British Government."

I had closely followed the trend of Eden's conversations in Washington. As regards the relationship of the United Nations to Soviet Russia, I learned that he had used all his very convincing and suave diplomacy to impress upon the American Government and political circles how indispensable it was to continue to apply great caution in dealing with the Soviets, and to avoid so far as possible any too forceful arguments which Stalin might resent and which might result in the loss of this powerful partner, who was bearing the brunt of the war against Germany.

On the whole, these arguments fell on willing American ears and appeared considerably to impress American official, political, and press circles in Washington. Mr. Eden's influence was at that time most clearly reflected in Walter Lippmann's columns.

So far as Polish problems created by Soviet Russia were concerned, Mr. Eden had discussed them in Washington, frankly expressing his concern, but he did not urge the United States Government to take action. On the contrary, I was told that he discouraged the idea of a strong intervention on behalf of Poland in Moscow.

Evidently the British Government was not averse to the idea of seeing Poland forced to accept the Curzon Line. It was especially noticeable that the British Government distrusted Soviet Russia and was afraid that Stalin might once again find a common language with Hitler. This had to be prevented at any cost, even if Poland was to be the price of Stalin's further participation in the war.

The picture was becoming clear to my eyes.

Both Britain and America appeared to understand fully the dangerous trend of Soviet policy and were probing the possibilities of influencing Stalin. Neither of them really trusted him. Both were considerably frightened at losing Soviet Russia as a partner in the war. Each was passing the buck to the other. The American Government contended that Britain, as Poland's ally, was in a better position to defend Poland's interests. The British Government was inclined to believe that the United States could intervene more effectively, being less directly interested in European issues.

As a result, Poland was becoming the subject of pending Power-political discussions regarding her ultimate fate. She was practically abandoned by her Allies and left alone to face her destiny of becoming the first victim of Soviet imperialism. Her government was paralyzed, having been promised Anglo-American support which was not forthcoming, on condition that it remain silent and make no attempt to enlist the powerful support of public opinion for its righteous cause.

CHAPTER XVIII

Soviets Break with Poland, April 1943

ON THE afternoon of April 26, 1943, I was called on the telephone by the Washington correspondent of Reuter's. He inquired whether I had received confirmation of a Reuter dispatch stating that the Soviet Government had, as said in the dispatch, "interrupted diplomatic relations with the Polish Government."

The inevitable had happened. The Soviets had carried into effect, with ruthless consequence characteristic of Stalin, a decision methodically prepared by the Kremlin.

The Soviet Government had chosen as its pretext the reaction of the Polish Government to the news of the mass murder of some eleven thousand Polish officers taken prisoner by the Soviets in the Polish campaign in September 1939. The graves of these fighters for Poland's independence had been "discovered" by the Germans, who broadcast the news to the world, accusing the Soviets of this unprecedented crime.

Whoever was responsible for the Katyn murders, this new outrage to civilization had deprived Poland of the flower of its officers. The news had been so great a shock to the Polish people that it was imperative for our government to react immediately. Always suspicious of Hitler's moves, and desirous to pursue his basic policy of maintaining good relations with the Soviets, General Sikorski decided to ask for an investigation of the massacre of Polish prisoners of war by some neutral body. In a dramatic message he informed me that the shock caused by the news of the murders had profoundly struck at the morale of the Polish Underground organization, of the Home Army, and of the Polish forces abroad.

"We have lost an irreplaceable contingent of our best soldiers," he said. "Our government must take immediate action to build up the spirit of the Polish nation and of our soldiers. I have therefore appealed to the International Red Cross in Geneva, the only international organization whose high standing and impartiality are unassailable and give the fullest guarantee of the lack of any bias. I have asked them to conduct an investigation on the spot with a view to verifying the information published by the Germans and to determine who is responsible for this crime."

The Soviet Government immediately took advantage of this move to break off diplomatic relations and accuse the Polish Government of connivance with Hitler.

Since July 30, 1941, when Polish-Soviet relations had been resumed, we had been repeatedly asking the Soviets for news of these Polish officers, prisoners of war of the Soviets. We had never obtained any definite or satisfactory reply to our inquiries.

The British and American governments had also repeatedly intervened at our request, in view of the growing importance of getting these officers to join the Polish forces. All these interventions elicited only evasive answers from the Soviet Government. These facts greatly increased the impact of the shock which the final revelation of this mass murder had been to all Polish people.

On that same afternoon of April 26 I called on Mr. Sumner Welles. As I came into his room at the State Department I noticed he was upset. I sensed for the first time a tense atmosphere in my relations with the Undersecretary. He started by saying that he could not understand how the Polish Government could have appealed to the International Red Cross to investigate an accusation made—as he put it—"by the German propaganda machine." How could the Polish Government expect an impartial result from such an investigation? He expressed his deep regret that the Polish Government had taken this course, giving an easy pretext to the Soviets to break relations with Poland.

I was taken aback by Mr. Welles's words. I reminded him that our efforts to locate our missing officers had gone on for a very long time. It was not Poland who had chosen this time of the greatest difficulties in its relations with the Soviets to break wide open this tragic problem. Did the American Government think that any self-respecting government could possibly pretend to ignore such an outrage on its fighting men? How, of all people, could Sikorski, who had so patiently and unswervingly pursued a policy aimed at friendly relations with the Soviets, hope to remain in office and to continue this policy, without at least making an attempt to clarify the unprecedented situation with which he was now faced? What could he have done except appeal to the only international institution which could, without delay, be brought into the picture and publish a report on its findings? Why should this move be interpreted by Russia as an acceptance by the Polish Government of the German version? On the contrary, any impartial person would surely see in General Sikorski's decision the proof that the Polish Government was determined not to accept at face value the German story before its investigation by a neutral organization, whose verdict would either confirm or disprove the German accusation.

I reminded Mr. Welles that since January 1943 I had been continuously warning the President, the Secretary of State, and himself, that it was becoming increasingly evident that the Soviets would seize on any pretext to bring about a break of relations with our government in order to get the green light for carrying out their designs on Poland.

I then asked Mr. Welles if he was aware that on April 15 Mr. Churchill informed General Sikorski that the British Cabinet had taken the decision, long overdue, to intervene in Moscow on the subject of Soviet-Polish relations.

Mr. Welles had been informed about it and knew that this intervention was to take the form of a personal appeal by Churchill to Stalin. He agreed that it was probable that the knowledge that such a step was being contemplated might have been a determining factor in Stalin's sudden decision to break off Soviet-Polish relations before it actually took place.

Referring to Washington rumors regarding a pending meeting of President Roosevelt with Churchill and Stalin, Mr. Welles told me that the President was trying to speed it up. He added, however, that it was impossible to say when the meeting would actually take place.

Mr. Welles again stressed the necessity for the Polish Government to avoid any public statements which might make it more difficult for the President to intervene in Moscow.

On my part, I drew Mr. Welles's special attention to the necessity of curbing the exaggerated pro-Soviet tendency of OWI propaganda at this delicate moment.

He promised he would try to do so.

A few days later I learned that Mr. Churchill, expected for some time, was about to arrive in Washington.

It was time for me again to see Lord Halifax. The British Ambassador naturally turned to the rupture of Soviet-Polish relations and asked me whether I did not think that if General Sikorski were to express his readiness to remove from his cabinet some of his Ministers who, "rightly or wrongly," were considered by the Soviets as unfriendly to Soviet Russia, it might make it easier to bring about the re-establishment of Soviet-Polish relations.

Being accustomed to such studiously naïve questions on the part of my British colleague, I jokingly inquired whether Lord Halifax had adopted the Soviet dictionary interpretation of the terms "independence" and "sovereignty" of nations, and pointed out that if General Sikorski were to take such a course, it would be equivalent to an acceptance of dependence of the Polish Government and a recognition of the right of the Soviet Government to influence the appointment of Polish Cabinet Ministers.

Lord Halifax at once admitted that I was right in principle and that he did not understand the conduct of the Soviets. He admitted that he had been impressed when Stalin so forcefully declared that he desired "a strong and independent Poland." He was depressed when, a few days later, Vishinsky launched a vehement accusation against the Polish Government, which made it more difficult for the British Government to pursue its attempts to save this perilous situation.

Regarding Stalin's declared desire for "a strong and independent Poland," I replied that his statement did not appear to be inconsistent with Soviet expansionist policies. It was merely a matter of specific Soviet terminology. The Soviet Government would probably describe the component republics of the Soviet Union, such as the Ukraine, as independent and sovereign States.

It was very characteristic of Stalin's and Soviet mentality that, after having made such a statement on the independence of Poland, Stalin had ordered the erstwhile prosecutor Vishinsky publicly to read an act of accusation against the Polish Government and nation. Viewed together, these two official Soviet statements were completely in keeping with Soviet custom.

Stalin said he wanted "a strong and independent Poland."

Vishinsky explained that to be free, Poland must have a government "friendly" to the Soviets. This, in the Soviet meaning of the word, meant a government totally subservient to Russia.

Such a government, composed of Soviet puppets, of well-known communists, was actually being constituted and indoctrinated in Soviet Russia. It was the group of so-called "Polish patriots" of Wanda Wasilewska. Similar Soviet-sponsored puppet governments were being got ready to impose Stalin's will on other countries.

To us, the pattern was a well-known one, and Soviet policy was by no means as "enigmatic" as it was fondly referred to in England and in America. It was only surprising that the British and American governments still preferred to discount reality and to indulge in wishful thinking, refusing to admit the Soviet threat to the independence of Europe.

Lord Halifax asked me what I thought would be the next phase in Soviet policy toward Poland.

I replied that it would probably be the announcement of the formation of a puppet government for Poland, and of an allegedly Polish armed force, flamboyantly dressed up in Polish uniforms, but commanded by Soviet officers and destined to become a military spearhead of Soviet domination as soon as the Soviets reinvaded Polish territory in their victorious march westward.

Lord Halifax became thoughtful, but said that he still could not believe that the Soviets wanted to dominate Poland or to Sovietize it.

I asked him if he was aware that Soviet broadcasts clearly pointed to this Soviet aim of communizing states bordering on Russia and especially Poland. There could be little doubt that Stalin was out to gain complete control of that country and of its government.

"If that is the case," replied Lord Halifax, "then we have very little hope of settling the Polish-Soviet dispute."

We then discussed the possible implications of the hitherto successful Soviet expansionist policy with regard to Poland and the

Baltic States, on the general situation and on the relationship of Soviet Russia to the Western Powers.

I said that we had been hearing a lot about "Stalin's realism," but, unfortunately, I saw no realistic arguments being used by the United States and Britain to balance even in the most friendly way this Soviet display of realism. On the contrary, a policy was being adopted by the Western Powers which made the relationship entirely onesided. We would not have to wait long for the results.

I quoted to Lord Halifax the conversation which a military colleague of mine had recently had with one of the dashing gold-braided officers of the Soviet Military Mission in Washington. After liberal drinks of vodka, in an atmosphere of friendly exuberance, my military friend asked the Russian to tell him what were the real Soviet war aims.

His Russian buddy answered without any hesitation: "We must have eastern and Central Europe. Peter the Great already had this aim. We shall control the Dardanelles, for the straits have been an axiom of Russia's basic policy for two hundred years. In the Middle East we will get hold of the Persian Gulf and blow the British out of India. In the Far East, we aim at regaining our frontiers of 1904, before the Russo-Japanese War. That will enable us to hold China in a firm grip."

Lord Halifax admitted that this was indeed a rather startling program.

Mr. Churchill arrived in Washington on May 11. He was accompanied by some hundred advisers and experts, mostly high-ranking military, naval, and air-force men. Continuous conferences were held bearing especially on the working out of details of what was to become the greatest amphibious attack in history.

The British were inclined to delay the opening of a second front on account of considerable German superiority. Mr. Churchill had brought with him the bold plan of relentless bombing of Germany, initiated by British Air Marshal Harris, and intended to soften Germany by disrupting her war industries and communications in preparation for the final attack on the European fortress.

I gathered from both sides that while at the outset the conference appeared to have started in a somewhat difficult atmosphere caused by considerable differences of opinion, it ended in a spirit of complete understanding and unity. Very positive and important decisions were jointly arrived at. Many points which were left unsettled at the Casablanca meeting were adjusted.

The President won his point of strengthening the war effort in the Far Eastern theater and of giving increased aid to Chiang Kai-shek. It was decided to take the offensive in Burma, to increase supplies of war matériel, and especially of air war matériel to China, to increase the pressure against Japan in the Aleutians and in the northern Pacific. I gathered that this latter decision was also calculated to impress Soviet Russia, pending the Big Three meeting, in the hope that she might decide to participate in the war against Japan.

The decisions taken at the Washington conference also showed that the American and British military leaders were eager to strike at the enemy in Europe, but realized how much preparation was still necessary before such a gigantic operation could be successfully launched. Both America and Great Britain were anxious to avoid too great sacrifices in manpower and matériel. After lengthy, and at times heated, discussions the suggestions of air experts won the day.

It was agreed to proceed with intensive bombing and the cleaning up of the Mediterranean by first taking the island bases, and then invading and occupying southern Italy, at least, in order to clear the way for further active offensive operations in Europe.

The decision regarding the attack on Europe through the Balkans after the completion of this preliminary program was put off for the time being because of strong Soviet objections.

It was planned to make the final decision about the location of a second front coincident with the development of a new German offensive in the east, in order to strike at the most vulnerable point where the Germans might be least able to organize their resistance, thus drawing some of the German forces away from Russia. This, in the opinion of the British experts, could best be achieved by an invasion through the Balkans, "the soft underbelly," as Mr. Churchill called it.

I noted that the decisions concerning American-British military and strategic co-ordination were being taken with due regard to the political situation, which had gradually arisen in connection with Stalin's expansionist tendencies.

Thus the problem of bringing Turkey into active participation in the war on the Allied side, or at least of assuring her friendly neutrality in the case of an Allied attack through the Balkans, was discussed in all its military and political aspects. Turkey had apparently clearly indicated that she could contemplate giving up her neutrality only if she received from Russia satisfactory guarantees of her territorial integrity and of nonintervention in her internal affairs. She added that such assurances would have to be endorsed by America and Britain. Turkey further indicated that the Soviet attitude in the case of Finland, of the three Baltic countries, and of Poland, made it necessary for her to request such concrete assurances.

The conversations between the President and Mr. Churchill proceeded on the theory that their early meeting with Stalin to discuss not only his demands on eastern Central European countries, but likewise his attitude on the Turkish and other problems, had become an urgent necessity. The already evident negative attitude of the Soviets toward an Allied offensive through the Balkans was regarded in Washington as an ominous sign that Stalin's expansionism would soon include the Balkans, and possibly Turkish territory.

I had had numerous talks with members of Mr. Churchill's mission, many of whom I had been constantly meeting informally during their stay in Washington.

I renewed my former acquaintance with Admiral Sir Dudley Pound and found him enthusiastic concerning the fighting qualities of the Polish Navy which, as he said, was rendering such signal service to the Allied cause. Mr. Churchill's naval experts were full of praise for the fighting qualities and spirit of our navy. During a dinner at Colonel Rex Benson's, then British Military Attaché, Admiral Cunningham told me that it was remarkable that the Polish Navy had, in so short a time, attained standards of quality which it had taken the British Navy many centuries to attain.

I had several very pleasant conversations with Air Marshal Sir Charles Portal, the brilliant young chief of the R.A.F. His enthusiastic comments on the Polish Air Force and his very frankly voiced convictions about the necessity of defending Poland's complete independence by plain speaking to Russia showed that, at least as far as Britain's military leaders were concerned, Poland could count on British support earned during the war by her gallant fighting men.

The Roosevelt-Churchill conference had achieved its basic aims. Most of the problems of British-American collaboration in the war, and especially the military ones, had been satisfactorily thrashed out and co-ordinated. Some measure of diplomatic co-ordination had likewise been achieved between the President and the British Prime Minister.

But the main difficulty, little known to the uninitiated, of drawing Russia into franker and closer collaboration with the Western Powers, still remained to be overcome.

My conversations with American and British military leaders, and with several close collaborators of the President, served to convince me of their apprehension that Stalin might reject some, at least, of the decisions taken by the President and Mr. Churchill, that he might frown at some of the strategic plans of the Combined Chiefs of Staff for the invasion of Italy, the location of the second front, and other details of the planned military operations.

A considerable step forward had been taken at the Washington meeting, but, as soon as the conference closed, to those of us who had followed its details it was again becoming evident that practically everything that appeared settled would have to wait for Stalin's consent.

A new period of expectant waiting for Stalin's pleasure to agree to meet the President and Mr. Churchill had begun.

CHAPTER XIX

Exit Comintern, Enter Wishful Thinking, May 1943

ON MAY 27, two days after the conference ended and Mr. Churchill left Washington, I called on Sumner Welles. I was especially interested to know what decisions had been taken at the conference regarding the President's promised intervention in behalf of Poland.

Mr. Welles replied that the President and Mr. Churchill had decided personally to intervene when next they met with Stalin, which they hoped would be soon.

He added that, for the time being, Mr. Joseph E. Davies, the President's special envoy to Stalin, had been instructed to touch upon this subject in his talks with Premier Stalin. Mr. Davies was not to go into details, but only to indicate that this was one of the subjects which the President intended to raise at the meeting.

I gathered that the aim of Mr. Davies's new mission to Moscow was primarily to insure whether or not the Big Three meeting would really take place, and that he had not been instructed by the President to go into the merits of any of the problems which the President intended to discuss personally with Stalin.

Mr. Welles was particularly interested in the announcement just made by the Soviets on the dissolution of the Comintern. He said the American Government attached considerable importance to this Soviet move, but admitted he had not yet fully grasped its meaning. He asked for my views on the subject.

I told him that I considered this Soviet decision as a move of considerable importance and hoped that the President and the American Government would draw the right conclusions.

Viewed together with other Soviet moves of the past weeks,

and especially the turn indicated by Soviet propaganda, it certainly was proof that Stalin was desirous, at least outwardly, to eliminate some causes of friction in view of the pending Big Three meeting. Stalin's Comintern move should help the President to realize the influence the United States could have in dealing with the Soviets. It could certainly be taken as an indication that Stalin was anxious to make some gesture which would favorably impress the President and American public opinion.

Mr. Welles shared my view and apparently thought that the dissolution of the Comintern had two angles: a diplomatic and an intrinsic one. He pressed me to tell him what I thought of this second aspect. Did it forecast actual cessation of Comintern activity?

I replied that the dissolution of the Comintern might not necessarily entail the cessation of communist activities and that this angle should now be carefully watched, considering that for a long time the Comintern had not been directly active.

In the decree dissolving the Comintern it was openly stated that the communist parties in other countries were sufficiently competent and no longer needed the directives of the Comintern. This appeared to imply that the dissolution of the Comintern had been dictated to Stalin by the fact that the influence of communism could perhaps be more effectively served in foreign countries by spreading it from inside.

I drew Mr. Welles's attention to various so-called "front" and anti-fascist committees in the United States, and to the American Slav Congress, which certainly was one of the most modern means inspired by Moscow for active infiltration of communism among the American working masses.

I told him that considerable loads of the communist Polish language paper *Free Poland*, published under Soviet sponsorship in Moscow, were being brought into this country on ships returning from Russia after delivering Lend-Lease supplies to the Soviets. These papers were extensively circulated among Americans of Polish descent in Chicago, Detroit, and other industrial centers.

The dissolution of the Comintern would indeed be of considerable importance if it meant that all other Soviet-sponsored communist activities in foreign countries would cease. But it might also only be a blind to calm growing anxieties, while subversive activities switched to the use of local communist elements within labor unions and utilized "fellow travelers" who now appeared to have become the most zealous propagandists of the Soviet system.

Mr. Welles said that he shared these apprehensions. He assured me that the American Government would keenly observe all further developments following the dissolution of the Comintern. For the time being, however, he considered it gratifying that the Soviets had given this proof of considering American public opinion and he thought that this fact provided instructive elements which should be taken advantage of in shaping American policy.

On this occasion Mr. Welles appeared to be clearly optimistic about the general situation. He regarded the Washington conference with Mr. Churchill and his experts as very successful. He thought that the war situation was reassuring. He complimented the Polish Government for its dignified attitude in refusing to be provoked into press and radio polemics "by the regrettable Soviet propaganda" which he frankly criticized. He promised me to do his utmost to discourage Soviet attempts at vilifying the Polish Government and Poland, but impressed upon me the importance of avoiding any unduly strong enunciations and hostile polemics on the part of the Polish Government, because he was sure that our calm attitude would be most helpful to the cause and would facilitate the President's personal intervention with Stalin.

In reply to a question of mine, Mr. Welles admitted that no date had yet been fixed for the Big Three meeting, and that the prevailing optimism then spreading in Washington that it would be held soon was still unfounded. There had been no definite indication that Stalin was agreeable to such a meeting at this stage of the war. However, there were some reasons for hope— that was all.

The dissolution of the Comintern, as could have been expected, changed nothing in Soviet activities in foreign countries.

To the enlightened few it soon became clear that the Comintern had been dissolved to mislead public opinion abroad, and especially to give an additional powerful argument to pro-Soviet propagandists in Britain and America.

The very fact of its dissolution was so effectively propagandized that it succeeded in taking in the bulk of public opinion. The reactions of sections of the American press clearly proved this result. For the most part, the American people were ready to welcome this Soviet gesture as conclusive evidence that the Soviets were preparing to adopt the American version of democracy.

Some noteworthy precedents were being established as a consequence of the trend of Soviet-Allied relations and of the intense desire of the President to meet Stalin. The importance of Soviet-American friendship was being actively urged by leftist and New Deal circles with full approval of the White House.

Mr. Joseph E. Davies used every opportunity to further pro-Soviet enthusiasm among the American public.

The open letter of Corliss Lamont was extensively publicized on May 7. It gave his very biased interpretation of the Casablanca conference, lauding in superlatives Soviet military achievements. It warned the American public against all attempts to draw America away from the Soviets, stressing the importance of American-Soviet collaboration, which he said was essential to America. In fact, it was a perfect illustration of the drive for "overselling" Russia to the American people in a way similar to that in which highly speculative shares were boosted on a rising market.

Any criticism of Russia's clearly expansionist claims and demands was being actively discouraged in conversations and in the press. The American people were being gradually misled into believing that there were no real difficulties on the way to an all-out brotherly understanding with the Soviet Union.

A glamorous picture of Russia, of her democratic sentiments, of her sincerity, of her admiration for America, was being drawn for American consumption.

The fast-dwindling few who dared to challenge the truthfulness of such blasts of pro-Soviet admiration were accused of unfriendly bias and suspected of fascist leanings.

In a bigger and better way this pro-Soviet propaganda drive was reminiscent of the artificially created psychosis for Russia which seized France in the old days of the Franco-Russian alliance. The rising tide of "fellow travelers" was rapidly penetrating American official and political circles, ready to criticize even the American Bill of Rights if it appeared to clash with Soviet ideology.

Curiously enough, the most enthusiastic pillars of this movement were prominent capitalists, parlor communists, theorists of the type which flourished in England at Oxford University and Chatham House in the early twenties, when these stately British institutions became centers of admiration of Soviet Red ideology and went "pink."

To the Washington diplomats, who closely observed President Roosevelt's every mood, it was becoming evident that he encouraged these tendencies as a means of creating a favorable atmosphere for his eagerly awaited meeting with the elusive Stalin.

Personally, I viewed with growing anxiety this dangerous pattern being woven into the fabric of American policy which appeared to be ever more ready to sacrifice its noble fundamental principles to the mirage of a doubtful understanding with Soviet Russia.

I had ample opportunity to know that, apart from actual war problems, President Roosevelt was concentrating his attention almost entirely on the realization of his great desire to meet Stalin. He had chosen Joseph E. Davies to entice the Soviet dictator to consent to such a meeting. In diplomatic circles we discussed this choice, and it was generally considered that the President had finally chosen Mr. Davies because of his enthusiastic pro-Soviet attitude, expressed with such crude naïveness in his incredible book and in its film version. This choice was supposed to show Stalin how favorably disposed the President and the United States were to Soviet Russia. Mr. Davies was expected to persuade Stalin that he had nothing to fear from a meeting with President Roosevelt.

I was told that Mr. Davies was instructed to explain all the advantages of such a meeting for Stalin. As regarded the Soviet-Polish situation, Mr. Davies was merely to mention it as a probable topic of discussion between the President and Stalin but was not to discuss its merits.

I must frankly admit that I blessed the President for his decision not to entrust the grave and delicate problem of Soviet-Polish relations to the arch pro-Soviet propagandist of America.

One other event took place at that time in Washington.

President Beneš of Czechoslovakia had very judiciously made his visit in Washington coincide with that of Mr. Churchill.

The Czechoslovak propaganda machine announced that President Beneš was "ready to undertake the task of mediation between the Soviets and Poland."

Considering the traditional pro-Soviet sympathies of this ever-opportunist statesman, the suggestion aroused some merriment in official and diplomatic circles. However, it was in line with the tactics which Mr. Beneš had always pursued in the past, of becoming the self-styled intermediary in all major disputes and of offering his services for conciliatory purposes mostly in order to attract attention.

State Department officials told me that Mr. Beneš had gone out of his way in official conversations to express his strong disapproval of any kind of confederation with Poland, which he had previously so strongly advocated. He explained that there could be no question of such a federation now that Russia was opposed to it. His speeches and conversations, which I followed attentively, showed that he was painstakingly getting in line to reap for Czechoslovakia all the possible advantages she might gain by becoming a willing front-row Soviet-Russian satellite. He was ready to give up all his ideas of European federation and for European security plans based on a system of alliances centered on France, and to sacrifice them all to pro-Soviet opportunism.

I had an amusing proof that Mr. Beneš's "statesmanship" was justly appraised in some authoritative circles in Washington when, commenting on the shrewd timing of his visit to coincide with Mr. Churchill's, a prominent American remarked: "In America we associate such methods with the jackal, who hunts with the lion, hoping to feed on what remains of the lion's prey."

With the coming of June, official Washington, sensitively reflecting the moods of President Roosevelt, was becoming watchfully expectant of the welcome news from Moscow that Stalin would finally consent to the holding of a Big Three meeting.

There was something dramatic in this atmosphere of anticipation.

America, the leading democracy of the Western world, with all its unlimited moral and material resources, wholly involved in an unprecedentedly gigantic war against totalitarian despotism, was soliciting for the fifth time the favor of a meeting with the absolute dictator of a communist totalitarian Power, whom destiny and Adolf Hitler had placed in the fighting camp of the democratic United Nations and who had become the most important military mainstay of this righteous camp, but insisted in dictating his own personal terms of partnership.

CHAPTER XX

Sikorski Killed—Poland Fights On

On SUNDAY, July 5, 1943, at seven o'clock, I was suddenly awakened by the insistent ringing of the telephone at my bedside. The First Secretary of our embassy was calling. He had just heard on the radio that General Sikorski was killed a few hours before in an airplane accident at Gibraltar.

I switched on the radio while I dressed rapidly. Details of the fatal accident were being broadcast.

Sikorski was on his way back to London, after spending several weeks in the Middle East and Egypt with the Second Corps of the Polish Army. He was accompanied by his daughter, who was an officer in the Women's Auxiliary Corps, a few staff officers, and his inseparable British friend, Major Victor P. Cazalet, M.P., who acted as British liaison officer between Sikorski and Churchill. They were all killed.

The general and his party had traveled on a Liberator bomber, placed at their disposal by the British High Command. After the trip from Cairo, the plane had been refueling in Gibraltar before setting out on the last leg of the journey, which was to land a few hours later in England.

From Sikorski's telegram received a few days before I knew that he was planning only a short stay in London. He was to get in touch with Churchill. He intended once more to urge the British Prime Minister and President Roosevelt, through my intermediacy, to declare their support for his efforts for an understanding with the Soviet Government. If he obtained this support, he was determined to fly to Moscow in order to make a supreme effort to clear up Soviet-Polish misunderstandings in direct talks with Stalin.

From information which began to arrive from London, Cairo, and Gibraltar, I learned that the plane had just left the runway, headed seaward, when, after a few seconds in the air, it suddenly dived into the waves, all four engines going full blast, and the steering gear blocked. Only the pilot was thrown out of his broken cockpit and rescued. A few of the bodies were recovered, including that of General Sikorski, in a state of terrible mutilation.

Thus, after an eventful and dramatic life, Sikorski met his death. He had started out as a Polish insurrectionist and legionnaire in 1914. He later became a soldier statesman, who, through his indomitable perseverance, succeeded in re-creating in France and, after her collapse, once again in Britain, an outstanding Polish fighting force. He was the man who had headed the Polish Government at this most crucial time. He had succeeded in forming and directing from abroad the powerful and efficient Polish Underground organization renowned for its fighting spirit. He had met his death at the height of his career before completing his efforts to restore his country's independence.

It was impossible at the time to gauge the full scope of the tragic consequences of his death on the future of Poland.

The news of General Sikorski's death echoed throughout the world. Innumerable tributes and expressions of sympathy were voiced. It was clearly evident that the camp of nations fighting for the common cause knew that through his death it had lost one of its outstanding champions.

President Roosevelt reacted immediately to the news of Sikorski's death in a telegram addressed to the President of the Polish Republic in London. Among other expressions of sympathy he said: ". . . During his several visits in Washington I had the opportunity of personally becoming well acquainted with General Sikorski. Through my association with him I learned to admire his integrity, his patriotism, and those great qualities of leadership which so fully justified the confidence which you and the Polish people placed in him. His high sense of statesmanship and devotion to the cause of liberty and democracy made him one of the outstanding leaders of our times. His passing represents a severe loss to all freedom-loving people."

The most stirring tribute was paid to General Sikorski by Mr.

Winston Churchill in a speech in the House of Commons on July 7. In expressing the feelings of the British House of Commons he said: ". . . His death in the air crash at Gibraltar was one of the heaviest strokes we have sustained.

". . . From the first dark days of the Polish catastrophe and the brutal triumph of the German war machine until the moment of his death on Sunday night, he was the symbol and the embodiment of that spirit which has borne the Polish nation through centuries of sorrow. . . .

". . . He persevered unwearied and undaunted. The powerful Polish forces which have now been accumulated and equipped in this country and in the Middle East, to the latter of whom his last visit was paid, now await with confidence and ardor the tasks which lie ahead. General Sikorski commanded the devoted loyalty of the Polish people now tortured and struggling in Poland itself. He personally directed that movement of resistance which has maintained a ceaseless warfare against German oppression in spite of sufferings as terrible as any nation has ever endured. This resistance will grow in power until, at the approach of liberating armies, it will exterminate the German ravagers of the homeland.

". . . He was a man of remarkable pre-eminence, both as a statesman and a soldier. His agreement with Marshal Stalin of July 30, 1941, was an outstanding example of his political wisdom. Until the moment of his death he lived in the conviction that all else must be subordinated to the needs of the common struggle and in the faith that a better Europe will arise in which a great and independent Poland will play an honorable part. We British here and throughout the Commonwealth and Empire, who declared war on Germany because of Hitler's invasion of Poland and in fulfillment of our guarantee, feel deeply for our Polish allies in their new loss.

"We express our sympathy to them, we express our confidence in their immortal qualities, and we proclaim our resolve that General Sikorski's work . . . shall not have been done in vain."

The death of Sikorski placed the Polish Government in a most difficult situation. It presented problems of considerable magnitude which had to be tackled immediately.

When the Polish Constitutional Government of National

Unity was formed on September 30, 1939, in Paris, Sikorski became simultaneously Prime Minister and Commander in Chief of the Polish Armed Forces. In those early days of the war Poland's military and political problems were inseparable. It was natural and almost automatic that the conduct of military and political affairs should be entrusted to one man.

At the time of Sikorski's death, Poland's war problems had reached a more advanced stage, and it was advisable to separate these two functions. It was more appropriate that the political direction of the government should be entrusted to a civilian, considering that the problems of postwar planning and internal reorganization of the State were growing in importance. Above all, there was no other man of Sikorski's stature whom President Raczkiewicz could appoint as his natural successor to carry on simultaneously the burden of Poland's military and political affairs.

General Kazimierz Sosnkowski was next in line of seniority among Polish generals. He was very popular with our armed forces. He had had a brilliant military career which started in Poland in the Legions of Pilsudski in World War I, and culminated in daring exploits at the end of the Polish campaign against Hitler's aggression in September 1939. He was the natural choice of the President of Poland for the post of Commander in Chief.

It was in line with the trend of Polish politics to select the leader of the Peasant party, Stanislaw Mikolajczyk, a small holding farmer from western Poland, to head the new Polish Government as its Prime Minister. He had been the speaker of the Polish National Council in London—a position to which he was elected on the death of Ignacy J. Paderewski—and had worked very closely with General Sikorski.

The new Cabinet constituted by Premier Mikolajczyk was essentially one of national unity and, compared with the Cabinet of General Sikorski, was even more radically democratic. It was composed of three representatives of the Peasant party, the party of small farm owners, presided over by Mr. Mikolajczyk; three members of the Polish Socialist party; two members of the National Democratic party and two of the Christian Labor party. Only the Ministers of War and of Foreign Affairs were non-party members of the Cabinet.

On assuming office, Premier Mikolajczyk pledged himself to continue the foreign policy of General Sikorski. He promised that he would pursue the work for good understanding with Soviet Russia.

His choice of one of our most able diplomats, Tadeusz Romer, for the post of Minister of Foreign Affairs, proved the sincerity of Mr. Mikolajczyk's intentions. In most trying and difficult circumstances, during the negotiations in Moscow in the winter and early spring of 1943, and until Russia broke off relations with Poland, Romer, as our Ambassador in Moscow, had succeeded in establishing the reputation that he was best equipped among our diplomats to negotiate with Soviet Russia and could do so in a friendly way.

On July 21 I had a long and very cordial conversation with Secretary Hull on all details concerning the new Polish Cabinet.

I emphasized its democratic character and its decision to carry on General Sikorski's policy. Mr. Hull showed great interest in the matter and asked many questions. He expressed his satisfaction that, as he put it, the new Polish Government had been "so wisely reconstituted," and asked me to convey to it his assurance on behalf of the American Government that it was "pleased to continue with the new Polish Government the close and friendly collaboration which had so satisfactorily developed with the Polish Cabinet headed by General Sikorski."

Apart from political and party considerations which prompted the President of Poland to appoint Stanislaw Mikolajczyk to succeed General Sikorski as Prime Minister of Poland, another important factor had been taken into account.

In the last two years of his life General Sikorski had entrusted to Mr. Mikolajczyk the task of continuous secret contacts with the Underground civil authority, which was not only the representation in Poland of our government abroad, but was headed by three political leaders, actual Cabinet Ministers of the Polish Government in London, who were delegated to carry out the government's policies in the occupied country. The methods of daily contact between the government in London and its Underground organization in Poland were necessarily "top secret," and it was most important to assure their continuity and further development by leaving them in the hands of the man who had successfully insured them in the past. It had been also a mark of the rising predominance of the Polish Underground in the conduct of our affairs of state.

A fortnight before General Sikorski's death I got word from my government that one of the actual fighters of Poland, an officer of the Polish Underground Home Army, acting as liaison between the Polish Underground and the government in London, would shortly report to me in Washington. I awaited this visit with eager anticipation, as it was to be my first personal contact with one of those heroic young Underground fighters who daily risked their lives in Poland and who undertook the perilous journeys between occupied Poland and London bearing secret reports and instructions.

On the morning of June 22 I received a tall, dark young man, of striking appearance. He looked as if he had gone through great suffering and hunger, and his burning eyes reflected keen intelligence coupled with childish candor.

He was Jan Karski, lieutenant in the Polish Underground Army, an integral part of our national armed forces. He had recently come to London for the second time from Poland at great personal risk as a confidential messenger of the Underground authorities to the Polish Government. He handed me letters from General Sikorski and Mr. Mikolajczyk, in which they asked me to hear his report on the activities of the Polish Underground organization and to put him in touch with the competent American civilian and military authorities.

In my first conversation with Karski I realized more fully the greatness of that Polish Underground organization which constituted the leadership of the secret Polish State and assured the continuity of Poland's life as an independent nation, regardless of German domination and oppression.

I invited Karski to stay with me at the embassy and spent hours listening to him. I had never met a man who could with such simplicity, such telegraphic brevity, and such absolute frankness, describe events and complicated situations.

I started to invite selected groups of prominent civilian and military officials, as well as friends of mine in political circles. It was necessary to keep all Karski's information on the Polish Underground and its workings strictly secret at that time, and all those who met him during his first visit to America were pledged to secrecy.

However, some enthusiastic comments concerning the facts reported by Karski had been reaching the President and, finally, I got an early-morning telephone call from the White House on July 28, asking me to call on the President at ten-thirty that same morning and to bring Karski along.

We were taken upstairs to the study, where President Roosevelt started immediately asking Karski a series of questions.

"Mr. President," Karski began, visibly moved, "I cannot express my feelings. I cannot find the right words. When I was leaving Poland on my journey to England and to America I could hardly promise the men who sent me abroad that I would be able to reach you. They did not dare to think that it would be possible for an Underground courier to report to you personally at the White House in Washington.

"And here I am, Mr. President.

"Permit me to tell you, Mr. President, that not only we, the Poles, but hundreds of millions of people in Europe look up to you as the only man on earth who can bring us liberation and organize a peace based on justice and human principles. . . ."

The President listened attentively and was visibly pleased, but apparently wanted to get to the point quickly. He asked Karski if the situation in Poland was really as bad as he had heard.

Karski went on to give details telling about the insufficient food rations, the lack of coal for the civilian population, adding with a smile: "When the population of Poland was completely deprived of sugar, Hans Frank, the German ruler of Poland, through loud-speakers placed on every street corner thanked the Polish population for 'offering their sugar to the heroic German Army which is protecting them from British and American imperialism, from communism, and from international Jewry.'"

"That is amazing," said Roosevelt. "We still fail to realize the extent of German perfidy."

Karski went on with his detailed explanation of everyday life in Poland under German occupation. He mentioned that after he reached Paris on his way from Warsaw to London, and ate there what the average Frenchman eats, he was sick for several days because the food in occupied France was so rich. "After two and a half years in Poland, Mr. President, my system could not take care of all the fats, the meat, and sugar which comparatively stringent rationing allows a Frenchman."

"Who guided you through France?" asked Roosevelt.

"The Polish Underground organization," replied Karski. "All through Germany, Belgium, France, Spain, and into Gibraltar, where I was picked up by a British plane, my only task was to let myself be transferred from one of our Underground cells to the other."

"Unbelievable!" exclaimed the President. "And I hear that more of your boys reached London after you. Well done! But tell me about the situation on the farms. How about cattle and horses?"

Karski gave an account of German requisitions of Polish property, and informed the President about Germans settling on farms from which their Polish owners were expelled.

"Was all the property taken away from the Poles?" the President asked.

Karski reported extensively on German expropriation and all the abuses.

"Are the Germans easy to bribe?" asked the President.

"Indeed they are, Mr. President," answered Karski. "I think that, apart from members of the SS Elite, some officers, and some of the Gestapo, every German in the occupied countries is out to make money.

"Of course we take full advantage of this situation. We buy their pistols and rifles, newsprint for our secret press, their uniforms and their documents, sometimes even small printing presses. And once we have bribed a German, we just keep on blackmailing him, thus forcing him to continue rendering us services. These people are by no means politically opposed to the Nazi regime. Far from it. They are just plain crooks who want money above everything else. But once they accept it, we have them in our clutches."

"Would you say that demoralization in the German Army and Administration has reached any considerable degree?" asked the President.

Karski said that it had, and dwelt on the point that from the time the Germans suffered their first defeats on the eastern front thousands of German deserters appeared in Poland, greatly contributing to the deterioration of the hitherto rather high German morale.

The President then asked Karski to give him a picture of German methods of political terrorism, and Karski gave a full account of it, stressing particularly the system of dragnets which, within two to three days in Warsaw alone, resulted in 35,000 persons being arrested and indiscriminately sent to concentration camps or to forced labor in Germany. He went on to describe the concentration camps in which mass murders were an everyday event. He spoke of Oswiecim, Majdanek, Dachau, Oranienburg, of the women's camp at Ravensbruck, and gave the President the nerve-shattering description of his own visit—disguised as a policeman—to the two murder camps; Treblinka and Belzec, where Jews were gassed in railway trucks.

"I am convinced, Mr. President," continued Karski, "that there is no exaggeration in the accounts of the plight of the Jews. Our Underground authorities are absolutely sure that the Germans are out to exterminate the entire Jewish population of Europe. Reliable reports from our own informers give the figure of 1,800,000 Jews already murdered in Poland up to the day when I left the country."

"Does your Underground co-operate with the Jews?" asked the President.

Karski replied in the affirmative, giving the President details about the Jewish Underground movement composed mostly of Jewish workingmen. He described the efforts to smuggle some particularly valuable Jewish individuals and scientists out of the ghettos in order to hide them among the Christian population.

"Whoever is caught hiding a Jew, however, is subject to execution by the Germans, and I do not know of any instance in which the death penalty was escaped," added Karski.

"I was instructed by the leaders of our Underground to tell the British and American military authorities that only through direct reprisals, such as mass bombing of German cities, after dropping millions of leaflets telling the Germans that they were being bombed in reprisal for exterminating Jews, could this mass extermination be stopped or at least limited. This is also the opinion given me personally by the leaders of the Jewish Underground in Poland, with explicit instructions to convey it to the leaders of American Jewry and to the Allied governments."

"I would like you to tell me in detail the methods of your Underground work and particularly the organization of your political authorities and your Underground army," was the President's next request.

Karski went on describing the structure of the Polish Underground State, the incredible story of the functioning of this branch of the Polish Government in London established in Warsaw in 1940. He told of the formation of the Home Army, of the skeleton of a civil administration and judiciary—explaining that its organization was based on a coalition of the four democratic parties, the leaders of which held secret sessions acting as Poland's Underground government.

He told the President about the functions of the chief delegate of the London government, of his daily work, and of the tremendous influence which the mere existence of these secret authorities exerted on the morale of the population.

He went on to explain the work of the newspapermen, who still managed to publish 112 secretly printed newspapers; of the work of army officers who armed and trained their detachments; and of the work of the secret judges, issuing verdicts against particularly dangerous German rulers—death sentences which were invariably carried out.

"Incredible, incredible," repeated the President. "It is unbelievable that men could create and maintain such an organization under these conditions. I see now why there are no Quislings and no collaborators in Poland. It is really magnificent," he said.

"I am sure," said the President, turning to me, "that only Poles are capable of such sacrifices."

"Don't forget, Mr. President," I replied, "that our tradition in this kind of underground fight is centuries old."

"How about the government's contact with Poland?" the President asked, turning to Karski. "How frequent are these contacts? How do you know what is going on in the world and how do you get help from your government?"

Karski plunged into a detailed explanation of the work of our secret radio stations, of couriers leaving the country and returning by parachute—every ten days five to seven of them, but fewer during the summer months when the nights were too short for British planes to reach Poland to drop the parachutists and equipment and return safely. He told of the arms, dynamite, microfilmed orders, money, which periodically reached the secret state authorities and all its branches.

"I, myself, Mr. President," said Karski, "brought to London, concealed in my ears, several hundred pages of typed reports microfilmed on a roll the size of three American paper matches. . . . Some neutral governments also help us a little. From time to time we manage to get hold of a diplomatic passport. Sometimes we get the opportunity of using a diplomatic pouch."

"I believe the Swedes have been helpful?" queried the President.

"I heard it said," answered Karski, "but I do not have any precise information. I know, however, that in 1942 there were some arrests among Swedish citizens in Poland who were our friends."

"Can planes coming from England land in Poland?"

"Not yet, Mr. President, and this is our greatest trouble in matters of liaison. We are trying desperately to prepare some hidden airdromes in the wooded parts of Poland, but I discovered in England that it is up to the British air force to get some kind of a new device which would permit long-distance planes to land on short and soft runways. The British have promised us to work on this and I know that they are doing so."

"Have you much snow in your country? Couldn't the planes be fitted with skis for landing purposes?"

"I do not know about that, Mr. President."

"Those things must be looked into, Mr. Ambassador," the President said, turning to me. "Soon we will have more planes than we can use, and I think that some of our 1942 vintage Liberators could be used for that purpose. We will have to work on it. I remember that I promised General Sikorski a few of these planes. Please take the matter up again with our air command, Mr. Ambassador."

I promised to do so.

"And now," addressing Karski again, "how about your contacts with Poles driven to Germany for forced labor?"

Karski explained to the President the network of the Underground, branching out into every camp of slave workers and even into individual groups assigned to farm work deep within Germany. He also mentioned in this connection the preparations made by the Home Army and its detachments for operating in Germany a general uprising of slave laborers when the time was ripe.

"But I understand, Mr. President, that the moment for the uprising will be determined not only by the situation in Poland, but as part of the over-all Allied strategy."

"Of course that is obvious. You should try, however, to keep your grip on your men in Germany."

Karski went on to relate about the organization among Poles working in German factories, and the preparations made for sabotaging German industry as soon as the Allied invasion began. He also gave details of sabotage conducted by the Poles in German industry.

"How deeply has the loss of General Sikorski affected the Poles?"

"Very greatly, Mr. President. But we do not rely on persons for our liberation. The Poles rely on their government as the expression of Poland's sovereignty."

The President wanted to know about the situation in East Prussia, and after Karski told him that in this part of Germany the Polish Underground cells were even more active than in Germany proper, the President turned to me as if thinking aloud:

"I wonder what we will do after the war with the Germans from East Prussia. Should we force them to leave? Would they leave of their own will? Poland would not like to keep them there, would she? Probably not. I think, however, that quite a number of those people are really Poles by origin, forcibly Germanized. Many might wish to stay on and again become Poles, as were their ancestors."

Karski interrupted with a rather grim smile: "I would rather be frank with you, Mr. President. Nothing on earth will stop the Poles from taking some kind of revenge on the Germans after the Nazi collapse. There will be some terrorism, probably short-lived, but it will be unavoidable. And I think this will be a sort of encouragement for all the Germans in Poland to go west, to Germany proper, where they belong."

The President nodded. "The Germans certainly deserve it, but this will not solve the problem. We will have to solve it, because East Prussia will belong to Poland." And, accentuating each word, he turned to me: "No more Polish Corridor, Mr. Ambassador, no more corridor this time."

And then, as if speaking to himself, President Roosevelt went on: "The problem of the Baltic States, and particularly that of Lithuania, will be much more difficult.

"You know, Mr. Ambassador"—he turned in his chair and raised his voice—"I am still unable to see Stalin, and this makes the settlement of many questions and problems very difficult. We have to discuss with those people, but I am rather disturbed by one possibility."

President Roosevelt looked straight into my eyes and, as if seeking my reaction, went on emphasizing every word: "What can we do if Stalin calmly announces, for instance, that the question of Lithuania must be left out of the discussions? I presume that he will also insist on his demands for some rectification of the eastern boundaries of Poland. He may make out of it a question of prestige. You know, Mr. Ambassador, the situation is best expressed by the Chinese saying—'standing pat to save one's face.' I am afraid that Stalin will raise a question which will be very difficult for us; namely, that of compensation for giving East Prussia to Poland."

The President paused, as if waiting for my answer, and I voiced the opinion that only a firm attitude on the part of the United States could stop Stalin's territorial demands and make him understand that his appetite would not be satisfied.

"Well, yes, but we cannot afford a war with Russia," said the President.

"I can only repeat, Mr. President," I replied, "what I told you before on this subject. Soviet Russia will try to make you believe that she is ready for anything in order to achieve her territorial aims. But, in reality, she is bluffing, because she cannot afford a war with Great Britain and the United States. If you and Mr. Churchill refuse to yield any of your principles, you cannot fail to impress a realist like Stalin."

"Personally, I believe you are right, but it will not be an easy matter." The President turned to Karski.

"How about your contacts with other nations?"

The young man told the President about the plans for a future federation being prepared between the Underground leaders of Poland, Czechoslovakia, and Lithuania, explaining that there was a common urge for closer postwar relations among those nations. "Unfortunately, Mr. President, when I arrived in London I soon learned that, viewed from the diplomatic angle, this problem presents quite a different picture."

"Well, couldn't you guess that?" smiled the President. "But tell me, Karski, something about the communists in Poland. Tell me all you know about them."

"In the first place, Mr. President, I must tell you that I was much surprised in London when some of the Englishmen I met told me that the Poles hate Russia, that they do not wish any friendship with Russia, and so on.

"That is absolutely untrue, Mr. President. I wish to assure you of that. We know very well that we cannot change our geographical position and that we must maintain good relations with Russia.

"It is particularly for that reason, it is especially because we want truly friendly Polish-Soviet relations, that we watch with growing anxiety the activities of communists and Soviet agents in Poland. Repeatedly we tried to establish co-operation with the small communist underground. But all the communist detachments, led by Soviet officers and political instructors, parachuted into Poland from Soviet planes, steadfastly refuse any kind of contact with us. They raid Polish villages and small townships, they carry away food, thus exposing our innocent people to dreadful German reprisals."

"But do they actually fight the Germans like your people do?" interrupted the President.

"No, they avoid fighting the Germans, and they evidently are out to conserve their forces for the future. However, what is more striking, because it is so dangerous, they incite the Polish population to all kinds of unprepared, silly, amateurish acts of diversion and sabotage without any preparation. Those poor people are led to believe that they will be covered by the communist detachments, but this never materialized, and they are just being exposed to ruthless German mass reprisals.

"Many attempts of our command to co-ordinate our guerrilla operations with the communists have failed completely. Every time we start conversations to bring about common action we are told that the communist detachments take their orders only from Moscow."

"How strong are they?" asked the President.

Karski explained that he had been asked the same question in London. He said that the Polish Underground was unable accurately to check their numerical strength. They certainly did not number more than a few thousand.

"We could take care of them and liquidate them easily with our own forces," he added, "but General Sikorski has ordered us to abstain from any hostile action toward the communists. 'I don't want to create a Yugoslav situation in Poland,' General Sikorski told us; 'I don't want to help the Soviets create a Mikhailovitch-Tito situation. Our most important task is to defeat Germany, and we must not waste our forces.' Those were his orders and we obey them."

Karski went on to explain another aspect of communist activities in Poland; namely, that the communists were trying to penetrate the ranks of the Polish democratic parties. The Communist party had recently assumed the name of "Polish Workers' party." This infiltration is considered very dangerous by the Underground because the communists were "too curious." They wanted to know the workings of the entire Underground network, the names, aliases, addresses, and functions of every man in the legitimate organization.

"It looked to us a little too much like spying, and we have to be very careful, as some of us believe that they are trying to do some spade work for the Red Army and the NKVD to scoop us up when the Soviet forces move into Poland," added Karski.

"They really create a very difficult situation in Poland, don't they?" interposed the President.

"Many people in England asked me whether their work in Poland is really dangerous in the long run," continued Karski. "My answer is *no!* because the Poles, much as they desire good relations with Russia, will never follow the communist line. The communist movement as such has never made any headway in Poland, despite suffering and poverty and all the propaganda which is flooding us from the Union of Polish Patriots organized in Moscow.

"The difficulty of the situation lies in the fact that under orders from our government in London we may not resist them actively because our government is afraid that this would hamper the chances of understanding with Russia. So they remain in Poland and are free to prepare the ground for a new attempt at penetration of our political life when the Red Army comes to back them up.

"This situation is very discouraging for our leaders, who realize that an attempt to force a Soviet system of government on Poland would undoubtedly stir up anti-Soviet feeling among our population.

"That is why, Mr. President, we all hope that when the moment of liberation of Poland comes, our army, now abroad, will return to Poland with Allied army detachments and march into our country, if possible, simultaneously with the Red Army.

"We also most urgently appeal for British-American missions to be sent into liberated Poland to supervise developments and duly to report to you on the situation which the entry of Soviet troops may create."

"Yes," nodded the President, "certainly we would like to have some of our troops in Poland. As concerns Allied missions, I think it is a good idea, and I will think it over. Yes, your idea appeals to me. . . ."

The President went on to say that what Karski had told him, added to the creation by the Soviets of the Union of Polish Patriots in Moscow and of the "Free Germany Committee," gave him much food for thought.

Then, placing both hands on his desk, he turned to me with a smile and said: "We have to admit that Uncle Joe knows how to play a wily game.

"Tell me one more thing," the President said, turning again to Karski. "What do the Polish people expect of us when the liberation of Poland comes?"

"Our Underground authorities are ready to take over all civilian administration. We have trained officials ready to take over every administrative position down the line to local authorities. We want our government to return and to include in the

Cabinet men who stayed during the war in Poland. Thus a new provisional government will be set up until we can hold our elections. This will not require much time.

"From our Allies we expect relief only. We need food, clothing, machinery, and raw materials, but we have the manpower ready to take over and to start work.

"One major problem exercised our Underground leaders considerably for a time. It arose when the German occupation authorities, realizing that they would never be able entirely to suppress our active resistance, offered to appoint Polish administration officials to local government posts, as they had done in other occupied European countries. This would have allowed us to save some of our population from persecution and extermination. We refused, being desirous of maintaining Poland's unique record of non-collaboration with the enemy. I have been instructed by the Underground command to ask you, Mr. President, and the British Government, if we were right in taking this momentous decision and if the Polish nation could count on its being appreciated and regarded as an exceptional proof of its outstanding loyalty to the common cause."

The President appeared to be deeply moved by Karski's question.

"Tell the Polish Underground authorities," he said emphatically, "that their indomitable attitude has been duly appreciated. Tell them that they will never have cause to regret their brave decision to reject any collaboration with the enemy, and that Poland will live to reap the reward of her heroism and sacrifice."

He then stretched out his hand to Karski. "I thank you, my friend, I thank you very much, but I am more than an hour late for my other appointments. What you told me is very important, and I wish you all luck in your work. I hope to see you back in the United States, and, once more, I wish you good luck."

Karski bowed and asked the President whether he had his permission to report this conversation to his superiors in Poland.

"Certainly, you may report every word of it," and, turning to me, the President said: "I am really thrilled, Mr. Ambassador. Thank you for having given me this opportunity of hearing Karski's report on the wonderful resistance and spirit of Poland."

Karski's report corroborated and supplemented what the President and the American military command had known of the strategic and political value of the Polish Underground for almost two years.

But they now realized more fully that our Underground was not only an effective secret military formation for active sabotage, guerrilla, and resistance, it was also an official Polish organ whose activities were controlled and co-ordinated with clocklike precision by our government. It was for our Allies a most valuable, in fact a unique source of secret-intelligence information which operated effectively in the very heart of the enemy camp. It was continuously helping the Allied command in the planning of war operations.

The President knew the increasingly important part played by the Polish Underground, but, as he told me later, it was only after Karski had given him this very complete picture of its workings that he fully understood the great advantages of its further development. He told me he now realized that it was a fully-equipped Underground Polish administration which in a truly miraculous way led and controlled a fighting nation. He saw in the Polish Underground the machinery of state which at the time of Poland's liberation would be ready to take over all state functions, thus preventing chaos and revolutionary movements.

At the request of General Sikorski, the President had been giving material support to the Polish Underground for some time past, realizing its efficient part in the Allied war effort. He said that his talk with Karski had confirmed his decision to continue his support, which consisted of special Lend-Lease matériel for guerrilla and sabotage purposes, of radio equipment and financial aid periodically parachuted to the Polish Underground by British and Polish fliers.

CHAPTER XXI

Seesaw at Quebec, August 1943

THE summer of 1943 brought the decisive turning point in the war. The victorious North African campaign was followed by the invasion of Sicily early in July. The advance into Italy had started, and under the pressure of the American-British advance the decomposition of the bombastic *fascismo* was marked by Mussolini's resignation in favor of Marshal Badoglio.

American forces in the Far East were advancing from island to island in their laborious and tough fight which was to blaze the road to Tokyo.

In the first half of August successful bombing of the Rumanian oil fields of Ploesti was gravely affecting the vital supply of oil for the German air force.

Kiska in the Aleutians was reoccupied by American forces.

All this meant that the tide of war had turned in favor of the United Nations, and of America and Britain in particular. The Russian advance westward continued amid bitter fighting.

London and Washington suddenly realized that, while the clockwork precision of the Combined Chiefs of Staff was slowly reaping the fruit of wise military planning, American-British statesmanship was insufficiently prepared to handle the political problems which the welcome Allied victories made it necessary to face and to settle without delay. The probability of early Italian surrender especially required immediate preparations.

The problem of the European second front had been left in abeyance at the last Roosevelt-Churchill meeting in Washington. It was now gaining in importance and urgency. Italy was a steppingstone for the future invasion of Europe, and the time was fast approaching for definite planning, for fixing its location and scope.

Diplomatic circles in Washington knew that it was comparatively easy for President Roosevelt and Mr. Churchill and their staffs to get together and work out further details of the campaign itself and of the terms of Italian surrender. But at this stage of the war, when co-ordination between the United States, Great Britain, and Soviet Russia had become indispensable and urgent, the failure to persuade Stalin to take part in direct talks with his Western Allies was in itself a pressing problem.

There were as yet no signs that the Soviet dictator had realized this necessity. On the contrary, Stalin appeared to be even more aloof in his relations with the Western democracies. One of the signs pointing in that direction was the recall from London to Moscow of Soviet Russia's top-notch diplomat, Ambassador Maisky, and his replacement by the young and inexperienced Goussev, who had been for some time Soviet Minister in Ottawa. In diplomatic language this could mean only that the Soviet dictator for some important reason desired to mark his determination to transfer the center of Soviet-British relations from London to Moscow. He implied that it was sufficient to appoint to the Court of St. James's a messenger boy who would have to refer the smallest matter for decision to the Kremlin. It was rumored in Washington that Ambassador Litvinov would also soon be recalled and replaced by a lesser diplomat.

In fact, Soviet-Allied relations had reached a stage where the smoothly running machine of Soviet propaganda, ably and wholeheartedly supported by the official information agency of America, became practically the only audible sign of Anglo-American-Soviet understanding and friendship, while official relations between Moscow and London, and especially between Moscow and Washington, appeared to be, to say the least, at a standstill.

The passive patience of President Roosevelt toward Soviet Russia was still, outwardly at least, the keynote of American-Soviet policy. But the rapid succession of war events pressed for action.

I remembered the saying of a great British diplomat who once told me in London years ago when we were discussing some of the characteristics of British statesmanship: "We British only see the obvious and only react to it when we see it."

From information I was receiving from London in the latter part of July 1943 it was becoming evident that the urgent necessity for joint Allied action had become plainly obvious to the British Government. Britain was more directly aware of it than America. The problems of the Mediterranean—that channel of British imperial communications—were fast ripening for solution as Italy's surrender approached. London realized that, Stalin or no Stalin, immediate action had to be taken.

Military and political strategy had to be discussed and coordinated. War events and Stalin's aloofness, more than any deep thinking, had suddenly shown to the least receptive British brains that the problems of further military operations and of future security required above all the closest possible collaboration of the United States and Britain.

Such a close association of the two English-speaking democracies had for a long time been Mr. Churchill's fondest dream. Circumstances seemed to open a chance for its realization. Moreover, contrary to the sincere wishes of President Roosevelt and Mr. Churchill to blend the operations on all the fronts of the conflict into one United Nations war against the Axis, at that stage there were still two wars: a Russian-German war and an Allied-Axis war.

The Western Allies were in a more difficult position than Russia, owing to the greater distance and greater difficulties of amphibious operations necessary to place their troops in Europe for the final stage of the march on Berlin. It was therefore necessary for the Western Allies to strain every nerve in an effort to achieve perfect American-British co-ordination which would place these two Powers in the best military and political position when finally war events and circumstances convinced Stalin he could no longer refuse to confer personally with President Roosevelt and Mr. Churchill.

These considerations gave birth to the momentous Anglo-American meeting in Quebec which opened on August 17, more unexpectedly and secretly than any of the conferences held in the past.

Before this conference opened we heard in Washington that

the President and Mr. Churchill met "somewhere in Canada" on a "fishing expedition" and had the opportunity of personal talks before opening the actual conference, to which Mr. Churchill had again brought a considerable number of military and civilian experts.

From personal sources of information I learned that the President and Mr. Churchill had not lingered over their "fishing expedition." Surrounded by only a few chosen closest collaborators, they left to take part in what was to be the first entirely secret Big Three meeting at which Marshal Stalin was to be present. The meeting was to take place on Manitoulin Island on Lake Huron. The secrecy surrounding this meeting was such that only very few members of the American Cabinet knew about it.

The President was accompanied by Harry Hopkins, Admiral Leahy, and James F. Byrnes.

For some time intelligence reports had been mentioning that Marshal Stalin had left Moscow in the latter part of July, presumably on his way eastward.

The meeting lasted only two days. On August 11 I learned that the President and the British Prime Minister were disappointed with its results. Apparently at the last moment Stalin had changed his mind, and considering, probably, that the time was not ripe for him personally to face discussion with his Western Allies, had decided to send Foreign Commissar Molotov to represent him.

I had reasons to believe that, apart from a few precisions on Soviet war strategy regarding the German front and insistent demands for a second front, the Soviet Foreign Commissar had given the impression to the President and Mr. Churchill that Stalin was determined to act in eastern Europe as he saw fit, and to take full advantage of the favorable strategic position gained by Soviet Russia.

The fact that this meeting was never openly mentioned did not unduly surprise me, considering that the President of the greatest Western democracy and the Prime Minister of Great Britain had been faced with the probably unique situation that the head of an Allied Power, whom they were scheduled to meet, failed to appear in person and sent a locum tenens in his stead. It was a situation somewhat awkward to explain to the public, especially as the results of the conference were far from satisfactory. This missing link in the history of the war certainly helped me to understand the character of the Quebec conference and of the Washington conversations between President Roosevelt and Prime Minister Churchill which immediately followed.

At Quebec the dynamic Mr. Churchill appeared to be the moving spirit. I learned that he had persuaded the President to adopt a more active line in dealing with the Soviets and to follow Stalin's realism in discussing and solving urgent problems of Allied military strategy and political planning, independently of Stalin.

The conference started as news poured in that the surrender of Italy was but a matter of days and that signs of depression were noted within Germany. Mr. Churchill was out to convince the President that there was no more question of Soviet Russia concluding a separate German-Soviet peace. The effective bombing of Germany and the breaking up of Italy had so considerably undermined the situation of the Axis Powers that it was urgent to revise all former plans accordingly, and to counteract the possibility that Russian armies alone would suddenly enter German territory, allowing the Soviets to play a lone hand in settling the German problem. Mr. Churchill realized that absolute unity of purpose and at least a realistic show of complete harmony in Anglo-American collaboration were essential to prepare for such an emergency.

Russia was by no means to be excluded or cold-shouldered. On the contrary, it was planned that Mr. Eden should fly to Moscow immediately after the Quebec meeting to inform Stalin of the decisions arrived at. The Chinese Foreign Minister, T. V. Soong, was invited to spend a few days in Quebec, and some problems of the Far Eastern campaign were discussed with him. The Quebec conference, however, was one at which European military and political problems were primarily discussed.

The considerable task of drafting the political and military conditions of Italy's surrender was completed at Quebec. This thick volume of clauses was rightly regarded as most important, as it was to be the first document to lay down the pattern of what President Roosevelt had defined as "unconditional surrender."

How urgent was the necessity of drafting the terms of surrender for Italy became evident to me a few days later, on the 27th of August, when the news of Italy's declared readiness to capitulate was suddenly brought by air to Lisbon by Italian emissaries in a most dramatic secret flight. It was also characteristic of Allied differentiation between Germany and Italy that, as I learned, already in those opening negotiations the co-belligerence of the Italian Army with the Allied invading forces was foreseen and discussed.

Among Churchill's suggestions to the President, the question of a more definite recognition of the France of de Gaulle occupied an important place. The Vichy representatives in Africa could now be disregarded. The time for an invasion of France was fast approaching, and it was high time to give effective support to the French forces of liberation symbolized by de Gaulle and his fighters.

Curiously enough, Churchill's plea regarding France and de Gaulle did not succeed in convincing President Roosevelt that the time was ripe for taking such a decision. I was told that Secretary Hull and Admiral Leahy were opposed to it and that their opinion, supported by that of Minister Murphy, who was reportedly still pursuing a complicated policy of placating the Vichy authority of Marshal Pétain, delayed the recognition of de Gaulle's French National movement.

The problem of Turkish neutrality was considered and discussed at Quebec. The conversations on Turkey naturally came up in connection with further discussions between the President and Mr. Churchill on the invasion of Europe by way of the Balkans.

I noted with interest and hope that this Churchillian suggestion had by no means been entirely abandoned by him. On the contrary, I was informed that Mr. Churchill was again trying to convince the President of the military and political advantages of such an operation. The President's acquiescence to this plan seemed to me probable when I was told of a conversation which the President had at the time with Yugoslav Ambassador Constantin Fotitch. The President spoke with high praise of the fine military achievements of General Draja Mikhailovitch, hailed his Serbian active resistance movement and effective guerrilla warfare against the Italians and Germans, and very significantly said that the Allies would soon need the support of Mikhailovitch in their military operations.

Mr. Churchill had for a considerable time favored the establishment of a firm second front through southern Italy and the Balkans. This was a masterful plan, militarily sound, especially at the time when Italy's resistance had crumbled. An invasion of the Balkans would help to speed up an early contact of the Western Allied forces with those of Soviet Russia and would forestall possible Soviet attempts to get into eastern Europe, Germany, and the Balkans ahead of the Allies and to play a lone hand there. But I was told that one reason finally determined the President to reject Mr. Churchill's plan: Stalin was very definitely opposed to a Balkan invasion by the Western Powers.

It was said that Mr. Churchill had difficulties in trying to convince the President that a new realistic trend in American-British policy required this decision of attacking Europe through the Balkans and that nothing could make Stalin realize more effectively that a united American-British front had really been established at Quebec. Stalin would certainly understand, argued Mr. Churchill, that it was to his advantage to collaborate with Allied policy and that this was a war to be won jointly in preparation of a peace to be established jointly.

However, President Roosevelt appeared to be primarily concerned with bringing about an early meeting with Stalin in an atmosphere of "personally mutual confidence," being convinced that the aim of establishing world security could best be achieved by "avoiding any decisions which might alienate Stalin or increase his distrust of the Western democracies."

The information which I was receiving at the time of the Quebec conference from British and American sources made me realize the main difference in outlook between Mr. Churchill and Mr. Roosevelt.

The unbroken series of insistent, ever-growing Soviet demands and claims, and the alarming information which the British Government was receiving from the European countries under German domination, made Mr. Churchill realize, as the war proceeded, that the greatest danger would be to allow the formation of a vacuum in Europe.

He considered that such a vacuum in famine-stricken areas, whose populations were crazed by Hitler's inhuman oppression, would result in chaos. He knew from past experience that chaos was the natural basis for communist revolution and that the Soviets would take advantage of it for the purpose of Sovietizing Europe.

He was determined to do his utmost by pursuing a policy which would compel Stalin to join Britain and America in the establishment of a joint United Nations security plan and, if Stalin insisted on playing a lone hand, he felt that it was indispensable to establish so close an association between America and Britain that it could impose solutions, even if this meant isolating Soviet Russia.

The President, on the other hand, was quite willing to create temporarily the appearance of a united military and diplomatic front with Britain, but he was carefully noting all Stalin's reactions in view of his main desire of bringing about a meeting with the Soviet dictator. He viewed the establishment of American-British unity at Quebec more as an argument and a tactical warning to Stalin than as a permanent solution.

At the same time President Roosevelt was already becoming increasingly aware of internal political reactions in America in view of the presidential election in November 1944. Harry Hopkins, with whom I discussed these matters at that time, bluntly told me that the President "had possibly oversold Russia to the American people." How can one expect him now, when, as Hopkins said, "we are getting busy preparing his re-election," suddenly to get up and express his doubt of the possibility of Soviet-American friendship and collaboration? That cynical witticism, so characteristic of Harry Hopkins, appeared to me to put the matter in a nutshell.

That the realistic Stalin understood the implications for Soviet policy of an Anglo-American rapprochement and unity of purpose was soon revealed when news reached Washington that Ambassador Maisky had suddenly returned to London from Moscow, this time as a special envoy of Stalin, for important talks with Mr. Eden. This prevented the projected trip to Moscow of Mr. Eden, who was about ready to leave.

The tone of Stalin's envoy in these circumstances, as we were informed in Washington, clearly showed a new tendency to conciliation on the part of Stalin. For Britain, Poland's ally, it was still impossible at that time to divorce the problems of Soviet-Polish relations from any discussions with the Soviets on matters of principle and policy. It was therefore natural that Mr. Eden discussed with Maisky not only the results of the Quebec conference and problems of military and political planning, but also signified to Maisky the anxiety of the British Government regarding the Polish issue. I learned that the British Government was surprised to find that even on this "vexatious" problem the Soviets were willing to make what the British considered at that time to be concessions.

At the outset, the conversations between Eden and Maisky, in which Ambassador Winant took part, showed considerable tension and began by a sharp exchange of mutual recriminations. Mr. Eden, however, apparently strengthened by the results of the Quebec conference, showed a new spirit which resulted in considerably toning down Mr. Maisky's aggressiveness. The holding of a tripartite conference with Marshal Stalin was discussed, but this time the Western Allies suggested that it should be preceded by a meeting of the three Foreign Ministers to clear up some of the differences on important problems before the Big Three met for their talk. Mr. Eden also broached the subject of granting East Prussia, with Danzig, to Poland at the end of the war, and, to his surprise, Mr. Maisky replied that this would be entirely agreeable to Stalin. When further pressed, he assured Eden that he was speaking with Stalin's authority.

CHAPTER XXII

Will America and Britain Pull Together?

As the Quebec conference came to a close and the echoes of the establishment of full understanding between the President and Mr. Churchill appeared in the press and were commented on in conversations, I noted with considerable interest how sensitively American opinion reacted to such news and how ready it was to welcome it without too much probing beneath the surface.

Contrary to OWI and fellow-traveler propaganda, American public opinion was becoming apprehensive that the Soviets were not turning out to be an ideal of "radical democracy" and beginning to wonder if it was not more judicious to seek reinsurance in world affairs in a more natural association between the two English-speaking democracies. Be that as it may, it was clear that, although somewhat timidly, American opinion appeared more ready to follow the President's lead for closer co-operation with Britain.

In informed Washington circles it was rumored that at the end of the conference the eventuality that collaboration with Soviet Russia might prove impossible had been discussed by President Roosevelt and Mr. Churchill.

Mr. Churchill was reported as having admitted that pro-Soviet sympathies in England would make it a difficult task to convince British public opinion that it had to abandon the hope of close collaboration with Soviet Russia. It was said that the President had replied that he would have no difficulty in making the American people realize such a situation should it arise. According to the President, pro-Soviet sentiment in America was superficial and, as a matter of fact, it had to be artificially fed. If the necessity arose, the American people would accept the inevitable without much comment.

Mr. Churchill came to Washington after the Quebec meeting. He prolonged his stay beyond schedule apparently for three reasons: (1) the necessity for conferring with the President while the Winant-Eden-Maisky conversations in London were proceeding and might require rapid decisions, and (2) the news that Maisky was receptive to the suggestion of a tripartite conference of Foreign Ministers to prepare the way for the meeting of Roosevelt and Churchill with Stalin.

British circles admitted that the third reason was Churchill's interest in the meeting of Republican party leaders then proceeding at Mackinac Island. At that party conference matters of foreign policy were being discussed, and particularly the degree in which the United States should participate in world affairs after the war.

I had reason to know that Mr. Churchill, in the course of his visit in Washington, intended to press the cause of Anglo-American unity which had superficially made good progress at Quebec. In British circles it was considered that Maisky's sudden arrival in London and the tone he adopted in his conversations with Mr. Eden and Winant, as well as the fact that Stalin had at last signified his willingness to meet Mr. Roosevelt and Churchill, were regarded as the immediate fruit of the show of Anglo-American unity at Quebec. Accordingly, Mr. Churchill hoped to advance his favorite idea of a close permanent association of the United States and Great Britain.

I knew from my British friends who accompanied Mr. Churchill how delighted he was when the potential Republican presidential candidate, Thomas E. Dewey, came out in Mackinac as the champion of an American-British alliance.

Mr. Churchill was determined to do his best to further his pet aim of a close permanent working partnership between the United States and Britain. He discussed it at great length with the President and with high American Government officials and politicians. From echoes of his conversations which reached me I noted how ably he urged the necessity of such an association.

Having sounded out the atmosphere, possibly encouraged by the unexpected support for his great idea from the Republican meeting on Mackinac Island, Mr. Churchill was prepared publicly to raise this subject in one of his speeches before leaving the United States.

On September 5 General Ismay, one of the closest friends and collaborators of Mr. Churchill, a man of keen insight in military and international affairs, lunched with me at our embassy.

My guest was especially interested in the internal political situation in America, and in particular wanted to know, in view of Mr. Churchill's plans, why there was still such a lack of understanding in America of the necessity of a British-American alliance. He wondered if pro-Soviet enthusiasm, so strongly fed from some official and semi-official American sources, might be the answer. Evidently echoing Churchill's views, he thought that there could be no better guarantee of peace for the world than a security system based on a British-American association which would inspire confidence because it could never be regarded as expansionist or imperialistic.

I told General Ismay how entirely I shared his opinion, but that I did not believe any communist or pro-Soviet propaganda was likely to influence the American people. Nor did I think that its temporary superficial effectiveness was a serious obstacle to a closer association between the English-speaking democracies.

I drew his attention to a paradoxical fact which I had once previously mentioned to President Roosevelt. The proof of how anomalous pro-Soviet propaganda was in England and in the United States was borne out by the curious fact that in England it was being fostered by the Anglican hierarchy and other normally conservative centers of opinion, while in the United States it had become a sort of salesman's hobby of such ultra-capitalists as Marshall Field, Joseph E. Davies, Thomas and Corliss Lamont, and some other prominent Wall Street personalities. It was symptomatic that British trade unions and the leading American labor unions remain definitely anti-communist. Although they voiced deserved admiration for the Russian war effort and were sympathetic to the Russian people, they appeared to realize the dangers of Soviet totalitarianism.

This surely showed that pro-Soviet propaganda in England and in America had only succeeded in gaining opportunist circles of opinion. Peoples of all countries were certainly full of admira-

tion for Russia's war effort and her splendid defense against the
German invader. But it seemed a pity to misrepresent the Soviets
as a democracy to democratic nations. It would certainly be
detrimental to Russia herself in the long run, because the propaganda bubble was bound to burst in the near future, and this
might cause a swing back of the pendulum, unfavorable to Russia
among those who were being misled by such irresponsible or
tendentious sales talks.

General Ismay shared my opinion. He told me that Mr.
Churchill was also apprehensive of the consequences of this exaggerated and artificial enthusiasm, which would do more harm
than good to Allied collaboration with the Soviets.

We passed to a discussion of Mr. Churchill's favorite scheme
of a British-American association. I warned General Ismay, and
expressed the hope that he would impress upon Mr. Churchill
that, however much public opinion in America might have
evolved as a result of the excellent results of Anglo-American collaboration in the war, the word "alliance" was traditionally distasteful to the American people and its use should be avoided.

Moreover, it was unnecessary to think in terms of a signed
alliance when American-British collaboration was already so close
and practically all the elements of a virtual alliance were in
existence.

Anglo-American collaboration could best be served on the
basis of already-existing ties. The Combined Chiefs of Staff were
the outstanding visible proof of the closest military collaboration
which could be usefully prolonged after the war as a post of
Anglo-American vigilance guaranteeing world security.

There was the Combined Food Board and other similar agencies which could be adapted to peace requirements. On this
basis one could establish Anglo-American joint postwar planning in the industrial field for peacetime production in general
economic and financial spheres of combined interests.

The huge development and almost unlimited future possibilities of air transport and air defense opened another vast field
of possible collaboration.

But, the idea of permanent Anglo-American collaboration
should be worked out around the greatest of all problems;
namely, the problem of world security. I reminded General Ismay

that since the fateful mission of Lord Haldane, then British Secretary of War, to Berlin in 1909 to ascertain whether Kaiser Wilhelm II was actually contemplating a war of conquest, the world had not enjoyed one moment of real security.

This meant that more than thirty years of insecurity had been affecting human psychology and international relations, hampering economic development and co-operation. Mutual suspicion ruled international relations.

In fact mutual suspicion and fear had become the keynotes of foreign policy.

One could truthfully say that no one at the present time was capable of thinking in terms of a world free from mutual suspicion in which one could indulge in a sense of real security.

These suspicions undoubtedly subconsciously lurked in the minds of the American people when they contemplated the eventuality of linking their interests with those of Great Britain, with her far-flung empire which so directly involved her in all potential conflicts of interest and forced her to participate in practically every war.

Notwithstanding the experience of the two world wars, the Americans had not yet realized that America was no less involved in world affairs and potential conflicts and that scientific progress in weapons and means of transport had made her as vulnerable to attack as any other country.

Apart from that, the American people had not yet realized their own power. They still underestimated the fact that at the end of the war the United States would probably be the only world Power unscathed so far as war destruction was concerned, with the greatest and most powerful navy, air force, a most modernly equipped army, and unlimited resources.

I told General Ismay that, having closely observed American reactions, I sensed that the American people still feared to enter into too close an association with Britain mainly because they had not yet gained the conviction that in its present stage of military power, of industrial development, and financial and other resources, the United States would inevitably be the senior partner and play first fiddle, and that war-weary and exhausted Britain would agree to play second fiddle.

They had possibly not even realized the implications of the

fact that for the first time in history the American Navy would be greater and stronger than the British Navy, and that the sense of inferiority, which British naval supremacy still so recently inspired, was a thing of the past.

It was therefore necessary to make the American people realize how powerful they had become and to help them understand their great responsibilities of leadership resulting from their newly attained power.

I told him frankly that I did not feel that this had ever been sufficiently emphasized by British Government spokesmen.

In time, I hoped not too late, the American people would suddenly see the enormous advantage of Anglo-American association for American and world security. They would realize how many Anglo-American problems, so difficult of solution between the two countries, could be automatically solved by such a close understanding.

General Ismay replied that Mr. Churchill had been trying to make that very situation clear to his American friends, and he asked me what I thought was the opinion of President Roosevelt on this subject.

I told him I believed that personally the President encouraged the idea of the closest collaboration between America and Britain, but he was primarily a politician and would be greatly influenced by popular reactions.

I added that I did not know to what degree Mr. Roosevelt's hope of establishing close understanding and collaboration between the United States and the Soviet Union might affect his final decision in this matter. I told Ismay that whenever my conversation with the President turned to British-American collaboration, he had always stressed the necessity of strengthening it, and had encouraged me to popularize Great Britain in my speeches and in my talks with American politicians.

On the other hand, some of the President's advisers and personal friends among the leftists of the New Deal group were inclined to minimize the advantages of an Anglo-American association and to boost a rather vague idea of what they were pleased to call an "organic American-Soviet alliance."

I did not regard these obviously immature ideas as deserving too much attention.

On September 6 Mr. Churchill delivered his famous address in Cambridge, Massachusetts, on the occasion of the bestowing upon him of the honorary degree of Doctor of Laws by Harvard University. His speech echoed all over the United States. He had planted a seed which, although it provoked criticism in many American quarters, was destined to sprout into a topic of continuous discussion for many years to come.

Personally, I thought it a pity that he had used the word "alliance," in view of the traditional American distaste for alliances. What was most interesting to note, however, was the immediate reaction to Mr. Churchill's speech on the part of President Roosevelt.

At his press conference on September 7 the President very definitely said that he shared the views of Mr. Churchill regarding the necessity of continuous closest collaboration of the United Nations for security in its postwar period and added specifically that it had been decided to maintain the offices of the Combined Chiefs of Staff for a considerable period of time after the end of hostilities.

An analysis of the importance of the Quebec conference and of its Washington follow-up disclosed that these momentous conversations had several distinct aspects.

The Churchill-Roosevelt meeting was, from the diplomatic angle, both a warning and an invitation to Stalin. It was a warning that if he further delayed accepting the invitation to meet his Western Allies he might miss the boat, because they could get along without him and settle most problems in his absence. However, this subtly implied hint to Stalin was wrapped up in the form of a pressing sixth invitation to a tripartite meeting.

My observation of this important aspect of the Quebec and White House conversations disclosed that, while Mr. Churchill was frankly aiming at permanent closest collaboration between Britain and America, whatever Stalin might decide to do, the President appeared to be mainly interested in its value as a convincing argument for drawing Stalin into closer collaboration with the United States and Britain.

The President's hesitant attitude on the question of an Allied European invasion through the Balkans was explained to me as one of the proofs of this attitude. Nineteen forty-four was fast approaching. The President already referred to it as his "political year." The war had become successful for the Allies and he certainly felt strengthened.

But the war was not yet won. And while it was convenient to refer to Soviet Russia as an "enigma," the President, as I knew from my conversations with him, was well aware and apprehensive of the implications of Soviet expansion and used to say that he "kept his fingers crossed."

The President was determined to avoid any moves which might alienate Soviet Russia. He still hoped to win Stalin over to his ideas on United Nations unity of purpose. Above all, he was not going to make any important decisions on world affairs before getting his chance for a frank talk with Stalin.

As a politician, he was faced with the difficulty which Harry Hopkins had so bluntly expressed to me: he had felt compelled by circumstances since 1941 to sell Russia to the somewhat reluctant American people. To get them to "buy" Russia as an ally at the fancy price imposed by a then-uncertain war situation, he had to boost her by means of superlatives current in American commercial advertisements. Under the circumstances he could not well afford, at the time, to weaken deliberately the purposely inspired pro-Soviet trend of public opinion. And he would probably run for re-election within a year.

I was often warned by the President's closest political friends that, unless forced by events on the international stage to modify his policy, the President would continue to maintain his passive attitude toward Stalin's increasing demands.

CHAPTER XXIII

Mr. Hull Flies to Moscow, October 1943

IN THE early part of September 1943 we heard that a new American Ambassador would shortly replace Admiral Standley. Several candidates were mentioned. Admiral Standley had asked to be relieved of his duties. It was said that he felt he was unable to get any satisfactory response to his very patient attempts to clear up the numerous problems arising between the United States and the Soviet Union.

The final choice seemed to waver for some time between Ambassador Winant, the American representative in London, General J. H. Burns, chief of the Munitions Assignment Board, who had recently visited Moscow, and W. Averell Harriman, whose candidacy was put forward by the group of New Dealers closest to the President. They regarded him as the most suitable candidate on account of his previous favorably reported contacts with Stalin.

For a few days the candidacy of Edward R. Stettinius, Jr., was much talked of, but I learned that the President considered it difficult to replace him as director of Lend-Lease administration.

The name of ex-Ambassador Joseph E. Davies cropped up as usual on such occasions. I heard that the President actually offered him the Moscow Embassy, hoping that the choice of Mr. Davies, who had so enthusiastically supported the Soviets in the field of literature and motion pictures, would inspire Stalin's confidence and convince him of the friendly disposition of America.

It was rumored that the President was much amused when Mr. Davies turned down the offer, saying that although he would gladly go to Moscow, his health prevented him from eating the indigestible Russian food.

When the President asked him how he reconciled this with references in his book and motion picture on the excellency and wonderful quality of Russian food, Davies reportedly replied that he had praised Russian food because propaganda made it necessary to do so.

"But," he added, "my digestive organs tell a very different story, and I really cannot take the risk."

For a few days General Marshall was mentioned as having been suggested to the President for the post of Ambassador to Moscow. But the idea was dropped, owing to the general feeling that he was irreplaceable at his post of Chief of Staff.

It soon became evident that W. Averell Harriman would be appointed. He was the personal candidate of Harry Hopkins, the power behind the throne, and Hopkins was seldom known to fail in putting through his appointments.

The conference of Foreign Secretaries of the United States, Great Britain, and Soviet Russia, which was to be a sort of dress rehearsal of the pending Big Three meeting, became the main subject of diplomatic communications between Washington, London, and Moscow.

Its foundations had been laid in the Maisky-Eden-Winant conversations in London. The eagerness shown by Stalin to see this conference materialize was regarded in London and Washington as the welcome consequence of the outwardly united Anglo-American front created in Quebec and solidified in the Roosevelt-Churchill conversations in Washington.

As the London talks with Maisky proceeded, Mr. Eden took advantage of Maisky's favorable disposition to review with him the major Allied-Soviet problems, and drew up the preliminary draft of an Anglo-Soviet agreement, by virtue of which both Powers were to pledge themselves not to sign any agreements with any other countries before the end of the war.

It was intended by Mr. Eden not only for the purpose of making it impossible for the Soviets to conclude a separate peace with Germany, but also as a reinsurance against possible agreements which the Soviets might be tempted to conclude with the Soviet-sponsored puppet governments or "freedom committees" established in Moscow for Poland, Finland, Rumania, and other neighboring countries. The British Government wished particularly to prevent the so-called Union of Polish Patriots, headed by Wanda Wasilewska, and composed of Comintern agents, from being recognized by the Soviets as a Polish government.

I was told that laborious and, at times, very heated discussions had taken place between Mr. Eden and Maisky. The Soviets were demanding the division of Europe into zones of influence, which the British Government still strenuously opposed.

Maisky then accused Britain of trying to organize a chain of buffer states in eastern Central Europe to separate Europe from Soviet Russia. Mr. Eden countered by pointing to the puppet governments set up in Russia and to the Free Germany Committee, which showed that the Soviets were trying to organize a definite and far-reaching zone of Soviet domination in Europe.

It was clearly understood in London that the Polish problem would be placed on the agenda of the conference of Foreign Ministers and, later, if still necessary, would be discussed at the Big Three meeting.

Soviet territorial demands on Poland had also come up in Eden's talks with Maisky, and while Mr. Eden did not entirely exclude the possibility of some changes of Poland's prewar eastern frontier in favor of Soviet demands, he made it clear to Maisky that these would have to be discussed with and fully approved by the Polish Government and would have to be only slight rectifications. Moreover, these eventual rectifications would have to be conditioned on compensating Poland with German territories in the west.

I also heard that the question of Soviet participation in the war against Japan was regarded as one of the subjects which the President and Mr. Churchill desired to raise with Stalin.

The place where the Foreign Ministers meeting would be held and who would represent the United States was still unsettled. Undersecretary Sumner Welles had previously been regarded as the President's most likely choice for this mission.

However, he had just resigned from the State Department, and it soon appeared that Mr. Hull was determined to represent the United States at this important meeting. The President wished

Mr. Hull to head the United States mission on account of his great authority in Congress.

I soon learned that the meeting was to open in Moscow in the first half of October. For security reasons the exact date was naturally kept secret.

At once I asked the Secretary of State to receive me, being anxious to discuss Polish problems with him before his departure.

As Mr. Hull rose to greet me when I entered his study on October 6, I noted that he appeared very much rejuvenated. He wore a light gray traveling suit. He told me he was leaving that very evening and that, knowing how much I wanted to see him and desiring on his part to discuss with me several points connected with the Moscow conference, he had reserved part of his last afternoon for our conversation. He told me that immediately afterward he would have his final talk with the President before leaving Washington.

Seldom in my talks with Secretary of State Hull had I seen him so keen and alert. I found him fully acquainted with all details of the problems which he was to discuss in Moscow, and got the impression that he was prepared to do some plain speaking. He asked me to review for him the problems created by the Soviets in their relations with Poland and the trends of Polish policy, and to give him my views on Soviet aims in Europe.

I told him that, having received very detailed instructions from my government that very morning, I was particularly well prepared to answer his questions.

The policy of the Polish Government at this crucial time of the war had been recently expressed in a resolution dated August 15, 1943, adopted in Warsaw by the four leading political parties represented in the Polish Underground and in our government. The basic aim of the Polish nation and government was to continue to contribute actively in the fullest possible way, inside and outside Poland, to the defeat of the common enemy.

I stressed in particular that my government was fully aware of the need of understanding between the United States and Britain on the one side and the Soviet Union on the other—an understanding toward which Poland had never ceased to strive, despite the unfriendly reactions of the Soviet Government and its claims, which were by no means directed against Poland alone.

The recently expressed readiness of the Soviet Government generously to support the claims of Poland to some German territories, with the view to inducing Poland to give up the eastern half of her territory to the USSR, was interpreted by the Polish Government and people as an attempt on the part of the Soviet Government to make Poland dependent on Russia, and possibly to use her as a springboard for extended Soviet domination of Central Europe, and of Germany in particular.

In the opinion of the Polish Government, the re-establishment of normal diplomatic Polish-Soviet relations was indispensable and should be brought about by the firm action of the United States and Great Britain. It would be a test of the good will of Soviet Russia as regards the sincerity of their collaboration with the Western Powers in war, and later in peace.

Such action should eliminate at this time the settlement of territorial problems—in accordance with the views repeatedly expressed by the President and the Secretary of State. Since the Polish Government was firmly determined to defend Poland's territorial integrity in the East, it considered that the question of frontiers should be postponed to a later date.

"This is a reasonable attitude on the part of your government," interjected Mr. Hull.

I told him that, anxious to maintain good Polish-Soviet relations in the future, my government would deem undesirable either temporary or partial occupation of Polish territories by the Soviet armies. However, if such occupation were unavoidable as a result of military operations against Germany, it should be dependent on a previous Polish-Soviet understanding, based on the re-establishment of diplomatic relations.

If such an understanding did not take place, one would have to reckon with an open attempt of the Soviet Government to communize Poland by means of the Union of Polish Patriots, supported by Soviet-sponsored allegedly "Polish" military units, as well as through extermination or deportation of leading nationally conscious Polish elements.

Such action on the part of the Soviet Government would unavoidably cause desperate movements of self-defense on the part of the Polish population. In the fifth year of the unceasing and uncompromising resistance of the Polish people to Germany, this eventuality would be a dire tragedy.

Mr. Hull agreed that "every effort must be made to prevent such a misfortune."

In the face of this danger the Polish Government felt compelled to appeal to the American and British governments for a guarantee of independence, of territorial integrity, and of security of the Polish population.

Should the entrance of Soviet troops on Polish territory follow a previous adjustment of relations, and take place in agreement with Poland, then, in conformity with the principle established at the Quebec conference, the right to take over the administration of the country by the legal and sovereign Polish Government should be guaranteed.

To safeguard such a guarantee, American-British troops, or at least small detachments of such troops, should enter and be stationed on the territory of Poland to protect the population against eventual Soviet reprisals and the creation of accomplished facts.

I added that I had also been instructed by my government to say that it desired to open negotiations with the United States and British governments regarding Polish participation in the future occupation of Germany.

The Polish Government also confirmed its intention of upholding in principle its program of federation in Central Europe, and once more emphasized that this program was in no way directed against Soviet Russia and her interests.

In view of the accelerated pace of the war in Europe and the advantages which the United Nations could gain by attracting other nations to join them in the war against Germany, the Polish Government considered countries which had become satellites of Germany, such as Rumania, Hungary, and Slovakia, as potential co-belligerents on the Allied side on the pattern similar to that established in the case of Italy. They might be of considerable service to the United Nations. In these countries the Polish Government could count on large numbers of Polish refugees and, moreover, it could influence these nations. The Polish Government could not be indifferent to the occupation of these countries by the Soviets, as such occupation would mean the encirclement of Poland by Soviet-controlled countries.

Mr. Hull appeared very much interested by these aspects of European problems.

I added that in case of a satisfactory adjustment of Polish-Soviet relations, the Polish Government authorized me to express its readiness to participate in a general security pact which, besides the directly interested countries of eastern Europe, would comprise Soviet Russia, America, and Britain.

Mr. Hull said that he welcomed our decision to declare such readiness, because it proved once more that Poland was willing to collaborate directly with Soviet Russia.

The Polish Government also suggested the creation of an official Allied body for dealing with problems of general strategy in Europe. Poland's participation in such a body was justified by the numerical strength of the Polish armed forces, which were still fifth in size in the United Nations camp. This Allied council should deal with all matters directly concerning Poland, such as the use in action of the Polish armed forces, their speedy access to Poland, the supply of weapons to the Polish Underground Home Army in preparation of its armed rising against the Germans, and with all decisions regarding the date of such a rising, in co-ordination with the general operational plans of the Powers.

I told Mr. Hull that never in the course of our three years' acquaintance had I called on him at so crucial a time and on such important and urgent matters.

Soon the Soviet armies would enter Polish territory. For the first time in this war the armies of a member of the United Nations would actually be liberating the territories and people of another member of the United Nations. Thus a precedent was about to be created which would set a most important pattern for the future.

In the case of Soviet-Russian troops entering Poland, special conditions had to be taken into consideration.

Poland was the oldest European member of the United Nations, having been first to offer armed resistance to Germany. Hitler's first major campaign in this war was fought in Poland. Apart from that, Poland had kept an unbroken record of active resistance inside and outside her country without ever flinching.

It was a regrettable fact that the last time the Soviet armies had entered Poland in September 1939 they came, not as good neighbors or allies, but as invaders and allies of Hitler. They had violated their signed treaties of non-aggression with Poland. In the course of their occupation of Polish territory, the Soviets had also been guilty of serious violations of international law. They had deported considerable numbers of our population. They had annexed our territory.

It was therefore most important at this time, not only for Poland, but also for Soviet Russia, to clarify in what character the Soviets would now re-enter Poland.

The Polish nation had agreed to follow the instructions and advice of its government in London and not only to continue its fight against Germany, but to give the fullest support of its well-organized Underground forces of resistance to the oncoming Russian forces. This made the problem of Soviet-Polish relations one of great military importance and an acid test of Soviet good faith. Not only Poland, but all the members of the United Nations camp were affected.

I told the Secretary that we regarded it as providential that at this time the important conference in Moscow was to take place and to be followed by the so-long-delayed Big Three meeting. We knew how much depended on how firmly Poland's just cause and that of the three Baltic countries would be defended by the United States and Britain. In fact, these next two momentous meetings would show whether the great concept of the United Nations could survive.

Mr. Hull assured me that he fully appreciated the importance of the problems which I had once more placed before him. He said that, in principle, he was entirely in accord with our views, and admitted that his decision to take part personally in the Moscow conference had been greatly influenced by his realization that issues were involved which for the good of the world and in the interest of peace and security had to be discussed and settled without further delay.

When I drew his attention to the necessity of a joint British-American-Soviet guarantee reassuring the Polish nation that Soviet entry on Polish territory would be caused only by temporary war necessities, Mr. Hull said that he thought it was "a logical request," but one which it might be difficult to get the Soviets to agree to.

On the other hand, he thought that our request that the Polish Government should be allowed to return to Poland and take over the administration as soon as the Soviets entered Poland was not only logical, but conformed to the principle established at the Quebec conference.

And here Mr. Hull defined his attitude in words which I have always remembered:

"The Polish Government," he said, "is entitled to act the part of host to the Soviets when they come into Poland. This is both just and logical and requires, as your government rightly maintains, the re-establishment of direct relations between the Soviet and Polish governments."

He also expressed his understanding of our suggestion that some American and British troops, or at least token detachments of such troops, and possibly American and British missions, should be on the spot to help avoid friction between the Soviet and Polish authorities.

Mr. Hull also appeared very much interested in our policy on European federations and questioned me closely on this subject.

I told him I had the impression that, in recent times, possibly under the influence of pro-Soviet propaganda, American circles appeared less partial to this policy. I stressed the fact that our policy on European federations expressed a traditional Polish policy which we were now anxious to see adopted because, in our opinion, it was the best guarantee of European security. The Soviet distrust of this policy and the accusation that it tended to build a *cordon sanitaire* against Russia were entirely unfounded. On the contrary, such a system of federations would materially strengthen Russia's security.

Mr. Hull replied that he remembered clearly General Sikorski's arguments on this subject, and said that the Soviet idea of the cordon sanitaire appeared to him to be "farfetched."

He then suddenly asked me whether the Polish Government was really prepared to enter into a world-security organization in which Russia would take part.

I answered emphatically that that was our determination, and that Poland would do this wholeheartedly, provided normal So-

viet-Polish relations were satisfactorily established and that Poland was fully guaranteed non-intervention by the Soviets in her
internal affairs and given a satisfactory guarantee of her sovereign rights and territorial integrity.

Mr. Hull agreed that these conditions were both essential and
fair.

By this time we had completed the discussion of all the points
which I had been instructed to submit to the Secretary of State.
Mr. Hull now turned to me and said that he would like to hear
any personal views and comments which I might care to offer
before he left for the Moscow meeting.

I thanked him for allowing me to think aloud in his presence,
and said that I would like to analyze Soviet-Allied relationship
on its merits and in its tactical aspect.

That relationship appeared to require the most speedy and
complete clarification if it was to become a normal and close
collaboration. As matters stood, it was better to face facts. It
was difficult to continue to regard as an ally a Power which,
while taking so prominent a part in a common fight for declared
principles of freedom and justice, was at the same time pursuing
a policy contrary to these principles.

The splendid defense put up by Soviet Russia should not blind
us to reality or make us indulge in wishful thinking by pretend-
ing that she acted as a democracy. We had to face the fact that
there was as yet no real unity of purpose and policy between the
Allies and Soviet Russia toward Germany. This was clearly
proved by the establishment by the Soviets of the Free Germany
Committee in Russia.

We were all inclined to hope wishfully that Soviet communism
had been entirely replaced by nationalism, more normal in a
people at war, and that the dissolution of the Comintern and the
adoption of outward signs of military rank reminiscent of tsarism
were proofs in point.

But we had to admit that Soviet activities and propaganda,
especially in the countries neighboring on Russia, and the creation
of puppet governments ready to take over in European countries were definite proofs that the Soviets had not given up communism as an instrument of their foreign policy, aimed at
political disruption of foreign countries from within.

The much-publicized "Soviet realism" called for the use of realistic arguments on the part of the Western Allies—of a realism which would clearly show Soviet Russia that the United Nations were apprehensive of her aims, and convince them that unity of purpose and of policy was essential to inspire confidence in her participation in an international security organization on a world scale.

As I was developing these ideas, Mr. Hull frequently signified his approval and said that he had no illusions about the Soviet attitude and that he shared my apprehensions. He added that he would like to hear what I had to say on the tactical aspect of this situation because he felt a certain difficulty in following the processes of Soviet thinking.

I replied that between the United States and Great Britain on the one side and the Soviets on the other there existed a whole series of problems of first-rate importance which might be defined as arising out of the respective basic policies of the three Powers.

The aims did not necessarily change with changes of governments and regimes. For instance, the basic aims of Soviet Russia's foreign policies were certainly the same as those of tsarist Russia. The basic policies of Great Britain, as far as empire and other fundamental British problems were concerned, had not greatly changed with time. The basic policies of the United States, such as the Monroe Doctrine and the Stimson declaration on Manchuria, still prevailed.

It was no use blinking the fact that the basic policies of Soviet Russia and those of Britain in Europe and Asia, and probably those of the United States in the Far East, were very different and, to say the least, difficult to adjust. Some were bound to clash. It might be necessary to put off their discussion until the end of the war, when they would ripen and could no longer be shelved. But one could, and, I ventured to think one should, prepare the way for their adjustment now on the basis of the greatest common problem which affected all Powers in equal measure and had become vital and urgent; namely, the problem of world security.

World security could not be achieved without a unified policy between the Great Powers on the security of all United Nations. No such unification existed and, if Soviet Russia continued to drift in the direction of her selfish aims, which appeared to be imperialistic, at a time when the United States and Britain had so firmly declared that their concept of security was based upon the fundamental principles of freedom, justice, and equality for all peoples, we were heading for disunity and disaster.

It therefore appeared advisable to open negotiations for the achievement of a unified security policy between the Powers by first solving the problems which did not directly involve the personal interests of the United States and Great Britain. In my opinion, no more urgent and appropriate problem could be selected for such an *entrée en matière* in discussions with Soviet Russia than the problem of Poland's independence and of her security. Soviet policy toward the Baltic States, Finland, part of Rumania, and some other European countries, was another problem ripe for immediate frank discussion.

It should be much easier for the Western Allies to discuss these problems and to condition future relations with the Soviets on their clarification and satisfactory solutions. It was so much easier to defend a cause involving principles and the defense of right against might, principles of security and legality, than to enter into discussions of policies which could never be dealt with in a spirit free from personal interests of the Powers directly involved.

Mr. Hull emphatically agreed with me, but wondered in what way one could get the Soviets into a discussion of principles.

I replied that above all it was necessary for the United States and Britain to speak with one voice and be prepared to counter any attempt of the Soviets to divide them on this issue or any other issue. To be successful, such conversations would have to be carried on in a spirit of realism. The Western Allies would probably have to invoke bargaining points, such as Lend-Lease supplies, the problem of the second front, and aid to Russia.

I added that I was sure the Secretary would regard it as fair in this case to point out to Stalin that nothing could better serve his cause in world public opinion than a gesture on his part which would clearly prove that he had no imperialist designs.

I put Mr. Hull on his guard against Soviet methods of negotiation. Observation of Soviet diplomacy made it permissible to foresee that the Russians would try to convince him that he had nothing to fear if he trusted their genuinely "democratic" tendencies, and that he could rely on them to act in line with American and British conceptions of justice and democracy.

Mr. Hull smiled and replied that he was prepared to be cautious and did not think he would allow himself to be taken in by such methods.

As he accompanied me to the door of his study, where we warmly shook hands and I wished him all success in his mission, he told me that he knew he had undertaken a very difficult assignment and he did not know how far he would succeed, but he assured me that "he was decided to defend the cause of Poland as he would defend the cause of his own country."

On the following day I heard that, in taking leave of Secretary of Commerce Jesse Jones, when the latter asked him what had finally determined him to undertake so difficult and dangerous a mission at his age, Mr. Hull had replied that, in the final analysis, the situation created by the problem of Poland had determined his decision. He said he felt that he "had to defend it to the end."

CHAPTER XXIV

Mr. Stettinius at the State Department

SUMNER WELLES'S RESIGNATION at the end of August 1943 started a new era in the history of the State Department. Washington rumor had it that Mr. Hull had been pressing the President for a change of undersecretaries.

The appointment of Edward R. Stettinius, Jr., the efficient Lend-Lease administrator, regarded as a devoted sympathizer of the New Deal although for all practical purposes not an inner-circle New Dealer, was at first commented on as proof that the President wanted to accentuate the close relationship between the policy-making department and the war agencies, such as the Lend-Lease Administration. There were also people who believed that the President wanted to give Mr. Hull an undersecretary with less individuality than Sumner Welles.

Stettinius had no direct experience in foreign affairs, and it was the general belief that he would be guided entirely by Mr. Hull, for whom he would be a convenient liaison officer with the White House. Everybody knew that Stettinius was Harry Hopkins's personal candidate.

The appointment of Ed Stettinius, whose charm of manner, straightforwardness, and efficiency had made him a favorite with all officials and diplomats while he headed the Lend-Lease Administration, was greeted as a popular move of the President at the time. His unanimous confirmation by the Senate clearly proved it. In appointing him the President had scored another political triumph. Few men started their career in so responsible a post, under such auspicious personal conditions as the handsome Ed.

Personally, I was very sorry to see Sumner Welles leave the State Department. I had learned to know him as an able and experienced diplomat who, behind his rather cold manner, was both human and full of understanding of world problems and, what was rather rare among high American officials, had a comprehensive knowledge of European problems.

He had always been sympathetic to Poland, a real friend of General Sikorski and a supporter of his policies. However, once the inevitable had to happen and Sumner Welles left, I admit that I welcomed the appointment of Stettinius, with whom I had had very pleasant and friendly relations both personally and in matters of Lend-Lease. We sometimes used to discuss European affairs, and he appeared eager and openminded. This encouraged me to think that he would take the utmost trouble to become conversant with foreign affairs, now that he was called upon to deal with them directly.

I called on him on October 28, shortly after he took over his duties at the State Department. As I came into the Undersecretary's study, the arrangement of which had been so familiar to me since days long past when, in the twenties, I had frequently called on my friend Joseph C. Grew, then Undersecretary of State, and more recently on Mr. Sumner Welles, I noticed that the furniture and the whole character of the room were changed.

It had been modernized and made to look more like a business executive's office. Mr. Stettinius, with his characteristic cordiality and his genial smile, rose to welcome me, expressing his pleasure "at seeing so dear a friend." I congratulated him on his appointment and asked him how he felt in his new surroundings. He replied that he felt "very bewildered."

Barely a few days after taking over his duties he had become Acting Secretary of State in the absence of Mr. Hull. With boyish frankness he admitted that he not only felt ignorant of the affairs he had to deal with, but, what made it even more difficult, he did not know most of the officials of the Department who had suddenly become his subordinates and collaborators.

When I cheered him up by saying that with his proverbial efficiency and capacity for work he would certainly have little difficulty in getting familiar with his new surroundings, he expressed the hope that I would continue our previous informal relationship and that I would, as he put it, "come to hold his hand from time to time" and help him understand the problems

of Europe which, as he amiably added, I had so helpfully discussed with him in the past.

I said I would be delighted to do so.

When I referred to my last conversation with the Secretary of
State on the day of his departure for Moscow, Stettinius appeared
very optimistic about the result of the conference. He suddenly
asked me what, in my opinion, would be the best line for him to
follow in order to fulfill his mission as Undersecretary of State
to the best of his ability.

This very direct and spontaneous question really charmed me.
I jokingly advised him not to think that foreign affairs and
diplomacy were a sort of mysterious magic mostly requiring
shrewdness. I hoped he would not try to become an American
Talleyrand. There was no time for such aspirations.

I told him emphatically and very sincerely that he had a wonderful chance for striking out in an almost unexplored direction
in furthering the new American policy initiated by the President
in establishing the United Nations. It was a splendid concept
for him to work on, full of vast possibilities, leading straight to
what the whole world of freedom-loving peoples most earnestly
yearned for; namely, American leadership. I told him that I had
watched with deep regret Mr. Roosevelt's great idea being allowed to depreciate because it was not being followed up in the
right way. It looked as if a Power-political concept had been
grafted on to it.

The representatives of the United Nations, except the United
States, Great Britain, Soviet Russia, and China, were practically
never asked their views on important matters of war, or of peace
and security. They were even seldom admitted to any actual
collaboration or planning. And yet it was of the utmost importance to get their fullest collaboration, to know their views on
problems which affected them directly.

At best they were called in to be photographed standing under
their respective flags at ceremonies or war-bond drives for propaganda purposes, as an outward show of an almost non-existent
collaboration.

I told him that, as I saw it, it was still difficult to foresee in
what measure the American people would finally agree to let
the United States become permanently involved in world affairs.

And it was so essential to world peace and security that the United States should not only take its due place in world affairs, but that its voice should be heeded and its leadership asserted.

Therefore, even from the American internal political angle, it appeared to me highly desirable that, in working out a United Nations world policy, all the United Nations, not merely three or four Powers, should be effectively brought into the picture and consulted. By avoiding to do so, as had been the case up to that time, the United States Government appeared to be assuming the responsibility for all world problems. It was a responsibility which should be shared by all the United Nations. Here, I added, was his great chance to make the United Nations concept a really living and active organization, well balanced and effective.

I told him that, being personally untrammeled by traditional restrictions of old-fashioned diplomacy, he could more easily strike out on this new idea and make it a real success. Nothing could better strengthen the President's great concept nor better assure American leadership in a natural and democratic direction than by thus broadening its base.

Stettinius said that he was "thrilled" by this suggestion which appealed to him, and assured me he would do his best to work it out. He asked me how I thought it could be started most effectively.

I answered that I thought it would be a welcome new departure if he started by initiating periodical conversations—at first with one or at most two representatives of the United Nations of a given region on all the problems of that region. Later, when he felt that he had learned some of the problems and noted affinities and differences between the various countries, he might enlarge such conversations to include representatives of several nations at a time. Thus, gradually, he would be drawing all of them in and learning quite a lot about problems which he would be only partially able to understand from divisional reports or dispatches of American representatives abroad.

Stettinius thought this an excellent idea, but I saw that he had not fully understood my suggestion when, after saying that he knew now how to put it into effect, he explained that he would have a big table placed in his room and would seat groups of representatives of the United Nations around it, with himself as their host, and would call in the photographers and newspapermen so that the public would know that collaboration was really progressing.

I begged him to refrain from doing any such thing. I explained that it was exactly what I thought should be avoided. No publicity was necessary. Really friendly exchanges of views and direct discussions, in very small groups at the most, were what I recommended. Publicity was not what was lacking. In fact, there had been too much of it. There had been too many klieg lights and too much Hollywood showmanship surrounding great ideas which remained unexplored and which could easily become inapplicable.

As an example of lack of consultation, I mentioned the fact that Yugoslavia and Greece, the victims of Italian and German aggression, who had put up a splendid fight against the invaders, had not only not been consulted on the terms of Italy's surrender, but these terms had not even been communicated to their representatives. How could one imagine a European settlement if European countries were to be kept in the dark on settlements involving them directly simply because they were not Big Powers in the antiquated sense of the word? Was that democracy about which so much was said and so little was being done?

Stettinius appeared really interested. "Your idea appeals to me more than I can say." He asked me to help him when, as he certainly hoped, he would be able to start carrying it out.

We parted in a most friendly way, and I hoped that he would succeed in adopting my suggestions.

It soon became evident, however, that no such innovation could be introduced, even by this new and dynamic man, unspoiled by officialdom and bureaucracy.

As time went on and my close friendly relations with Stettinius developed, I saw that he did not appear to realize how much he could achieve by initiating real collaboration among the United Nations.

He appeared to me to regard foreign relations as a mixture of publicity and propaganda, rather than as an art of cultivating delicate plants of thought and policy which had to be nursed and sheltered from the crude rays of spotlights and publicity until they were strong enough to stand them.

As I observed his very sincere efforts during the time he was Undersecretary of State, and especially when he became Secretary of State, it seemed to me that his pursuit of efficiency was mostly aimed at streamlining, while, as concerned the merits of international problems, he acted partly as showman, partly as would a chairman of a big board of shareholders.

He did not seem to see the difference between running a meeting of shareholders and an association of nations. He appeared to regard even superficial unanimity as more essential than the merits of the solution. He seemed to think that it was possible to buy unity, sometimes even by sacrificing fundamental principles, without appearing to realize that only on the basis of fundamental principles could such unity be sincere and durable in a United Nations association.

He seemed to forget that at a shareholders' meeting, although some members held enormous quantities of stock and others only a few, one could safely press for "unity above all other considerations" because all of these shareholders held stock in the same concern, which made their interests coincide; individual nations, in an association embracing the globe, had only some identical interests and many very divergent ones.

Real unity could be created only after co-ordinating these divergent interests around some great principles. It could not materialize usefully or permanently by any artificial means.

The divergence between the aims and policies of totalitarian Soviet Russia and those of the United States were, as I often told Stettinius, the best example of the deep differences of ideologies which could at best be made co-operative but could never be adjusted on the basis of compromises with principles for the sake of a fictitious and precarious unity.

With the departure of Sumner Welles the State Department entered on a series of so-called streamlinings.

With the arrival of Stettinius it was rejuvenated with a view to making it technically more efficient. In diplomatic circles we were sorry to see Assistant Secretary Breckenridge Long, Financial Adviser Herbert Feis, and others leaving the Department.

A great friend of mine, considered by all us diplomats as one of the greatest American experts on Russia and the eastern European countries, Loy Henderson, had been appointed Minister to Iraq in June 1943. His place at the State Department was taken by Charles E. Bohlen, a younger official, with some experience of Russia.

It was with real regret that I saw another friend, Ray Atherton, leave the State Department to become United States Ambassador to Canada. He had with great tact and subtle judgment occupied the important post of Chief of European Affairs. He was replaced by H. Freeman Matthews.

Washington received very little information from Moscow in the course of the conference of the three Foreign Ministers in which Secretary Hull was taking part. An atmosphere of optimistic anticipation, crowded with rumors, prevailed and was reflected in all conversations at diplomatic and social gatherings.

On November 1 the communiqué closing the Moscow conference was published to the accompaniment of enthusiastic, officially inspired comment. The Administration was boosting the conference as an enormous success and as a definite step on the way to co-ordination of relations between the three Big Powers.

In reading the Moscow communiqué on the results of the conference, one had the impression that very little had actually been achieved. Official enthusiasm further contributed to blur the picture.

It surprised me when, in conversation with some officials of the State Department and with politicians of the inner White House circle, I realized that, contrary to the artificial enthusiasm regarding the results of the Moscow conference, their private opinions were mostly pessimistic. I gathered that, as far as could then be ascertained, America and Britain had had to sacrifice the three Baltic countries and half of Poland to Russia "for the sake of understanding with the Soviets."

I actually met with expressions of sympathy and condolence on the part of numerous political friends and I grew more than ever apprehensive and impatient to know what had really happened in Moscow.

In the face of the increasingly rapid Soviet advance westward, the situation of Poland was becoming daily more serious as the probability increased that the Soviets would enter Polish territory without having resumed diplomatic relations with the Polish Government. Their tendency to create accomplished facts and to take full advantage of them, their declared determination to incorporate almost half of Poland into Russia, and the absence of any indication from Moscow that the Polish problem had been at all discussed, let alone settled by the three Foreign Ministers, appeared to justify our worst fears.

When Mr. Hull returned to Washington on November 10 I was in Atlantic City attending the inaugural meeting of the United Nations Relief and Rehabilitation Administration.

I had requested the State Department to ask the Secretary to see me as soon as he returned, and to let me know the date so that I could rush back to Washington. I was told, however, that Mr. Hull, having agreed to appear at a joint session of Congress to deliver a comprehensive report on the Moscow conference, had decided not to see anybody before appearing on Capitol Hill on November 18.

I could not even see Jimmy Dunn, because, as he explained when I called him on the telephone from Atlantic City, he was entirely absorbed by his work with Secretary Hull. All I could get was a promise that Mr. Hull would see me on the day following his appearance in Congress.

I went to Congress to hear Mr. Hull's statement. There was nothing in it to show that the problem of Soviet-Polish relations had been settled or even discussed. But I was told by a close friend that, immediately after the return of Mr. Hull and the Secretary's conversation with the President, Harry Hopkins had made the comment that "the President was worried about the Moscow conference" because it showed that Allied-Soviet relations demanded immediate clarification and the situation was far from favorable. In thus commenting on the conference which was being simultaneously boomed in the press as a "triumphant success," Harry was quoted as having added these words: "We are prostrate about the Moscow conference."

I ran into Harry Hopkins a few days later and he not only confirmed this saying, but hinted that Britain and America had not succeeded in appearing entirely united in Moscow, and that from Eden's attitude the Soviets might have concluded that Britain was trying "to ease America out of European problems." This struck me as an interesting comment from the lips of a man so close and friendly to Britain.

When I asked him why such enthusiasm had been aroused around the results achieved in Moscow and was being fed to the American public, he snapped back with a smile: "Perhaps because we want to show the Soviets that we harbor no suspicions of their conduct."

"Your specific diplomacy," I replied, "appears to me to be a New Deal form of Machiavellian naïveness."

He laughed good-naturedly at my remark and said that this diplomacy had served him fairly well in the past.

At that time Harry Hopkins became undoubtedly the most important figure behind the Washington scene. Beloved by some, envied and disliked by many, he seemed to glory in his role of *eminence grise,* content to remain in the shadow of his great master, the President, for whom he had absolute devotion and fidelity.

It was difficult not to like Harry. Under a veneer of crudeness, which he purposely exaggerated, he had an elemental driving power, an almost superhuman capacity for work, a total disregard for his own very frail health, and a ready and caustic wit well nigh irresistible.

His nimble intelligence, coupled with aggressive and, I believe, sometimes assumed disregard and lack of respect for class or rank of the statesmen and leading personalities in America and abroad whom the President sent him to get in touch with, made one forget his lack of education and culture. The better one knew him the more difficult it was to say whether he was a radical or a conservative at heart. He was identified with the New Deal group, yet he had many of the characteristics of the easy-going playboy.

In my fairly numerous contacts with Harry Hopkins I always found him receptive to new ideas on international affairs and keenly interested to hear opinions on the diplomatic aspects of a given situation or problem. But I soon realized his genuine contempt for diplomats and diplomacy, so characteristic of those who had never tried to understand it, and who regard it as a suspiciously mysterious profession which Mark Twain had defined as the "gentle art of lying in state."

As I sometimes listened to his views on international problems of that time, and especially on those created by Soviet policy, I admit I shivered to think that at this crucial period of history a man like Harry Hopkins was entrusted with the prodigiously difficult task of interpreting American policy to the wily Stalin.

In one of my conversations with the President in 1943, when I was appealing for his intervention on behalf of Poland in Moscow, the President said he would like to send Harry to carry out such an intervention but could hardly do so on account of Harry's health. Hopkins had then had one of his periodical relapses and was undergoing treatment.

The President must have noticed I showed no enthusiasm for the choice of Harry for this particular intervention, because he eagerly asked me: "Don't you like Harry?"

I replied that I did, but that I was afraid he knew too little about the Soviets and Russian mentality to negotiate with Moscow.

The President appeared taken aback and assured me that "Harry gets on like a house afire with Stalin—in fact they seem to have become buddies."

I replied that I had no doubt this was true. Harry's breezy manner was so disarming. But, I added, surely the President would agree that personal ease of contact and even friendship alone could hardly suffice to influence Stalin to change his basic policy.

If we hypothetically reversed the situation and were to admit for a moment that Stalin wanted to persuade the President to alter some important item of American policy to suit Stalin's book, what chance would any personal envoy of Stalin have of achieving such a result, even if he enjoyed the President's confidence and friendship?

"What chance then has any diplomacy?" countered the President.

"We know, Mr. President," I answered, "that even in diplomacy there comes a moment when only decisive arguments, strong bargaining points, and the statement of conditions can succeed, and at such moments it is difficult to press these forceful arguments in the 'hail-fellow-well-met' atmosphere which Harry Hopkins has created at the Kremlin."

The President said he agreed with me in principle but that Harry knew how to bargain and his instinct could be relied on to appraise correctly men and situations.

What made me apprehensive of Harry Hopkins's ability to negotiate with Stalin, was his real or assumed indifference to the human angle of world problems. I once told him so, hoping that he would disperse my fears. He smiled his attractive crooked smile and answered simply: "You are right, I have no patience with the human element. I love only F. D. R."

CHAPTER XXV

The Pattern Crystallizes

WHAT appeared to me more ominous than the whispered rumors about the Moscow conference was the unexpected change in the attitude of the Combined Chiefs of Staff on the matter of supplying our Underground forces with war matériel and munitions for guerrilla and sabotage warfare in preparation for an uprising against the Germans when the Soviet forces entered Poland. During Sikorski's last visit to Washington it had been agreed that in a series of parachute operations war matériel would be supplied to our Home Army. All the plans had been co-ordinated with the R.A.F. and the Polish High Command in London.

Now, suddenly, immediately in the wake of the Moscow conference, our military mission was informed by the Combined Chiefs of Staff that this decision had been revoked. As an explanation it was hinted that the Soviet-Polish tension might make it dangerous to arm our men in Poland and also that the Russians might object.

I was privately told that the Russians had indeed objected, and that their objection was the reason for this undeserved blow dealt by our Western Allies to the valiant Underground Army of Poland.

I did all I could to have this decision changed. In conversations with the American and British representatives on the Combined Chiefs of Staff as well as at the State Department I noted that they were all embarrassed and anxious to assure me that this decision might only be temporary and had been taken in view of the pending Big Three conference "which would certainly clear the way and open new possibilities for Poland's rearmament against Germany."

My military friends went out of their way to praise the organized resistance of the Polish Underground and nation. They readily admitted the importance and value of the intelligence activities of our Underground in Poland, in France, in Germany, as well as in other German-occupied countries. They stressed the fact that at times they had relied entirely upon Polish intelligence and that its information had frequently saved them from making mistakes and had prevented the loss of a great number of men not only on land, but also by supplying them with secret information on the movements of German submarines. They told me that they considered the Polish Underground as "unique of its kind" and that they had counted greatly on its effective collaboration in the period of the Russian advance through Poland. Personally, they told me, they were deeply disappointed by this military decision dictated by political considerations. They realized the value of well-conducted offensive guerrilla operations of our troops on the rear of the retreating German Army which, they said, could save many American and British lives.

Nevertheless, I was faced with the brutal fact that Poland was not to be given "the tools with which to finish the job." Obviously, the policy of placating Russia at all cost had begun to affect even purely military decisions, arrived at after mature study by the American and British General Staffs.

On November 19, Mr. Hull greeted me with the remark that I was the first among the Ambassadors in Washington whom he was seeing after his return from Moscow. He excused himself for having delayed our meeting, explaining that he had been very much pressed with work, having to report on his mission to the President, to discuss its results with members of the Cabinet, and to prepare his statement made the day before in Congress.

After this introduction, Mr. Hull said that he wanted to give me a frank and accurate account of his views on the Moscow conference. He began by saying that he found himself in an unfamiliar setting. As he had been frequently described as unsympathetic to the Soviets, he had tried to dispel this suspicion in Moscow. He had had to discuss a whole series of important and difficult problems with a partner who, to say the least, was difficult and whom he did not know sufficiently well.

On his arrival in Moscow he realized from the outset that it would be impossible to cover all the subjects he had intended to raise. It was most important, he repeated, to create a favorable atmosphere of mutual confidence which would allow for future frank and more detailed discussions. He believed that he had succeeded in creating such an atmosphere, and had carried away the impression that the Soviets did attach importance to the creation of bases for permanent collaboration. He added, after a pause, that he "wanted to believe they were sincere" in giving him this impression.

On the question of Poland Mr. Hull said that he had gone to Moscow considering that his main aim was to bring about the re-establishment of Soviet-Polish relations. He could not imagine any further normal development in Soviet-Polish affairs while the two countries were not "on speaking terms."

He assured me that in his conversations with Molotov he had taken every opportunity to impress upon him that the re-establishment of Soviet-Polish relations was of primary necessity, but he gained the impression that the Soviets regarded the refusal of the Polish Government to enter into any compromise on the territorial issue as the main obstacle.

He immediately added that he did not want to imply that he thought we ought to make such concessions, but he saw that the Soviets were pressing their territorial demands in so realistic a way that it had become practically the condition of a renewal of relations. And, he added, since Soviet Russia was strategically in a very advantageous position, while the Allies still had no armed forces in Central Europe and thus were deprived of the means to support their arguments, it was unlikely that the Soviets would change their attitude on the Polish question.

"One can insist, and even press," the Secretary said, "if one has the means to do so. We have no such means for the time being, and could therefore only use persuasion. We could not resort to more forceful arguments."

Here the Secretary referred to the example of China. At the beginning of the Moscow conference he had little hope of obtaining Soviet agreement for China to be admitted to affix her signature to the joint declaration of the Powers issued after the Moscow meeting. It took him the better part of two weeks of constant work to obtain this result. He added that the attitude of the

Chinese Ambassador, who patiently remained in the background and made no attempt to bring any pressure to bear, certainly greatly contributed to the satisfactory solution of this difficulty.

In the matter of the eastern territories of Poland Mr. Hull said that he regretted to have to tell me that he had not met with any encouragement from the Soviets when he made several references to this subject. He saw clearly that the Soviets were taking full advantage of their exceptionally favorable military position and were determined to regard this matter as solved in their favor. They resented any outside interference on the part of their Western Allies. Mr. Hull admitted that this was an "entirely unreasonable point of view," but, faced with the choice of forcing the discussion of this topic, or putting it off to further meetings, he thought it more judicious to take the latter course.

When he raised the question of the presence of Western Allied forces at the side of the Soviet forces in the liberation and occupation of European countries neighboring on Soviet Russia, he met with a very determined show of opposition on the part of the Soviet representatives. He doubted if the Soviets could ever be persuaded to change their policy. They had strongly pointed to the exclusive character of the British and American activities in North Africa, Sicily, and Italy where, as they said, a precedent had been established of which the Soviets wanted to avail themselves in eastern Central Europe.

With regard to another matter; namely, of admitting the Polish authorities to take over the administration of Poland as it became liberated from German occupation, Mr. Hull had come to the conclusion that it was premature to raise this point in Moscow on the basis of the formula adopted at the Quebec conference. That formula still remained in the form of a joint American-British suggestion which had not been accepted by the Soviets and it was to become a subject of further negotiations.

In view of this fairly black picture of the Moscow conference, I asked Mr. Hull if he would kindly tell me whether he considered that the optimism which had been spread in Washington was justified.

Mr. Hull replied that, according to him, the conference "should be regarded only as a preliminary step and a first attempt at understanding and co-operation." Generally speaking, he considered that this attempt had been successful, but he certainly did not think that one could draw any final optimistic conclusions. The most one could say about the conference, he thought, was that a framework for understanding, as well as a propitious atmosphere for future talks, had been created. Once more he stressed the fact that the situation of inequality between the weaker position of the Western Allies and the powerful and advantageous position of the Soviets in Europe had forced him to be very careful. He was convinced, however, that, as the war situation developed in favor of the Allies, the position of the Western nations would become more favorable for pressing for agreement on the more important problems of Allied-Soviet relations.

He admitted that the situation of Poland was, for the time being, extremely difficult. Great Britain and the United States would have to take advantage of every opportunity to press in a form "which would be friendly but firm," for a satisfactory solution of Polish questions. He did not think speedy results could be expected. But he was confident that the Soviets realized the deep interest of America and Britain in a just solution of the problems of Poland, and that they would finally agree to "go along."

I asked the Secretary whether one could consider that the United States had in any way changed its views regarding the fundamental principles of the United Nations.

He answered emphatically that it had not changed its views nor its devotion to these principles. He said that his words had been misunderstood by the press when it reported after his press interview that he had said that the Atlantic Charter would have to be revised. He was glad to assure me that he had said only that the most pressing matters had to be taken up first—matters pertaining to war problems—before going into the application of the principles of the Atlantic Charter to territorial and political problems of the postwar period.

He asked me what I thought of the comprehensive picture of the Moscow conference he had drawn for me.

I replied that I had to admit that his very interesting description had by no means allayed my fears. We expected the entry of the Soviet troops on Polish territory in the near future. If this happened in the present circumstances, and if the Soviet armies brought with them communist Polish Quislings, it was certain that Soviet Russia intended to create accomplished facts in Poland.

The Polish people had been unswervingly loyal Allies, who would see their country actually become, through the force of events, the victim of ruthless imperialist expansionism of a Power allegedly allied to Poland in a common struggle. These events, as Mr. Hull said, could not be checked because Britain and the United States were not in a position to press for such a change.

What could the Polish people think when they knew that the Emperor of Abyssinia had already returned to his liberated country and taken over its rule? What would they think when they knew that even Italy, one of the Axis Powers, was allowed to form her own government, which was taking over the administration and was to be admitted to participate at the side of Allied forces in further action for her liberation? Surely Poland had the right to demand that she should not be treated less well than those countries, and I ventured to think that her exceptional conduct in the war entitled her to more favored treatment.

The Polish people had one birthright, I said. They had the right to fight for their own liberation, on their national territory. This birthright was being denied them. The supply of arms had been cut off. The Poles wanted to continue the fight against the German invader, with whom they had steadily refused to co-operate in any way. It appeared unthinkable, I added, that after having ceaselessly defended our territory, regardless of inhuman oppression and retaliation, of unprecedentedly brutal methods of extermination, we were to give it up and to hand it to an allegedly friendly neighbor just for the asking.

I said I feared that the fact that the Secretary had agreed not to insist on the discussion of the Polish problem with the Soviets in a more positive and insistent way had been taken by Stalin as a proof that American and British interest in justice for Poland was only superficial. He certainly interpreted their passive attitude as a sign of weakness and of their decision to pursue a policy of appeasement of Russia. I reminded the Secretary that a similar situation had arisen in Munich in 1938 but it had not averted the terrible catastrophe of the present world war.

The Secretary appeared to be impressed by my arguments and

asked me if I could suggest anything that could be done at present.

I answered that I knew that the Big Three conference was about to start. I regarded it as absolutely necessary and urgent that at that conference, where the heads of the three Powers would discuss all problems of common interest to the United Nations, Polish problems should be discussed in a more determined manner, taking advantage of that "friendly atmosphere of understanding" which, according to the Secretary, he had succeeded in creating in Moscow.

Mr. Hull asked me what argument I thought could be used to persuade the Soviets to renew relations with the Polish Government.

I answered that at this stage Stalin would have to be told very finally by the President and Mr. Churchill that America and Britain would refuse to recognize any other but the legal Polish Government in London. Another point which should be taken under advisement was the restatement of American and British non-recognition policy regarding territorial changes. It was likewise time to warn the Soviets that if they wanted to avoid coming up squarely against this firm determination, they should realize that, so far as America and Great Britain were concerned, the recognized territorial status of Poland would be regarded as legal and binding. It should be added that the American and British governments would under no circumstances change their decision on this matter.

Mr. Hull said that he could not give me any promise that such an attitude would be adopted. However, he would immediately suggest it to the President. He said that he thought the initiative of conducting discussions at the Big Three meetings in such a way should be taken by Great Britain, who was bound by an alliance with Poland. He was sure that the President would follow suit if Mr. Churchill put the matter squarely on such a basis.

I expressed regret that the President had already left Washington. I admitted to the Secretary that I knew he was on his way to the momentous Big Three meeting, and asked Mr. Hull whether he did not think that, in view of the considerable importance of the problem and of its urgency, it might be helpful if Premier Mikolajczyk joined the President at some spot on the way to the conference in order to discuss the matter with him and see what could be done to achieve a satisfactory solution. I added that Mr. Mikolajczyk was ready to undertake such a journey. It might be all the more useful because it would give the President a chance to discuss the whole problem with the head of our government together with Mr. Churchill.

Secretary Hull thought this over for a moment and said he could give me only his personal view on this suggestion. He would be quite frank. He did not know whether I should advise my government to undertake this move. In principle, he certainly agreed with me that such a discussion before the Big Three meeting might be of considerable help. On the other hand, it might complicate the situation for the President if the Soviet Government became suspicious of it.

Finally, after a moment's hesitation, he admitted that both Eden and he had come to the conclusion that the Soviets would not change their attitude toward the Polish Government if it did not suggest some compromise on the territorial issue. Having gained this impression, he felt that the journey of Premier Mikolajczyk could bring results only if he had some "concrete new suggestions" to make on this subject.

Mr. Hull was certain that the President intended to raise the Polish problem with the fullest understanding and that he was aware of its urgency. In fact, he added that the President and Mr. Churchill had accelerated the date of the conference, which was to have been held later, because they understood that war events and the unexpectedly rapid retreat of the German Army, "as well as the acute Soviet-Polish situation," had necessitated the immediate holding of the meeting. He thought that before deciding whether the Polish Prime Minister should join the President and Mr. Churchill this matter should be discussed with Eden, not only because the British Government, as Poland's ally, was in the best position to express its opinion on such a subject, but because he was sure that if Mr. Churchill approved of it, the President would also approve.

Before I took leave the Secretary asked me to believe that he had in no way changed his attitude and that he continued to be most friendly and well disposed to all Polish problems. Nor had he abandoned any fundamental principles. He was deeply concerned by the tragic situation of the Polish nation. He assured me that "we do not differ as regards principles or on the merits of Poland's just cause. We may possibly differ somewhat in our views on the tactics to be followed in order to bring about a satisfactory solution."

Once more he repeated he was certain that only by advancing gradually on the way to an understanding with the Soviets could one hope for good results. He had tried "to take the Soviets by the hand in Moscow and to lead them along the way to understanding and collaboration." The Big Three meeting would probably succeed in making further progress.

I replied that I would like to add only a few words as a European speaking from the point of view of world problems. I was frankly apprehensive that the logic and realism of the Soviets made them interpret the passive Anglo-American policy toward them as implied readiness to depart from fundamental principles, which I regarded as the only sound basis for harmonious collaboration between the Powers and, in fact, between all the United Nations. That relationship required that all conferences and exchanges of views should take place on a footing of equality.

Nobody could believe that the Soviets really thought they could insure their security by annexing bits of territory to their already-enormous holding. They attached no more importance to having a cut of Poland, or the Baltic States, than Hitler actually cared for the territory of the Sudetenland or even of the whole of Czechoslovakia.

We, the United Nations, should face facts. The pattern of Soviet policy was becoming clear. I asked the Secretary to realize that, by annexing Poland, Soviet Russia was out to create for herself a convenient political springboard for communist infiltration into Central and western Europe. We knew that the Germans were quite capable of allowing themselves to be Sovietized because, as totalitarians, they realized that this did not mean sacrificing much, and especially not their militarism. We were aware that in France, in Italy, and in Yugoslavia, communism had already made considerable progress. Any Munich policy applied to the Soviets was bound in time to result in their continuous expansion westward, and suddenly they might appear on the banks of the English Channel and on the French and Iberian coasts of the Atlantic. What then would be the situation of British and American security?

I admitted that, from all reports published by the Soviets or by the American press, and even from what Mr. Hull had just told me so frankly about the Moscow conference, I did not see a single proof that the Soviets were tending in the direction of a system of world security within the framework of the United Nations. On the contrary, all their moves and enunciations were negative and unilateral. Their strong opposition to any form of European federation had to be regarded as ominous, because you could not reject the idea of federation if you wanted to reinforce effectively a sound security system.

The Secretary listened attentively, signifying from time to time that he agreed with my arguments. Once more he assured me that our views were not far removed. But he insisted that, while the considerations I had just mentioned were correct and should be borne in mind, it was all the more necessary to "advance cautiously on the way to understanding with Soviet Russia."

As we shook hands to say good-by I felt that this conversation marked a definite turning point in my previously too hopeful expectation of American leadership in world affairs.

I had just had a conversation with the same Cordell Hull with whom I had so frankly discussed these problems a few hours before he left for the Moscow conference, from which he had just returned. It flashed through my mind that these problems had not only been explored by the Big Three Foreign Secretaries in preparation for the discussions between the President, Mr. Churchill, and Stalin which were about to open at Teheran, but that their solutions had already been far advanced in Moscow in a way which would set a pattern imposed by the will of Stalin.

It appeared to me that not only had the international situation deteriorated, but that the Moscow conference had left its seal on Mr. Hull himself. I had seen him on October 6 much rejuvenated by his determination to go to an unknown land in order to defend and, if necessary, to force through the acceptance of American fundamental principles from which he said he was not prepared to depart. It seemed to me he had returned aged by his experience, a man who felt helpless to turn the rising tide of events, a man who had begun to doubt America's power to assume moral leadership. The Moscow conference was to have been the high-light of his eventful life. And it had turned into a show of help-lessness in the face of stern brutality.

Mr. Hull had just told me that he remained hopeful because he felt he had succeeded in creating confidence which had been lacking on the part of Stalin before the Moscow conference. He told me he thought that, having in a friendly way taken Soviet Russia by the hand, he could gradually lead her through future frank exchanges of views to deeper mutual Allied understanding and convince her of the advantages of future harmonious co-operation on the basis of mutually agreed democratic principles. But it was hard to believe that he did not realize, as fully as I did, that Stalin, after preparing the ground by five refusals to meet his Allies, after securing his militarily advantageous position, and after a final barrage of overbearing propaganda, had, in fact, car-ried out in Moscow a first successful direct attack in a personal diplomatic offensive aimed at softening his American and British Allies and of setting the scene for more advanced American-British appeasement at Teheran.

Moreover, the conference had been boomed as an enormous success in view of the even more important pending conference of the Big Three. That in itself appeared to be a fatal mistake. If the American people had been told the truth about Moscow, and had been made to realize how remote was the hope that the rush-ing force of Soviet expansion could be stemmed by passive silence interpreted by Stalin as tacit agreement, they would have reacted in a way which would have strengthened the hand of their Presi-dent, who was about to open negotiations with Stalin. As matters stood, Stalin had won the first round of an uneven contest of statesmanship, and the artificially aroused public enthusiasm for the results of the Moscow conference had confirmed his belief that he was dealing with weak partners who preferred to conceal the truth from their people rather than face him squarely.

CHAPTER XXVI

From Moscow to Teheran, December 1943

THE secret that the President was conferring with Churchill and Stalin could, of course, not be kept long. The tension caused by Stalin's previous refusals to meet the President now gave way to hopeful anticipation. In official and political circles, among the diplomats and in Washington drawing rooms, the conference at Teheran was practically the only topic of conversation. When, finally, the short closing communiqué was published, it came as an anticlimax. Its very wording made it evident that the curtain would not be raised on what actually happened at Teheran.

On President Roosevelt's return to Washington this was further confirmed by the fact that, after having allowed the announcement that he would personally report on the Teheran meeting to Congress—a prospect which aroused the greatest interest—the President decided not to do so, and refused to give any detailed information to the newspapermen.

He skillfully dodged questions regarding his acceptance of Stalin's hospitality at the Soviet Embassy in Teheran during the conference—a fact which had not only been rather freely criticized, but appeared to have shocked many important political personalities in Washington.

At first I found it impossible to obtain any reliable information through normal official channels. In conversations with high officials of the American Government I met with the usual assurance that the Big Three had been very successful "in attaining unity of purpose." Nobody seemed to be able to say on what particular problem, among so many, this unity had been achieved, nor, especially, at what price. I had to pursue my research work mostly behind the scenes, and it took me nearly two weeks to form a picture of the Teheran conference.

Outwardly it was being boosted as a great success, even a triumph, especially by New Dealers. The Cairo Roosevelt-Churchill conference had aroused hopes that Turkey might soon join the United Nations. The fact that Stalin had agreed to sign a Three Power declaration guaranteeing the complete independence of Iran was held up as a personal victory won by the President.

On the other hand, the triumphant note of the Soviet press and radio comments on the Teheran conference was in itself revealing.

Moscow proclaimed the Teheran conference as a great success and, for the first time, injected a note of praise for the United States, even admitting the importance of American aid to Russia in her now victorious war with Germany. At the same time the anti-Polish accents of Soviet propaganda markedly increased, and direct attacks on the Polish Government continued with renewed vigor.

Before the return of the President from Teheran I learned that the date of the meeting had been advanced because of the rapid progress of the Soviet offensive. I was told that Mr. Churchill especially had urged the earlier holding of the conference. British military circles expected the Germans to make a firm stand on the Dnieper River, and hoped to make the Big Three meeting coincide with this development, which would in some degree restore equality in discussions with Stalin. American and British military successes, though considerable, were as yet insufficient to balance the fact that the Soviets were advancing rapidly and their victorious forces were fully engaged with the bulk of the German Army, while the Allies had less than twenty divisions engaged in actual combat.

I learned that what had struck the President, Mr. Churchill, and their delegations rather forcibly on their arrival in Teheran was the disproportion between the very considerable staffs which accompanied the President and the British Prime Minister and the Soviet delegation, which in effect consisted of three men: Stalin, Molotov, and Voroshilov. The remainder of the Soviet delegation was made up of lesser officials and of innumerable numbers of agents of the Soviet secret police. I was told that the American delegation numbered 285 persons. In that imposing number W. Averell Harriman was the only ranking American diplomat present, the President having taken none of the higher officials of the Department of State. The British delegation was somewhat smaller than the American, but also very numerous.

In commenting on this numerical disproportion, one of my closest New Deal friends admitted that these figures were most revealing. According to him, they proved that the President desired to bring his most important military experts in direct contact with Stalin and the experts of the Soviet delegation and to put at the disposal of the Soviet dictator all the data on American war plans in their greatest detail. In fact, he had made the gesture of showing all his cards to Stalin, and Churchill had done the same.

On the other hand, while Stalin certainly appeared eager to be informed on all subjects, he did not seem prepared to confide much of the workings of Soviet strategy or policies to his Western partners.

I gathered that the Big Three had mostly and almost exclusively discussed military problems and the planning of future strategy. So far as co-ordination of military movements was concerned, the date and location of the so-called second front were apparently discussed at length and, according to the general surmise, the date had been fixed for the early spring of 1944, after having established that technical difficulties, especially those of supplies and gasoline to insure perfect mobility of forces on land and in the air, had shown the impossibility of completing this titanic job earlier. One thing had become certain at Teheran. Churchill's plan of attack through the Balkans suffered a complete setback. Stalin had succeeded in pressing his demand for a British-American invasion of western Europe.

I was greatly interested to hear optimistic comments about the possibility of Turkey's entry into the war. I knew that at the meeting held by President Roosevelt, Churchill, and Eden, the problem of Turkey had been discussed, and her government had been consulted on such possibilities. The matter now appeared to hinge on the condition placed by Turkey for a Three Power guarantee of her territorial integrity and full independence, which meant that, until Stalin definitely joined in such a guarantee which the Western Allies on their part appeared ready to give, Turkey would continue to remain neutral.

I was told that at Teheran this matter had been discussed and that Stalin had declined to join in any guarantee for Turkey.

It also appeared that agreement was reached which turned Allied support to Yugoslavia away from King Peter's government and General Draja Mikhailovitch to support of the communist agent Broz-Tito.

My friends who had accompanied the President admitted that Stalin had succeeded in holding the initiative in all discussions throughout the conference and had a way of discouraging talks on any subjects he did not want discussed. He played the role of the gracious host to the President and took every opportunity to impress upon him that he was a "regular guy," a democrat, not a communist of the Lenin type, and that he had no ambitions either for world revolution or conquest.

I was told that the President made several attempts to bring up all the subjects he had prepared for discussion with Stalin. He expressed his interest in Finland and in the fate of the three Baltic countries. He explained to Stalin the advantage to the Allies of helping Finland to get out of Germany's grip. Stalin replied that Soviet-Finnish peace talks were already proceeding smoothly in Sweden, and assured the President that he would be generous to Finland. He said he did not intend to change her territorial status and would respect the frontiers fixed after the first Soviet-Finnish war in 1940. He added that he did not intend to interfere in Finnish internal affairs, or to influence Finland's choice of a government. He admitted, however, that he would insist on the Finnish statesman, Passaikivi, a man "friendly to Russia," becoming president of that country. He laughingly added that Passaikivi was known to be a democrat and not a communist, but nevertheless had Stalin's full confidence.

These and similar statements of Stalin had greatly pleased the President.

Stalin apparently did not want to give any assurances concerning the three Baltic countries. He said that he had not yet made up his mind about their future. He was not yet clear whether he would leave them as three distinct states or would integrate them

into one composite state. He admitted, however, that these countries would have to remain in the closest union with the Soviets,
especially on account of their important strategic and economic
position. This did not necessarily imply, he added, that they were
to become actual Soviet republics within the USSR. He said that
he might devise for these countries some new type of close union
with the Soviets, but could not yet say how close he would have
to make it.

In reply to a question by Mr. Churchill, he said that the
Soviets would naturally establish their air, sea, and land bases on
the territory of the Baltic countries, but added that, so far as
their governments were concerned, he did not attach too much
importance to this matter, and did not even exclude that he might
ultimately allow them to continue to exist under a capitalist
regime. Anyway, he assured the President and Mr. Churchill
that they would be allowed to retain their internal autonomy.

I was told that the President asked Stalin on what his final
decision regarding the Baltic countries would depend. Stalin gave
the disarming reply that it would depend on further investigation
by the Soviet dictator of the wishes of the local population.

The Polish problem had been discussed in detail by the President, Churchill, and Eden in Cairo, and with Stalin at Teheran.
My friends told me that the great difficulty, of course, was the
fact that Soviet Russia had severed relations with Poland and it
was of "such great importance" that they should be resumed.
This had been pointed out by the President and Mr. Churchill
to Stalin, who answered that he also considered it important to
establish good relations with Poland, but he had to insist on
Poland having "a friendly government."

He added after a pause: "If only I could find a Polish Passaikivi matters would be so much easier."

I heard that, in view of this unreceptive attitude of Stalin
whenever they broached the general subject of Poland, the President and Mr. Churchill had switched to the question of Poland's
eastern boundaries, and that it was Mr. Churchill who suggested
the Curzon Line, with a suitable compensation for Poland in the
west.

So now Stalin not only could see that by refusing to discuss
Poland he could have a free hand in dealing with her, but had

been told, on the highest authority, that by calling his territorial demands on Poland "the return to the Curzon Line," he could count on the support of Poland's British ally.

I was interested to know what Stalin's attitude had been with regard to the all-important German problem. I was told that the assurance the President had gained from Stalin was the acceptance of the formula of unconditional surrender, provided it was to be clearly understood that Germany would have to surrender to all three Powers simultaneously.

What had reportedly struck the President most in his talks with Stalin was his unexpected admission that Russia was weakened by the war and, consequently, very exhausted and war weary; that the Soviet war effort had strained all the fibers of the Russian people. Stalin admitted that, as a consequence, he foresaw the possibility of political and social difficulties in Russia after the war. He mentioned the return of the huge Russian armed forces to their country, after having been outside its frontiers during the war. He said that, as a realist, he foresaw that his soldiers would return with an altered ideology. He said he was ready to face these problems and would possibly change "the present communist system of Soviet Russia" to one which would be "a middle course between communism and capitalism." Such a system would admit of private ownership, freedom of religion, and would possibly even encourage some degree of private enterprise. He told the President that he thought the time had come to change even the name of the Union of Soviet Socialist Republics and to revert to the name of Russia.

This possibility appeared to be borne out when, a few weeks later, on the occasion of a banquet in Washington for the fortieth anniversary of aviation, the Soviet Ambassador was listed on the program as the "Russian" Ambassador for the first time in twenty-five years.

At this dinner I sat next to General Henry Arnold, chief of the American Air Forces. He had accompanied the President to Teheran and I was interested to hear his impressions of that important meeting. He told me he could sum them up in one sentence: He saw no great difference in Stalin's and Roosevelt's ideologies, and he believed it was a mistake to think that Stalin was a communist.

I asked him jokingly whether this meant that Stalin had become a democratic president, or that President Roosevelt had become an autocratic tsar. General Arnold laughed good-naturedly and replied that possibly he had exaggerated the situation, but Stalin had impressed him rather as a democrat, or at least, he added, "he succeeded in giving me that impression."

As the fog of secrecy slowly lifted and more of the details of the Teheran conference were disclosed, one could see that the foremost result of this Big Three meeting was the granting of final sanction to the dictatorship of the Three Powers.

It was later to be reaffirmed at Dumbarton Oaks, at Yalta, at San Francisco, and ultimately embodied and signed in the United Nations Charter drawn up in San Francisco, which appeared symbolically to open the way for the war-battered United Nations, not toward any Western democratic conception of freedom for all peoples envisaged by the President in 1941, but in the direction of the rigid concepts of Power-politics.

It appeared to me that at Teheran the President and Mr. Churchill had been compelled to agree to precipitate the United Nations from the heights of the Atlantic Charter to depths lower than those of the Congress of Vienna, with its superannuated theory of spheres of influence and its doctrine of precarious balance of power.

Owing to the artificially fed enthusiasm which for several months continued to obscure the picture, the consequences of Teheran were not fully realized by the American people. As Constantine Brown defined it, "It took six months to debunk Teheran."

I regret to say that, personally, I had little chance for illusion. Realism forced me to see that the tendency to suppress the lofty principles embodied in the Atlantic Charter dated back to the fateful day of June 22, 1941, when Hitler's double-crossing attack suddenly projected Soviet Russia into the unprepared lap of the United Nations. Teheran merely proved that even a Roosevelt and a Churchill, magicians though they were in the arts of statesmanship and diplomacy, could not turn magic into reality, and that, in the words of Ernest Bevin overheard in 1940 when he commented upon Mr. Churchill's praise of "Lord Beaverbrook's magic" in organizing British war economy: "Magic was always 90 per cent illusion."

CHAPTER XXVII

The Veto Sneaks In

IT WAS known to only a few people in Washington—outside the secret inner sanctum of the Big Four Powers, the United States, Britain, Soviet Russia, and China—that the pattern of Power dictatorship was first secretly introduced through the innocent-looking greatest relief organization in the world—the UNRRA.

It was this pattern of Power dictatorship with its right of "veto" for each of the Big Four which was confirmed and sanctified at Teheran and Yalta, and at San Francisco became the very essence of the United Nations organization.

Between December 21, 1942, and April 1943, at the time when war events marked a decisive turn in favor of the United Nations, when the Soviet victory at Stalingrad had dealt a staggering blow to Hitler's might, the Ambassadors of Great Britain, Soviet Russia, and China, with the United States represented by Assistant Secretary of State Dean Acheson, were holding a series of "top-secret" meetings to work out the draft statute of the UNRRA.

It was in the seclusion of these meetings that the Soviet Government, through its most experienced diplomat, Maxim Litvinov, succeeded in smuggling into the UNRRA statutes the Soviet-sponsored Power-political concept. It happened at the time when America and Britain still continued to proclaim their faith in the Atlantic Charter and the American Government in particular still persisted in declaring its fidelity to democratic forms of international collaboration.

I followed from behind the scenes the progress of these Four Powers meetings as they took place. They were a revelation which disclosed to my unbelieving eyes the inside story of what, in Washington, was beginning euphemistically to be called "realism."

The story as it unfolded at those five fateful meetings at the State Department has too great a bearing on the present world setup to be left untold.

After preparatory soundings by the Department of State, the draft of August 13, 1942 (Draft No. 2, Revised), for the organization of a United Nations Relief and Rehabilitation Administration, had been submitted by the United States to China, the Soviet Union, and the United Kingdom, for an expression of their views. That first American-sponsored draft already suggested that membership in the so-called Policy Committee of the future relief organization be limited to the Four Powers exclusively.

The Chinese were the first to reply, on November 24, 1942, accepting the draft proposal but making certain suggestions of which the most important was that the democratic rule of majority vote be adopted. T. V. Soong, the Chinese Minister, explained in his reply that ". . . the provision for unanimous consent appeared to be undesirable because such a provision might sometimes cause difficulty through political trading." This was the subtle way in which the great Far Eastern Power expressed its doubts concerning the admission of the "veto."

On December 21 Lord Halifax reported to the Secretary of State that Britain was opposed to the idea of confining membership of the Policy Committee to the Four Great Powers. "The limitation of membership of the Policy Committee in this way would not, in practice, be conducive to smooth working," the British reply stated, "since the scheme as a whole would thereby be rendered less acceptable to other important countries whose whole-hearted co-operation it will be essential to secure."

In particular, the British Government considered that Canada "has a very strong claim to membership of the committee."

And further, as a happy afterthought, the British memorandum concluded with this passage, which proved that, at that time, London was not unconscious of its role of leadership in Europe. "The United Kingdom government state that they feel it important to obtain the views of the other United Nations, and particularly of the European Allied governments, on these proposals at the earliest possible date."

Eight days later Litvinov transmitted to the State Department a memorandum which in its first two paragraphs expressed the typical "hands-off-Russia" policy, excluding any relief activities by non-Russian organizations inside the Soviet Union.

The third Soviet suggestion stated that "All decisions of the Policy Committee should be *unanimous.*"

The Soviets had thus, for the first time, definitely demanded the right of veto for the four principal Powers. It happened on December 29, 1942—twelve months before Teheran and twenty-six months before the Yalta conference.

The Secretary of State, Mr. Cordell Hull, held a meeting with the three Ambassadors on January 11, 1943, after which Lord Halifax, Maxim Litvinov and Dr. Wei Tao-ming accompanied Dean Acheson, Undersecretary of State, to his room, where they proceeded to discuss the draft point by point.

In regard to the British suggestion that "the membership of the Policy Committee be expanded to seven so as to include Canada and two other countries," the Soviet Ambassador insisted on the draft as it stands on this point. "A decision to add to the Policy Committee other members in addition to the Big Powers," said Litvinov, "would set a pattern which might be embarrassing on other occasions when quite different matters might require decisions or action by the Four Powers."

Lord Halifax declared that, although instructions from his government were very explicit on this point and he was firmly bound by them, he was so much impressed with the Soviet Ambassador's reference to "the influence which this pattern might have on future decisions regarding other matters," that he would be glad to refer once more to his government on this point.

Further discussion of the Soviet suggestions disclosed that the representative of China alone was still opposing the idea of the rule of unanimity which was to be adopted instead of the democratic majority voting rule. Mr. Acheson then declared his support of the Soviet suggestion, while Lord Halifax did not appear to oppose it.

Opening the next meeting on February 17, Mr. Acheson presented a memorandum dated February 9 from the Canadian

Legation, the substance of which was the request of Canada to be represented on the Committee of UNRRA—a rather natural request in view of the fact that Canada was to become one of the main countries supplying relief.

I should mention that none of the British Dominions had been asked to take part in the working out of the UNRRA statute. It was explained to me at the time in a "hush-hush" way that this decision had been reluctantly taken, especially as regarded Canada, for two reasons: The first was that the Soviets had set their minds on excluding all other United Nations except the Big Four from participation on the most important Policy Committee; the second, that if Canada and the other British Dominions were admitted, it would be difficult to exclude European and Latin-American countries from participation. Some of them had already been asking insistently to be admitted, and Soviet Russia, supported by the United States, discouraged this tendency.

The discussions on February 19 disclosed for the first time that Ambassador Litvinov had been instructed by Moscow to say that his government "was concerned regarding the governments which would be members of the proposed UNRRA," and he added very definitely that in this case "his government's concern extended beyond its own territories."

The most interesting and enlightening debate, however, took place at this meeting, when suggestions submitted by the British came under consideration. The British Government stuck to its proposal that the membership of the Policy Committee be expanded to seven nations, to include Canada and at least one European ally. Lord Halifax strongly stressed the fact that this extension of the committee should be made. He had reported to London Ambassador Litvinov's fear of the possibility "that a decision in this case might set a pattern for international organization in other spheres," but London had replied that "there was a distinction between relief and political or economic subjects," and that it would be possible to provide for a UNRRA Policy Committee of seven "without prejudicing later decisions in other fields."

Ambassador Litvinov dryly replied that his government was just as insistent on a committee of four and could not alter its views.

The Chinese Ambassador communicated his government's agreement to a policy committee of four, while Mr. Acheson very definitely stated that "although the United States Government recognized that strong arguments could be made in favor of both positions, it considered it best, in view of the difference of opinion, to continue with the plan for a policy committee of four." He said that the importance of Canada to the scheme was recognized, and that the desire of Canada to be a member of the Policy Committee was given considerable weight, but that the United States Government felt that any extension of the membership of the committee would create difficult new problems.

Lord Halifax then inquired whether the question of the membership of the committee could not be left for the general meeting of the United Nations to decide. This arrangement might avoid the possibility of forcing through an agreement which "would be jealously regarded and only grudgingly accepted by many of the smaller nations."

Voicing the so typical Soviet apprehension of any "open forum," Ambassador Litvinov expressed the fear that the conference of the United Nations would not only favor a committee of seven rather than four, but would be led to a considerable extension of the number. He then suggested that Lord Halifax should take this problem before his government again, pointing to the fact of agreement between the Soviet, Chinese, and United States governments on a policy committee composed of four members.

Emphasizing the fact that the leadership of the Four Powers was already widely accepted, Litvinov suddenly inquired what position the British would take in the event that some controversy arose at the proposed general conference. Would the British Government be neutral, or would it expect to take a position for either a committee of four or a committee of seven?

Mr. Noel Hall, Minister at the British Embassy, who by that time had replaced Lord Halifax in the discussion, as the Ambassador had to leave to keep another appointment, reiterated the statement that England could not commit herself to press for a committee of four and that at the general conference she would prefer not to vote against a reasonable proposal for an amendment of the draft providing for a committee of seven, if a substantial majority should support such a proposal.

The next meeting of the three Ambassadors with Mr. Acheson was held on March 24.

The purpose of this meeting was to consider amendments to the draft proposed by the Soviet Government. All present first readily agreed to the restrictive clause suggested by Litvinov, that in Soviet territory the Soviet Government would be free to assume full responsibility for relief and rehabilitation measures.

It was also readily and finally agreed that the Policy Committee should be composed of only four members, as the Soviet Government had demanded. Likewise, the unanimity clause, or veto right, was agreed to. Litvinov's triumph was complete.

There was, however, some lively discussion before accepting the Soviets' next suggestion, providing that of the two deputy directors general proposed for the European region, one should be a Soviet citizen. The remaining deputy director general in that region would be a British subject.

Here Lord Halifax explained the position taken by the British Government favoring the appointment of the administrative personnel of UNRRA purely on a basis of merit and usefulness for given functions, without any reference to nationality. Lord Halifax reminded Litvinov it had been agreed that the responsibility for measures within Soviet territory should be the responsibility of the Soviet Government, and asked why the Soviet Government should be concerned with the appointment of a Soviet director for the entire European region.

In reply, Ambassador Litvinov said that two quite separate questions were involved. The Soviet Government did desire to have full responsibility for the work to be done in the Soviet Union, but it also had a real interest in the measures to be undertaken elsewhere in Europe.

Mr. Acheson curtly expressed the hope that the British Government would be able to accept the Soviet proposal.

A final meeting took place on April 12 at which Mr. Noel Hall, Minister at the British Embassy, Mr. Andrei Gromyko, Counselor of the Soviet Embassy, and Mr. Tswen-ling Tsui, First Secretary of the Chinese Embassy, met with Mr. Acheson and Mr. Roy Veatch of the Department of State.

Mr. Acheson referred to a communication received from the Canadian Government, who had confidentially been shown the text of the draft. The Canadian Government stated that it was "to be understood that Canada's acceptance of these arrangements in the particular case of the relief administration does not indicate any withdrawal from the position the Canadian Government has taken that the Four Power pattern is not in principle an acceptable form of international organization, and that representation on international bodies should, whenever possible, be determined on a functional basis, and that the proposed form of the Central (Policy) Committee will not be regarded as a precedent in other connections."

Democratic Canada appeared to be well aware of the danger which the application of the Four Power pattern to international organizations presented. However, its warning proved to be a voice crying in the wilderness. It could no longer stem the tide driven by the insistent demands of the Soviet Union for just such a Power-political world setup.

To me it appeared most characteristic that in these meetings the Soviets at times came up against British views and objections aiming at a more extensive and liberal interpretation of United Nations collaboration. On the other hand, the Soviet demands were steadily supported by Mr. Acheson on behalf of the United States.

After studying the course adopted at these five meetings, I realized that, although the final draft of the proposed statute of the UNRRA would in due course be submitted to my government and to those of all the other United Nations for their approval, it had already been frozen into a final shape by the combined will of the Four Powers. Their draft statute for UNRRA included the "dotted line" upon which the remaining United Nations would have to affix their signatures.

The Power-political pattern, with its despotic veto, had sneaked into the United Nations concept by the back door of the world relief administration.

CHAPTER XXVIII

First Fruits of Moscow and Teheran

EARLY in December 1943 I was delighted to hear from London that the United States Ambassador to Poland, Anthony J. Drexel Biddle, Jr., was on his way to America for a short stay.

Tony Biddle was more than an American Ambassador in the eyes of the Polish people. He was Poland's best friend, the most popular of foreign envoys, beloved for his human qualities, his wonderful spirit, and his charming manners. Tony and his wife Margaret knew everybody in Poland. They were familiar with all of Poland and were most welcome guests in Polish city and country homes.

Tony's sporting instinct appealed particularly to the Polish people. He had a ready smile and a welcome for rich and poor alike, and if that were still possible in a country where America was a magic word which opened every door, Tony and Margaret had certainly succeeded in opening all Polish hearts even wider to the United States.

Apart from their great qualities there was an even more important reason for the loving admiration of the Polish people for the Biddles. Throughout the tragic September and October days in 1939, when the Polish Army and the entire nation fought their desperate struggle against Hitler's might, Tony and Margaret had, with the utmost courage and serenity, faced all the dangers and hardships at the side of the Polish Government, whom they never abandoned, and with whom they ultimately crossed into Rumania, driven there by the German onslaught from the west and the Soviet invasion from the east.

Tony dropped in at the embassy to see me on December 16 and we had a very frank conversation. He admitted that he had chosen this moment to come to Washington to see the President and his friends at the State Department, realizing the gravity and urgency of the situation of Poland. He was deeply concerned and disturbed by the trend of events, and what little he had heard of the results of the Moscow and Teheran conferences had increased his anxiety. He told me that he had seen the President on his arrival in Washington, but had only had a few minutes' conversation and was expecting to have a longer talk with him in the course of the next few days.

He would tell the President very frankly and clearly, he said, that, if the legitimate interests of Poland and his hopes that Poland's sovereignty and territorial integrity would be energetically defended by the President were not to be fulfilled, he could no longer remain in his post as United States Ambassador to the Polish Government. He had for many years been so closely knit with Poland in her good days as in all her difficulties, that he knew he could never face the Polish nation if the cause of Poland were to be abandoned by the United States.

The President had returned very tired from Teheran, and Tony Biddle had to wait longer than he expected before seeing him. When I saw Tony after his conversation with Mr. Roosevelt, he told me the President had assured him that he would not give up the cause of Poland, but had added that he had found Stalin so recalcitrant on this subject that he had had difficulties in pressing the point.

I found Tony evasive concerning his plans, and a few days later I heard that he had asked to be relieved of his functions as Ambassador to Poland.

"I have come to the conclusion," he told me, "that I can be more useful to Poland if I get into uniform and join the American staff as an expert on East European countries. I hope that, as the war develops, American detachments, or at least military missions, will be sent to your country. I will then join them and help in solving Polish problems from the military angle."

His decision depressed me. It proved that Tony Biddle, the honest American, was losing hope that the American Government would press for a just solution of Poland's problems by diplomatic means.

On January 4, 1944, news reached Washington that the victorious Soviet armies had entered Poland on the heels of the retreating German forces.

The Polish nation had been tensely waiting for this moment. As early as October 1943 the Polish Government had issued orders to the Underground to intensify its action against the Germans. These orders were being carried out efficiently, with perfect discipline. But it was urgent to clarify the situation and to explain to the Polish people the attitude they should adopt toward the oncoming Russians. These people had the right to know whether the Soviets were coming as the long-awaited liberators, as friends, or as new invaders. The Soviets had deliberately chosen to leave this burning question unanswered.

I called on Secretary Hull on the same day, having asked him to receive me immediately. I told him that the Polish Government was about to publish a declaration on the occasion of the Soviet entry into Poland which would be conciliatory in tone and once more would suggest to the Soviets the immediate resumption of relations and the co-ordination of the action of our Underground Home Army against the Germans with the Red armies.

The Secretary expressed his hope that this move would be well received by the Soviets. When I asked him to give me more particulars about the Teheran conference in regard to the Soviet-Polish problems, he appeared embarrassed. He repeated what he had already told me after his return from Moscow, that the Soviet position was so much better than that of the Western Allies, as far as the war situation was concerned, that it had been impossible for the President to coerce or threaten Stalin, and he could only try to persuade and request. He assured me that the President had tried to raise the Polish problem "time after time," but had met with no encouragement from Stalin, who gave every indication that he was not prepared to admit any interference on this matter.

The Secretary was of the opinion that the British Government, as an ally of Poland and of Russia, was in a better position to initiate appropriate steps than the American Government. I assured him that Premier Mikolajczyk was in close touch with Mr. Eden and that I felt sure, now that Mr. Churchill was back in England, that the British Government would certainly take some action in view of the urgency of the situation. I added, however, that it was important the American and British governments should act jointly in the case of Poland, so as not to give the impression to the Soviets and to other European nations that America was losing interest in European affairs.

Mr. Hull asked me if I did not think that the Polish nation would be greatly relieved to see the Germans retiring from Poland and whether this might not help to prepare a favorable background for good relations with the Soviets.

I replied that we had laid great hopes on this aspect of Soviet-Polish relations. But, as the Secretary had rightly said in one of our previous conversations, "it was necessary to be on speaking terms" if one wanted to agree. Obviously the Soviets did not appear to share this view, as they persisted in their refusal to resume relations, disregarding all the openings we had given them.

I assured the Secretary of State that there was no fear of the Polish people giving up their fight against the Germans. They were eager to continue it. The question did not arise of their giving up the fight. The question was, would the Soviets allow them to go on fighting. It was much more probable that they would try to suppress and disrupt our Underground organization than admit its collaboration. I explained that while the Germans had applied mass reprisals for every act of our Underground, they had never succeeded in penetrating the core of the organization and destroying its foundations and its leaders. Soviet Russia applied different methods. Through infiltration, her agents ferreted out individuals and groups and went to the roots of the organization which she was determined to destroy.

There were signs pointing to the fact that, through the destruction of the Underground, the Soviets would pave the way to ultimate domination of Poland by imported puppet rulers.

The Secretary appeared to be impressed by this argument, which he said he had not realized. His very human instincts were evidently disturbed by the trend of the Soviet-Polish situation, but he was obviously helpless to do anything about it.

The Polish Government's declaration of January 5 was simple and dignified in tone. It offered the collaboration of the Polish Underground Home Army to the Soviets and emphasized the importance of friendly relations between the two neighboring countries. It was a clearly worded proposal to renew relations in the name of good neighborliness and in the interests of the fight against the common enemy.

The Polish Government had once more stretched out its hand in friendship to Soviet Russia.

On January 11 came the brutal answer. The Soviets stated that "the exiled Polish Government," as they called it, had made "an erroneous affirmation concerning the Soviet-Polish frontier," because ". . . as is known, the Soviet constitution established a Soviet-Polish frontier corresponding with the desires of the population of western Ukraine and western White Russia. . . . The territories . . . were incorporated into Soviet Russia."

The Moscow answer further lauded the Soviet-sponsored Union of Polish Patriots, clearly indicating what was in store.

On January 15 the Polish Government officially asked the British and American governments for mediation ". . . with a view to securing . . . the discussion by the Polish and Soviet governments . . . of all outstanding questions, the settlement of which should lead to friendly and permanent co-operation between Poland and the Soviet Union."

The Soviets replied in a statement of January 17 that ". . . as regards the Polish Government's proposal for the opening of official negotiations between it and the Soviet Government, the Soviet Government is of the opinion that this proposal aims at misleading public opinion, for it is easy to understand that the Soviet Government is not in a position to enter into official negotiations with a government with which diplomatic relations have been severed."

On January 26 Moscow officially rejected an offer of the United States Government to mediate in Polish-Russian conversations, asserting that "the conditions have not yet ripened to a point where such good offices could be utilized to advantage."

Nevertheless, the Polish Government decided to confirm its orders to the Underground Home Army to co-operate with the Red Army in the fight against the Germans, without any reservations whatsoever.

In its declarations the Polish Government had given a supreme proof of Allied loyalty and of patient perseverance in pursuing good-neighbor relations with Russia. In its only condition it expressed its adherence to the principles of legality and to those of the Atlantic Charter.

In their two answers the Soviets openly stated their annexationist designs on Poland, making it quite clear that good relations with the Polish Government depended on Poland's acceptance of accomplished facts by which her independence and sovereignty would virtually be wiped out.

The world was faced with a situation unilaterally created by the USSR and bound to become a dangerous precedent in the future. It happened within a month after the first full-dress Big Three meeting at Teheran, which was still being sold to the American people as a triumph of President Roosevelt's statesmanship.

CHAPTER XXIX

Marking Time in Washington

In the atmosphere of silence inspired by the OWI on all Soviet-Polish matters, the publication of excerpts from the Polish and Soviet declarations suddenly revealed to public opinion the existence of an acute Soviet-Polish problem.

This revelation coincided with the rising anxiety that, contrary to officially inspired enthusiasm, the Teheran meeting had not been the unqualified success it was made out to be. I frequently heard expressions of criticism of the President for his "secret diplomacy," and suspicions that, behind the curtain drawn around Teheran, secret agreements had been concluded. The approach of the election campaign was making public opinion noticeably more alert and critical.

As frequently happened when I felt the necessity of a frank discussion of matters weighing on my mind, I asked Justice Felix Frankfurter if I could see him. We used to meet often in the course of my mission in Washington, and he was a frequent guest at our embassy, especially at my stag dinners, which, since August 1941, had become almost regular weekly features. We used to call them, jokingly, our debating dinners, because in a restricted circle of six or eight men who mostly belonged to the New Deal group closest to the President, we indulged in heated but very friendly informal debates on all the problems of the hour pertaining to the war, to foreign and internal politics. Ben Cohen, then adviser to James F. Byrnes, War Mobilization chief, Oscar Cox of the Lend-Lease Administration, the rotund and irresistible Edward F. Prichard, Isador Lubin, Archibald Mac-Leish, Assistant Secretary of War Jack McCloy, and a few others were the pillars of these pleasant gatherings at which Justice Frankfurter was the central and most dynamic figure.

On this occasion, on January 18, he asked me to lunch with him in his chambers at the Supreme Court. For nearly two hours we discussed the world situation, with special reference to the Teheran conference.

Having for several years closely followed the evolution of Polish problems, Justice Frankfurter was eager to know the latest developments which preceded and immediately followed the entry of the Soviets into Poland. When I described the situation, he agreed it was very disturbing.

We both knew some of the still generally unknown details of the Teheran meeting and discussed them in the light of the Soviet policy of accomplished facts, which apparently Teheran had not changed. We knew how confident the President had been that he would succeed in influencing Stalin and persuading him to co-ordinate his policies with those of the United States and Great Britain. This had evidently not happened.

We wondered if, after having made so many attempts to meet Stalin before the latter finally consented to do so, the President had not gone to Teheran convinced that he would meet an untractable Eastern autocrat, and possibly had been too easily charmed and too ready to accept at face value Stalin's clever ways of ingratiating himself when he assumed the role of a broad-minded and very human statesman, of a man both sincere and frank, knowing when to flatter and how to disarm the President by making him believe that he was anxious to meet him halfway and, above all, to enter into close and friendly collaboration with him.

We deplored the fact that at the Cairo conference, which preceded the meeting at Teheran, differences of opinion had arisen between the President and Mr. Churchill. Anglo-American unity achieved at the Quebec and Washington talks was impaired. Stalin was undoubtedly aware of it and, we had been told, took advantage of this fact to play one against the other. This had been the case in the discussions on the problem of Turkish neutrality and on several other questions relating to the location of the second front and of unified command.

We agreed that, instead of becoming more active after Teheran, as had been expected, American policy remained passive and still hesitated to make use of the test case of Poland, although it offered such a good opportunity for adopting a firmer tone in dealing with the Soviets, whose growing demands on European countries were becoming dangerously insistent.

I asked Justice Frankfurter to use his influence in pointing out to the President the danger of continuing this passive policy at the time when the Soviets were creating precedents which might entirely change the aims of the United Nations. He promised to do his utmost, in view of the serious situation, but admitted that he was not very hopeful of success.

American policy appeared to him to be going through a dangerous phase, which, under the pretext of a wrongly conceived realism, had made it drift away from American fundamental ideals and principles under the influence of selfish interests of big business and finance.

"There is big business to be done with Russia" was now the slogan which tended to replace the principles of the Atlantic Charter. Frankfurter said that he was disturbed by these trends, the more so because he sensed growing criticism of American policy and of the President spreading among the American people. He deplored the fact that in view of the approaching presidential election internal political considerations were beginning to influence and, at times, to paralyze American foreign policy.

In reviewing the details of the Teheran conference, we came to the conclusion that Stalin had scored on practically all points.

A conversation I had on the succeeding day with Louis Fischer, eminent writer, and one of the leading American experts on Soviet affairs, confirmed the accuracy of Justice Frankfurter's analysis.

I had not seen Louis Fischer for some time and was struck by his deep concern regarding Soviet-Allied relations. He was distinctly pessimistic. Just before our conversation he had discussed the situation with Secretary of State Hull and with some of the President's closest friends at the White House.

He did not believe in the possibility of changing the passive course of American policy toward Soviet Russia, and greatly deplored this fact. He feared that the moment for applying an active policy had been overlooked.

I admitted that I was also beginning to doubt whether, at this time, after having advanced so far in the direction of appeasement, President Roosevelt and Mr. Churchill would still summon the necessary energy to change their policy.

Fischer agreed with me that the elements for pursuing a firm policy still existed and that, given the necessary impulse on the basis of principles and of the democratic aims declared by the United Nations, such a turn could be made. But he drew my attention to the fact that at this stage, when it was so indispensable to show Stalin that his Western partners, Britain and America, were entirely united in purpose and policy, and spoke in one voice in closest understanding, we were witnessing the growth of differences of views between the British and American governments which, unfortunately, were apparent and well known to the Soviet Government.

In his opinion, the President and American official circles had become so personally engaged in pro-Soviet propaganda that it was difficult to imagine how they could "go into reverse" at this time, when internal political considerations were playing such a big part.

This, together with the difficulty of re-creating a fully-united Anglo-American diplomatic front, made him think that no considerable change in the trend of passive policy, which had encouraged Stalin to press his demands, could be expected in the near future.

Fischer did not believe that the President would more actively defend the Polish cause. He would certainly continue to declare his interest in Poland's future and his moral support of its rights, because that could be done in a theoretical way and was, in fact, necessary, in view of the growing apprehensions on the part of Americans of Polish descent, whom the President would naturally want to reassure before the elections.

He feared that, in the present circumstances, the President was getting resigned to the idea that accomplished facts would solve these problems without engaging his personal responsibility, and that he would then be able to accept eventual solutions of the Polish problem, possibly under protest, but in a way which would not directly involve him in any serious controversy with Soviet Russia.

He did not think that Secretary Hull could change this tendency. Mr. Hull had returned from Moscow under the sincere but erroneous impression that he had saved the principles of the Atlantic Charter by not admitting their discussion or their open repudiation.

To Fischer, who knew Soviet mentality so well, it was clear that the Secretary's refusal to discuss matters of principle, or to insist on the case of Poland as the test case of these principles, had been interpreted by Stalin as implied, though perhaps reluctant, agreement to let matters take their course. This was borne out by the Teheran conference.

From my conversations at the Department of State in connection with Premier Mikolajczyk's visit, originally scheduled for January 1944, I noticed a tendency on the part of the President to put it off to a later date.

It was explained to me that the President felt it most important for Premier Mikolajczyk first to clear the whole "Polish-Soviet problem" with Churchill before coming to talk it over with him in Washington.

In Poland, as the Red Army advanced, the Soviets methodically had begun to liquidate our Underground Home Army.

In London, in the wake of the Teheran conference, the Polish Government was being pressed by the British to enter the way of concessions.

Washington was marking time, and, in the words of Louis Fischer, was expecting "self-made solutions" which would not involve American responsibility.

CHAPTER XXX

London Compromises, Washington Hesitates

JANUARY 22, 1944, marked a definite turning point in the British attitude to the Polish-Soviet problem.

Mr. Churchill, assisted by Mr. Eden and Undersecretary Sir Alexander Cadogan, conferred with Premier Mikolajczyk and Foreign Minister Tadeusz Romer on the impression created by the advance of the Red Army into Poland. Considering the situation as very grave and requiring immediate intervention, the British Prime Minister offered to intervene in Moscow and urged the acceptance of the following five points by the Polish Government:

1. The Polish Government to agree to accept the so-called Curzon Line (prolonged through eastern Galicia) as a basis for negotiations with the Soviet Government.

2. The final settlement of the eastern frontier to be linked with the grant to Poland of East Prussia, Danzig, and Upper Silesia to the Oder River.

3. All Poles left on the Soviet side of Poland's eastern frontier would be given the right to return to Poland.

4. All the German population within Poland's new boundaries to be removed from Poland.

5. The solutions as enumerated above would receive the approval and guarantee of the three principal United Nations.

If the Polish Government accepted his plan, Mr. Churchill was ready to cable Premier Stalin, suggesting this solution on his own behalf, and asking the Soviet Government to engage itself to refrain from any further calling in doubt of the Polish Government and any interference in the internal affairs of Poland. He would likewise indicate to Premier Stalin the indispensable necessity of bringing about an understanding between Poland and Russia regarding the co-ordination of military action and the safeguarding of Polish Underground forces fighting in Poland against the Germans.

Churchill's suggestions raised grave doubts in Mikolajczyk's mind. Such an *a priori* acceptance of the Soviet demands would render further negotiations futile. In the form of a surrender to a Russian dictate, it would create a situation highly dangerous to the national unity of the Polish people. At the same time it gave to Poland no effective guarantee that the Soviets would respect her sovereignty, or that the program of her territorial adjustment in the west would be carried out.

Before deciding on his final reply to Churchill's suggestions, Mikolajczyk wanted to consult the Polish Underground authorities in Poland and the United States Government.

I was instructed to communicate immediately Churchill's proposals to President Roosevelt and to ask:

1. Whether the United States Government considered it advisable to enter upon the final settlement of territorial problems in Europe.

2. Whether the United States Government was prepared in principle to participate in bringing about such settlements and to guarantee them.

3. Whether the United States Government regarded it possible to lend its support to Churchill's plan and to its realization.

The President, who had been in bad health, was temporarily absent from Washington. I therefore turned to Secretary Hull, whom I saw on January 27. After stressing how urgent it was for Premier Mikolajczyk to ascertain the views of the President before taking any decision, I asked him to convey immediately the British suggestions and Mikolajczyk's three questions to the President, asking for a speedy reply.

Mr. Hull was anxious to know whether Mikolajczyk, having told Churchill that he was going to sound out the opinion of the Polish nation through our Underground, desired to have the President's answer before or after receiving his reply from Poland.

I told the Secretary that in my opinion it was desirable that the President's answers should be obtained as soon as possible. The opinion of President Roosevelt was of the greatest importance and was, in fact, most urgent. I added that, as General Sikorski, Jan Karski, and I had so frequently pointed out, the President held a unique position in the minds and hearts of the Polish people. He had in the past frequently sent messages of encouragement directly, or through our intermediacy, to Poland, fighting and suffering under the German yoke. The Polish nation had been repeatedly assured that it could count on the President of the United States in its struggle for independence and sovereign rights. That is why I was sure it was important that the President's reply should reach the Polish people without delay, possibly at the same time or immediately after the communication of Mr. Churchill's suggestions, which were being held secret for the time being.

Mr. Hull agreed that this was highly desirable and said that he would submit the case to the President without delay. He asked me then what reply we expected from the President and what would be the attitude of the Polish people to Mr. Churchill's proposal.

I replied I felt convinced that the Polish nation would continue to have full confidence in its legal government. In my opinion, the Polish people would not agree to cede to Russia almost half of Poland as outlined by the Curzon Line. Such a partition would not only deprive Poland of very valuable agricultural land, of Poland's only oil fields, of her best timberland and other natural resources, but it would also deprive her of the ancient bastions of Polish culture and European civilization—Wilno and Lwów. I added that I was sure that the Polish people would expect the President to take these circumstances into consideration in his reply.

The Secretary expressed his understanding of this point of view, but refrained from giving any personal opinion. He told me that after lengthy delay he had just received a reply from Moscow to a joint American and British intervention in behalf of Poland carried out in August 1943. The Soviets had replied that "the Polish problem was not yet ripe for a broader discussion" and, in its very wording, the reply clearly showed that Moscow rejected outside intervention in Soviet-Polish affairs. Mr. Hull admitted that it looked very much like a flat refusal. He asked what I thought the expression "not ripe" applied to the Polish question might mean. I answered that in the Soviet vocabulary it appeared to imply that it would duly become "ripe" when the Soviets had unilaterally finally "solved" it, which would come after they gained more complete military control of Poland.

The Secretary was noncommittal.

On January 31 the President returned to the White House after a ten days' absence and immediately took up the matter of drafting his reply to Premier Mikolajczyk's questions. Mr. Hull lunched at the White House and spent several hours with the President.

On February 2 Jimmy Dunn called me on the telephone and asked me to come around to see him. He explained that Mr. Hull, having to attend another conference, had asked him to see me instead. Dunn then handed me a White House memorandum containing the reply of the President to Mikolajczyk's questions.

I was taken aback when I noted that in this rather briefly worded statement the President had obviously reversed his former attitude. For the first time he stated that, in the case of Poland, his adherence to the American principle of non-recognition of territorial settlements in time of war did not exclude attempts to bring about "amicable settlements between countries."

Clearly suggesting such a settlement, the President offered his "good offices" to the Polish and Soviet governments. Simultaneously he insisted on this settlement being "freely negotiated." Finally, he waived the possibility of an American guarantee for Poland's independence, as suggested by Mr. Churchill.

I did not conceal from Jimmy Dunn that the President's answer appeared to me somewhat equivocal. I drew his attention to what I considered most important; namely, that the President, referring to an understanding between the Soviets and Poland, had used the words "freely to reach a settlement" and that he "would welcome the solution by friendly accord. . . ." That was as far as the President went in lending his support to Poland.

On the other hand, however, the President had clearly indicated he agreed with the idea of having Polish-Soviet relations renewed after the settlement of the territorial controversy. This was a new way of putting the matter as compared to that in which it had always been previously put by the President and Secretary Hull. They had repeatedly urged the necessity of "getting on speaking terms" in order to discuss the outstanding difficulties. Now, however, the President appeared to consider it necessary "freely to reach a settlement" first, or, in Churchill's more direct way of putting it, to make concessions to the Soviets in advance, in order to obtain the resumption of relations.

After having heard so much about the meeting at Teheran, I was not unduly surprised by this change of attitude. It showed that from his conversations with Stalin the President must have gained the conviction that only definite concessions on the part of Poland could induce the Soviet ruler to agree to re-establish relations with the Polish Government.

In further analyzing the President's important reply, I came to the conclusion that Mr. Roosevelt had exercised the greatest caution in wording his statement. He had once more insisted on the continued interest of America in the solution of the Polish problem. On the other hand, however, I understood the President had been anxious to imply that, contrary to Mr. Churchill, who took upon himself the unpleasant duty of pressing Mikolajczyk into submission, Mr. Roosevelt did not wish to assume any such responsibility.

Be that as it may, the Polish Government rightly interpreted the President's answer as a gesture expressing his desire to avoid intervening for the time being in the Soviet-Polish controversy.

I had an additional proof of this cautious American attitude when I was told at the State Department that the visit of Mikolajczyk in Washington, officially scheduled for January, had been indefinitely postponed by the President. Thus, all indications appeared to show that the President did not wish Stalin or Churchill to infer that he was giving support to the Polish Government at this critical moment.

The Underground representation of the Polish people replied to Mikolajczyk's soundings, as was to be foreseen. They unequivocally rejected the suggestion of making territorial concessions to Russia.

The situation of our government became very precarious indeed. British pressure increased with each conversation of our government with British officials. America was clearly avoiding any commitment and standing on the side line. The Polish nation refused to authorize its government to make unjustified concessions to an alleged ally.

It was becoming urgent to take some decision, and my government wished to consult with me directly on these matters.

After I had communicated to London the President's evasive reply, I was requested to come to London for consultations.

I felt that I ought to see the President personally before going. I requested Stettinius to ask the President to receive me, and he transmitted my request immediately to the White House. Two days later he telephoned to say that the President was feeling "unwell" and was "under terrific pressure of work." The President had asked him to tell me that "much as he would like to see me, he could not do so at this time, and sent me his best wishes for a safe journey and a rapid return."

Over the telephone I expressed my deep regret that I could not see President Roosevelt at a time so exceptionally difficult for Poland, and asked Stettinius whether he would not once more ask the President to see me, adding that I was ready to delay my departure if I could hope to be received at the White House.

On the following day Stettinius called me up, asking me to come to the State Department to get the President's answer. When I arrived Stettinius told me that the President had once more looked over his appointments and found that he could not find time to see me in the near future. However, he sent me a polite message which he personally dictated to Stettinius and which ran as follows:

"The President regrets very much that he cannot see the Ambassador at this particular moment before he leaves for London. The President assures the Ambassador that the interest of the American Government in a friendly and satisfactory solution of the present difficulties is deep and abiding, and that this government is doing and will continue to do everything it properly can within the framework of our interests in the larger issues involved. The President adds that the United States has a great and sincere friendship for the Polish people."

I asked Stettinius to thank the President for me and told him that I would leave for London as soon as possible.

I flew to London on a plane of the Air Transport Command.

My first conversations with my old British friends at the Foreign Office gave me the opportunity of verifying my impression that both in Washington and in London the Polish problem had been going through a phase of passing the buck. This situation had previously been expressed by Mr. Hull, when he told me that it was easier for Great Britain, who was officially an ally of Poland, than for the United States, to show more initiative and to adopt a firmer attitude. In London I frequently heard the opinion expressed that surely the strong position of America as chief supplier of Lend-Lease goods should make it easier for Washington to intervene in Moscow than it was for London. Moreover, very often the argument was advanced that America, with some six million Americans of Polish descent, could not long remain passive on the Polish problem.

My arrival in London coincided with another new, decisive development.

Just before my arrival Mr. Churchill suddenly resorted to the method of open pressure upon the Polish Government, in addition to the pressure he had brought to bear in secret diplomatic conversations. On February 22 he delivered his momentous speech in the House of Commons in which he bluntly stated his attitude on the Polish problem. He declared that a compromise on the territorial issue was necessary; that the British Government was pressing for it, and regarded it as indispensable that Poland should make territorial concessions to Soviet Russia.

In this way, openly, Mr. Churchill very definitely broke with his own previously declared principles. Britain was now committed to press the Polish Government to yield to all Soviet demands.

Naturally Mr. Churchill's speech was received as a deadly blow by the Polish people in Poland and abroad, and particularly by our armed forces fighting alongside the British. I was surprised to find how few British statesmen and officials, even among those closely associated with Mr. Churchill, appeared to understand this Polish attitude of disappointment and national tragedy.

I had a curious proof of that lack of understanding for the most elemental human feelings when Brendon Bracken, the British Minister of Information, with whom I lunched in one of the London clubs, asked me candidly to explain why Mr. Churchill's speech had so deeply upset us that several instances of suicide among our army officers were recorded.

I tried to be as diplomatic as possible in my reply. I explained that Mr. Churchill had offered, on his own initiative, to intervene in Moscow on behalf of Poland and that we had understood that he was negotiating our problems with Moscow as the advocate of our just cause. His speech, however, showed that Mr. Churchill had changed the very character of his intervention. He had now openly come out as the advocate of the Soviets, whose demands he was publicly supporting. He was openly pressing Poland, the weaker party, obviously dependent on his protection, and was coercing her into submission to demands supported by a show of force and every kind of ruse.

I am not sure that Brendon Bracken understood my point.

My continuous conferences with the President of Poland and with Mr. Mikolajczyk and the members of his Cabinet revolved around one all-important question: Can we or can we not rely on President Roosevelt's support?

It was my duty to explain the American situation thoroughly and sincerely. Despite the fact, however, that in my explanations I touched upon every angle of the American internal situation, on the consequences of the continuous passivity of Mr. Churchill's policy, and on the additional difficulties encountered in the formation of a united political Anglo-American front, I found it difficult to make my Polish friends understand the President's attitude. The confidence in Mr. Roosevelt and in his word, in his pledges and promises, was too deep-rooted in every Polish heart and mind to be dislodged by reasons of a political nature.

Polish official circles and public opinion regarded Mikolajczyk's delayed visit in Washington as indispensable to clarify the position of the American Government with regard to Poland.

In view of the repeated postponements of this visit, Mr. Mikolajczyk gave me, before I returned to Washington, a long personal letter to Mr. Roosevelt. It was not a document written by a diplomat. Mikolajczyk, the peasant leader of Poland, was not a diplomat. It was a straightforward man-to-man letter, and the thoughts it expressed had the elements of an earthy human statesmanship, compelling through its simplicity.

Here are the most striking paragraphs of Mikolajczyk's letter which I handed to the Department of State on March 25 to be forwarded to the President:

. . . Owing to circumstances I am temporarily unable personally to present to you my views at this time so critical for Poland and, indeed, for the problems of peace . . .

. . . I need hardly stress that the Polish people regard you, Mr. President, and the American people as the trustees of the principles for the triumph of which our United Nations' camp is fighting.

. . . I am fully conscious of the considerations which, for the time being, prevent the United States Government from publicly defining its stand on particular European problems. My urgent desire to pay you a personal visit at this time was not inspired by the intention of appealing to you to do so. . . .

. . . I will not enter into a detailed recapitulation of the course of events relating to the difficulties encountered in our attempts to find a solution of the outstanding differences existing between the Soviet and Polish governments. . . .

. . . The Polish Government sincerely tends to reach an understanding with the Soviet Government which would allow their fullest and most effective joint action against the common enemy, thus forming a solid basis for postwar neighborly collaboration. . . .

. . . I am sure that you will agree that at this time, when the whole future of mankind is involved, it is imperative to face reality in a spirit of sincerity and truth on which alone the future of international relations and durable peace can be founded.

. . . I am firmly convinced that Nazi totalitarianism and its drive for world mastery shall be destroyed. But will not Poland, and later Europe, be overwhelmed against their will by a new wave of communist totalitarianism? Can the nations condemned to the rule of such a new totalitarianism agree to accept its tyranny?

Never, as far as Poland is concerned.

The masses of Polish small farmers, anxious to build their prosperity not in collective farms but in individual farmsteads, will never agree to it. . . .

. . . The present war has proved that wars cannot be localized. The development of technical means of total war makes it impossible, even for the strongest Power, to win a world war single-handed. Collaboration of all of us is indispensable if autarchic systems are to disappear and nationalisms are to be reduced. Political and economic collaboration must be closer than before to bring about the establishment of the future world order. That is why the co-ordination of the policy of the Great Powers and their collaboration with the smaller Powers already in the course of the war is so important to the future peace.

. . . The responsibility of the Great Powers will be ever greater inasmuch as they will be called upon to safeguard, apart from their own security, that of smaller nations, their freedom and especially the freedom of the individual throughout the world.

To achieve this aim it appears to me essential to realize the full truth of the existing situation.

Unfortunately public opinion is frequently being led to accept entirely false views on Europe, and particularly on Poland.

I fully share the admiration inspired by the heroism of Soviet soldiers fighting in the defense of their country against the German invader. I also appreciate the realism of Marshal Stalin whose word can limit the political aims of world communism.

I am afraid, however, that public opinion may be bitterly disappointed should it discover that the widely publicized social changes and the alleged democratization of the Soviet Union are in fact but a combination of old Russian imperialism with communist totalitarianism which has not abandoned its former ambition for world rule.

Therefore it appears to me wrong to lead public opinion to believe that democracy exists where in reality it does not and cannot exist for a long time, as this is fraught with the danger of causing deep disillusionment and even unhappiness in nations who may be subjected to a rule which, while recognizing the freedom of the State, denies that of the individual.

It may also create disillusionment in business circles which expect freedom of trade relations in the future. The deepest disappointment, however, will be that of the working classes now rightly impressed by the fighting valor of the Soviet people but misled to believe that labor's greatest aspirations and democratic ideals have been achieved in the Soviet Union.

I regard the maintenance of Allied solidarity as essential and imperative in our common fight.

I therefore observe with profound misgiving the activity of German propaganda, hitherto completely disbelieved, which now succeeds in rebuilding the German morale—shattered by military defeats—by attempting to prove that the Allies are aiming at a compromise which would open the door of Europe to communism.

It is difficult to estimate how far the declared Soviet intentions toward Poland and the Baltic countries have already influenced the attitude of Turkey and Finland—thus affecting directly military operations. It is likewise difficult to say what consequences it may cause in European countries under German occupation.

One thing is certain—Nazi-occupied Europe was decidedly anti-German and the hope of its rapid regeneration after its liberation was justified. The activities of communist agencies brought about disunity and fear of chaos, for these agencies have endeavored in every country to achieve supremacy, less for the purpose of strengthening the struggle against the Germans, than for that of establishing communism in the countries concerned.

The concealment of truth on which this situation is based is more detrimental to the Polish nation than to others. Once more I must stress that I am most anxious to preserve Allied unity. History will reveal how, in spite of violent criticisms of the Polish opposition at home and abroad, General Sikorski's and my own Cabinet have refrained from publishing the true facts which would have enlightened public opinion regarding Poland's situation and the methods used by Russia in her dealings, and her intentions as regards my country. We have refrained from publishing such facts, although this is clearly against our interests, because we were anxious to reach an understanding with the USSR and to safeguard the unity of the Allies. Our reticence is, however, exploited by Russia, thus placing us in an intolerable position. Thus, the Polish Government, responsible for the welfare of our country, is deprived of the elementary right of defense *of its national interests and the right of the weaker to appeal for help to the stronger, in the name of the principles and ideals enunciated by you, Mr. President, in the Atlantic Charter, the Four Freedoms, and many other statements which have won the respect and approval of the entire world. . . .*

. . . The accusation that the Polish Government is undemocratic, when in reality it is composed of men who by their origins and by their lifelong struggle for democracy have proved their sincere attachment to democratic ideals, is slanderous. It is a serious wrong to insult that Government which enjoys the confidence of its nation and is its expression, merely because it refuses to countenance the cession of eleven millions of its citizens to a country where individual freedom is unknown. Nor can one blame it for refusing to hand over half of its national territory, to agree to the transfer from eastern Poland of at least five million Poles, in exchange for the transfer of millions of Germans, or because it apprehends the prospect of a turning tide which within fifty years or so, in accordance with the changing European political situation, may once more cause the shifting of populations on its territory.

It is the greatest insult to accuse the Polish soldiers, who have fought since 1939 in Poland, France, Norway, Africa, and Italy —in the Battle of Britain in the air, and on the Seven Seas—of a lack of fighting spirit. While American and British soldiers are rightly promised employment and better conditions after their return home, the Polish soldiers, airmen, and sailors, who come from eastern Poland, are told that they may never be allowed to return to their homes and their families.

Mr. President, the Polish people . . . cannot understand why its great sacrifices appear to have been forgotten. It does not claim payment or reward, but only justice. It still believes that the rights of the weak will be respected by the powerful.

The Polish nation cannot understand why, in the fifth year of war, it does not receive sufficient armament and supplies for its underground struggle, at a time when Allied mass production of aircraft and weapons has reached a wonderful peak, and the contribution of the Polish Underground Army can be of considerable importance. Poland needs these weapons for its final struggle against the Germans. . . .

. . . In fact the supply of equipment for the Polish Underground Army has been virtually stopped since the autumn of 1943. . . .

Mr. President, your name is revered by every Pole. The Polish nation looks upon you as the champion of the principles which you have proclaimed with such deep faith and conviction, presenting to mankind a vision of human freedom in a better world.

Our people fighting in Poland's Underground Army have lost everything. They lay no value on life. They may not reckon sufficiently with realism, while being threatened with the loss of their last hope of freedom and by the prospect of another enslavement. They have faith in you, Mr. President. I am convinced that their faith will be justified.

At the present moment the situation in Poland can be summed up as follows: As far as the attachment to principles is concerned the Polish nation is united and unfaltering.

Its attitude toward the war is expressed in the following points:

1. *Poland is determined to carry on to the end the struggle against the Germans and asks for adequate supplies of arms and equipment for that purpose.*
2. *The Polish people decided, in full agreement with the Polish Government and on its instructions, that our Underground Army will come out into the open and offer its collaboration against the Germans to the Soviet armed forces as they enter Poland, even if diplomatic relations between the Polish and Russian governments are not resumed. The Polish Underground took this decision although it is aware of the dangers resulting from disclosing its organization to the Soviets.*

I hope that you will kindly forgive this very frank and long letter at this tragic moment for my country. On behalf of the Polish nation and government I appeal to you, Mr. President, to do all in your power to prevent the creation in Poland of accomplished facts; to safeguard the sovereign rights of the Polish State and of its lawful authorities; to insure the respect and safety of the lives and property of Polish citizens; to safeguard the Polish Underground Army and administration from the dangers that threaten them after their disclosure to the Soviet forces.

I am convinced that in your great wisdom and statesmanship, and realizing that the case of Poland has a direct bearing on the future peace, you will find the best way to give support to her just cause. . . .

On April 5 I was given by the State Department the following rather surprisingly short reply of the President to Mikolajczyk:

April 3, 1944.

My dear Mr. Prime Minister:

I have read with interest your letter of March 18 which was delivered to Ambassador Ciechanowski, and I wish to thank you for your courtesy in explaining in such a frank manner your position and that of your colleagues on various problems confronting your Cabinet at this time.

In regard to your desire to come to Washington in order that we might discuss these various problems in person which you referred to in your letter and which your Ambassador reiterated to the Secretary of State, I feel that a useful purpose would be served by such discussions. As you have undoubtedly heard, however, I have been suffering from a slight case of bronchitis and my doctors impressed upon me the desirability of taking a rather extended rest. I purpose, therefore, to leave Washington shortly for a few weeks' rest. I have, moreover, already made plans for a visit by Prime Minister Curtin at the end of this month.

Under the circumstances I regret that I shall not be able to receive you sooner than the early part of May. I hope you will be free to come at that time, and I will let you know as soon as I possibly can the exact date I will be free to see you.

Very sincerely yours,
(*Signed*) Franklin D. Roosevelt.

CHAPTER XXXI

D-Day and Politics

In the spring of 1944 Washington tensely awaited the pending Allied invasion of Europe. The rapid advance of the Red armies in their offensive against Hitler's retreating forces was making it increasingly urgent for the Western Allies to put the final touches on that gigantic military enterprise.

In diplomatic circles we lived in an atmosphere of anxious expectancy created by the question: Would the Soviets reach Berlin before the American and British forces, or would the balance be restored in time by the Western offensive, so long awaited and so carefully being prepared?

Alongside of military preparations, work had also started at the State Department in preparation for the establishment of a future international organization for peace and security destined to replace the League of Nations.

The thin veil of secrecy which surrounded these labors, personally conducted by Secretary of State Hull, did not prevent diplomatic circles from following its evolution.

In conversations with State Department officials and among ourselves in the diplomatic corps we expressed regret that this most important work of setting up the framework of a bigger and better League of Nations, which we had hoped would be in line with the United Nations concept, was clearly tending to adopt a pattern of Power-political domination.

We called it following the line of least resistance inspired by the subconscious anxiety that Russia might still break away from her allies and elect to play a lone hand in the postwar world. These considerations seemed to impair the natural instinct to reassert American principles of freedom, justice, and equality in framing the New World's security charter.

American foreign policy continued to be passive. It appeared to me to be a result of the fact that American war successes were still only intermittent and inspired the American Government to be timid and to adopt a policy of "wait and see."

At that time, when so many important decisions were shaping in the military field and in the preparation for the alignment of the United Nations in a future system of peace and security, I realized that the absence of more direct leadership on the part of President Roosevelt was making itself felt. The President was frequently absent from Washington. I knew that after the Teheran conference, when criticism of his so-called "personal diplomacy" began to spread, he had entrusted the actual conduct of foreign affairs more completely to Secretary Hull. The internal political situation was daily becoming more tense as the date of the elections approached. Close friends of the President used to say that he was anxious to avail himself of Mr. Hull's influence in the Senate and the House to prove to public opinion that the conduct of foreign relations was, in fact, in the hands of the competent Department.

Harry Hopkins's illness and his prolonged absence from Washington fitted into this picture, and contributed to strengthen the impression that "personal diplomacy" had, for the time being at least, been abandoned. On the other hand, I was told that the President, accustomed to discuss practically all matters with Harry Hopkins, was impatiently awaiting his return.

The coolness which, since Teheran, characterized Roosevelt-Churchill relations continued to prevail. Friends of the President explained that it was owing less to differences of opinion on specific matters of conduct and strategy of the war or on specific European problems, than to personal reasons.

In his "political year," as 1944 was being termed, and in view of the approaching European invasion, the President was avoiding enunciations and declarations on world problems. Mr. Churchill, however, pressed by British parliamentary and public opinion, had no such reasons for keeping silent. His speech of May 24 in the House of Commons was a comprehensive program which caused American political and press circles to try to ascertain how the President and the American Government reacted to Mr. Churchill's bold plans. On May 30, at his press conference, the President, in reply to questions, dissociated himself from Mr. Churchill's friendly reference to Spain. He did so courteously, but very definitely.

As usual before elections, criticism of the President and of the Administration was on the rise and, for a time, it took the shape of pressing for a firmer policy toward Russia. On the occasion of Poland's Independence Day, on May 3, one hundred and forty-seven speeches were delivered in Congress in praise of Poland, mostly stressing the necessity of justice to Poland and criticizing Soviet expansion. An important organization of Americans of Polish descent, embracing almost the entire group of six million American Poles, was organized in May under the leadership of Charles Rozmarek, the dynamic chairman of the Polish National Alliance, and incorporated under the name of Polish American Congress, as a permanent organization for the defense of principles and their application to American policy.

I observed that the White House and the American Government were becoming increasingly sensitive to these proofs of the awakening of public opinion to the realities of an explosive international situation which had been concealed from the American people.

Another development aroused my attention; namely, the sudden appearance in political circles and in some sections of public opinion of a movement of sympathy for the Germans. I traced it to two reasons. As victory was becoming more and more certain, the natural sporting instinct of the American people was beginning to reassert itself. I had always found it difficult to persuade my American friends and American audiences of German inhumanity and barbarism in the war. The American people had for a long time nourished a friendly admiration for the Germans, for their literature and music, for their efficiency and thoroughness. They were reluctant to accept the idea that the German population was entirely Nazified, cruel, ruthless, barbaric.

There were other reasons why this sudden reaction of sympathy for Germany became more pronounced and more evident. The elections were approaching. The numerically strong and well-organized group of Americans of German descent constituted an influential body in the electorate.

This fact was openly admitted by American politicians. On one occasion, in May, I met a prominent senator at lunch and we discussed Hitlerism and Germany.

His arguments struck me as distinctly pro-German. According to him, Germany should not be destroyed or broken up. There were more good Germans than bad Germans. The Germans were not the only people guilty of atrocities and barbaric acts. All other nations, he said, had committed such acts in times of war.

The senator was opposed to any form of summary justice being applied to the Germans. That matter, he contended, should be put off and dealt with, after a cooling-off period, by American judges and American juries. He went even further, saying that it would certainly be necessary to resort to occupation of Germany, especially in order to defend the Germans from the vengeance of such peoples as the Czechoslovaks and the Poles, who resented German occupation during the war.

In some American circles, especially outside Washington, pro-German sympathy was growing because of increasing fear of Russia and of communism. The idea was spreading that Germany, after having been purged of Nazism, might be used as a convenient barrier against Soviet expansion.

The feeling of apprehension inspired by Soviet Russia's ever-growing demands ran parallel to the process which Constantine Brown had defined as "debunking Teheran." It was also heightened by the rumors that a security system was being prepared in the form of a United Nations organization in which the Big Three Powers would wield virtual dictatorship. In the last days of May indiscretions appeared in the press, giving a tentative outline of this organization. As Stettinius told me, it was an outline unauthorized by the State Department and "very different" from the actual plans then under discussion in the committee of senators and high-ranking officials set up by Mr. Hull to work out the tentative draft. I noticed that Mr. Hull was greatly irritated by these "untimely comments" and when, on June 1, the press published a statement of the Dutch Foreign Minister, van Kleffens, defending in a significant way democratic principles in a future world-security organization, the Secretary of State, in an off-the-record press conference, gave vent to his annoyance, and attacked foreign and American critics who had no idea of real democracy but were trying to teach him democratic principles and criticizing matters they knew nothing about.

Some of my European colleagues in the diplomatic corps were greatly concerned about their countries.

From the representative of de Gaulle's France, Minister Hoppenot, who called on me shortly after my return from London, I learned how anxious he was about the continuous reluctance of the American Government to follow Mr. Churchill's advice of granting recognition to the de Gaulle Committee at this advanced stage of the war, although the invasion of France by the Western Allies was pending. He confirmed what I had heard in London, that this attitude on the part of America was pushing France into the arms of Soviet Russia.

From Constantin Fotitch, the eminent Ambassador of Yugoslavia, I learned that he was worried by the increasing signs that the Western Powers were changing their policy of support of the legal Yugoslav Government, and appeared to be on the verge of giving support to the communist adventurer, Tito. Fotitch deplored the British pressure on King Peter and his government and the British tendency to give active support to the communist organizations of Tito, abandoning General Draja Mikhailovitch and his valiant resistance forces.

My Greek colleague was also anxious about the difficult situation of his country, and particularly disturbed by the reported decision of the President to give part of the Italian Navy to the Soviets.

From all my contacts with American political and press circles I was gaining the impression that in this pre-invasion period American policy had reached a stalemate. Uneasiness was growing. The President had been almost inaccessible in the course of many weeks. He was in poor health and greatly overworked. He was seldom in Washington, and it was up to the Secretary of State to bear the brunt of more and more searching questions concerning the Teheran conference. But, as one of the senators put it, he either did not wish to discuss the conference, or did not know the details of the President's discussions with Stalin.

Secretary Hull did not conceal from me his own uneasiness. He complained he was in a difficult situation. The President was sick. He would return to Washington unexpectedly, but would leave again soon and would attend only to current matters, having little time for problems of foreign policy.

According to Mr. Hull, the pre-election atmosphere was already very evident. Senators and congressmen were pressing him for explanations on the Polish situation. He did his best to reassure them, as he tried to reassure me, that the American Government was not prepared to abandon the Atlantic Charter, but considered that for tactical reasons it was not yet possible to stress its principles to the Soviets, who were still in an exceptionally advantageous position so far as the war was concerned. He told me there was no reason for the Polish nation to get the impression that America was giving up any of her principles or withdrawing her support of Poland's just cause.

I asked the Secretary how he could interpret the reply he had recently given to the press when reporters asked him for some statement concerning European territorial matters. He had been reported as having said that those were "microscopic matters" which could not be taken into account for the time being.

Mr. Hull explained he had been misinterpreted by the press. He had merely meant that these matters, as compared to the enormous problems of the war, appeared microscopic and had to be temporarily shelved. But he seemed disturbed and embarrassed by the fact that, as he put it, "the general situation was not yet sufficiently favorable to allow of more energetic American action."

In the beginning of June, it looked as though the American political scene was undergoing a phase of near crisis in foreign and domestic affairs. In an atmosphere of uneasiness regarding the future part which the United States would be called upon to play in world affairs, the lack of any constructive and active policy was now generally felt, and the desire to see the United States snap out of its role of "playing second fiddle to Stalin and Churchill" was becoming at times very vocal.

These instinctive reactions on the part of the American electorate at the start of the election campaign were vigorously combated by the radical New Dealers and the leftists of the CIO, organized in the PAC, powerfully backed by some representatives of big business, who had definitely become the enthusiastic supporters of Soviet Russia at any price and under any circumstances, in view of the alluring prospects of "doing business with Russia." These groups were strongly supported by the so-called "Palace Guard" around the White House. It surrounded President Roosevelt as a sort of political bodyguard, analyzing every move of American policy from the angle of its possible influence on the President's election.

I kept in touch with some of them and was able to follow their activities. They used to tell me bluntly that "this was no time for the President to modify his policy toward Russia." According to them, that policy had helped him to obtain the support of leftist elements and of the powerful labor unions. They used to point to big-business circles which, as they said, had willingly "gone along" on that very policy, had become firm supporters of the President, and would help re-elect him, while the "idealists and dreamers" had little to offer in that line.

The shortsighted crudeness of these sayings made you realize that these cynical politicians did not think in broader terms of American leadership in world affairs. It seemed that their vision embraced only the electoral arena upon which it was essential, above all, to assure the re-election of President Roosevelt and their own survival. They used to tell me that "the time for other matters would come later."

In this atmosphere of political maneuvering and lobbying, of high hopes on the eve of D-Day, when American, British, and Canadian troops, supported by thousands of ships and planes, were just about to land in northern France, Premier Mikolajczyk arrived in Washington as the guest of President Roosevelt, and was ceremoniously received and installed at Blair House by Ed Stettinius, surrounded by other high officials of the Department of State.

Stettinius was then Acting Secretary in the temporary absence of Mr. Hull. He appeared to have become the President's favorite liaison officer with the Department of State and, as I had occasion to notice during Mikolajczyk's stay in Washington, the relationship between the President and Stettinius had grown very close, friendly, and informal.

From the moment of his arrival on June 5, up to his departure on June 14, Mr. Mikolajczyk was surrounded by constant proofs of most friendly hospitality and of the greatest readiness to facilitate his personal contacts with the President.

Mikolajczyk arrived literally on the eve of D-Day, when the entire American Government was wholly concentrated on this momentous event and the President was under the greatest pressure of work. And yet, during those nine days, Mikolajczyk had four long talks with the President. His contact with Stettinius was practically uninterrupted. They saw each other daily, and sometimes several times a day, either at the State Department or at Blair House, where Stettinius would drop in from the State Department whenever Mikolajczyk expressed the wish to see him in order to follow up his conversations with the President.

CHAPTER XXXII

Red Carpet for Mikolajczyk, June 1944

MIKOLAJCZYK'S first conversation with President Roosevelt took place at noon on June 7. Stettinius had warned us that the President's health was still poor and that on account of D-Day he was especially busy and would probably see us for only a brief moment.

The President, however, appeared to be in the highest spirits and the conversation lasted an hour and a half. It was quite evident that the President was out to create a very friendly atmosphere. He greeted Mikolajczyk, whom he had seen only once before in 1941 on his visit as the vice-chairman of the Polish National Council, as if he had known him for years. He excused himself for having so long delayed the visit and, turning to me, he added that he hoped that he had not "worn out" my patience or discouraged me too greatly by doing so. He added that only pressure of work and doctors' orders had prevented him from seeing Mikolajczyk earlier. But there were so many things regarding Poland which he wanted to discuss, that he was extremely glad the Prime Minister could come and hoped they could have several comprehensive conversations which perhaps might help to solve the problems which he "had followed with the greatest attention and with some concern." He said that "he was optimistic regarding the final settlement of Polish problems" and fully convinced that "Poland would again arise strong and independent."

The President, as was his custom when in good spirits, kept the ball rolling and obviously wanted to do the talking in his easy and charming way, punctuating the conversation by questions.

He launched immediately into a vivid description of his impressions of Stalin at Teheran. He said that Stalin had impressed him "as a realist who was neither an imperialist nor a communist." He realized that he was "very deft."

Here the President turned to me and said that the French word *adroit* best expressed his meaning, but that he had realized that Stalin's was a very specific mentality. He found him very suspicious, but this did not prevent him from appreciating a good joke. He certainly had a sense of humor, the President added.

He admitted Stalin was not easy to confer with, because when he did not want to be drawn into a discussion on any particular problem "he simply let the matter drop." He went on to say that he had been interested and at times amused by the attitude of the people surrounding Stalin, who never appeared to take their eyes off him and were attentive to his every gesture, every smile, or frown.

Then, with a note of playful irony, the President said that personally he had found no difficulty in adapting himself to Stalin's moods, and that he was pleased to say he appeared more readily to understand his specific sense of humor than "my poor friend Churchill," who did not seem to have much affinity with the Soviet dictator's personality.

As an example the President, with visible relish, related an incident of the conference. When Stalin suddenly proposed a toast to the death of at least 50,000 German officers, the President said he immediately understood that Stalin meant German Junker militarists. But Churchill failed to grasp the jocular tone of Stalin's toast. He answered testily that he could not drink such a toast "because Great Britain could never admit the killing of war prisoners." Stalin was visibly displeased. He gave Mr. Churchill what the President called "a dirty look," and the atmosphere between the British Prime Minister and Stalin became icy. The President laughed heartily, saying that he saved the situation by suggesting "an amendment to Stalin's toast," and proposed a revised one "to the death in battle of forty-nine and a half thousand German officers."

The President said he was much amused when, during the Teheran conference, several incidents of this kind showed him the psychological difference between the Eastern chief, Stalin, and the "Victorian statesman, Churchill, who had kept a nine-teenth-century British mentality."

Mr. Roosevelt then switched to his talks on Poland with Stalin at Teheran and pointed out that neither he nor Stalin had referred to the Curzon Line as a final frontier between Poland and Soviet Russia. It was Churchill who brought up this subject and, the President added that, naturally, Stalin took full advantage of the opening.

As regarded the present phase of the Soviet-Polish conflict, the President had heard from Stettinius that Mikolajczyk thought there might be some signs of improvement and he said he also had the impression that, now that the Red Army was in Poland, Stalin would be more inclined to make some gesture, especially if he noticed he could not easily "get on with the Poles" without going through the Polish Government. This might help to find a way out of the difficulty.

The President admitted, however, that he did not yet see the best method to adopt. He referred to 1933, when he finally agreed to recognize the Soviet Government and to enter into normal diplomatic relations with Russia. He said that at that time he took the decision, although it was greatly opposed by a big section of American public opinion. He did so because he was sure that it was the right thing to do. Since then he had constantly applied to the Soviets a policy calculated to show them that he trusted their pledges and promises.

"But with the Russians I always keep my fingers crossed," added the President with a smile, crossing his fingers on both hands and holding them up for Mikolajczyk to see.

The President said he thought that it was indispensable for Poland to reach understanding with the Soviets. Without such an understanding "they would continue to create accomplished facts.

"When a thing becomes unavoidable, one should adapt oneself to it," he said, and he asked Mikolajczyk what he thought of this theory.

When Mikolajczyk reminded the President that the Soviets had placed, as a condition of understanding, demands irreconcilable with the idea of Poland's independence and sovereignty, the President said he was aware of this fact, but that we must remember "there are five times more Russians than Poles," and that Russia was "a neighboring Power which could swallow up Poland if she could not reach an understanding on her terms." He said he could not believe Russia wanted to destroy Poland and, moreover, he knew how difficult it would be to do so, even for Russia. Stalin knew that the United States Government and American opinion would be very much opposed to such a solution. But, the President thought, some concessions were necessary in order to achieve the aim which he knew Premier Mikolajczyk and the Polish Government so much desired; namely, to reach understanding and establish collaboration with Russia.

To Mikolajczyk's question as to whether the President thought it possible to agree to considerable territorial concessions and to Soviet interference in Poland's internal affairs, which included even the choice of members of its government, the President answered that he thought one should certainly try to avoid any final settlement of territorial matters, but, so far as the composition of the Polish Government was concerned, he thought "it might be advisable to find some way of making changes in the personnel of the government if this were to lead to understanding with the Soviets."

He then added that he thought it would be well if Mikolajczyk could get into personal conversation with Stalin or, at least, with Molotov. What did Mikolajczyk think of this suggestion?

Mikolajczyk replied that he had been thinking of it, but he realized the difficulty of getting Stalin to agree to such conversations, and he added that without the President's support he felt sure Stalin would insist on his acceptance of the conditions placed by the Soviets as a preliminary to any negotiations.

The President turned to Mikolajczyk, as if he were taking him into his confidence, and said that "as a politician" Mikolajczyk would understand that for the time being, in this the President's "political year," he could not officially start a new intervention with Stalin on the Polish problem or propose mediation on his part.

But while he could not be a "mediator" in the official sense of the word, he would very much like to play the part of a "moderator" in the Soviet-Polish conflict. He explained that in the Presbyterian Church a moderator was neither priest nor bishop, but one who "interpreted ideas and views and facilitated understanding."

He then asked Mikolajczyk once more to give him the details on the latest developments of the Soviet-Polish situation. He was especially interested when Mikolajczyk told him about soundings started by Soviet emissaries, which had preceded his departure from London, and amused to hear that, on the eve of Mikolajczyk's departure, President Beneš had again suddenly come into the picture as intermediary to communicate to the Polish Premier that he had been asked by Moscow to tell him that the Soviets would be willing to open "informal discussions" which might lead to an understanding with the Polish Government, but insisted on the acceptance of two preliminary conditions: one, that the Curzon Line be accepted as the basis of the final Soviet-Polish frontier; two, that the Polish Government be reconstituted and certain personalities, including the President of the Polish Republic, be eliminated. These, added Mikolajczyk, were conditions which even the Soviet intermediary, with whom he had previously spoken, had not ventured to mention to Mikolajczyk.

The conversation drew to an end. In saying good-by the President very graciously reminded Mikolajczyk of his invitation to a dinner which he was giving at the White House in his honor that same evening. He then complimented him on his fluent English.

The dinner at the White House was a full-dress affair, to which the President and Mrs. Roosevelt had invited about fifty persons.

Mrs. Roosevelt, Mrs. Boettiger, the President's daughter, Madam Perkins, Secretary of Labor, and Dorothy Thompson were the four ladies in the party.

General Marshall and General Arnold attended, though they were to fly that same night to the European front where the two-day-old invasion was making rapid progress. An atmosphere of most hospitable friendliness prevailed, notwithstanding the formality of the occasion. The Cabinet was fully represented. Secretaries Ickes, Morgenthau, Stimson, Francis Biddle, James F. Byrnes, Stettinius, and others were present.

The President was in the best of spirits and, as we sat down, called over the table to Mikolajczyk, who was sitting on the right hand of Mrs. Roosevelt, that this was a great occasion because he had just received encouraging news from the Normandy front and was so glad to have with him on this day "the head of the government of Poland, which was fighting so splendidly against the common enemy."

As usual on such occasions, in the course of the dinner the President raised his glass to propose the health of his guest. But on this occasion President Roosevelt departed from the customary protocol and, instead of saying only a few perfunctory words of greeting to his guest, he made a remarkable fifteen-minute impromptu speech, in which, in most brilliant form, he spoke of Poland, with references to her long history, to her precarious geographical situation, to her great mission as the bulwark of Christianity and Western civilization. He spoke of the partitions of Poland in the eighteenth century, of "the injustice of these shameful acts of imperialism" which had been righted after World War I, of the present "indomitable fight" of the Polish nation, of the achievements of the Polish Army, Navy, and Air Force in this war, of Poland's allied loyalty, and of the necessity of insuring Poland's full independence in a future peaceful world.

It was indeed a magnificent speech in which the President said that, knowing history and geography, he wanted all his guests to know and understand more fully "the greatness of the nation" which Premier Mikolajczyk represented. When the President finished speaking we all felt that this man, so frail in health and so engrossed in the conduct of the greatest war in history, had made a point of going out of his way to express his deep understanding and sympathy for Poland.

Mikolajczyk was deeply moved by this unexpected tribute to Poland. He leaned over and asked me whether I thought he should just thank the President, or whether he could say a few words in response. I urged him, and Mrs. Roosevelt also asked him to say whatever he felt he wished to say, because it would be appropriate to do so after the President's speech.

I must admit that I felt proud of Mikolajczyk when I heard the tactful way in which he rose to the occasion. In very good English, very simply, he thanked the President for his kindness and hospitality. He admitted that he was overwhelmed by his understanding and the solicitude expressed in his speech, and welcomed the President's determination to help in restoring Poland's independence. He said he was heartened by the President's words, which showed that he understood that, in a democratic world, freedom and independence were a birthright and not a privilege. He then referred to the American citizens of Polish extraction as the living proof of the understanding and adaptability of the Poles to the ideals of freedom and democracy. That was what the Poles in Poland were craving for, and what they had been deprived of under foreign imperialist domination.

After dinner the President and Mrs. Roosevelt entertained their guests in the drawing room of the White House. There the President and Mikolajczyk sat together, and the President invited Cabinet members and military and civil officials one after another to engage in conversation with his guest of honor.

At ten o'clock, after the guests departed, the President asked Stettinius to take Mikolajczyk, General Tabor, and myself to his private study for further discussion of Polish matters.

The President showed great interest in General Tabor. He had arrived secretly in London from Poland by plane only a few days before. We did not know even his true name. "Tabor" was the pseudonym he used in his most dangerous work as Chief of General Staff of the Polish Underground Army, under the command of the legendary General "Bor." The President plied the lean, dark officer with questions concerning his activities in Poland, asking him how he got out, wishing to know the details of his flight to England. He then asked him to give a complete picture of the organization of the Polish Home Army. General Tabor spread out his secret maps, showing the disposition of the Polish Home Army centers and detachments all over Poland. He explained the ways of contact between these units, their methods of grouping into larger detachments and of breaking up after guerrilla action. He gave figures of sabotage activities, of the number of bridges, railways, and German trucks, trains, guns, and ammunition dumps destroyed. He spoke at length of the situation in the rear of the German Army.

The President said he was "thrilled" by this information, and suddenly turned to Mikolajczyk, saying that he realized now the importance of the Polish Underground military organization and was sure that if Stalin realized it, he would see his advantage in co-ordinating its action with that of the Red Army. He felt "this was the missing link in Soviet-Polish relations," and that at pres-

ent, when the operations of the Western Allies had been so successfully started in Europe, it was of the greatest importance not
only to Poland and Russia, but also to the Western Powers, that
co-operation between the Polish and Soviet forces inside Poland
should be achieved without delay.

The President showed his great alertness by saying that now
that the Polish Home Army was coming into the open, in connection with the Soviet advance through Poland, he realized how
necessary it was to supply our Underground forces with sufficient
arms and ammunition. He thought one could advantageously
make use of the new "shuttle-bombing" bases, functioning between Russia and the Western Allies, to supply Poland with war
matériel. One could parachute arms, munitions, supplies, and
funds to the Polish forces.

The President turned to Stettinius and asked him to put General Tabor immediately in touch with the Combined Chiefs of
Staff, so that he could discuss all these matters from the technical
point of view, and asked that he should also talk with Admiral
Leahy, the President's Chief of Staff, who was to return in a few
days from a short absence.

After the first part of the conversation with General Tabor,
punctuated by many questions addressed to Mikolajczyk and myself, the President once more returned to the political aspect of
the Soviet-Polish difficulties. Referring to his morning's talk with
Mikolajczyk, he said that what he had learned about the Polish
Underground military action confirmed his conviction that it was
necessary to do everything possible for Mikolajczyk to get into
personal contact with Stalin.

He thought the action of the Polish Home Army had an enormous bearing for Russia and for the Western Allies at the present
phase of the war. The President said that, "thinking aloud," it
had just occurred to him it might help if he sent a personal telegram to Stalin, expressing his interest and appreciation of Mikolajczyk and General Tabor, and of the great possibilities of
co-ordinating military action through the Polish Premier. He
would urge Stalin to talk with Mikolajczyk "as man to man."

After a short pause he added that he had not yet made up his
mind whether he could do this, but he was convinced that the
Polish Government should make every effort to establish such

contact. It was in the interest of Poland and of Russia. It could materially shorten the war, and this was a consideration of paramount importance to all the United Nations.

Mikolajczyk said he had been sure that the President would appreciate the war effort of the Polish people, that, as he had already told the President, he had been thinking of establishing personal contact with Stalin, but saw great difficulties ahead. He feared that, as matters stood, Stalin would not agree to restrict these conversations to matters of military co-ordination, but would inject his territorial and political demands which he had been so insistently pressing. As soon as one started talking about co-ordinated action, the question of the administration of the territories of Poland now being liberated would necessarily crop up. It was normal that the Polish Underground authorities should take over the administration in Poland until elections could be held. This would automatically raise the question of the various Polish provinces. It was difficult to imagine that the Soviet dictator would not press Mikolajczyk to give up the territories east of the Ribbentrop-Molotov line of 1939, now conveniently referred to as the Curzon Line, and insist that they were outside the administration and jurisdiction of the Polish authorities, because he had annexed them and considered them an integral part of Soviet Russia.

The President admitted this view was probably correct, but he still thought that direct conversations were necessary if real collaboration, so indispensable to all the Allies, was to materialize.

He then described to us very vividly what he did when he wanted to bring about understanding between labor and management. That, he said, would explain better than anything what he meant by the role of "moderator." He told us when he noticed that labor-management controversies had reached a stalemate, and could not be advanced in any direction by further discussion or by arbitration—and he thought that the Polish-Soviet situation had reached such a stalemate—he knew that "some outside impulse had to be given to the stationary machinery of negotiation to move it in the right direction."

When such a situation arose between labor and management, the President would call in Philip Murray, chairman of the CIO, and say to him: "Philip, I want you, without insisting on any preliminary conditions, to sit down here with the representative of the employers, and, in a human way, as man to man, talk over with him not the problems that divide you, but the interests common to you both." The President said that he had found this method of "moderating" the best form of mediation. He thought that Mikolajczyk should have "just such a human conversation" with Stalin. He suddenly turned to me and asked what I thought of it.

I said that I would like to take the President at his word and remind him that he had stressed two points in his most interesting suggestion. Without those two points the understanding he hoped to facilitate would be impossible. And this certainly fully applied to the Soviet-Polish conflict. Namely, the President had said that he demanded from Philip Murray and from the representatives of the employers that they should talk to each other in a human way, as he had put it—"as man to man"—without placing any preliminary conditions, and by starting the discussions on points of common interest, and not on matters on which they were divided. I felt that, if there was any hope such a conversation should take place between Mikolajczyk and Stalin, this could happen only if the President took the same initiative in their case and suggested this method to Stalin and pressed him to accept it. It was, above all, necessary that Stalin should agree not to place any preliminary conditions and not to insist on the acceptance of the Curzon Line or on a forced reconstruction of the Polish Government as preliminaries to such talks.

The President readily acquiesced. He said he would see what he could do about it.

Mikolajczyk then assured the President that, so far as he was concerned, he was ready to make every effort. He was prepared to go to Moscow, to talk with Stalin if he could be convinced that such conversation might really be of use and that the Soviets would not take advantage of it to create an even more difficult situation which might so complicate matters as to make any solution impossible.

We left the President at midnight, definitely under his spell.

CHAPTER XXXIII

Diplomacy or Politics?

THE following morning, in the seclusion of the Secretary's study at the State Department, Mikolajczyk opened our conversation with Stettinius by saying that he had given much thought to the President's advice of entering into personal contact with Stalin. He once more assured Stettinius he would willingly undertake such a venture, but would like to know whether he could tell him in all sincerity whether this idea had suddenly come to the President or if it had been previously thought out and discussed. Did Stettinius think that the President would cable his suggestion to Stalin?

Stettinius, with his usual kindly frankness, replied that he still could not say for certain whether the President would finally decide to send such a telegram. It was certainly a spontaneous idea of the President, about which the Secretary had not heard before. The President did not always follow up his initiatives at this time. He was still in poor health and very pressed by affairs of state and war. Moreover, it was, as he had told us, his "political year," which, in certain cases, made him exercise caution before deciding to take an initiative. What was important in this case—as Stettinius put it—was to know whether Mikolajczyk wished to enter into conversations with Stalin now or preferred to put them off to a later time.

Mikolajczyk answered with equal frankness. He said his only concern was to know whether any move on his part could help the cause he was so anxiously defending. The matter, as he saw it, resolved itself to the question whether he should take the great risk of being forced by Stalin into a discussion of the territorial issue. This issue was regarded by Poland, and by the United States, as one which should not be discussed or settled during the war. In view of the impossibility for Mikolajczyk to make any concessions on this matter, he wondered if it would be better to put off conversations with Stalin for the moment, risking the creation of further accomplished facts, or should he try to reach some understanding with Stalin on military co-ordination and the taking over of the administration by the Polish authorities in the territories now being liberated. He admitted he was in a quandary and would like to know the views of Stettinius.

Stettinius replied that officially he could offer no advice, but, as a real friend, he would like to put the matter squarely in the following way: In the present political atmosphere in America, so near elections, and in view of the new phase of the war opened by the European invasion which had only just begun, he thought, personally, that the President was in no position to adopt a more decisive attitude toward Soviet Russia. The President would certainly be true to his word and do his utmost to help Poland, but he could not come out just now with any really firm support of the Polish Government in its difficulties with the Soviets. Perhaps later, say in a month or two, perhaps in six months, when the war situation became more favorable, the balance between the Western Allies and Soviet Russia might be restored. Then, thought Stettinius, the President might be able to give more definite support to the Polish Government. He was sure that, while certain matters of principle had to be kept in abeyance for the time being, the American Government and the American people would certainly ultimately revert to fundamental principles and Poland could then count on their support for her just cause.

Our next conversation with the President took place on Monday, June 12, in the presence of Stettinius.

The President opened the conversation by asking Mikolajczyk what he had done on Sunday, and expressed his pleasure when he learned that he had driven over the beautiful Skyline Drive in Virginia. This led the President to tell us that he had just become interested in a scheme for the building of a unique skyline drive over the mountains from Vermont to the Mexican border and up to the Panama Canal. It would have the advantage of preventing unemployment. It would be the most beautiful and longest mountain route in the world, leading through magnificent scenery. It was to be conceived as a toll road, which, however, would never entirely pay for its construction. The President added that one would have to think of building good roads in Poland after the war.

The President then asked what phase had been reached in the talks which he had asked Stettinius to arrange for General Tabor with the heads of the War Department and the General Staff.

Mikolajczyk informed the President about the very extensive discussions which General Tabor had had at the War Department, the American General Staff, G-2, and the Office of Strategic Services. It appeared that these contacts would lead to closer military co-operation, and that the Polish Home Army would be supplied with the weapons necessary for its final rising against the Germans.

The President once more returned to his suggestion that Mikolajczyk should take steps in seeking personal understanding with Stalin. Stettinius reported briefly that in discussing with Mikolajczyk the matter of personal conversations with Stalin, both he and Mikolajczyk were inclined to think it might perhaps be more judicious to wait some thirty or more days before taking any decision, in view of the changes in the war and political situation, which might affect Allied relations. Mikolajczyk also shared this view.

The President did not appear to be of this opinion. He said that if one faced realistically a situation which he could only term as "compulsory," in view of Soviet demands and their presence in Poland, he considered it advisable to attempt direct conversations with Stalin without much delay. He foresaw the difficulties, and shared the apprehensions of Mikolajczyk that Stalin would press his political and territorial demands, but the President thought it advisable to face this emergency and to be prepared to make some concessions, especially as regards the composition of the Polish Government. He once more reminded Mikolajczyk that the Polish nation was numerically much smaller than the Russian nation. It could not effectively resist Russian pressure. Moreover, he knew that, as Mikolajczyk had told him, Poland desired good relations and collaboration with Russia.

The President added that if he found himself in such a situation, "he would unhesitatingly agree to make concessions if he considered them unavoidable." Unexpectedly he confessed he would even be ready to make changes in his government "if he could thus inspire confidence in a much stronger adversary and thereby open the door to understanding" which, in the case of Poland, was of such great importance, not only to her, but to all the United Nations. The President explained that even if the United States, vast and powerful though it was, found itself in the situation "of having to choose between a matter of prestige and the establishment of good relations with a powerful neighbor," and could remove a permanent threat by so doing, he would not hesitate to sacrifice prestige to the more important aim of security.

Mikolajczyk said that the President's simile greatly impressed him but that, as the head of a democratic government, he had, above all, to consider the will of his people, with whom he was in constant touch, and without whose directives he did not feel entitled to undertake any action. It would not be easy to obtain authority from the Polish nation to make such concessions even to a powerful neighbor.

The President said that being the head of a democratic government he realized how difficult it was, and fully understood Mikolajczyk's misgivings. He then suddenly asked if it would not be a good idea for Mikolajczyk to return to Poland as soon as possible, to try to explain the whole situation personally to the Polish people, and there to reconstruct his government by removing certain personalities regarded as objectionable by the Soviets and replacing them by people chosen among the leaders of the Underground State.

Mikolajczyk replied that he would willingly go to Poland, but that for the time being he could go there only by way of Russia, and this would curtail his freedom of action and movement.

The President once more returned to his plan of sending a telegram to Stalin. He said he would like to word it so as to tell Stalin how impressed he was by the personality of Mikolajczyk, and that he was sure Mikolajczyk would make as good an impression on Stalin. He said that while he had not entirely made up his mind to send such a telegram—and again he mentioned his "political year"—he had asked Stettinius to prepare a tentative draft.

Mikolajczyk then told the President of his conversations with high-ranking American officials concerning the supply of arms, munitions, and credits necessary to the Polish Underground and the Home Army in their fight. He dwelt on the importance of these supplies and pointed to the fact that the Polish people had been greatly disappointed that supplies of war matériel had been stopped on account of the Polish-Soviet difficulties. He said he realized that in the past there had not been enough planes to carry war matériel to Poland on any larger scale. At present there was no such difficulty, as the President himself had admitted, and it was urgently necessary to give the Polish people the means of carrying on their fight against the Germans and of proving to the Soviets that their support was really effective.

The President expressed his complete agreement, and promised to give instructions to the proper authorities. He then referred to the question of Poland's future boundaries. He thought that if contact with Stalin could be satisfactorily established and if a more friendly atmosphere could be created, Stalin might be less insistent in his territorial demands. If an easier relationship existed, the President thought, he might help personally in getting Stalin to agree that Poland should retain the city of Lwów, the city and oil fields of Drohobycz, and the region of Stanislawów. Wilno, he said, appeared more doubtful, but he did not entirely exclude Stalin's ultimate agreement to leave Wilno to Poland. Then turning to the question of the western boundaries, Poland, he said, should get East Prussia. When Mikolajczyk interjected that Stalin claimed Königsberg for the USSR, the President said he did not think Stalin's claim to that city should be regarded as final, and that he might ultimately persuade him to drop it.

According to the President, Poland should obtain the whole of East Prussia, including Königsberg, which, as he remembered, was so situated that it could strategically threaten Danzig if it were in foreign hands, thus endangering Poland's free access to the sea. The President said he wanted Poland also to have Silesia. He knew that Stalin had suggested Poland be extended westward up to the Oder River and Stettin. He asked what Mikolajczyk thought of this suggestion.

Mikolajczyk replied that regarding Silesia and western territories, generally speaking, he was of the opinion that the German territories, with large percentages of population of Polish origin, should be joined to Poland. This certainly applied to Silesia. But there was another important reason why Silesia should be incorporated into Poland; namely, to prevent Germany from preparing future wars, which the highly developed Silesian industries had so greatly facilitated in the past.

On the other hand, Mikolajczyk said, he was definitely opposed to any exaggerated expansion of Poland westward, as this would burden Poland with a large German minority. Moreover, experience had taught the Poles that the British and American people quickly forgot what Germany really stood for and were only too ready to become sympathetic to Germany after defeating her.

The President agreed with Mikolajczyk, and expressed approval of his sober views on this problem.

This was to have been Mikolajczyk's last conversation with the President. Before taking leave, the President asked Stettinius what arrangements had been made for Mikolajczyk's return to London.

Stettinius replied that the Premier was to leave for England on a British plane. The President said that as the Polish Premier had arrived on a British plane, he would prefer him to return to England on an American plane, and asked Stettinius to make the necessary arrangements. He asked the date of Mikolajczyk's departure. When he heard that arrangements were made for Mikolajczyk's departure on the fourteenth, the President expressed the desire to see him again on the fourteenth "to wish him Godspeed." He then offered him his framed photograph with a very friendly dedication.

As Mikolajczyk stood up to say good-by to the President and to thank him once more for his hospitality and for his kindness in wishing to see him again before he left, he asked the President if he could take a personal message to the Polish nation. The President's face lit up and he replied with force that he would be grateful if Mikolajczyk would "assure the Polish people of the abiding friendship of the United States Government and of the American people for Poland, and express the President's conviction that Poland would regain her full independence."

Our last conversation with the President, on June 14, which was to have been just a few minutes to say farewell, lasted nearly an hour.

Before referring to Polish matters, the President asked Stettinius if there were any new developments concerning the news published that morning of the refusal of General de Gaulle to accept the authority of the British and American High Command over the French officers who were to re-enter France with the Allied forces.

On our way to the White House Stettinius had mentioned this to Mikolajczyk and had deplored the attitude of General de Gaulle which, he said, "made things so difficult."

By a coincidence, on the same day the news appeared in the press that the Polish Government had recognized General de Gaulle's Committee of Liberation as the Provisional Government of France.

When Stettinius replied to the President's inquiry that he had no further information on the subject of de Gaulle's attitude in regard to the French officers, the President turned to Mikolajczyk and said de Gaulle was creating great difficulties at a time when American and British forces were giving their blood for the liberation of France. He made no reference to the recognition of the de Gaulle committee by Poland, but expressed his regret that de Gaulle was "as difficult to deal with as a prima donna."

The President continued that de Gaulle wanted the United States to recognize his committee without appearing to realize that it was well nigh impossible to recognize a committee which represented no continuity of government and could speak for only a limited percentage of Frenchmen. It was still impossible to ascertain whether de Gaulle's committee was acceptable to the majority of the French population. The President added that "there could be no comparison between the de Gaulle committee, however excellent its aims, and, for instance, the Polish Government which, in the fullest sense of the word, was a constitutional government assuring the continuity of the Polish State."

The President added that he expected de Gaulle in Washington shortly, but felt it would be difficult to reach understanding with him "because he was obstinate and politically minded at a time when military considerations were of paramount importance."

Mikolajczyk refrained from making any comment.

The President then spoke of Finland, expressing his regret that Finland had rejected Soviet peace conditions which he called "quite acceptable." Finland, he thought, was now placed in a "lamentable situation."

Mikolajczyk countered that, in all sincerity, he had to express his deep regret that so splendid and democratic a nation, with such a fine record, was threatened in its very existence, and expressed the hope that everything would be done to prevent Finland losing her independence. The President nodded his approval and said he also had great sympathy for the Finns, but he could not see how he could help them in their present predicament.

The President then once more broached the subject of the Soviets and said how pleased he was that Premier Mikolajczyk had agreed to see Professor Lange, because he thought "it was necessary to do so." He asked whether he had also seen Father Orlemanski, who had accompanied Lange to Moscow.

The President said he had heard that Orlemanski was a good man, "pure and decent, possibly too naïve, but with good intentions." With irony the President added, laughing, "He is what we call a man who means well. I was asked to receive Father Orlemanski." He added that he had not made up his mind whether he would do so. What had interested him about this Catholic priest was that in the report of his conversation with Stalin he said that when he talked of freedom of religion in Russia, and particularly of freedom for the Roman Catholic Church, Stalin had answered that he had nothing against religious freedom, but that there were so many religions in the world that it was difficult to decide how largely to apply religious freedom. Stalin had apparently added that, once you gave freedom to one or two denominations, a dozen or several dozens of religions would apply. It might be better, he thought, to unify religions.

The President admitted this saying of Stalin had struck him, because it might be an indication that Stalin would favor a union between the Russian Orthodox and Roman Catholic churches. The President thought this might be a hint in the right direction.

Stalin certainly did not have the ambitions of the tsars to become the head of the Church. He might possibly admit the Pope's leadership and allow him to become the head of the two united churches.

"Perhaps it would be well to help Father Orlemanski to go to the Vatican, as he had suggested, to submit this plan to the Pope," added the President thoughtfully, and asked what Mikolajczyk thought of it.

Mikolajczyk answered that, without going into the merits of the case, he would like to say he would be ready to believe in the sincerity of Stalin's declarations concerning freedom of religion only after Stalin freed the many Catholic priests whom he still held in Soviet prisons. That was the least one could ask as a proof of sincerity from a "realist."

The President admitted the logic of this view, and once more referred to Polish matters. He said that the more he thought of it, the more he liked the idea of a visit of Mikolajczyk to Moscow for direct conversations with Stalin.

When Mikolajczyk reminded him again that Stalin had by no means withdrawn the preliminary conditions which he insisted would have to be accepted before entering into any negotiations, the President countered that, after all, one had to be realistic. "You must remember what I told you before. There are five times more Russians than Poles, and you cannot risk war with Russia. What alternative remains? Only to reach an agreement."

Such an agreement, according to the President, might require making concessions "on matters of prestige." He thought territorial claims would not be so strongly pressed by Stalin if the other conditions, especially that relating to the composition of the Polish Government, were accepted. And here again the President said that if he found himself in a similar position he would not hesitate to change the composition of his government to meet the situation.

Mikolajczyk answered he had thought the matter over since his last conversation with the President. He did not think it right for a big Power to force the harshest of conditions upon the government of another nation, especially if the big neighbor was sincerely aiming at an agreement which was to become the foundation of real friendship and understanding. He admitted that he could not ask the Polish people to agree to change their President under any foreign pressure. That, in his mind, would be such a violation of democratic principles that it was unthinkable. Moreover, a government formed under foreign pressure would not only be unconstitutional, illegal, and unrepresentative of the people, but it could conclude no binding agreements. It would therefore be of little use even to Stalin, unless he wanted to make Poland become a Soviet satellite.

Summing up our conversations, the President explained once more that at the present time and in view of his "political year" he did not think he could take any definite engagement or pledge himself to support Mikolajczyk directly.

"Once more I wish to stress," said the President, "that I want to be the moderator in Polish-Soviet negotiations."

He added that he wished to assist Mikolajczyk in bringing about direct conversations with Stalin and in giving the necessary impulse to help move the Soviet-Polish problem from its "stalemate," possibly through a personal telegram to Stalin, which he was decided to send.

"I want you to rest assured," he said, grasping Mikolajczyk by the hand, "that I will watch over this matter and will do all I can to help you."

Two days after Mikolajczyk's arrival in Washington Professor Oscar Lange, a recently naturalized American citizen very active in pro-Soviet circles, returned from a visit to Russia undertaken, as we were told, on the invitation of Stalin, to discuss Polish problems.

Shortly upon his arrival in Chicago, where he made his home, Professor Lange wired to Mikolajczyk in care of the Polish Embassy, saying that he had just returned from Russia where he visited the Union of Polish Patriots and the Polish Army and would like to see Mr. Mikolajczyk before his departure "if agreeable to him."

When I handed this telegram to Mikolajczyk immediately after its arrival and asked what reply he desired to send, he put off sending an answer, saying that he was not anxious to see Lange, whom he regarded merely as a pro-Soviet propagandist.

Two days later Lange telegraphed the State Department re-

peating his message to Mikolajczyk and stating that he had received no answer to his telegram and adding, in characteristic
Soviet fashion, that he was afraid it had been "suppressed by the
embassy."

On June 9, after an official dinner at the Polish Embassy, the
chief of the State Department's Eastern European Division,
Charles E. Bohlen, and his assistant Elbridge Durbrow, stayed on
with us to continue their conversations with Mikolajczyk, and
Mr. Bohlen communicated the text of Lange's reminder.

Mikolajczyk said that he saw no good purpose in seeing Lange,
whom he could regard only as the mouthpiece of the Soviets.
Bohlen and Durbrow used every conceivable argument to press
Mikolajczyk to see Lange. They admitted that Lange was somewhat unreliable and "certainly a Marxist," but feared he would
publish the fact that Mikolajczyk had refused to see him. This
might be wrongly interpreted by American public opinion as a
proof that Mikolajczyk did not want to explore this additional
channel of Polish-Soviet understanding.

In view of this insistence on the part of high officials of the
State Department, Mikolajczyk agreed to see Lange, and I telegraphed him, fixing the appointment for June 13 at Blair House.

The conversation lasted two hours. Mikolajczyk asked many
questions concerning the attitude and disposition of the Polish
people in Russia, with whom Lange had been in contact, but expressed no personal opinions.

From the text of the conversation, as dictated on the same day
by Mikolajczyk, it appeared that Stalin had told Lange he understood the hesitation of the Polish Government in agreeing to a
territorial compromise so long as they could not be sure of receiving the compensation which Poland was to obtain in the west "up
to Stettin inclusively." As soon as Russia would be in a position
to give these German territories to Poland, Stalin said it would
be easier for the Polish Government to make concessions in the
east. He added, according to Lange, that Poland could not turn
down so generous an offer, which would give her a wide access
to the sea, with East Prussia and Silesia up to the Oder River
and territories in the west to Stettin inclusively.

Lange admitted that Stalin had said he wanted to keep Królewiec (Königsberg) in East Prussia for the Soviets, but Lange did not think this condition was final.

Lange further stated that Stalin told him he was aware that the attitude of the Polish people, and even of the soldiers in the Soviet-sponsored Polish Army, was untractable on the subject of Lwów, but explained he had to consider his Ukrainians who regarded it as Ukrainian territory.

According to Lange, even this very crucial point was advanced by Stalin in a way which made one think he might be willing to reconsider it in the future. He assured Mikolajczyk that Stalin had convinced him he had no intention of governing Poland. There would not even be a military Soviet administration. Should no Polish-Soviet agreement be reached before Poland was occupied by the Soviet forces, Stalin said he would entrust the administration to the local government authorities. He added that he was not in the least interested in the internal regime of Poland. He did not think Poland was adaptable to a communist rule. But he had added that he was greatly interested in Poland's foreign policy and her foreign relations. The whole attitude of the Soviets would depend, according to Lange's version of his talk with Stalin, on the direction of Poland's foreign policy. This certainly confirmed Mikolajczyk in his belief that Russia was especially anxious to sever Poland from its close contacts and friendships with the Western world.

The trend of Lange's talk with Mikolajczyk appeared to show that Stalin had used the Chicago professor as a possible intermediary between himself and the Polish Premier. Mikolajczyk gained the impression that Lange was not only anxious to become the intermediary, but the interpreter of Russian demands on Poland, and was trying to make them appear acceptable to the Polish Government.

On the 14th of June Stettinius and I saw Mikolajczyk off at the Washington airport. Stettinius kept up a running conversation with our Premier, stressing the "excellent impression" which he said Mikolajczyk had made upon the President, and summed up the visit as a great success. He assured Mikolajczyk that he could count on the President's support in his attempts to reach an understanding with Stalin. Stettinius was kind, friendly, spontaneous, and frank. As the great C-54 plane started on its way, he turned to me and said of Mikolajczyk: "Our friend Stan is a regular guy, and we shall do all we can to help in his undertaking."

As I drove back to the embassy, I tried to weigh in my mind the real importance of Mikolajczyk's visit in its exceptionally friendly setting.

I had been so often warned by well-informed American and British friends that Poland had been made the object of "a deal" by the President with Stalin at Teheran. I still wondered if that could be true in the light of all the publicity given officially to the visit, and of President Roosevelt's reassuring remarks to Mikolajczyk. On the other hand, he urged him to "arrange things" with Stalin. He had hesitated in promising his support. He had referred so repeatedly to his "political year," and explained that it prevented him from taking too definite initiatives in European affairs.

The six million Americans of Polish descent had recently given frequent signs of their anxiety about the fate of Poland. According to my Palace Guard friends, what they called the Polish vote was of considerable importance to the President in Illinois, Michigan, Pennsylvania, New Jersey, and especially in the state of New York, which they regarded as Dewey's stronghold.

Was I being "unrealistic" if I continued to believe in the sincerity of the President's assurances? Should I, on the contrary, regard all these latest innumerable and unusual proofs of hospitality, of kindly solicitude and understanding, lavished by him on the Polish Premier during his stay, as merely a glamorous window-dressing for internal consumption?

Washington press circles had closely watched the details of Mikolajczyk's visit and were conducting an inquiry to ascertain its true importance.

Three days after Mikolajczyk's departure, the newspapermen at Secretary Hull's press conference asked Mr. Hull for an explanation of the terms of support promised Mikolajczyk by the American Government. Mr. Hull answered, off the record, by referring to a Tennessee custom: "When in Tennessee two farmers get into a quarrel, their friends do not go into the merits of their differences, but press them to get together and thrash it out between themselves. This method is usually successful. It was this method that the President had applied in the case of the Soviet-Polish controversy. He had simply advised Mikolajczyk to talk matters over directly with Stalin."

Was that the official interpretation of Mikolajczyk's visit?

Ever since the resignation of Tony Biddle as United States Ambassador to Poland I had been asking the President and the Secretary of State to appoint a successor to Biddle. As month after month passed and the appointment was delayed, the American Polish Congress and several members of the House of Representatives of Polish descent petitioned the President to appoint a new Ambassador to the President of Poland in London. Mikolajczyk had once more personally asked for such an appointment, pointing out to the President the importance of such a step as an indication to Stalin that the United States Government had not weakened in its determination to continue its full recognition of the Polish Government. The President expressed his willingness to make the appointment very shortly. Three months later, on September 20, 1944, Arthur Bliss Lane, United States Ambassador in Colombia, one of the most able American career diplomats, who had been in Poland as First Secretary of the American Legation re-established after World War I under Minister Hugh Gibson, was appointed to replace Anthony J. Drexel Biddle.

The news was hailed by Polish public opinion as a proof of American friendship for Poland. The Polish language press in the United States commented on it enthusiastically. Members of the Palace Guard anxiously questioned me whether I thought this new proof of the President's interest in Poland would help the President politically.

By that time I had become hardened to such "undiplomatic" questions. I answered jokingly that it would largely depend on whether Arthur Lane was sent to London in time to present his credentials to the President of Poland before the November elections.

CHAPTER XXXIV

Soviet "Realism" versus Good Will

ON HIS return to London from Washington, Mikolajczyk informed me that he had reopened through intermediaries his confidential talks with the Soviet Embassy in London. True to the promise he had given to the President, he was sounding out the chances of his projected visit to Moscow.

I told Stettinius on July 11 that, in their first phase, these conversations had made Mikolajczyk hopeful, as they appeared to open the way to a possible understanding. However, in their further development it appeared that Soviet territorial claims on Poland and their demands of changes in the composition of the Polish Government were not only maintained, but, in fact, even accentuated.

While it was impossible to ascertain whether this attitude on the part of the Soviets was mainly tactical and temporary, or if, on the contrary, it expressed a definite policy, it forced the discontinuance of the direct conversations discreetly conducted by Mikolajczyk. The Polish Government, however, again confirmed its instructions to the Polish Underground to continue collaboration with the advancing Soviet armies, and the Underground organization was obeying these orders and fighting very effectively against the German forces.

Regardless of renewed attacks by Soviet and pro-Soviet propaganda, the Polish Government continued to maintain its conciliatory attitude.

I told Stettinius that the British Government had assured Mikolajczyk of its friendly support and that he counted on further moral support by the United States Government in accordance with the assurances given him by the President.

Stettinius agreed that we had fully demonstrated our good will, and expressed regret that we had not met with more understanding on the part of the Soviets. He told me the President had received an answer to his personal telegram to Stalin, sent the day after Mikolajczyk left Washington. He regretted to say that Stalin's telegram was negative. Stalin had said that, considering his views on the Polish question, which were known to the President, he did not think any good results could be obtained from his direct contact with Mikolajczyk.

In view of the unsuccessful attempts of Premier Mikolajczyk in London, and of Stalin's negative telegram, I asked Stettinius what he thought could still be done to break the stalemate.

Stettinius could not make any suggestion. He said he was aware that the Soviets were making matters more difficult for Poland. He hoped that events on the war fronts would alter the general situation and make it possible to adopt a firmer tone in negotiations with Russia. For the time being, the Soviets were in a most advantageous position because they were actually in Poland, while the Western Allied offensive was proceeding very gradually.

He agreed with me that, in the meantime, it was important to give outward proof to the Polish people that their cause was sympathetically viewed by the American Government and to supply the Polish Underground with arms, munitions, and funds necessary to keep up their fight against the Germans. He promised to bear this in mind. He intended to see the President and to use his influence to speed up military supplies to the Polish Underground Army. He did not conceal from me the fact that the President was disappointed by Stalin's reply to his telegram. It not only confirmed the Soviet dictator's attitude of discouraging Allied intervention in the Soviet-Polish problem, but could be regarded as a proof that the personal friendly relationship, which the President thought he had established with Stalin at Teheran, was not being interpreted by the latter in the way it was understood by the President.

In the meantime the Soviets were going ahead in Poland and piling up accomplished facts. The Polish Home Army had come out into the open and, as my British military friends of the Combined Chiefs of Staff admitted, had most brilliantly succeeded

in inflicting heavy losses on the common enemy near Wilno, which
they helped the Soviets to take, as well as in the provinces of
Volhynia and on other eastern Polish territories. At first the local
commanders of the Red Army were impressed by these effectively
conducted military operations of the Polish Underground. As
the Polish officers at the head of their units presented themselves
to the Soviet Army staffs, they were congratulated, thanked, and
told they would be supplied with the necessary equipment and
arms to continue the fight. A few days later, however, while the
Polish detachments were regrouping, the Polish commanders,
apparently on orders from Moscow, were put under arrest, some
of them were shot, some hanged, and others deported. Their men
were given the choice between joining the Soviet Army or being
disbanded. This Soviet attitude aroused tremendous indignation
in Poland. However, it still did not prevent the disciplined Polish
Home Army from continuing to obey the orders of the Polish
Government in London to carry on the fight against the Germans.

In a personal letter from Mikolajczyk to the President, dated
July 21, a copy of which I handed to Secretary Hull on July 24,
all the developments, about which Mr. Churchill had also been
fully informed, were stated in detail. Mr. Hull, appearing greatly
concerned by the conduct of the Soviets, promised me to take the
matter up with the President.

We discussed this message in which Mikolajczyk urgently
asked the President that American officers be dispatched to the
Soviet front in Poland because their presence might favorably influence the Soviet Government and stop its violence. Mikolajczyk
also asked that American intelligence officers be parachuted into German-occupied Poland in order to be in contact with the
Polish Underground.

The Secretary of State readily admitted that the situation of
Poland was becoming exceptionally tragic and that the Polish
Government "had done and was doing all that was humanly possible to arrive at an understanding." He admitted it appeared
that the Soviets were out to reject every offer made by the Polish Government which did not in every way comply with their
demands.

The absence of the President from Washington made it im-

possible for me to see him personally. However, Mr. Hull promised to use his influence in presenting the case, as a most urgent
one, for the President's consideration.

I took advantage of this exchange of views with Mr. Hull to
ask him about the pending conference of the representatives of
the Four Powers, which was to be held at Dumbarton Oaks in
the second week of August. Mr. Hull explained that this was a
further step in the policy he had initiated during the Moscow
conference. He aimed at a co-ordination of purposes and views
between the Four Powers in view of establishing an international
body which would replace the League of Nations. It was to be
conceived on stronger bases. He thought that "in the present circumstances, when some Powers," as he put it, without specifically mentioning Soviet Russia, "appeared to tend to unilateral
action, it would be no easy task to form such an international organization. But," added Mr. Hull, "we have to go on trying. We
may suspect one another. We may even dislike one another, but
we must persevere in our attempts to establish a constructive
system of security." That, he said, was the aim he was pursuing
in calling the conference to Washington. It was, above all, necessary, he thought, to ascertain in what degree the nations would
be ready and willing to place their military forces at the disposal of such an organization for the maintenance of peace and
security. It would later be necessary to create "some kind of
Council of Four Powers" which would undertake the direction
of such an international force. This might necessitate, as a further
development, the creation of a sort of general staff of the Powers,
possibly of several regional general staffs.

Mr. Hull thought that at a later phase an executive committee
of the Powers would take the head of the future United Nations
organization, while a council of all the United Nations, big and
small, would act as a sort of parliament of nations which would
assemble from time to time to formulate and to unify policy on
security and peace. He emphasized that the Dumbarton Oaks
meeting would be an "entirely informal preliminary conference"
whose aim it would be to explore the possibility of unifying the
views of the Powers on matters pertaining to world security. It
would not deal with any territorial or other problems, European
or non-European.

I asked the Secretary of State whether Soviet Russia had agreed to send a representative to this conference. The Secretary smiled and answered that for a long time he could get no reply from the Soviets, but finally he had been informed that Ambassador Gromyko would be the Soviet representative at the meeting.

In defining American policy at the conference, the Secretary said very emphatically that he could assure me that the United States would continue to oppose the division of the world into spheres of interest and would discourage all attempts to revive any theories of balance of power which had proved so ineffective in the past.

He then asked if I wished to give him my views on the forthcoming conference.

I replied that my views could be expressed in one sentence: I was sure that it was essential for the world, and especially for the smaller nations, that American leadership should make itself felt as the only safeguard of justice and freedom in a postwar peace settlement.

Shortly after my conversation with Secretary Hull I got word from London that, after several conversations with Churchill and Eden, and after lengthy meetings of the Polish Cabinet, Premier Mikolajczyk had left for Moscow by plane on July 27.

He stopped in Cairo. Simultaneously, in Poland in the dead of night, from a secret flying field of the Polish Underground, a British plane piloted by a Polish military flier, picked up a venerable old man of seventy years, Thomas Arciszewski, for forty years a prominent leader of the Polish Socialist party, who from the outset of the war had led the left wing of the Polish Underground organization.

The Polish Premier, Mikolajczyk, and the Underground leader, Arciszewski, met in Cairo. As they shook hands and eagerly discussed the problems of Poland before Arciszewski continued his flight to London and Mikolajczyk his journey to Moscow, the press announced that Stalin had officially handed over the administration of the "liberated parts of Poland west of the Curzon Line" to what he was pleased to call "The Committee of Liberation."

Thus, while awaiting the arrival of the Polish Prime Minister who, on behalf of the Polish Government, was to explore with him the possibilities of a Soviet-Polish understanding, the Soviet dictator had again deliberately created a situation which placed a new, almost insuperable obstacle to understanding between the Soviet and Polish governments.

The very composition of the Soviet-sponsored Committee of Liberation clearly showed Stalin's intention. He had placed at the head of this outfit a notorious communist, an agent of the Comintern, who used the alias "Bierut." This agent had for years been a Soviet citizen, though he was of Polish origin. He had always been entirely subservient to Moscow.

The committee took over its functions of administration in the city of Lublin which, by order of Stalin, was to become Poland's temporary capital. The members of the Liberation Committee were ordered by Stalin to appear in Moscow in view of the pending conversations with the Polish Premier.

On learning in Cairo the news of the appointment of this committee, Mikolajczyk hesitated whether he should continue his journey to Moscow or return to London. He decided to go to Moscow. He cabled me that he had taken this decision in view of the fact that the Soviet armies had reached the Vistula River, and were only a few miles from Warsaw. In continuous broadcasts the Soviet radio kept calling on the Polish Underground Army and the people of Poland to rise against the Germans and join the Soviets in their victorious march westward. German and Soviet guns were thundering over Warsaw, the Polish capital. Mikolajczyk said he felt he had to sacrifice all other considerations and face this urgent situation.

From Teheran, where his plane stopped for refueling, he cabled to President Roosevelt to inform him that he was on his way to Moscow at the urgent request of Churchill and following the President's advice. He said that, regardless of the difficulties created by the Soviets through the setting up of the communist Committee of Liberation, he attached the greatest importance to the attempt he was making to reach understanding with Marshal Stalin. He assured the President that he would once more demonstrate the good will of the Polish Government in trying to reach an agreement. He reminded the President of his promise of support and said how badly he needed it.

As soon as he arrived in Moscow, Mikolajczyk realized that Stalin had very cleverly prepared the setting for his talks. By appointing the Committee of Liberation and summoning it to Moscow to meet him, the Soviet dictator wanted to force Mikolajczyk to negotiate with an allegedly Polish group of communists who had already signed on the dotted line the surrender of nearly half of Poland's territory by "accepting" the Curzon Line. They were a living specimen of the sort of government which in Soviet terminology was regarded as "a government friendly to Soviet Russia."

The whole Soviet-Polish problem was thus reduced by Stalin to the low level of an artificially created conflict between "two rival groups of Poles," thereby allowing the Soviet dictator to assume a sort of benevolent role of arbiter or, to use President Roosevelt's expression, of "moderator," in a "quarrel between Poles." The Lublin Committee, a puppet group, unrepresentative of any Polish political party, had obviously one main mission to perform. It was to appear as a Polish administration opposing the legal Polish Government and to prepare the way for Poland's domination by the Soviet Union.

As Mikolajczyk found on his arrival in Moscow, the very independence of Poland had now become the real issue. The Soviets had arbitrarily created a government of their own choice. Stalin's repeated declarations that he desired "a strong and independent Poland" had now obviously become a sinister joke.

I was informed on August 5 that, in the first Moscow conversations with Molotov and Stalin, only the most urgent questions were discussed; namely, those concerning the relationship of the Red Army to the Polish Home Army in operations against the Germans.

The Polish tragedy, however, was reaching its climax. In view of the Soviet approach to Warsaw, of the Soviet radio appeals to the Home Army and to the population to rise against the Germans, General Bor-Komorowski, commander of the Polish Underground Army, gave the order for the rising, called "Operation Tempest."

On August 1 the desperate fight of the Polish Underground started in Warsaw, barely nine miles behind the German-Soviet front. It opened an unequal and unprecedented battle carefully planned by the Polish General Staff to coincide with the speedy entry of the Soviet forces into Warsaw. It was to give strong support to the Red Army, in accordance with the plans which General Tabor had disclosed at the White House and discussed with the President and the British and American staffs.

It was now of the utmost importance for Mikolajczyk to obtain from Stalin active support of the Red Army for the heroic fighters of Warsaw. Contact and co-ordination would have to be established immediately between the Red Army command and the Polish Home Army. Arms and munitions, food and supplies would have to be parachuted to the Polish fighters to allow them to develop their initial success which, in the first days of the Warsaw rising, had given them control of more than half of the city and allowed them to save the waterworks, the gasworks, the electric plant, and the vital bridges over the Vistula by which the Soviets were to force their way into the embattled city.

It soon became apparent, however, that Stalin did not intend to give any such support. The Russian offensive, which had made such rapid headway to Warsaw, was suddenly stopped. Instead of pressing on the Polish capital, the Red Army forked out southward, headed for the conquest of the Balkans, leaving Warsaw to fight its own battle.

On August 9, in a conversation with Stalin, Mikolajczyk obtained the Marshal's promise to look into the matter and to give the necessary aid to our Warsaw fighters. But Stalin did not fulfill his promise to Mikolajczyk and later, when the Premier, back in London, reminded him of his promise in a telegram dated August 13, Stalin replied on the sixteenth of August by a blunt refusal, saying that the Soviet Army had failed to establish contact with the commanders of the Warsaw rising, which, Stalin added, had not been previously co-ordinated with the Soviet High Command.

Mikolajczyk replied on August 18, reminding Stalin that the commander of the Home Army ordered the rising at the time when the Soviet armies were within reach of Warsaw, at a point only a few miles distant from the capital. He referred to the Moscow radio appeals, and reminded Stalin that he had told him that the Red Army would be in Warsaw on August 6. He repeated his appeal for Soviet support for the Warsaw fighters. This appeal remained unanswered.

The British Government then decided to act. It realized the urgency of supplying the Polish garrison in Warsaw with arms, munitions, and food. However, very little could be done. Technical difficulties were very great. Moreover, the Soviets not only refused to co-operate, but refused to allow the British and Polish R.A.F. planes to use the shuttle-bombing bases in bringing supplies to Warsaw. The British Government repeatedly intervened in Moscow. Mr. Churchill and President Roosevelt personally requested Stalin for help, but without avail. The situation was fast becoming desperate.

On August 11 the Germans sent an ultimatum to General Bor, together with an order for the Polish population to evacuate Warsaw. The ultimatum was ignored, but tens of thousands of inhabitants of Warsaw were chased out by the Germans and herded in a concentration camp in Pruszków, a small town about twelve miles west of Warsaw.

Aid to the Warsaw fighters was first flown by the British from Mediterranean Allied bases after August 10. British, Polish, and South African air crews, sustaining heavy losses, participated in these flights and dropped munitions and arms in quantities which, however, were by no means adequate. A slightly larger force of R.A.F. planes flew over the Polish capital on August 16, contributing to raise the morale of the Polish soldiers and civilians rather than their matériel strength.

The insurgent population of Warsaw faced increasing difficulties as their small stocks of food and water became exhausted. On the fifth anniversary of the German attack on Poland, September 1, 1944, it seemed that the Polish capital would be unable to hold out any longer, but with almost inconceivable heroism the fight raged on throughout the entire month.

The Russian attitude toward the uprising finally underwent a slight change. On September 13 the Red Army eventually captured the suburb of Praga on the eastern bank of the Vistula. The Red artillery and air force then started shelling and bombing German positions inside the capital. Even some supplies of food and munitions were dropped by the Russians for General Bor's army, arousing public expressions of gratitude from Bor and Mikolajczyk. However, no parachutes being used by the Soviet air force for this purpose, the major part of the supplies dropped were smashed and useless.

Eventually, on September 18, the long-awaited help of the United States air force materialized. Ammunition, food, and medical supplies were dropped to the Polish insurgents by a strong force of American Flying Fortresses based in England. Under the pressure of rising public opinion abroad, the Russians had finally allowed the American fliers to land on the shuttle bases behind the Russian front. However, this too-long-delayed help could not save the decimated Home Army and the population of the Polish capital.

With the complete exhaustion of all supplies, the spread of epidemics, mass starvation, and the methodical destruction of the city, all hope of success vanished. General Bor, a few days before identified as Lieutenant General Tadeusz Komorowski, was forced to surrender to the Germans. He had no other choice. Although by that time the eastern bank of the Vistula was captured by the Russians and contact had finally been established across the river with Marshal Rokossovsky's army, to which ample information on the strength and location of German troops inside and around Warsaw was given by General Bor's men, the spokesman of the Committee of Liberation, Osobka-Morawski, after a conference with Stalin, broadcast the astounding news that there would be no immediate Russian attack on the western bank of the Vistula and on the city of Warsaw itself.

Moreover, the Soviets, through the communist Lublin Committee, announced that General Bor, just then appointed Commander in Chief of the Polish Army by the Polish Government, was a traitor and a criminal, and would be court-martialed along with his entire staff after the capture of Warsaw by the Red Army.

The Germans, with inhuman barbarity and ruthlessness, destroyed what remained of Warsaw. They inflicted the most cruel reprisals on the population. They looted, burned, and pillaged. They executed and exterminated tens of thousands of civilians, including women and children. With barbaric ruthlessness, they drove to concentration camps what remained. But, being primarily militarists, they could, apparently, not altogether suppress their admiration for the heroic fight of the Polish Underground. They agreed to treat its officers, men, and auxiliary women's detachments as military prisoners of war.

Over 100,000 Polish men, women, and children lost their lives in the Warsaw rising.

During those two months I was continuously receiving in Washington, day and night, telegrams describing these terrible events and instructing me to do my utmost to obtain American help for the Warsaw rising. I was in daily contact with Stettinius, and discussed with General McNarney the possibility of joint British-American air operations over Warsaw. Conferences took place at the Combined Chiefs of Staff and at the War Department to study the possibilities of supplying the Warsaw garrison with arms, munitions, and food. Apart from technical difficulties, the Soviet refusal to allow the use of the shuttle-bombing bases was the main obstacle. This made it impossible to undertake more extensive air operations. However, my American military friends thought that even that difficulty could be overcome by simply disregarding Soviet protests and making use of the shuttle-bombing bases, considering it unthinkable that the Soviets could actually prevent American planes from using these American-operated air fields. Finally, however, it was decided that no larger operations could be undertaken.

Apart from my almost daily talks with Stettinius and other State Department officials, I appealed to President Roosevelt through his Chief of Staff, Admiral Leahy, who received me at my request on Labor Day, September 4. Admiral Leahy showed full understanding of the tragic situation of the Polish Underground forces, and it was he who finally obtained the President's consent for the joint British-American air operation over Warsaw.

Mikolajczyk's visit to Moscow and his talks with Stalin and Molotov did not bring any definite results, but, as he later explained in a message sent through me to President Roosevelt, they had allowed him to get a full picture of the Soviet attitude and arguments.

Mikolajczyk thought the tension was somewhat eased and, as he expressed it, although the Soviets still refused to make any gesture of recognition of the Polish Government and placed between themselves and our government a serious new obstacle in the shape of the hand-picked Committee of Liberation, they had appeared to wish to remain, for the time being at least, on speaking terms with the Polish Government.

He also informed the President that Stalin had promised him help for the Polish Home Army fighting in Warsaw. He had not kept his promise. He had discussed the question of Poland's western frontier and had declared that he would see to it that Poland was extended to the Oder and Neisse rivers, including Breslau, and in the northwest to Stettin. He had likewise said that he would clear that territory of all its German population. He promised Poland East Prussia, but without Königsberg, and the region northeast of that city which was to be incorporated into the Soviet Union. He insisted on the Curzon Line as the "future Soviet-Polish frontier," but did not appear to close the door entirely on the question of the city of Lwów and of Poland's only oil fields in the district of Drohobycz. Suggestions were made of forming a new Polish government as soon as Warsaw was liberated. Stalin had stated that "Mikolajczyk and some of his colleagues could come to Warsaw, where the government could be constituted" in understanding with the Soviet-sponsored committee.

At Stalin's request Mikolajczyk had discussed the formation of a new government with the representatives of the Lublin Committee of Liberation. But new demands were made of him, some directly by Stalin and Molotov, others through their mouthpieces, Bierut and Osobka-Morawski of the Lublin Committee.

In addition to their previous demands, the Soviets were now insisting on the scrapping of the Polish constitution of 1935 and on the return to the more radical one of 1921. This demand, naturally, could not be accepted, such a decision being the exclusive prerogative of the Polish nation.

Having thus explored at close range the Soviet attitude, which clearly disregarded Poland's territorial status, her sovereignty and independence, Mikolajczyk asked me to inform the American Government that, while he intended to maintain the contact he had so laboriously established in Moscow, he was returning to London for consultations with the President of Poland and his Cabinet, and with Churchill and Eden. He left Moscow for London on August 10, in search of a new formula of understanding with Soviet Russia.

CHAPTER XXXV

Pressure Diplomacy

THE embers of Warsaw were still smoldering at the end of the battle which had lasted sixty-three endless days, when I was informed by cable from London that on October 10 Mikolajczyk, accompanied by Foreign Minister Romer and the aged Professor Grabski, chairman of the Polish National Council in London, had once again left for Moscow, where Prime Minister Churchill and Minister Eden had preceded them.

This second visit of Mikolajczyk to Moscow took place in very different circumstances from those of his first visit in August.

Ever since his return from the second Quebec conference with President Roosevelt in September 1944, Mr. Churchill had been insistently pressing Mikolajczyk to yield to Soviet demands. In Washington, Mikolajczyk had gained the conviction that, while he could count on sporadic proofs of moral support from America, President Roosevelt's "political year" would, to say the least, make him delay taking any more direct part in an attempt to settle the Soviet-Polish problem. After his return from his first trip to Moscow, Mikolajczyk had been exploring with the Polish Cabinet every possible formula of understanding which would justify his return to Moscow to continue conversations with Stalin. He had found it impossible, however, to get agreement on the acceptance of Soviet territorial and political demands. After sounding the Underground State in Poland, which finally established that the Polish nation rejected the Soviet demands, the situation again became static.

I learned that on the ninth of October Prime Minister Churchill and Mr. Eden had suddenly left for Moscow and that this unforeseen trip had been necessitated by the urgency of co-

ordinating war operations with Russia and especially of fore-
stalling open controversy between the Soviets and Britain on the
subject of the Balkans.

It should be remembered that, after their sudden halt on the
Vistula River in Poland, the Soviets had launched a strong and
rapid offensive toward the Balkans which, as the British Government feared, they would reach before American and British troops
could get there. It was also feared that the Soviets would take
advantage of this situation to play a lone hand, creating new
accomplished facts.

Apparently, together with this important problem involving direct British interests, Mr. Churchill was determined to make a
final attempt to solve the Polish problem.

His departure for Moscow had been so sudden that he had not
had time to discuss the latest aspects of his plans with our government. He had, however, addressed a letter to Mikolajczyk before
leaving London in which he said that his visit in Moscow might
be a good occasion to advance the solution of Polish-Soviet problems and suggested that Mikolajczyk should join him there to
take part in the talks.

In his reply, Mikolajczyk declared his readiness to go to Moscow but warned that if he went he would be guided by the decisions of the Polish Government, known to Mr. Churchill, which
did not allow him to make territorial concessions or to admit
Soviet interference in the forming of a Polish government. This
reply crossed a telegram from Mr. Eden from Moscow, asking
the Polish Premier to come at once, and expressing the belief
that the atmosphere was propitious for a settlement of the difficulties.

On October 12, Mikolajczyk, Romer, and Grabski were already in Moscow and had their first conversation with Eden.
They learned that, in his preliminary talks with Stalin, Mr.
Churchill had touched upon the Polish problem and regarded
the atmosphere as favorable to a settlement. Ambassador Harriman, who visited Mikolajczyk on the same day, appeared to share
this opinion.

On October 13, Mikolajczyk, together with Romer and Grabski, paid a courtesy call on Molotov. Later that same day, in the
guesthouse of the Soviet Commissariat of Foreign Affairs, the

first conference on Polish-Soviet problems took place in the presence of Marshal Stalin, Mr. Molotov, Ambassador Goussiev, representative of the Soviets to the British Government, Prime Minister Churchill, Mr. Eden, Ambassador Clark Kerr, and Mikolajczyk, Romer, and Grabski. Ambassador Harriman, accompanied by a Secretary of the American Embassy, was present as an observer.

At this meeting Mikolajczyk defined the attitude of the Polish Government along the lines of the Polish Cabinet's latest proposals. These were based upon the expressed opinions of the Polish Underground State, which favored the establishment of good-neighbor relations and the closest collaboration between Poland and Soviet Russia, including the conclusion of a Polish-Soviet military alliance. At the same time the Polish Government and its Underground representatives refused to agree to the cession of eastern Poland and to any Soviet interference in the reconstruction of the Polish Government, which they regarded as an infringement on Poland's independence and sovereignty.

Stalin then took the floor. He said that the Polish attitude had two main defects which made understanding impossible. The first was that the Polish Government appeared to ignore the existence of the Polish Committee of Liberation. That, he contended, was wrong, because it was a fact which could not be ignored. The committee existed, and he had handed to it the administration of Poland's liberated areas. According to Stalin, the committee had organized meetings, from which it appeared that a part of the Polish population was beginning to admit its authority. According to Stalin, there now being two rival Polish governments, the best way out of the difficulty would be to form a government by reaching a compromise between the two.

The second defect of the Polish Prime Minister's statement, Stalin said, was that the Polish Government had not given any answer on the question of the new eastern frontier of Poland. He added forcefully that if the Polish Government wished to have any relations with the Soviets, it could achieve this end only by recognizing the Curzon Line as the permanent Soviet-Polish frontier. On the other hand, he admitted that what Mr. Mikolajczyk said concerning good neighborly Polish-Soviet relations was acceptable to him. But this envisaged the future. One had to face present facts and necessities. There could be no understanding, Stalin repeated emphatically, if the Poles rejected the Curzon Line and were not prepared to settle the composition of a new Polish government on the basis of an understanding with the committee he had established in Lublin.

Prime Minister Churchill, on behalf of the British Government, supported Stalin. He said the great sacrifices of Russia for the liberation of Poland entitled her to the Curzon Line, but that Poland, of course, would have to receive a compensation of "equal balance" in the north and west, and this would be in the form of the incorporation into Poland of East Prussia and Silesia.

Mikolajczyk objected that he could not presume to decide the matter of Poland's frontiers, this decision being constitutionally reserved to the Polish nation. He appealed to the conference, saying that if he were to act as Stalin desired in the matter of Poland's territorial status, they would form a very bad opinion of him. How could they expect him to express his willingness to give up more than 40 per cent of Poland's national territory and thirteen million Polish citizens?

A discussion followed in which Stalin, stressing the sufferings and sacrifices of the White Ruthenian and Ukrainian nations, called Mikolajczyk an imperialist. Mikolajczyk protested that on his part he had to remember the sufferings and heroism of the Poles.

"If I agreed to these frontier suggestions," added Mikolajczyk, "it would mean that the Polish politician was ready to sell what the Polish soldier abroad and the Polish soldier of the Home Army had fought for and given their lives to preserve."

Seeing that the proceedings were taking an unfavorable turn, Churchill stepped into the breach and suggested a compromise formula, by which the Polish Government would accept for "practical purposes" the Curzon Line, reserving the right to appeal to the future peace conference on this matter after the war.

At this point Molotov made a surprising statement. He said that he saw it was necessary to remind those present that at Teheran President Roosevelt had expressed his complete agreement with the Curzon Line as the Polish-Soviet frontier and regarded it as a just solution which should be satisfactory both to the Soviet Union and to Poland, and that the President had merely added that, for the time being, he preferred his agreement on this point should not be made public.

If this was the case, Molotov said, then we may conclude that the Curzon Line has not only been agreed upon by the Soviets and Britain, but has been accepted by all the Three Powers.

Molotov added that he thought it useful to bring this matter up. He then turned to Churchill and Harriman and challenged them to deny his statement if they considered it inconsistent with the truth, "because it appears to me," he said, "that Mr. Mikolajczyk is not aware of this fact and is still in doubt regarding the position of America on this subject."

Molotov paused dramatically for a while to see whether Churchill, Eden, or Harriman would take up his challenge, and when it became evident that they were not prepared to do so, the conversation switched to the subject of the western frontiers of Poland.

Churchill and Stalin stated they were determined that the western frontiers of Poland should be on the Oder River, Stalin adding: "including the town of Stettin, and in the north East Prussia up to a line running northwest and southeast of Königsberg, which will be incorporated into the Soviet Union."

Mikolajczyk finally said he was not empowered to sign any such frontier settlement.

Before this meeting adjourned, Churchill summed up by saying that the whole controversy was now narrowed down to two points: first, the acceptance of the Curzon Line as a *de facto* eastern frontier of Poland, with the right of Poland to raise this subject at the future peace conference; second, the arrival at a friendly understanding between the Polish Government and the Committee of Liberation in Lublin, which would lead to the constitution of a new government by means of the fusion of these two bodies, in accordance with a compromise which they would reach.

At this point Minister Romer asked whether Mr. Churchill's formula was accepted by the Soviet Government, to which Marshal Stalin very firmly replied that the Soviet Government rejected it. He said he would only accept a definite agreement of the Polish Government to the Curzon Line as the frontier which, at its final delimitation, might possibly be altered slightly one way or another from three to six or possibly to seven kilometers east or west.

After this first meeting, Churchill and Eden made several attempts to explore new compromise formulae. It was apparent that Churchill regarded it as most important and urgent to reach an agreement in Moscow and, as the formulae successively suggested by him were rejected, his pressure on Mikolajczyk and Romer increased hourly.

Churchill and Eden received the representatives of the Lublin Committee on the following day at the British Embassy in Moscow, and on October 14 Churchill told Mikolajczyk that he intended to have a personal talk with Stalin on the Polish problem in the afternoon and that he was anxious to clear up matters in his conversation with Mikolajczyk beforehand, in order to be able to make definite suggestions to Stalin and to reach an understanding.

As he put it, this was the crisis of the fortunes of Poland. No such opportunity would return, and the damage done would be irreparable if one lost the chance of concluding an immediate agreement. Everything hinged on one thing: 'the eastern frontier of Poland. He reminded Mikolajczyk that in January 1944 he had urged the Polish Government to agree to the Curzon Line. How much easier everything would have been if his advice had been followed! There would have been no Lublin Committee of Liberation. Diplomatic relations would have been resumed.

At present "these Lublin people," as Churchill called them, would be "an awful nuisance." They would build up a rival government. Civil war would break out. Fighting might break out in Poland, with the Russians siding with the rival government. Then Churchill started to threaten Mikolajczyk. He told him that he would tell the House of Commons he entirely agreed with Stalin, and would publicly define His Majesty's Government's attitude. He entreated Mikolajczyk to settle upon the frontier question. He urged him to take responsibilities. If he would accept Churchill's formula, Churchill would go to Stalin and would certainly succeed in concluding an agreement. What other alternative was there? Ample compensation was promised in the west as well as the evacuation of the German population from the territories, which Poland was to receive.

If Mikolajczyk agreed on the frontier issue, continued Churchill, then certainly the Russians would withdraw their support of the Committee of Liberation. He said that when he had criticized the Lublin Poles in talking to Stalin, the Russian dictator also criticized them. Stalin evidently considered them unworthy of his support.

Churchill pointed out to Mikolajczyk that if he accepted the Curzon Line as the future frontier, he might possibly obtain some further concessions from Stalin. After all, what did it matter if Mikolajczyk lost the support of "some of the Poles"? He should think of what he was gaining for Poland. He would be able to return to Poland, and there to form a government. The British and American Ambassadors would be with him. They would support him. It was indispensable for Mikolajczyk to agree. If he missed this chance, he would lose everything.

In reply to this impassioned torrent of words Mikolajczyk declared that he had thought the situation over all through the night. He had been struck by Molotov's declaration that the decision regarding Poland's territorial status had been agreed to at Teheran by Churchill and Roosevelt, without even consulting the Polish Government, and without even admitting to it that the matter had been settled in such a way. He was now asked to sign this Three Power settlement on the dotted line. In addition he was asked to agree to exorbitant Soviet political demands concerning the setting up of a compromise government dominated by the so-called Committee of Liberation. That would mean agreeing to give up Poland's independence. "What guarantee have I," said Mikolajczyk, "that the independence of what would remain of Poland after such a transaction would be respected?"

Churchill reminded him that Britain and America were involved in the settlement and would see to it that Poland's independence was respected. Mr. Eden added that if agreement was reached on the Curzon Line, one could certainly obtain a guarantee of Poland's independence from Stalin.

"But," objected Mikolajczyk, "territorial matters are for a nation to decide, not for one member of the government."

Mr. Churchill then gave vent to his violent irritation. He said that he "washed his hands of Mikolajczyk," that if he persisted in his obstinacy "the British Government would give the whole busi-

ness up." Because of "quarrels between the Poles," he was not going to "wreck the peace of Europe." He accused Mikolajczyk of being obstinate, and said that in his obstinacy he did not see what was at stake. He warned him that if they parted on this matter, "they would not part in friendship." He would tell the world how unreasonable the Polish Government had been. Poland would then "be responsible for starting another war in which twenty-five million lives would be lost. But what did Poland care?
. . ."

Mikolajczyk, bewildered by this torrent of abuse and threats, replied that he now knew Poland's fate had been sealed at Teheran, to which Churchill shouted: "It was saved at Teheran!"

When Mikolajczyk said he was not so completely devoid of patriotic feeling that he could give up half of Poland, Churchill answered that twenty-five years ago Britain had helped to reconstitute an independent Poland. Now she was trying again to prevent Poland from disappearing entirely, but Mikolajczyk "would not play the game." He was "absolutely crazy." But unless he accepted the frontier, he "was out of business forever."

"The Russians will sweep through your country and your people will be liquidated. You are on the verge of annihilation!" shouted Churchill.

"Anyway, the Polish Government would not be giving anything up because the Russians are already in Poland," he added after pausing for breath.

Mikolajczyk pointed out that it appeared in either alternative that Poland was to lose everything.

"Poland would lose only the Pripet marshes and five million people, mostly of Ukrainian origin, not Poles," interjected Churchill.

Mikolajczyk observed that, after all, if the question had already been settled by the Big Three, as Molotov had said, why should Poland be required to sign her own death warrant? Eden took advantage of this to suggest that one might, perhaps, reach agreement under protest from the Polish Government, putting the blame on the Three Powers. He said he saw Mikolajczyk's difficulty and his apprehension that he would be disavowed by the Polish Government and nation.

Finally Churchill decided he would in any case try to draw up a new compromise formula, and would ask Stalin to accept it. If Stalin's answer were negative or unsatisfactory, which Churchill doubted, the Polish Government would have lost nothing, and Mikolajczyk could go to London strengthened, and continue to have British support. But if Stalin accepted it, then he was sure the Three Powers would also accept it, and Mikolajczyk was finally bound to accept the decision of the Great Powers.

Mikolajczyk replied that he could not agree to such a solution. He asked Churchill whether he would accept it if Britain found herself in such a situation. Churchill answered impatiently that "he took no interest in him."

To a question of Minister Romer whether Churchill would agree to a cession of British territory, Churchill replied: "I certainly would, and be blessed by future generations. There is no other alternative. Poland is threatened with virtual extinction and would be effaced as a nation."

At this point Mr. Grabski, on behalf of the National Council, interposed, assuring Mr. Churchill that no Polish parliament would ever accept such a solution. "Well," answered Mr. Churchill ironically, "then there is nothing to prevent Poland from declaring war on Russia after she is deprived of the support of the Powers. What is public opinion, after all? What are you fighting for, the right to be crushed? I want to save the Polish nation," he concluded.

Before leaving the room Mr. Churchill, in his inimitable way, suddenly turned to Mikolajczyk with a friendly smile and said that after having met the people of the so-called Committee of Liberation he had to admit that he did not envy Mr. Mikolajczyk having anything to do with them. He said, laughing heartily, that he had taken "a considerable dislike to them."

CHAPTER XXXVI

Teheran Commitment Confirmed

THE new formula which Mr. Churchill intended to discuss with Marshal Stalin referred to the Curzon Line as the "line of demarcation" between Poland and the USSR. As regards the future Polish Government of National Unity, he had suggested it be set up at once on Polish territory liberated by the Russian armies and that it be presided over by Premier Mikolajczyk.

Stalin, while accepting the part of Churchill's formula relating to Poland's expansion westward to the line of the Oder, insisted that the Curzon Line should be definitely accepted as Poland's eastern frontier and not as a line of demarcation. He also crossed out the passage about Mikolajczyk's premiership of a new government. He insisted on its replacement by a passage stating that "the Polish Government of National Unity would be set up in agreement and understanding between the Polish Government in London and the Polish Committee of National Liberation in Poland."

The Moscow conversations continued until the nineteenth of October without any concessions on the part of Stalin. While the attitude of the Soviet Government continued to be uncompromising, Mr. Churchill's insistence on Mikolajczyk agreeing to Soviet demands increased as time went on.

As the various formulae suggested by Churchill and Eden were consecutively rejected by Stalin, Mikolajczyk finally agreed that Churchill should suggest one which would define the future Polish-Soviet frontier "on the basis of the Curzon Line, but leaving to Poland the city of Lwów and the Polish oil fields." At the same time Professor Grabski had conversations with Molotov urging him to realize the importance of Lwów as a center of Polish culture and industry.

Both Stalin and Molotov rejected all these suggestions.

After this failure to reach an understanding, Churchill put forward a final formula, which was to take the shape of a joint Soviet-British declaration, in which the Curzon Line would be determined as a line of demarcation and in which he again suggested a new Polish Government of National Unity, to be formed in Poland under the premiership of Mikolajczyk.

This also met with Stalin's refusal.

In a conversation which lasted two and a half hours Stalin insisted on his previous demands.

Even Churchill finally agreed that, under the circumstances, the Polish Government could do no more and that the responsibility for failure to reach understanding now rested on the Soviets. Whereupon the last Moscow conversation between Churchill, Eden, Mikolajczyk, and Romer took place in a very friendly atmosphere. It was decided to leave the door open for further conferences. The Polish Government was to remain "on speaking terms" with the Soviets and to try to find some way out as soon as Mikolajczyk returned to London.

Churchill promised his support in exploring new formulae.

Before leaving Moscow Mikolajczyk decided to try to reach some understanding with the Lublin Committee, but his talks with Bierut simply proved that these fervent Comintern agents were as insistent as Stalin on the acceptance of the Curzon Line as the eastern frontier of Poland, and would not budge from their attitude that in a new Polish government "the London Poles," as Bierut called our government, could have only one fourth of the portfolios, while the Lublin Committee would hold three fourths, all the most important departments to be included in that number.

Mikolajczyk turned down this proposal.

In his last interview with Marshal Stalin, on the eve of his departure from Moscow, Mikolajczyk once more raised the subject of Lwów and of the Polish oil fields.

Stalin again refused to make any concessions. He intimated, however, that if and when Mikolajczyk reached agreement within his Cabinet on the Soviet demands, he could proceed to

Lublin to take part in the formation of the new government in understanding with the Lublin Committee.

During their stay in Moscow, Premier Mikolajczyk and Minister Romer remained in constant touch with Ambassador Harriman, who tried to be helpful but was careful to preserve his position of mere observer. He explained to Mikolajczyk that as an observer he had not been able to take any active part in this Moscow conference, nor could he enter into discussions with Molotov regarding the latter's statement about the alleged agreement on the Curzon Line between the Big Three Powers at Teheran. He said he had been instructed not to depart from his role of observer. He added that any rectification of Molotov's statement on his part might have caused a crisis in Soviet-American relations, which would have highly undesirable repercussions in America, especially at this phase of the presidential election campaign.

Mikolajczyk addressed a letter to Ambassador Harriman asking him for a reply clarifying Molotov's statement on the President's alleged acceptance of the so-called Curzon Line. Harriman was shortly to fly to Washington. He promised to submit a report to the President on the Moscow conference, to explain the attitude of Mikolajczyk, and to ask the President to reply to Molotov's statement.

On his return to London, Premier Mikolajczyk reported the details of the Moscow conference to the Polish Cabinet and National Council. He sought new compromise formulae which would prove his continued good will and sincere desire to reach an understanding with the Soviets. He informed me he was greatly concerned by the continued passive attitude of the American Government. He was now aware that the Soviets would remain adamant on the territorial issue and would continue their pressure to force our legal government to accept a compromise arrangement, which would not only give the communists an unjustified majority of 75 per cent in a newly constituted Polish Government, but would also leave in their hands the most important political portfolios in such a cabinet. Churchill's pressure made him realize that the British were determined to support Stalin's territorial demands. He felt that, even on the question of the formation of a new government, the British Prime Minister would finally yield to Stalin.

Mikolajczyk's exceptionally difficult situation was further complicated by the fact that, with the exception of the representatives of his own Peasant party, all the members of his Cabinet were opposed to any further concessions to Russia's demands. He reported the results of his Moscow talks to the Polish Underground State and ascertained that it was also opposed to accept conditions which would turn Poland into a Soviet-ridden satellite state.

His faith in the United States had been profoundly shaken by Molotov's statement that President Roosevelt had agreed to the Curzon Line at Teheran. And he could get no definite denial or confirmation of this fact from Ambassador Harriman. He felt he had to know where he stood with President Roosevelt. He could not take any decision without ascertaining the attitude of the United States. The Polish Underground State also clamored to be told the truth about America's attitude on the problems of Poland.

On October 27 Mikolajczyk cabled to me the text of a personal appeal to the President, instructing me to communicate it immediately to the President. In this message he referred to his talks with Harriman who, he said, was to report the details of the Moscow conference to the President. He reiterated that he had not ceased to realize the necessity of Polish-Soviet understanding in the interest not only of Poland, but of the United Nations as a whole. He drew the President's attention to the fact that the Polish nation, while it might make some concessions for the sake of peace, under pressure, could not, without a feeling of deep wrong, admit the loss of nearly half of its territory, including great centers of national and cultural life and considerable economic values. He explained that it was therefore impossible for the Polish Government to agree to solutions which would make it lose the confidence and following of its nation.

He said that in the course of the Moscow conversations he had applied his best efforts to convince Stalin and Churchill of the importance of these considerations. He had particularly asked for a gesture on the part of Russia which would at least leave to Poland the city of Lwów and the Galician oil fields, even if they insisted on imposing the so-called Curzon Line as a frontier. He admitted that his endeavors had been fruitless, but that, in the face of his responsibilities, he could not regard them as exhausted until the President had clearly defined his stand in this matter. He reminded the President that in his conversations in Washington he had shown understanding, particularly in the case of Lwów, which for six hundred years had been a Polish city no less than Cracow and Warsaw, and had never in history belonged to Russia. He still trusted the President's assurances of support which, he said, "Mr. Molotov's one-sided version" that the President had acquiesced to the Curzon Line at Teheran "had not dispelled." He asked the President "once more to throw the weight of his decisive influence and authority on the scales of events," and appealed to him to address a personal message to Marshal Stalin, asking that at least the city of Lwów and the Galician oil fields be left to Poland. He begged for prompt action in view of the obvious emergency.

The President had left that very morning for Pennsylvania and Chicago in connection with his election campaign. I immediately called on Freeman Matthews, the chief of the European Section of the Department of State, who received me in the presence of Mr. Bohlen, chief of the Eastern European Division and his assistant, Elbridge Durbrow. After reading the text of Mikolajczyk's letter, Mr. Bohlen promised to send it immediately to Chicago, where it would reach the President on the following morning. We then discussed the situation.

Mr. Bohlen was anxious to know whether, if the President decided to intervene regarding the city of Lwów, the Polish Government would "finally accept" the Curzon Line as the future eastern frontier. I could give him no definite assurance on this subject and referred him to our conversations with the President during Mikolajczyk's visit. I reminded him that the President had shown special interest and understanding regarding Lwów and our oil fields. He had then promised Mikolajczyk his unqualified support should he need it.

Mr. Bohlen admitted that this was true. He thought the President would certainly wish to intervene, but regarded it as most unfortunate that the necessity for his intervention had arisen a few days before the date of the elections.

Except for a brief message which I received from the Presi-

dent through the State Department that he had read Mikolajczyk's appeal and would reply as soon as he could, the American
Government took no action.

Finally, on his way back to Moscow from Washington, Ambassador Harriman called on Premier Mikolajczyk in London on
November 21 and handed him a letter from the President dated
November 17. The President's letter, dated thirteen days after
his re-election, entirely omitted the points raised by Mikolajczyk,
and, by implication, appeared to encourage the Polish Government to make the territorial concessions demanded by Stalin.

Because of its importance, this letter deserves to be quoted in
full:

November 17, 1944.

My dear Mr. Prime Minister:

*I have had constantly to mind the problem you are facing in
your endeavors to bring about an equitable and permanent solution of the Polish-Soviet difficulties and particularly the questions
which you raised in your message of October 26. I have asked
Ambassador Harriman, who will bring you this letter, to discuss
with you the question of Lwów.*

*While I would have preferred to postpone the entire question
of this Government's attitude until the general postwar settlement
in Europe, I fully realize your urgent desire to receive some indication of the position of the United States Government with the
least possible delay. Therefore, I am giving you below in broad
outline the general position of this Government in the hope that
it may be of some assistance to you in your difficult task.*

*1. The United States Government stands unequivocally for a
strong, free, and independent Polish state with the untrammeled
right of the Polish people to order their internal existence as they
see fit.*

*2. In regard to the future frontiers of Poland, if mutual agree-
ment on this subject including the proposed compensation for
Poland from Germany is reached between the Polish, Soviet, and
British governments, this Government would offer no objection.
In so far as the United States guarantee of any specific frontiers
is concerned I am sure you will understand that this Government,
in accordance with its traditional policy, cannot give a guarantee
for any specific frontiers. As you know, the United States Govern-*

ment is working for the establishment of a world security organization through which the United States together with the other member states will assume responsibility for general security which, of course, includes the inviolability of agreed frontiers.

3. If the Polish Government and people desire in connection with the new frontiers of the Polish state to bring about the transfer to and from territory of Poland of national minorities, the United States Government will raise no objection and as far as practicable will facilitate such transfer.

4. The United States Government is prepared, subject to legislative authority, to assist in so far as practicable in the postwar economic reconstruction of the Polish State.

Very sincerely yours,
(Signed) FRANKLIN D. ROOSEVELT.

Ambassador Harriman told Mikolajczyk that the President had instructed him to explain that he wanted to emphasize his concern regarding the situation in which the Polish Government found itself after the Moscow conference, and to confirm his promise of support within the limits of his present possibilities. He also suggested that Ambassador Harriman should take up with Stalin the problem of Lwów and of the oil fields, if Mikolajczyk still thought it desirable.

Mikolajczyk promised to communicate the President's letter to the Polish Cabinet and to consult with them and with the Polish Underground before giving his final answer regarding Harriman's intervention concerning Lwów.

Mikolajczyk had two more conversations with Harriman—on November 23 and 24. He told him that, after consulting the leaders of the four Polish parties, he had found them opposed to the now-belated American intervention on behalf of Lwów. The Polish people realized that their agreement to such an intervention would be interpreted as their acceptance of the Curzon Line, which meant the cession of 47 per cent of Poland's national territory. They felt they had no right to do so. To the government it appeared all the more inadvisable, considering Ambassador Harriman had made it clear to Mikolajczyk that personally he did not see much chance of changing Stalin's attitude on the subject of Lwów and the oil fields.

In the last Mikolajczyk-Harriman conversation, at Claridge's Hotel in London on November 24, Mikolajczyk informed Harriman that, in view of the impasse reached in the Soviet-Polish situation, he would be compelled to resign. He was under constant pressure from Churchill. Although he appreciated the President's straightforward statement of policy and his readiness to intervene about Lwów, the President's letter proved that the United States did not see its way, at least for the time being, to take a more definite attitude in regard to Stalin's demands on Poland. Mikolajczyk added that, personally, he could not take upon himself the responsibility of accepting a compromise on the territorial issue, knowing it was contrary to the wishes of the Polish nation and that he could not "deliver the goods."

As he had told Harriman, Mikolajczyk was seriously thinking of resigning. He knew that, if he remained in office and discontinued his efforts to reach an understanding with Soviet Russia, he would lose the support of Mr. Churchill. If, on the other hand, he agreed to yield to Soviet demands, he would lose the confidence and support of the Polish people.

He was painfully aware that the Soviets were continuing to create new accomplished facts in Poland, that, together with the stooges they had established in Lublin, they were ruthlessly "liquidating" not only the Polish Underground State and our invaluable Home Army, but all the leading patriotic national elements which had so splendidly led the nation along the Calvary of German oppression and extermination for more than five years of the war. That consideration made him, personally, lean to a policy of concessions.

Mikolajczyk resigned on November 24, 1944.

In addressing a meeting at Chatham House in London on December 14, as a private citizen, he explained fully his situation and the implications of the Soviet-Polish problem.

He said that many well-meaning people had pressed him "to reach a compromise with Russia." He had looked up the word "compromise" in the dictionary and found that it meant "an adjustment of differences by mutual concessions." There was nothing "mutual" about the compromise which the Polish people were asked to make. It reminded him of the story about a household where the problem of redecorating a room arose. The husband wanted it painted green, and the wife pink. A compromise was reached. The room was painted pink.

He said he felt he had carried on General Sikorski's policy of conciliation with Soviet Russia in the fullest sense of the word. Instead of encouragement, the Soviets had ceaselessly denounced the Polish Government and himself as unrepresentative, as "a handful of reactionaries and fascists," although in fact it was a democratic government of radical tendencies.

The Three Powers appeared to have difficulties in adjusting their policies on European problems and on Poland's problem in particular. As they had taken upon themselves to make decisions, they would have to accept the responsibility. The Three Powers had been unable to agree whether frontier problems were to be settled during the war or after the cessation of hostilities. If the Great Powers themselves could not reach agreement on such a fundamental matter, how could any Pole take upon himself to decide in favor of definite territorial settlements and face his nation with such an accomplished fact without being regarded as a traitor? How could he put his signature to what amounted to a new partition of Poland and a premature surrender of her rights? As a matter of fact, how could one settle frontiers while the war was still on, while it was impossible to fix simultaneously, for instance, the western and northern frontiers of Poland which Germany still controlled?

It was all very well, continued Mikolajczyk, to say that Poland would be free, independent, and strong. Those were great words. But the Three Powers were disregarding these very words by making decisions without the participation of the nation directly interested. The Powers were arbitrarily settling questions of security for the postwar world. Only after such a system was set up would Poland and other smaller nations know how far their security had already been prejudged.

Soviet Russia did not appear to realize that a settlement satisfying her demands would leave the Poles with a profound feeling of wrong which would forever poison Polish-Soviet relations. No just solution could consist in imposing upon Poland a communist government, abhorrent to the Polish people, and in exploding all foundations of Poland's state legality. The legal Polish Government had as much right to function freely in Poland as had any other legal government on its own national territory. The Polish people were surely no less entitled than other peoples to express freely their will concerning the kind of government and political system under which they desired to live. International friendship could never be imposed by pressure or force, concluded Mikolajczyk.

The Polish Government in London was reconstituted under the premiership of the aged socialist leader, Thomas Arciszewski, the same man who, after having led the left wing of the Polish Underground for five years, left Poland secretly for London in August 1944.

The majority of the Peasant party followed its leader, Mikolajczyk, and refused to participate in the new Cabinet.

CHAPTER XXXVII

Operation "Four Freedoms"

THE fall of 1944 was full of momentous developments.

The Dumbarton Oaks conference opened on August 21 and continued until October 9. The second Quebec conference—"an unfinished symphony" in the concert of Anglo-American co-operation—was held early in September.

War events of great importance were taking place on the Allied western front in France. The fall of Paris, the lightning offensive of the Soviet forces in August and September in the Balkans, and events on the Far Eastern front, were keeping Washington on its toes. At times it looked as if German resistance might break down at any moment.

Notwithstanding all these dramatic happenings, the Washington atmosphere was dominated by the electoral campaign, culminating in the triumphant re-election of President Roosevelt for a fourth term on November 4.

I was deeply interested in the electoral campaign. I had closely followed the campaign which resulted in the election of President Hoover in 1928. There seemed to be a big difference between those two campaigns. Nineteen forty-four was, above all, a crucial war year, and this fact weighed heavily on the character of the campaign. The President was so busy with war problems that he started his campaign very late in the year. Contrary to custom, internal problems and the comments they elicited, were less prominently stressed in pre-election speeches than foreign policy, friendship with Russia, unity of the Three Powers, and their domination in the future world organization. The appearance of Ambassador Harriman and his political activities showed the prominent part American-Russian relations were playing in the election campaign.

The reactions of the various national groups of the American electorate closely interested in the European countries of their origin were being minutely observed by both party machines. I was frequently asked by various campaign managers, and especially by election agents of the New Deal, what I thought would be the most appropriate way to obtain the support of what they called "the Polish vote" for the Democratic machine. Of course I steadily refused to discuss these matters, but these questions showed how anxiously the vote of the Americans of Polish descent was being watched and nursed.

On the eleventh of October the President received a large delegation of the Polish-American Congress, who were desirous to ascertain at firsthand his views on the application of the Atlantic Charter to American foreign policy, and particularly to the problem of Poland's independence in the light of Soviet demands. I was struck by the fact that the White House gave out a press report of this meeting, published together with photographs of the President surrounded by the American Polish delegates. I was repeatedly told bluntly by New Dealers of the Palace Guard that the appointment of Ambassador Lane to replace Biddle as Ambassador to the Polish Government on September 22, 1944, was not only a proof of the President's "abiding" interest in Poland, but also a political move, which they hoped would be reflected by "the Polish vote."

The Polish language press in America did not appear wholly satisfied with the results of the talk which the President had had with the delegation of the Polish-American Congress. I learned privately that the President was aware of this fact and intended to see the chairman of that organization, Charles Rozmarek, on board his special train in Chicago on October 28. In the beginning of November, in Chicago, where I went to head the delegation of Poland to the Civil Aeronautical Conference, I learned that the President had seen Mr. Rozmarek and had definitely promised him to take active steps to insure Poland's independence. I noted from the press that the chairman of the Polish-American Congress had come out fully endorsing the Democratic ticket immediately after his interview with the President.

The electoral campaign was proceeding on the level of a bitter fight, somewhat incongruous in the light of the momentous world events of the war, now in its decisive stage.

The lightning progress of the war necessitated another personal contact between the President and Mr. Churchill. A meeting was held in Quebec where Mr. Churchill, Mr. Eden, and a fairly big staff of experts suddenly arrived in September. Many problems of military importance had to be discussed. Some problems of the immediate postwar period also required discussion and co-ordination.

Mr. Churchill had been exceptionally active in the course of the summer. I was told that it was on his initiative that this Quebec conference was being held. He was apparently optimistic that the war might finish sooner than had been expected. He was aware that many questions had been left in abeyance which might suddenly have to be settled. He had become increasingly concerned by the President's passivity.

Churchill was rejuvenated by the favorable turn of the war. He was buoyant and full of initiative. He found the President in poor health and hesitant. I learned that Churchill and Eden soon realized that, apart from some very urgent war matters, they could not count on a more active policy on the part of the President before the elections.

Military matters mostly were discussed. The problems of China were reviewed, particularly the necessity of activating Chinese operations in the Japanese campaign, and defining the attitude of the Powers in regard to Japan and the Dutch East Indies.

So far as Europe was concerned, the two statesmen found that, apart from the formula of "unconditional surrender," they had not yet settled finally in their minds how to deal with the various political and economic problems of a defeated Germany.

It was at Quebec that the decision was taken to appoint a special committee, headed by Secretary Hull, to study and define Allied policy toward Germany, especially with regard to Germany's industrial potential and her further economic status. Secretary of the Treasury Henry Morgenthau became the most active member of this committee. In a short time he brought out his comprehensive plan suggesting the virtual liquidation of Germany's heavy industry.

I was informed that Churchill once more tried to get the President's support for an Allied invasion from Italy through the Balkans, but met with no encouragement from the President, who apparently thought that it could not be contemplated in view of Stalin's opposition.

The Quebec conference ended as suddenly as it had begun. The health of the President was causing considerable concern at the time. He was greatly overworked, and the strain had been telling on him, arousing the anxiety of Mr. Churchill and his other friends.

In this atmosphere the Dumbarton Oaks conference closed on October 9. The principle adopted at that conference was most disturbing to the lesser United Nations. In discussions on this subject in diplomatic circles in Washington we expressed the hope that the Dumbarton Oaks plan would be considerably revised and adjusted, to make it more acceptable as a project in line with democratic ways of conducting international relations. As it stood, the draft statute which emerged from Dumbarton Oaks was a caricature of democracy in international relations. It gave the Big Powers complete control in the future security organization.

In a memorandum, which I handed to the State Department analyzing the Dumbarton Oaks plan, I very frankly drew the attention of the Secretary of State to this aspect of the Dumbarton Oaks suggestions. Even if one agreed that only the Big Powers were materially in a position to safeguard world peace, this did not appear to me to be a reason for excluding smaller States from playing an effective role in the assembly and in the Security Council, in which only a very restricted part was reserved to them in the proposal.

A glance over the record of the League of Nations sufficed to show how beneficial to international co-operation the activities of representatives of smaller Powers had been in the past. The Big Powers were involved, at least to a certain degree, in the solution of every international conflict, their interests being widespread practically all over the world. This very fact called for participation of the smaller Powers, whose interests were limited and could have a beneficent and somewhat more detached influence in discussing some of the Big Power problems.

I pointed out that in the nineteen years of the functioning of the League of Nations no conflict between two small Powers (Turkey vs. Greece, Greece vs. Bulgaria, Yugoslavia vs. Hungary, et cetera) had actually led to war. On the other hand, it was a fact that, whenever a Big Power became involved in a conflict, it had proved impossible to reach a peaceful solution through the medium of the League of Nations (Japan in Manchuria, Italy and Abyssinia, the Spanish civil war with its German, Italian, and Russian intervention, and, finally, the long series of Germany's unilateral accomplished facts which resulted in the present world war).

These considerations, coupled with the generally recognized inappropriateness of giving to a Big Power, when it became a party involved in a conflict, a judge's seat on the court by means of its veto power, pointed to the necessity of amending the original text of the Dumbarton Oaks proposal.

There was, however, one more important basic problem to be considered: One could not forget the sequence of events which led to the establishment of peace and of the League of Nations after the last war.

President Woodrow Wilson announced his Fourteen Points, thus putting before the world his program of liberation, based on the self-determination of nations. This basic program having been accepted and applied, a new world status was created and the League of Nations was set up to guard it.

What was the present situation? The victorious Powers proclaimed a one-world security system. In effect they were proceeding to carve up the world into spheres of influence, and were passively watching on the side line, while Soviet Russia was carrying out a policy of territorial expansion and communist infiltration at the expense of the smaller nations.

The latter were being converted into buffer states with puppet governments. Thus a world organization was being established by means of pressure which would declare it unlawful for anyone to try to change anything in this unhappy arrangement. It was therefore of primary importance that an international status be first established, based on the untrammeled rights of peoples freely to express their will, and that only after this was done, should an organization be created to make the new system secure and lasting.

Should the opposite course be taken, the new world organization would be reduced to the role of guard over a huge international prison, in which previously free nations would find themselves helplessly locked up as the direct consequence of the unilateral activities of some Big Powers in search of their own security by expansionist methods, rather than by relying on the creation of an effective world-security organization.

It was futile to expect that it would be possible to open the jail and to free the imprisoned nations after the creation of such an organization. It was clear that the world was faced with a situation in which a totalitarian Power, such as the Soviets, expert in the art which it defined itself as "social engineering" and which it now used for "taking countries from within," was busily at work.

Before the doors of the jail could be opened, the countries which, through military occupation, found themselves in the claws of a totalitarian system, would be thoroughly "engineered," their social and political systems changed by legislation arbitrarily introduced by puppet governments, their nationally conscious elements uprooted, and the nations would by that time be made ripe "voluntarily" to declare their "will" to remain permanently jailed.

Thus an international security organization, coming into being without first making it possible for the peoples to express their untrammeled will freely, would be but a right frame for the perpetuation of a political and territorial status achieved by a series of unilaterally accomplished facts. Such a peace, if it could be called by that name, would thus be established, which would not be a peace of free peoples, but a mock peace, in which the rights of small nations would be frozen into a semi-permanent state of dependence.

The framework for this kind of peace had been created at Dumbarton Oaks.

I listened to the results of the elections, and learned that President Roosevelt had been re-elected and that the Democratic party, contrary to its own somewhat pessimistic expectations, had achieved another sweeping victory by increasing its hold in the House of Representatives and in the Senate.

From my friends among the political bosses in the Democratic party I heard triumphant exultation concerning the so-called Polish vote which had so fully responded to the President's assurance given to the chairman of the Polish-American Congress on the presidential train on October 28, that he would use all his mighty influence to assure the restoration of Poland's full independence. I was told that these assurances had caused the Americans of Polish descent to vote overwhelmingly for Roosevelt.

A new Roosevelt era was opening—the era of a victorious Roosevelt, who was winning the war now in the final stages; a Roosevelt who, contrary to American political tradition, was returned to the presidency for a fourth term. How could anyone doubt that, so mightily strengthened by success, he would now rise to his full stature as a statesman and actively apply a new policy, asserting American leadership for the common good of a regenerated postwar world?

The general consensus of opinion, strongly supported in official American quarters, expressed the conviction that the President "would become tough" in reasserting American fundamental principles in his world policy and in calling a halt to Soviet expansion.

I admit that, having so closely studied New Deal tendencies for four years in Washington, I had become somewhat skeptical and "kept my fingers crossed." The disquieting news of the President's failing health, borne out by his recent photographs, contributed to make me anxious. So many accomplished facts of world importance had already been created, it appeared to me that a situation was reached which would demand not only a display of "toughness" on the part of the President, but a determined move in reverse in the American policy of appeasement, before one could hope for any tangible results, let alone for the assertion of American prestige and leadership.

I doubted whether the President, however strengthened he might be by his re-election and his victorious war leadership, was still capable of the enormous energy necessary to reorientate American policy so completely. The advantageous position of the Soviets in Europe, their most recent expansion in the Balkans, their ruthless tactics, and the impetus of their strongly backed propaganda in America, were so many ominous and alarming factors.

As weeks went by, I saw no indication that the United States Government would make use of its great bargaining points, of timing its military moves, of conditioning its co-operation, or of opposing its democratic principles or the weight of American public opinion to Soviet demands.

Dumbarton Oaks had fully confirmed America's acceptance of the pattern of Power domination first introduced in 1943 by way of the UNRRA.

The smaller United Nations yearned for freedom and for collaboration within the framework of the United Nations in the establishment and maintenance of a just and durable peace. And yet, unthinkable though it was, they were being deprived by the Three Powers of their rightful chance to participate in the great task, or to demonstrate their constructive and cultural capacities in the shaping of a really democratic peace.

Not the American pattern, declared by the President in the Atlantic Charter and in his Four Freedoms speech, but the Soviet pattern of Power-political domination, glamorized in Walter Lippmann's best-selling books, was becoming the *leit motif* of international relations.

A new misconception of realism was being forced upon the war-weary world by opportunist statesmen and writers. It appeared to me to be the most cynical interpretation of the realism of brute force, unworthy of our enlightened times. It was profoundly unrealistic because it refused to face facts and entirely ignored the human element, without which realism was but a farce.

The gallant way in which the men and women of Poland, of Norway, of Belgium, Holland, and of the other United Nations had fought in the war, the generosity with which they had sacrificed their lives in the cause of justice, should have taught the statesmen of the Three Powers that the noble principles of humanity still continued to prevail. It should have made them understand that the now-certain victory was in itself the best proof of the dominant part which ideals still played in true realism.

There was much talk of a "one world," united in one peace system. The cause of the "common man" had become one of the pet slogans of prominent New Dealers. It had conveniently helped them to rally the leftist elements in the election campaign. But when I frequently discussed its implications with those self-styled apostles of human rights, I invariably had the distasteful impression that, engrossed by their anxiety to remain in office, they had little time or inclination to ponder the meaning of that slogan.

One thing was becoming painfully evident. The actual trend of American policy was preparing not "one world" of united peace and security, but at least two worlds, vastly different. In the Western Hemisphere, the nations of the Americas were to continue to enjoy the blessings of the good-neighbor policy which, above all, was the basis of security and peace. At the same time, it was becoming increasingly certain that these blessings would not be made available to many countries of the Eastern Hemisphere which, for the sake of unity among the Three Powers, were being handed over to the totalitarian domination of one of the Big Three.

I took every opportunity to stress my apprehensions in conversations with American official and political personalities, with newspapermen, and fellow diplomats, as well as in my public addresses, and to draw attention at that crucial time of the war to the implications of the policy of appeasement of Russia, which now held sway and appeared to have vitiated both United Nations' ideals and realism. I pointed out that no nation, however powerful, was secure from attack in our modern times of scientific achievement. I stressed the meaning of "realism"—not in the cynical sense of Power-political concepts unworthy of a victorious America. I urged them to be sufficiently bold and realistic to face facts. Instead of launching new slogans about world unity, to help create that unity on the firm basis of principles which all free human beings understood and demanded. In fact, to realize the greatness of American concepts and to apply them to the world in establishing security and peace.

At the time of their proclamation by Woodrow Wilson the world had been unripe to adopt them. But at the end of this terrible total war all mankind was demanding freedom and justice.

I met with very little encouragement. Official America appeared to me to be going through a psychosis of misunderstood "internationalism." I was regarded as a "perfectionist" who "put the cart before the horse." I was told that the President would certainly rise to the occasion "at the appropriate moment." Was he not a "past master at timing his moves?"

It was considered of primary importance "to gain the confidence of the Soviets." Then, when this was achieved, "friendly coercion" would follow, and make Stalin realize he had everything to gain by following the President's advice. Such sayings alternated with bombastic reassurances: "You just wait awhile. You will soon see how tough we can get, now that the war is practically won."

Such talk, which I listened to daily through the winter months until the Yalta conference, made me wonder whether these American officials and politicians would ever realize that time did not remain at a standstill, awaiting their good pleasure to act.

And yet it was abundantly clear that the problems created by the war, which had shaken the world to its very bases and destroyed practically everything tangible and solid except the fundamental qualities of humanity, could not be solved by petty compromises or short-lived Power-political agreements. To solve them one had to start from the foundations, by applying sound, human, and solid principles with simplicity and courage, urged by firm determination to build a new and better world for its duration, and not merely to set up a precarious structure of antiquated concepts of balance of power on the quicksands of temporary appeasements and of wishful thinking.

Humanity had gone through too much to accept anything but real peace, founded on real freedom and on real justice. It was time to simplify, not to complicate problems. The solution of really great problems called for boldness of statesmanship.

The time had come to adopt and to apply to the world the proposal announced by President Woodrow Wilson in his magnificent address to the Senate on January 22, 1917, when he suggested "that the nations should with one accord adopt the doctrine of President Monroe as the doctrine of the world: that no nation should seek to extend its policy over any other nation or people, but that every people should be left free to determine its own way of development, unhindered, unthreatened, unafraid, the little along with the great and powerful."

As matters stood at the end of 1944, it appeared to me that

America, perhaps unconsciously, was taking part in the establishment of a mock peace which, at best, would delay conflicts between the Big Powers—a peace which would have the cold stillness of a cemetery, in which the human rights of smaller nations were being ruthlessly buried.

CHAPTER XXXVIII

Total Surrender at Yalta, February 1945

IN DECEMBER 1944 and January 1945, after a successful drive into the Balkans, Russia resumed her lightning offensive in Poland and East Prussia. Warsaw was finally captured on January 17 and the Soviet armies were driving through western Poland, meeting practically no German resistance, and getting daily nearer Berlin.

The Western Allied offensive had been making steady progress, but in the beginning of January the Germans launched a temporarily successful counteroffensive on several sectors of the front. In December, civil war broke out in Greece. To the well informed there could be little doubt that the Soviets were inspiring the subversive action of the Greek Communist party, and that the situation there had become a threat to British interests. We learned in Washington that Churchill and Eden had flown to Athens to end the civil war. By that time the Russians had reached Budapest.

As matters stood, in the middle of January 1945 the hoped-for restoration of balance on the war fronts between the Soviets and the Western Allies still appeared remote. The Soviets continued to hold the initiative of bargaining, and Washington had every indication that they intended to make full use of it.

The President was getting ready for the Big Three meeting, scheduled to take place immediately after his inauguration on January 20. I repeatedly tried to see him, but was told that his health was bad, that he was too busy with war events and the preparations for the Big Three meeting, and could not possibly find time to receive me.

On January 20 I attended the inaugural ceremony at the White House, together with all my colleagues of the diplomatic corps. I watched the President being sworn in, and listened to his firmly delivered inauguration speech, reminiscent of the dynamic Roosevelt I had known in past years. But I could not help noticing how thin he had become, how tense was his expression, and what a great physical effort he appeared to be making to impress upon his listeners the fact that he was sufficiently well and strong to face the arduous fourth term to which he had been re-elected.

I got no opportunity to speak to the President, who, after his speech, retired to one of the White House reception rooms, where only members of the government, of the Supreme Court, and a few of his closest personal friends were admitted. The diplomatic corps was entertained at a buffet luncheon in the main drawing room.

I talked with Admiral Leahy, with whom I discussed the pending Big Three meeting, to which he would accompany the President. I took this opportunity to draw his attention to the increasingly difficult situation of the Polish nation and government in connection with the imposition of the Soviet-sponsored Lublin Committee as the government of Poland.

As usual, Admiral Leahy showed full understanding of the situation created by this new accomplished fact, and tried to reassure me by saying that the President attached great importance to the satisfactory solution of the Polish problem and was fully informed of its details.

I also ran across Harry Hopkins, who was getting ready to leave Washington immediately on his way to London for conferences with Mr. Churchill before joining the President on his way to the Big Three meeting. He greeted me heartily, in his usual easy and debonair fashion. I buttonholed him and asked him very earnestly to realize the gravity of the Polish problem and to do his utmost in helping to bring about a solution consistent with a free Poland and with democratic concepts as opposed to totalitarian Soviet aims.

Hopkins was in jovial mood. He assured me that he would do his best, although it was no easy matter to oppose Stalin. He then added jokingly: "We have to think of other very important things." I asked him what things could be more important at this time than to lay the foundations for United Nations' collaboration in a secure postwar world on the basis of American principles. He laughed and answered in his humorously cynical way: "Why, we have to prepare the President's election campaign of 1948."

It appeared to me that my friend Constantine Brown, the eminent diplomatic commentator, gave the most accurate definition of the Yalta conference when, referring to a previous remark that it had taken six months to debunk Teheran, he said it required only six days to debunk Yalta.

From the point of view of the interests of the Western Powers, of the principles of democracy, of the Atlantic Charter, of the Four Freedoms, of the rights of smaller nations and "the common man," I regard the Yalta conference as the final act in the bankruptcy record of the policy of appeasement of Russia.

While such a policy might have been justified by the trend of events in the first years of the war, it could never be justified in its final stages, once the Western Allies had gained a solid foothold on the European continent. It could never be understood by those who had been led to battle and had nobly sacrificed their lives and all they possessed for the very ideals which, at Yalta, were finally trampled down and sacrificed on the altar of what was cynically termed the "unity of the Big Three Powers."

The Yalta communiqué in itself was a revelation of failure which, as I realized from numerous conversations with prominent Americans following its publication, was justly appraised as a surrender of American leadership, principles, and prestige. Many Americans admitted that they wondered what was the real price of the concessions granted by the President, and hoped that he had at least obtained something in exchange for this final surrender. Suspicion that secret agreements had been concluded was gaining ground.

On the President's return, when, together with many Ambassadors of foreign countries, I was present at the momentous meeting of the United States Congress to hear the President's report on the Crimea conference, I realized that there was no room for illusion.

The President looked desperately tired, and his speech was on the defensive. For the first time, instead of standing on the speaker's dais to address Congress, he sat in his wheel chair on the floor of the House. Every word he said spelled his profound fatigue and his moral discomfort.

Contrary to Churchill's speech in the House of Commons, in which the British Prime Minister tried to create the impression that the Yalta conference was a success, and especially stressed the "fairness" of the settlement of the Polish problem in presenting it as a square deal for Poland, the President made no such attempt in his Yalta report. He called the Polish solution a compromise—a compromise "which he did not like," but which he felt had become inevitable.

As I left the House of Representatives I knew that Poland had been "sold down the river," that an illegal act had been committed, by virtue of which, contrary to international law and justice, the sovereignty of the Polish nation, vested in its legal government, had been appropriated by the Big Three Powers, without giving the Polish people or their legal representatives the chance of having any say in the matter, without consulting the wishes of the Polish nation, in violation of the principles of self-determination and of all the traditions for which the United States had always stood in the past.

From that moment I knew it was merely a matter of weeks or months before Poland would be handed over, with the consent of the President of the United States and of the Prime Minister of Britain, allied to Poland, as the victim of Soviet domination and a prey of communism.

I discussed this aspect of the Yalta conference with various American officials. They were frankly disturbed by the concessions made to Soviet Russia at Yalta, still mostly unknown to the public, such as the agreement to grant Russia additional votes for some of the Soviet republics in the future United Nations organization, and the cession to Russia of some of the Japanese islands, although the Soviets were not at war with Japan.

In the face of these facts I understood that, if the President had made such concessions in matters so directly affecting American security, Poland could not hope that he would apply to the solution of the Polish cause any of that "toughness" which I had been told he would use at Yalta.

On the President's return I tried again to see him. I repeatedly asked Jimmy Dunn, Durbrow, the chief of the Eastern European Division, and Mr. Bohlen, then liaison officer between the White House and the State Department, who, as I was told, had played a prominent part in the "solution" of the Polish problem at Yalta and in the drafting of all the famous Yalta agreements, to help obtain an audience for me with the President. At first I was told that the President was too busy, but would probably see me shortly. Later I was advised "in a friendly way" not to try to see the President, who was "in a highly nervous state and did not see anybody except a few of his very closest collaborators."

When I discussed the results of the Yalta conference, protesting against the chapter entitled "Poland," and analyzed its meaning and implications from the point of view of international law with Acting Secretary Joseph Grew and other State Department officials, I had the impression that they were embarrassed and at a loss to find arguments to convince me that the Polish cause was not lost. They kept on repeating that the territorial issue could not be waived, that Mr. Churchill had advanced the Curzon Line as a British solution, and the President could not change a decision made by two of his partners. However, they tried to assure me that, at the price of this territorial concession, the United States Government "would see to it that a truly democratic Poland, entirely independent of the Soviets, would be re-established." They explained the fact that the United States had assumed part responsibility for the formation of the "Polish Government of National Unity" as a decision prompted by the President's determination to refuse to recognize any puppet government imposed by Russia.

When I asked how this could be done technically, I was told that the American and British Ambassadors would remain in consultation with Molotov, that possibly they would go to Poland in order to choose the most appropriate Polish personalities before constituting "the new Polish government." I was assured most emphatically that if the first or second attempt to form the new government did not entirely satisfy the American and British governments, that it was in reality a government representative of all Polish democratic parties equally balanced, they would reject it.

I was told that "possibly five, six, perhaps ten governments might be rejected before the United States Government would finally be satisfied and would agree only to a government it considered really representative of the Polish people." Moreover, I was assured the American Government would supervise the holding of "free and unfettered elections" and would never allow Russia to impose her pattern of "one-party elections" in Poland.

However, pressure on the leader of the Polish Peasant party, Mikolajczyk, to accept an unequal partnership in a government of communists and Soviet stooges was daily becoming more apparent, and I felt that the American Government would probably not "risk precious American-Soviet unity" by upholding Poland's right to freedom and democracy.

I encountered considerable difficulty in obtaining firsthand information on what really happened in Yalta, in the weeks which followed the return of the President. Stettinius had gone directly to Mexico City, without stopping in Washington. He was participating in the Pan-American conference on world security, which worked out the resolutions later defined as the Act of Chapultepec. I was very anxious to see him personally because I knew he would tell me frankly the details of the conference which my other friends at the State Department either did not know or tried to conceal from me.

Finally, on March 14, a few days after his return from Mexico City, I called on Stettinius at the State Department. I told him the difficulties I had encountered in getting details of the Yalta conference, and asked him to tell me frankly all he could say on the subject.

Stettinius, in his usual friendly way, told me that the President had been prepared "to fight for the Polish cause." However, on reaching Yalta he found the situation so tense and Stalin so stubbornly resolved "to carry out his designs on Poland," that the President immediately realized that he could not insist on rejecting the Soviet territorial demands without risking a complete break with Stalin. This decided him to accept the territorial demands and to defend, above all, Poland's political independence and her western frontier.

He told me that what had made it even more difficult for the President was the fact that Churchill had expressly accepted the so-called Curzon Line as Poland's eastern frontier and refused to revise his attitude. According to Stettinius, the Yalta agreement on Poland made it possible for the President and Churchill to insist on the formation of "an entirely new Polish Government of National Unity." This had forced them to agree to regard both the legal Polish Government and the so-called Lublin government as unrepresentative.

When I told him that the wording of the Yalta agreement did not clearly state that an entirely "new government" was to be formed but implied that a compromise government, dominated by the Lublin communists, had been accepted, Stettinius kept on insisting that this was not the case and that it was clearly understood among the Big Three that there was to be "an entirely new government and not a reconstructed Lublin government." That, he added, was the only reason which had determined the President not to insist on mentioning the London Polish government at all in the Yalta communiqué.

I saw that, without saying it in so many words, Stettinius was trying to imply that a tacit agreement had been reached on this subject, an agreement which would be favorable to Poland, and that the Ambassadors of America and Great Britain would insist on the participation of truly representative elements of the Polish nation in a newly constituted Polish government. But when I asked him if, in the meantime, the Russians had given any sign they had adopted a similar version of a "new government" for Poland, and if they had agreed to the scrapping of the "Lublin government," he admitted Stalin and Molotov did not appear to interpret Yalta in the same way.

I drew Stettinius's attention to the numerous memoranda I had been communicating to Acting Secretary Grew in his absence, which clearly showed that the government of Soviet stooges in Lublin was busily Sovietizing Poland, liquidating the Polish Underground State, deporting and killing Polish national elements, and disrupting political life—all this on orders from the Kremlin.

He replied he was aware of this situation, and regretted that owing to the illness of Ambassador Clark Kerr there had been some delay in holding meetings of the three foreign diplomats entrusted at Yalta with the task of presenting the Polish people with the "new" government. He said he was sorry that this delay had enabled the Russians to proceed with their policy of Sovietizing Poland. He spoke most highly of Mikolajczyk, saying that the American and British governments were certain that he was the best man to head the new government, but he admitted that the Russians had not agreed to give him so important a place in that government.

When I pointed to the necessity of a more active American policy to save Poland's independence, Stettinius assured me that the President and the American Government understood the situation and that "one could only hope" they would succeed in convincing Soviet Russia to honor the Yalta decisions.

We then discussed the acceptance by the American Government of the Soviet demand that the Polish Government should not be invited to take part in the San Francisco conference. I referred to the strong note which I had personally presented to Acting Secretary Grew on this matter, proving conclusively the illegality of this decision. That note remained without any reply. Perhaps because it was unanswerable.

Stettinius tried to defend the American attitude in this matter. He admitted it was most regrettable that such a decision had to be taken. According to him, the United States Government had to give in, in view of the fear that the Soviets might refuse to participate in the conference altogether. I noted that he was especially anxious that a Polish government should be appointed in accordance with the Yalta terms in time to insure some kind of Polish representation at the conference. He told me the American Government was under considerable pressure of public opinion, especially by members of Congress and by Americans of Polish descent "whose indignation he understood," but added that he could do nothing about it for the time being. He continued that he was hopeful a satisfactory solution could still be reached which would "save Poland's independence."

I realized more fully that President Roosevelt's re-election was not going to modify his policy of appeasement of Russia.

My conversation with Stettinius confirmed my impressions, gained in previous conversations with Acting Secretary Grew and other high officials of the State Department after Yalta, that they were embarrassed, helpless, and still under the psychosis of the power of Russia and of the impossibility of risking an open showdown with the Soviets on any subject.

I had almost daily contacts with the State Department, but I was finding it increasingly difficult to see Stettinius, wholly engrossed by the San Francisco conference, to which he attached the utmost importance and which he was personally supervising in its smallest details, including even technical arrangements and hotel accommodations. Whenever I asked Durbrow, then chief of the Eastern European Division, to arrange for me to see either Undersecretary Grew or any of the assistant Secretaries, he would promise to do so but later invariably said that they regretted, but were "too busy" to see me.

I saw Durbrow continuously, keeping him informed of all that was happening in Poland, and communicating to him, for the Secretary of State, numerous memoranda and messages from my government, describing the tragic situation of our people in Poland under the ruthless communist regime of the Soviets and their puppets. I noticed that even my best friends at the Department of State, such as Undersecretary Grew, Jimmy Dunn, and Freeman Matthews, always friendly and helpful in the past, gradually became "too busy" to receive me.

In this atmosphere of continuous strain, suddenly, on April 12, the death of President Roosevelt was announced.

We all knew in Washington that the President's health had been declining. His frequent absences from Washington and the considerable reduction of his personal contacts were freely commented on. His death, practically on the eve of victory and on the eve of the San Francisco conference, the importance of which had been so played up as a means of cementing the unity of the Big Powers and of opening a new era of collaboration in the establishment of a world-security system, appeared to throw everything out of balance. How would it affect American policy? That was the question uppermost in the minds of everybody in the capital.

I had personally met Mr. Truman when he was Vice-President. I had called on him in February and had had a very pleasant conversation on the problems of Poland. He had shown ready understanding of the situation and had expressed his concern. From what he told me I realized that he was apprehensive of Soviet Russia's policies. By a curious coincidence I had met him on April 11, on the eve of President Roosevelt's death, at a big

luncheon of the Rotary Club, and sat next to him on this occasion. Senator Tom Connally was the chief speaker at this
luncheon. He had chosen this forum to emphasize the importance
of the San Francisco conference and to define America's world
policy. Once more I found Mr. Truman sympathetic to Poland.
He impressed me as a man of sincere and direct approach to all
problems.

He was regarded as a simple American, expected to be less tied
by the trends with which war problems and war necessities had
inspired American foreign policy. Hope was expressed that he
would insist on reasserting American leadership. It was generally expected he would surround himself with new men, who
would replace some of the much-criticized Palace Guard, that
Harry Hopkins and other close personal friends and collaborators
of President Roosevelt would leave the White House. Having
been a senator, Mr. Truman was expected to admit the closer
participation of Congress in shaping American policy.

It soon became evident, however, that the very personal way
in which President Roosevelt had governed for twelve years, and
the secrecy which had surrounded his moves in foreign policy,
made it difficult for the new President to dispense with the
closest collaborators of President Roosevelt, who had been permitted to know some at least of his views, who had been with
him at Big Three conferences, and who now appeared to assume
the role of personal executors of President Roosevelt's policies.

The war was not over, though it had reached its final stage.
It still appeared difficult to initiate new policies, and especially
to halt and reverse the policy of appeasement of Russia, which
had gained such momentum in the last months of President
Roosevelt's life. Harry Hopkins was soon recalled to the White
House and once more became the chief adviser on Soviet affairs.

And yet public opinion was becoming more alive to the realities
of Soviet aims. The results of the Yalta conference were generally regarded as a setback to American foreign policy and
prestige. Hope was expressed in political and press circles that
President Truman would soon re-direct American policy so as to
strengthen United States prestige and leadership.

The San Francisco conference was then considered in Washington as a test case of President Truman's policy. There was

even talk of delaying it on account of President Roosevelt's death and the possible reconstruction of the Cabinet. Harry Hopkins was sent to Moscow, from whence rumors were reaching Washington that the Soviet Government was becoming apprehensive about reported changes in American pro-Soviet sentiment.

I was told that Hopkins was sent to explain the new situation to Stalin. He was to assure him of the new President's desire for good American-Russian relations, and also to imply that the Soviets would do well to modify the unilateral course of their policies, and to realize the importance which the United States Government attached to the San Francisco meeting. He was also to urge the Soviets to send a representative delegation to the Golden Gate.

From my conversations after the return of Harry Hopkins I gained the impression that, while he had frankly warned the Soviets of the change in American public opinion, he reassured them that the new administration in Washington would not alter the line of President Roosevelt's policies. In fact, he appeared to have left Stalin with the conviction that a mere change in tactics would suffice to regain the confidence of the American people.

As a result, Stalin decided to send Molotov at the head of an impressive delegation to San Francisco. Probably desiring to ascertain directly the new situation in Washington, he agreed to send Molotov to a preliminary meeting of the three Big Power Foreign Secretaries in Washington. And the fact that Stalin very shrewdly decided to send Molotov, instead of Gromyko, to San Francisco, was duly hailed in Washington New Deal circles as an "initial triumph of President Truman."

Stettinius and Eden were already in Washington and had started their conversations before Molotov arrived. The arrival of Ambassadors Harriman and Clark Kerr enhanced the importance of the meeting. Molotov was expected to arrive on Friday, April 20. Time was pressing, as the San Francisco conference was to open on the twenty-fifth. Finally, on the evening of Sunday, the twenty-second, Molotov arrived in Washington. Conversations started at once, and Molotov paid a short courtesy call on the President, accompanied by Stettinius. A continuous conference then took place between the three Foreign Secretaries.

I learned that the Polish problem came up in the discussions in connection with the Soviet veto against the invitation of the Polish legal government to the San Francisco conference. No headway was made, but Molotov was finally told not to count on the invitation of the representatives of the puppet Lublin government to the meeting.

From the first moment Molotov took the attitude that the Lublin government, sponsored by Russia, was the legal government of Poland, that it was an entirely independent government, and that it should be represented at the conference. When the American and British Foreign Secretaries explained that this was not the case, and that the Lublin setup was only a temporary administration in accordance with the agreement reached at Yalta, Molotov insisted that President Roosevelt had agreed with Stalin that even if the Lublin government were later to be reconstructed or completed by co-opting "additional democrats from Poland," it had never been said that this provisional government was not to be represented at international conferences. Therefore he said that he had no instructions from Stalin to admit that the Lublin government was not to be represented.

This was a serious controversy which showed that the Soviets would take advantage of President Roosevelt's death to invoke alleged secret commitments made by the President to Stalin, realizing that not even the few officials who had been with the President at Yalta would be in a position to deny their existence. An impasse was reached. The whole matter of the interpretation of the Yalta agreement concerning the future Polish government was once more discussed, Molotov steadfastly refusing to admit that the American and British interpretations were correct in their version that a really "new government" was to be formed, as Stettinius had so earnestly assured me.

Durbrow had recently returned to Washington after two months in Moscow, where he had been sent to help Ambassadors Harriman and Clark Kerr carry out the Yalta agreement on the Polish issue. I learned from him that no understanding had been reached on the formation of the Polish government.

The situation was greatly complicated by the fact that sixteen leaders of the Polish Underground, invited by the Soviet authorities in Poland to confer with them, in order to establish a *modus vivendi* and to help solve the difficult problem of Polish-Soviet relations, had been summarily and treacherously arrested and deported to Russia, the Soviets refusing to admit or to deny this fact when the British and American governments intervened in their behalf.

The Stettinius-Eden-Molotov conversations in Washington showed that there was hardly any prospect of Allied-Soviet understanding. On all subjects Molotov remained obdurate and would make no concessions. This applied not only to the Polish problem, but also to the problems of the occupation of Germany, to Chinese and Korean affairs, to Lend-Lease and long-term credit questions.

It was difficult to see how, in this atmosphere, and in view of the desire of the American Government to avoid making further concessions, the conference of San Francisco could achieve any success. However, the main keynotes adopted were: to achieve Allied unity at any price, and to mark the continuation of Mr. Roosevelt's policy.

My friends at the State Department kept reminding me that President Truman came from Missouri, "renowned for its hard horse trading." But I could not banish from my mind the view expressed by Stettinius that, whatever happened, the American Government had, above all, to achieve "Big Three unity." I knew that the New Deal Palace Guard was still around the White House and had certainly not changed its opinion that Soviet-American unity came first and the defense of principles and ideals "might perhaps be attempted later."

The empty chair of Poland at the San Francisco conference weighed heavily on that assembly. There was something uncanny in the fact that, at the end of a victorious world war, by a unilateral decision approved by democratic America, Poland, an Allied nation, with a splendid record for loyalty and active contribution in the war, was prevented from taking her part in a gathering of nations allegedly held to apply the terms of justice and democracy to a future system of world security.

Although the veto power, insisted upon by Soviet Russia as the privilege of each of the Big Three Powers, had not yet been voted by the conference, Russia had been allowed to use her veto to prevent the participation of Poland's legal government at this, the first great United Nations conference.

At San Francisco, Molotov suddenly disclosed to Stettinius and Eden in a casual way, at a dinner party, that the sixteen Polish Underground leaders, lured into a trap in best kidnaper fashion, had been arrested and deported to Russia, that they were regarded as enemies of the Soviets and would be tried as "traitors" by a Moscow court.

Even this outrage did not appear to affect American and British appeasement of Russia, although Eden made a statement expressing the disapproval of the British Government, and Stettinius reluctantly followed suit with a weaker declaration.

The die was cast. The illusory "unity" of the Big Powers, determined to dominate the postwar world, was being laboriously achieved at the price of fundamental principles of justice and democracy, sacrificed to that precarious "unity."

I listened on the radio in Washington to the opening speech of Stettinius at San Francisco. I heard the Secretary of State of George Washington's, Lincoln's, and Wilson's America declaring that unity must not be sacrificed to idealism.

And yet, this was a meeting sponsored by the United States and Britain, acclaimed by all civilized nations as the great leaders of justice and democracy.

Victorious America and Great Britain had allowed Soviet Russia to impose her totalitarian domination on a major part of the continents of Europe and Asia, and to sow the seeds of future conflicts.

CHAPTER XXXIX

The World Looks to America

THROUGHOUT April and May, and until June 26, when the San Francisco conference closed, the political atmosphere in Washington was as changeable as its climate. As Soviet pressure increased at San Francisco and forced concessions from the United States and Britain on the veto of the Big Powers, on the additional Russian votes for Byelorussia and the Ukraine, I sensed growing uneasiness and, at times, irritation among American officials and politicians.

Some senators and congressmen with whom I discussed the situation were losing patience with the persistently hesitant line of American policy. Criticism was rife regarding the agreements reached at Teheran and Yalta and which, in the light of Molotov's intractability, were now regarded as "futile attempts to placate Stalin."

At times a really "tougher policy" appeared probable, in view of ceaseless Soviet demands. Such hopes were followed by discouragement and even by the sporadic reappearance of isolationist tendencies.

The sudden political crisis in Great Britain complicated matters. The great authority of Winston Churchill, the victorious leader of fighting Britain, had finally been challenged. The pending British elections aroused considerable interest and comment in Washington. The British Embassy almost unanimously expressed the certainty that Churchill would be overwhelmingly reelected "by a grateful British electorate."

I did not share this opinion. Personally, I believed that the traditional political sense of the British people had made them realize the necessity for new leadership in peacetime and that they were pressing for elections because this natural tendency had become widespread. Besides which, the pendulum was swinging leftward everywhere in the wake of the war. The dictatorship of Winston Churchill, indispensable in wartime, had become inappropriate in a peacetime England, beset by internal and social problems.

In America, matters had taken a different course. A President, who had virtually held dictatorial power for nearly thirteen years, had died. A new President had taken over, a man very different from his predecessor, although belonging to the same party and surrounded by the same men who had been closest to President Roosevelt.

However, the world situation had greatly changed. V-E Day dawned on May 8. Japan's resistance was crumbling. It appeared logical, and at times probable, that the new President would redirect American policy to fit a victorious democratic Power which had just played a decisive part in defeating the world's leading militarist totalitarian coalition.

As I watched the evolution of the general situation from my Washington observation post, I realized the implications resulting from the fact that, at that crucial time, the dynamic Churchill was politically paralyzed by the British crisis, while the new American President was having difficulty in ascertaining the extent of his predecessor's international commitments, which were being gradually unearthed from secret files and placed before him.

Mr. Hull was in the hospital, a sick man. He had taken no part in international affairs for a considerable time. Stettinius had been rushed into his post during a period when a Secretary of State would have to act hastily, to travel to distant conferences without having sufficient time to study thoroughly the great new problems facing American foreign policy.

In fact, in that momentous time the only one among the Big Three who could fully develop his dynamism and initiative was Stalin, the totalitarian dictator of Soviet Russia.

As a consequence of this situation a new, unfortunate, and untimely slogan was launched in Washington; namely, that "the United States should act as mediator between Great Britain and Soviet Russia" without taking a more active part in its own right in the working out of solutions of world problems, complicated by the imperialistic trends of Soviet policy. There could be no doubt that this slogan was inspired from pro-Soviet sources and was intended to intimidate American officials. It appeared to be the opening wedge of a policy bent on disrupting Anglo-American unity at the very time when real world security depended on Anglo-American cohesion and closest collaboration more than ever before.

In May and June I had many conversations with American Government officials, with New Dealers, with prominent politicians and newspapermen whom I tried to convince of the necessity of more active American leadership in world affairs. At first I was encouraged as I observed a growing understanding of this necessity among some of them.

I went on repeating that, as a result of the decisive part played by the United States and its armed forces in the war, the American people had become conscious of their great military power. On the other hand, they still failed to realize that America, through her military, naval, and air power, her industrial development, and her financial resources, had attained a new and exceptionally strong position for international negotiation.

I became aware that the tragic events of the last thirty years of world history had disclosed a paradox of democracy. Most unexpectedly, democracy had proved invincible in two world wars against perfectly organized military Powers, but was proving lamentably weak at solving peace problems.

In the course of the twenty years of the peace period following the Versailles Treaty, the democracies proved incapable of defending a sound peace, based on the democratic principles, in defense of which they had not hesitated to fight with indomitable courage at the cost of untold sacrifices.

At the end of World War II democratic statesmanship was once more showing weakness in its timid attempts to win a democratic peace after the victory over the totalitarian imperialism of the Axis Powers.

My conversations with leading American officials appeared to confirm this paradox. In practically every discussion on American-Soviet relations, in connection with the Soviet unilateral policy of accomplished facts, they would throw up their hands and exclaim that there was nothing to be done, as "it was unthinkable for the United States to fight Russia." In my opinion, nothing could better demonstrate that the American people appeared to ignore the force that American arguments would have in peaceful but determined negotiations. They still believed that there were only two alternatives: to agree to all Soviet demands, or to fight Russia.

I regarded this as a sad proof of the inferiority complex of some of the high officials of the great American nation which, in the past, had steadfastly refused to assume the role of a world Power. It also showed profound ignorance of Russian psychology and of Russian methods of negotiation by means of bluff and blackmail.

The misconception of realism on the part of American public opinion was a direct result of the fact that in the course of the war the American Government and its agencies had been overselling Soviet Russia to the American people, for obvious reasons arising from the war situation. As a result, Soviet Russia was generally regarded as a kind of newfangled radical version of democracy with which one could deal in a normal, frank, American way, and persuade her to modify certain tendencies of her policy.

Official Washington appeared to me to be curiously unclear about the real issues at that time. One could detect a growing uneasiness regarding Soviet designs. But instead of leading to a more energetic insistence on American principles, it seemed to encourage passivity.

I urged my American colleagues to realize that America had the right to dictate her terms, not only because she had actually won the war, but especially because her own security depended on the setting up of a democratic world, and not of a Power-political one, pregnant of future wars.

I noted with dismay the unusual phenomenon that American radical and rightist elements joined hands, not in denouncing untimely Soviet imperialism, but in accusing Britain of being a potential mischief-maker, anxious to involve the United States in a war with Russia. Even among highly placed officials and some prominent politicians the antiquated British bogey appeared to obscure their vision. They ignored the fact that the British Commonwealth of Nations was as democratic as the United

States, and that in an American-British association the United States, with its strongest navy, with the greatest and most modern air force, and its unlimited capacity for industrial production, would certainly play first fiddle, while Britain would willingly play second fiddle for the sake of real security.

They did not seem to realize that the joint power of the two English-speaking democracies, consisting of America's newly created military potential, of her vast industrial development and economic and financial resources, with her hemispheric Latin-American backing, added to the power, the prestige, and the experience in international affairs of the British Commonwealth of Nations, with its conveniently distributed defensive bases all over the world, constitutes the natural outer circle of democratic world security, which no single aggressive Power or coalition of aggressive Powers could ever effectively oppose.

On the other hand, they did not appear to understand that a permanent association of democratic America with totalitarian Soviet Russia, on Soviet terms, was unworkable, because, being an abnormal partnership, it could never become a harmoniously functioning basis of democratic world security and peace.

I explained that if realism meant anything, to study the map of the world would be sufficient to understand the basic aims of Soviet Russia, which already then had become so obvious.

As a result of unilateral accomplished facts, Soviet Russia, in addition to her own vast territory of over 8,000,000 square miles, with her population of some 170,000,000, already controlled Finland, Esthonia, Latvia, Lithuania, an important part of Germany, all of Poland, Czechoslovakia, Hungary, Austria, Rumania, Yugoslavia, and Bulgaria. Nazist totalitarianism was already being transformed into a Soviet totalitarianism. This meant that Russia had acquired an additional population of some 150,000,-000 people, whom she controlled by force, whose contacts with the outer world she had entirely severed, and whom she was rapidly and ruthlessly "Sovietizing" with the ultimate aim of forcing them to become part of a greatly extended Soviet system.

It meant that, to the primitive and inefficient Soviet Russian population, the populations of enlightened, democratic, efficient nations of Central Europe were being forcibly added. Their scientific development, their technical skill and greater efficiency were already being used for the rehabilitation, reconstruction, and technical development of Soviet Russia.

A glance at the map showed that, apart from these populations and vast territories, some of which were highly industrialized, Soviet Russia held almost the entire agricultural area of eastern and Central Europe: the territories which supplied most of the potato and wheat crop, most of the cattle, meat, pork, fowl, and timber of Europe. In addition, the vast coal, oil, metallurgical, chemical, and textile industries of those countries were now entirely controlled by Soviet Russia.

That Russia was in earnest as regards her aims was proved by the fact that she had already started to dismantle and to transfer to Russia valuable modern machinery, from the industries of Poland, Hungary, Austria, Czechoslovakia, and Germany.

Under the pretext that they could not find work in their own countries, Russia was deporting thousands of engineers and technicians for work in Russian industry.

What was even more noteworthy, Russia was rapidly building military airports in those countries. She was calling up and training vast local armies; she was training considerable numbers of officers in newly opened officers' training schools in Poland and elsewhere. These officers were taught by Soviet military experts, in accordance with Soviet methods and standards, obviously in order to unify them in due time with the Soviet armed forces. They underwent a course of political indoctrination in communist ideology.

Germany was defeated. The question arose: Against what Power or Powers were these vast armed vassal forces being formed by Soviet Russia under unified Soviet command?

It was becoming ominously evident that Russia had started to carry out what Hitler had failed to do; namely, the most grandiose geo-political plan.

The Haushofer dream of a German Eurasian "Hartland" could have succeeded only if Germany had defeated Russia and had been able to harness her vast resources for the achievement of German world hegemony.

This plan, however, opened greater vistas when centered from Moscow by Stalin than it did when Hitler attempted to establish its center in Berlin. The enormous size of Russia, her wealth in natural resources, her native and foreign slave labor, the inaccessibility of the vast Russian domain, with the almost unlimited possibilities of Siberia for absorbing millions of deported slave workers and technicians, opened incomparably greater possibilities of achievement and presented far greater dangers than Hitler's plan.

Even those Americans who appeared to be somewhat disturbed by such possibilities made the mistake of thinking that "it would take Russia from twenty-five to fifty years to carry out such plans." Nothing was wider of the mark. It might be difficult for Americans to consider those Russian plans otherwise than from the viewpoint of high American standards of living. They were inclined to think that Russia would first have to devote many years to the task of rehabilitation and reconstruction and to the restoration of prewar standards of living before launching such ambitious plans. They appeared to forget that Russia's prewar standard of living was one of the lowest in the world, that it was no higher than her present war standard, and that general poverty and lack of any comforts, let alone modern appliances and luxuries, were, in fact, the normal standards of Russian existence.

Soviet Russia did not regard the attainment of a higher standard of living for her people as a primary aim. On the contrary, the Soviets were much more anxious to lower the standards of living of eastern and Central Europe. They had already started to carry this out in the countries they occupied, and their aims were better served by bringing those comparatively higher standards down to the level of the Russian workers' standards of living.

If Russia were allowed to pursue her plans, with the help of the brains, the labor, and industrial wealth newly acquired in Europe, she might complete her aim of attaining a vast industrial potential and be ready for a possible future war in a few years' time. Russian industrialization would then express itself in a rapid development of production of basic foodstuffs and goods, turned out by countless populations of working men and women, living at extremely low standards of human existence and wages. This was a real threat to the high American standards of living and would tend to deprive the United States of its world markets.

By these arguments, based on cold realism, I tried to show that, for the sake of peace and to prevent future conflicts, it was urgent for the United States and Great Britain, acting together in closest co-operation, to force a clear-cut showdown with Soviet Russia without delay, rather than to apply the bankrupt methods of appeasement, which had failed previously with Hitler's Germany, and allow Russia to choose her own time to make a bid for world hegemony by force or threat of force.

The Soviets had an additional weapon which Hitler had lacked. Contrary to the assertions of pro-Soviet propagandists, even under Stalin Russia had never ceased to be the "Vatican" of communism. Her basic policy of communizing the world by means of revolution or infiltration might, at times, be opportunely shelved, but it had not been given up. She was, in fact, already ruthlessly using this sinister weapon in the countries she had occupied. Communist Sovietization was being rapidly enforced in all of them, and especially in Poland, which appeared to be more openly refractory to communism than others.

Soviet Russia's designs might still be peacefully checked and the future peace of the world could still be saved if the United States was prepared boldly to assume moral leadership in world affairs and to proclaim a new American world peace policy.

During the war official American policy and tactics had followed the line of least resistance when dealing with the Soviets.

American democracy was loath to make use of threats, even when it had the necessary force to back its arguments.

Up to the time of World War I the United States and, indeed, the entire Western Hemisphere, was safe from outside aggression and could complacently rely on its geographical position for its security. This was no longer the case. The experience of two world wars had proved beyond doubt that, under modern conditions of scientific progress, America could no longer escape being involved in every major conflict in defense of her own security. Not only had the United States been involved in the two world wars, but it had played a decisive part in both as regards actual fighting and war production, without which the present war could never have been won by the United Nations.

A Power which was the decisive factor of victory in world conflicts had the indisputable right and indeed the obligation to be

a decisive factor in peace and to determine its conditions according to its views, especially in accordance with the requirements
of its own security.

American security now depended on world security, since
every major conflict involved the United States. America was
not an imperialist Power. She sought no territorial gains by conquest or other means. That in itself entitled the United States
to dictate the conditions of a peace settlement which would
effectively insure its security and uphold the democratic principles of freedom and justice, in defense of which the American
people had sacrificed their lives and spent their resources in two
world wars, and upon which alone a sound and durable peace
could be founded.

The future peace settlement could be based on a world-wide
application of the basic principles of the Monroe Doctrine. America had a right to demand this. As a matter of fact, some of the
important principles of the Monroe Doctrine had been restated
and suggested as the conditions of a world peace settlement by
President Woodrow Wilson in his historic Fourteen Points. They
were again restated in the Atlantic Charter and the declaration
signed by all the United Nations on January 1, 1942.

They constituted the pivot of American ideology, of American
principles, and of the American concept of security.

Their reaffirmation, restatement, and application to world
security would be but the logical outcome of traditional American policy and the safeguard of American and world security.

I suggested that it would be useful to add an official American
redefinition of democracy to a declaration announcing the decision of the United States to demand the application of these
principles on a world scale.

In view of continuous misleading assertions issuing from Soviet
and pro-Soviet sources, all tending to misrepresent communism
as an advanced form of democracy, it had indeed become urgent
that the government of the nation recognized as the leader in the
democratic way of life should authoritatively state its definition.

The importance of such a timely statement should not be
underestimated. An American declaration defining true democracy should expressly state that the American people rejected
other definitions of democracy. This would go a long way to

stabilize democratic ideology among the freedom-loving nations of the world and would enhance American prestige.

It would clear the atmosphere by implicitly reaffirming the profound difference between democracy and communism and between democracy and fascism.

The San Francisco conference had shown up the profound ideological differences between the Soviet Union and the democratic nations. It had also, unfortunately, proved that Soviet agreement and collaboration could be bought only by sacrificing democratic principles to totalitarian doctrines.

The issue was becoming increasingly clear. It was a choice between continued appeasement, which inevitably led to war, and a definite stand on democratic principles and the rallying of all democratic nations in their support.

Russia, weakened by the war, would have to reckon with such a powerful ideological alignment of nations and would undoubtedly prefer to enter the way of concessions, rather than be deprived of the benefits of international collaboration, which she still needed.

Some Americans, for whom any opposition to Soviet Russia had become unthinkable, might consider it provocative even to issue a declaration giving the American definition of democracy. However, in the present world situation, and in view of the mounting concern all over the world as a result of Soviet expansionism, the favorable response which such an American declaration would undoubtedly arouse would surely convince them of its urgency as an element of international stabilization.

I drew attention to the fact that American policy appeared to ignore Europe. I expressed the belief that such a policy would create between the Atlantic and the Russian border a vacuum which Stalin might communize. This would directly affect American security.

I urged that the eleventh hour had struck for reasserting American prestige and moral leadership.

In principle, my arguments and suggestions were well received, generally speaking. But, despite my unceasing efforts, I found nobody in authority in Washington bold enough actively to support them.

CHAPTER XL

Test Case Dismissed

Notwithstanding the daily contact of Molotov with Stettinius and Eden at San Francisco, no progress had been made in clearing up the stalemate on the Yalta decision to set up, under the auspices of the Big Three Powers, a Polish Government "of National Unity." The deep difference in interpretation regarding the character of such a government continued to prevail.

While Britain and America were "hoping," as Stettinius had expressed it, that the Soviets would agree to the formation of an entirely new government in which all the democratic elements of Poland would be represented, including some of the members of the legal Polish Government in London, Molotov obstinately insisted that this was an erroneous interpretation, President Roosevelt having agreed at Yalta to recognize *any* government which Stalin would consider as friendly to Soviet Russia.

According to Molotov, this meant a slight reconstruction of the Soviet government of Lublin, by means of co-opting two or three Polish politicians willing to co-operate in such a setup.

A stalemate having thus been reached, the long-established method was once more resorted to. Harry Hopkins and Charles E. Bohlen were dispatched to Stalin as personal envoys. They were to discuss the details of the next Big Three conference, at which President Truman was for the first time to meet Stalin and to conclude the Yalta settlement on Poland.

When I learned that Hopkins and Bohlen had been chosen for this mission, I had no doubt they would continue to appease Stalin, insisting at most on a face-saving formula, even if it required the nullification of the assurances given me by Stettinius and others of the State Department. I had been repeatedly assured that, whatever happened, "the United States Government would refuse ever to recognize a Polish government predominantly communist and unrepresentative of Poland."

Unfortunately, my apprehensions proved entirely correct, and as a result of Hopkins's mission it was decided that the Soviet stooges, with the addition of only three "ex-London Poles," would be regarded by the American and British governments as the "realistic" fulfillment of the Yalta deal.

The subtle face-saving formula which qualified this final agreement was expressed in one word: The government would be called "provisional."

I was told that this was a great achievement. One could now rest assured that Poland's independence would be safeguarded, because a provisional government could always be dissolved later. Moreover, the Allies "would insist on supervising the Polish elections foreseen in the Yalta agreement" and would see to it that they were "free, unfettered, and democratic."

These American officials appeared to ignore the old saying: "Provisional things last longest." They also conveniently ignored the fact that, under a communist government, however provisional it might be, there could be no question of freedom of speech, of press, or of assembly, indispensable to "free and unfettered elections."

In American official eyes Mikolajczyk had become the sufficient proof that even such a version of the "Yalta-sponsored government" could be regarded as "Polish." If he agreed to participate in it, even in a minor role, Stalin having refused to allow Mikolajczyk to be its Prime Minister, contrary to President Roosevelt's hopes, "why should the American Government worry?" Surely Mikolajczyk, late Prime Minister of the legal Polish Government, leader of the Polish Peasant party, numerically the largest political party in Poland, would add, through his participation, the respectability and Polish character which, without him, the Soviet puppets lacked.

A friend of Harry Hopkins and mine told me that on Harry's return from Moscow he had remonstrated with him for having agreed to conclude with Stalin "a deal so unfair to Poland." He quoted Harry Hopkins's reply: "After all, what does it matter?

The Poles are like the Irish. They are never satisfied with anything, anyhow."

The time had come for the recognition of this so-called "new
provisional Polish government." This necessitated withdrawing
recognition of the constitutional legal government of Poland in
London, already for six months cold-shouldered by the British
and American governments in preparation for this final act.

During this last stage of my official mission in Washington I
did my utmost to persuade the State Department that it was
clearly in the interest of the United States at least not to grant
full *de jure* recognition to the so-called Polish provisional government. It would not prevent the United States from establishing
diplomatic relations with that government, if it was merely
recognized *de facto*. But it would give a "handle" which the
American Government could use, if necessary, to insist on the
holding of elections. It was obviously the thing to do from the
diplomatic point of view and from that of reason and logic. It
would allow Washington to make it clear to the provisional government in Poland, and especially to its sponsor, Stalin, that de
jure recognition could be obtained only after the holding of su-
pervised elections.

Despite all my insistent efforts, I found it impossible to get
any consideration at the State Department for this suggestion.
In the words of Elbridge Durbrow, "the matter of de jure or
de facto recognition was a mere technicality." He told me that
"no such subtleties" had been discussed at Yalta and that "Stalin
certainly would not agree to anything less than full recognition."

When Durbrow, by that time the highest Department of State
official whom I was still admitted to see, thus rejected my suggestion, I recalled another instance of his contempt for what he
termed "mere technicalities."

On the appointment of Arthur Bliss Lane as Ambassador to
Poland I had stressed to Durbrow that, whatever the future
developments, it was essential and consistent with legality to
send him to London to present to the President of the Polish Republic the letters accrediting him as American Ambassador to
Poland.

Mr. Durbrow also summarily rejected this request, saying that the accrediting of Ambassadors to heads of States "was a mere technicality."

In one of my final talks with him, a few days before the actual recognition of the provisional Warsaw government, I once more tried to explain to this very modern diplomat that if the American Government finally yielded to the Soviets on the test case of Poland by granting unqualified de jure recognition to a government imposed on Poland by a foreign Power, a really dangerous precedent would be established for the future, which might force the hand of the United States Government to accept similar situations in other Russian-dominated European countries.

Durbrow rejected my suggestions with great finality.

Still I went on arguing with him, reminding him of the numerous bargaining points which gave America the possibility of insisting on certain fundamentals. But Durbrow, like so many other American officials, replied that there were only two alternatives: to yield to Russia's demands or fight her, which the United States could not do.

"Mr. Ambassador," Durbrow said, "you appear to have an exaggerated opinion of the power of the United States. You are wrong. America is not sufficiently powerful to impose her will on Soviet Russia."

This statement, made by a responsible American official to a foreign Ambassador, after a victorious war, forever impressed itself on my mind. Durbrow had put the crux of the situation in a nutshell. Official America was still unconscious of the almost unlimited power of the United States. It ignored the decisive weight which the word of the United States carried all over the world.

In the last months of my mission in Washington I had to discuss all Polish problems with this high official of the Department of State. Durbrow did his best to be kindly and considerate. But in the last weeks he would sometimes exclaim with disarming juvenile petulance that the Polish problem had to be settled, because it had become "an intolerable headache."

I recalled my earlier conversations with President Roosevelt: his many spontaneous expressions of tribute to and high appreciation of Poland; his written and spoken promises of American support for the cause of Poland's independence; his stirring declaration about Poland's war effort and her "unsurpassed Allied loyalty"; his public definition of Poland as "the inspiration of nations."

I recalled President Roosevelt's promises to the Polish-American Congress of Americans of Polish descent, "that he would never allow Poland again to be dominated by a foreign Power."

What remained of all these and other solemn pledges?

In the words of the youthful official spokesman of the "stream-lined" State Department, Poland had become "an intolerable headache."

Statesmanship had indeed traveled a long downward path in the last five years. . . .

Toward the end of June the Polish Foreign Minister informed me that the withdrawal of recognition of the legal Polish Government by Britain and the United States was imminent.

I asked Durbrow to warn me in time of the precise date so as to allow me to make the necessary arrangements, and also to avoid my hearing it first from the radio and press. He promised to do so.

On July 2, having heard privately that the withdrawal of recognition by the United States was fixed for July 4, I reminded Durbrow that the fourth was American Independence Day. I suggested it would perhaps be more tactful not to withdraw recognition of a legal government on that day, if only as a mark of respect for certain, perhaps naïve, susceptibilities on the part of the Americans of Polish descent and of the Polish people, who attached a sentimental importance to this historic date.

Durbrow appeared somewhat annoyed. He admitted that he had not thought of it, but promised to do his best about it.

On Thursday, July 5, at 2 P.M., President Truman's statement granting recognition to the "provisional Polish government" was broadcast on the radio, and appeared in the early afternoon editions of the press. Two hours later Durbrow telephoned to tell me that I would shortly receive an official note from the Secretary of State.

At 6:15 P.M. I received this final official note, signed by the Honorable James F. Byrnes, one-time Justice of the Supreme Court of the United States, who on July 4 had just assumed his functions as Secretary of State.

By a curious coincidence, the note addressed to me was the first official act of policy initialed by him in his new and exalted position. It informed me of the recognition by the United States Government of the provisional government in Warsaw, and of the withdrawal of recognition of the legal Polish Government.[1]

I replied by an official note at 6:45 P.M.[2] protesting on behalf of my government the illegality of this act.

On the following morning I held my last press conference at the embassy.

In a written statement[3] which I commented upon, I explained to the numerous newspapermen who attended this conference what had really happened to Poland. It was not merely a change of government. By arbitrarily determining Poland's territorial and political status, in violation of her constitutional and sovereign rights, the Big Three Powers had actually interrupted the continuity of the Polish State. They had entirely disregarded the will of the Polish people. They had carried out the fifth partition of Poland. They now imposed upon her an alien, communist-dominated puppet government. I announced that, rather than be, even for a moment, the Ambassador of an illegal communist government, I resigned my functions as Poland's Ambassador in Washington.

The officials of our embassy and all the Polish consuls in the United States resigned with me.

My mission to the United States had come to an abrupt end.

[1] Text of note appended.
[2] Text of note appended.
[3] Text of statement appended.

Appendix

Note from Secretary of State to Ambassador of Poland Notifying Him of the Recognition by the United States Government of the "Provisional Polish Government of National Unity"

THE Secretary of State presents his compliments to His Excellency the Polish Ambassador and has the honor to quote below for the information of the Embassy the text of a public statement the President is to make at 7:00 P.M., Eastern War Time, today:

It is with great satisfaction that I announce that effective today as of 7:00 P.M. Eastern War Time the Government of the United States has established diplomatic relations with the newly formed Polish Provisional Government of National Unity now established at Warsaw. The establishment of this Government is an important and positive step in fulfilling the decisions regarding Poland reached at Yalta and signed on February 11, 1945.

The new Polish Provisional Government of National Unity has informed me in a written communication that it has recognized in their entirety the decisions of the Crimea Conference on the Polish question. The new government has thereby confirmed its intention to carry out the provisions of the Crimea decision with respect to the holding of elections.

Mr. Arthur Bliss Lane, whom I have chosen as United States Ambassador to Poland, will proceed to Warsaw as soon as possible, accompanied by his staff.

For the further information of the Embassy, there is quoted below the substance of a communication the American Chargé d'Affaires ad interim near the Polish Government in London has been instructed to deliver to the Polish Foreign Minister:

Since the Government of the United States of America has, in conformity with the decisions of the Crimea Conference, decided to recognize effective at 7:00 P.M. Eastern War Time, July 5, the new Polish Provisional Government of National Unity as the Government of the Republic of Poland, I have the honor to inform Your Excellency that the Mission of the American Embassy near the Polish Government in Exile in London will terminate as of that time.

The Secretary of State, as can be appreciated, will not be able in the circumstances to transact official business with His Excellency the Polish Ambassador after the effective date of the recognition of the new Polish Provisional Government of National Unity.

J. F. B.

Department of State,
Washington,
July 5, 1945.

Note of Ambassador of Poland in Reply to the Note of the Secretary of State

THE Ambassador of Poland presents his compliments to the Secretary of State and has the honor to acknowledge receipt of the note of the Secretary of State of July 5, 1945, quoting the text of a public statement which the President is to make at 7:00 P.M., Eastern War Time, today, and the text of the communication which the American Chargé d'Affaires ad interim near the Polish Government in London has been instructed to deliver to the Polish Foreign Minister.

In reply to this note informing him that the Government of the United States has recognized effective at 7:00 P.M. Eastern War Time, July 5, the new Polish Provisional Government of National Unity as the Government of the Republic of Poland, and that it has withdrawn the Mission of the American Embassy near the Polish Government in Exile in London as of that time, the Ambassador, acting on instructions of his Government has the honor to state the following:

1) I was appointed to my present functions as Ambassador of Poland to the United States by the legitimate Polish Government which has not recalled me nor instructed me to relegate my functions to any other person. The Polish Government has not ceased to exist for the Polish Nation whose sole constitutional and independent representative it continues to remain. Being an official of the Republic of Poland I am pledged to remain loyal and obedient to that Government and without instructions from it I have no right to relegate my functions and powers to anyone appointed by the so-called Polish government headed by Messrs. Bierut and Osóbka-Morawski.

2) The authority of the Polish Government to which I owe my allegiance is based on the Constitution of April 23, 1935, which the Polish Nation has not changed and which it is not in a position to change freely and according to its own will in the conditions of pressure under which it finds itself today.

On the basis of the aforesaid Constitution the Polish authorities have maintained diplomatic relations with the Government of the United States and on the same basis they concluded agreements with that Government. When Poland entered into the present war against Germany, the Constitution of 1935 was in force. It is also in accordance with this Constitution that the President of Poland, before leaving his country in September, 1939, relegated his powers to the present President of Poland, by appointing him as his successor. The powers of the latter have until now not been questioned by any Power with the exception of the Soviet Union.

Throughout the war the Polish Nation made enormous sacrifices for the cause of Freedom. The Resistance Movement in the Homeland as well as the Polish Armed Forces on all fronts—on land, on sea, and in the air—fought the enemy unceasingly. The occupied Homeland and the leaders of the Resistance in Poland never ceased to recognize the authority of the Polish President and of the Government appointed by him.

Consecutive Polish Governments formed on the basis of this Constitution concluded the principal agreements concerning Poland with other States. Among these, which include in their number also all the bilateral undertakings entered into during the war and concerning military, naval, aviation, financial, economic, and shipping matters, I wish in particular to mention:

a) The Agreement between Poland and the United Kingdom signed at London on August 25, 1939, concerning Mutual Assistance.

b) The Polish-French Protocol, signed at Paris on September 4, 1939, concerning the execution of the Polish-French Alliance.

c) The Agreement between Poland and the USSR, signed at London on July 30, 1941.

d) The Agreement concluded at Washington between the Polish Government and the Government of the United States on July 1, 1942, concerning Lease and Lend, known as "Mutual Aid Agreement."

Furthermore, multilateral agreements to which the Polish Government is a party include:

1) Declaration of the United Nations, signed at Washington on January 1, 1942, embodying the Atlantic Charter and known as the "Declaration by the United Nations."

2) Inter-Allied Declaration against acts of dispossession committed in territories under enemy occupation or control, signed at London on January 5, 1943.

3) The final Act of the United Nations Food and Agricultural Conference, signed at Hot Springs on June 3, 1943.

4) Agreement to set up a United Nations Relief and Rehabilitation Administration, signed at Washington on November 9, 1943.

5) Final Act of the Monetary and Financial Conference of the United Nations, signed at Bretton Woods on July 22, 1944.

6) Agreement on Principles having Reference to the Continuance of Co-ordinate Control of Merchant Shipping, signed at London on August 5, 1944.

7) International Sanitary Convention, signed at Washington on January 5, 1945.

8) The International Agreement and the Final Act of the International Civil Aviation Conference, signed at Chicago on December 7, 1944.

When all the said Agreements were being concluded not one State questioned the validity of the Constitution of 1935 or of the powers of the Polish President and of the Government of his appointment. Neither was any doubt ever raised by such States as to the right of the Polish President and

Government to lead the Polish Nation in the struggle against the German aggressor and to exercise supreme command over the Polish Armed Forces fighting at the side of the Allied Nations.

3) Poland, still now remaining as it does under a foreign occupation and under the ruthless control of foreign military and police forces, is not in a position to change its Constitution by legal means and to choose freely a parliament and executive authority; nor is it in a position to carry out these changes, if it so desired, by revolutionary means. Any changes, therefore, which have occurred in Poland are not the result of the will of the Polish people, expressed legally or by revolution. The war which started in Poland in defense of her independence ended in depriving her of that independence and in placing our country under the direct control of a neighboring Power.

In these circumstances neither my Government nor I, as its Representative, are in a position to recognize such changes.

4) The first attribution of the independence of a State is its freedom to choose its Government. In the present circumstances, the source of the authority of the government headed by Messrs. Bierut and Osóbka-Morawski is a decision made not by the Polish Nation but by three foreign Powers, one of which controls de facto the whole administration of Poland through its army and police forces. The legal basis of the authority of that government cannot be regarded as better founded than that of the so-called governments set up in occupied countries during the war by Germany. In both cases they are based on the will of a foreign Power.

The persecution which thousands of Poles are enduring in Poland today, and which affects in the first place those who have given active evidence of their desire for an independent State by opposing with arms the German invader, is a further proof that the government of Messrs. Bierut and Osóbka-Morawski in no way represents the will of the Nation but constitutes a puppet government imposed on Poland by force from without.

5) In these circumstances, acting upon instructions from my constitutional Government, I protest most solemnly against the recognition of Messrs. Bierut and Osóbka-Morawski by the Government of the United States, for this amounts to recognition of the suppression of Poland's independence and of the foreign rule in Poland which is already being exercised there in actual fact. For the second time in history the Polish Nation is being deprived of its independence, though this time not as a result of events which took place in Eastern Europe alone, but as a result of a war which the United Nations waged in the name of law and justice. Notwithstanding the recognition of this state of things by other States, the Polish Nation will never give up its right to an independent State, and for this right it will struggle unwaveringly.

J. C.

Polish Embassy,
Washington,
July 5, 1945.

Statement of Jan Ciechanowski, Ambassador of Poland, on Leaving His Post as a Result of the Withdrawal of Recognition of the Constitutional Polish Government by the United States Government.

As A result of the withdrawal of recognition of the Constitutional Polish Government by the Government of the United States, I am compelled to leave my post, and I do so with deep personal regret. Before leaving, however, I feel it my duty to stress the tragic situation in which the Polish Nation now finds itself as a result of a world conflict which brought victory to Poland's Allies, while to Poland, who was first to fight and so fully contributed to the common victory, it has brought defeat and loss of her independence.

The fate of Poland will be better understood when it is realized that even defeated Nazi Germany loses less of her territory through this war, than Allied Poland has been forced to give up as a result of victory. Moreover, Poland has been left under the continued uncontrolled occupation of a foreign Power which is imposing upon her a government and a political, social, and economic system alien to her.

Poland's record as a fighting member of the United Nations during this war is unassailable. Her initial armed resistance to German aggression in Poland in September 1939 gave to France and Britain the time necessary to prepare their defenses. Later, her army, navy, and air force fought in Norway, in France, in the Battle of Britain, in Africa, in Italy, in Normandy, Belgium, Holland, and Germany, and her Underground Home Army performed miracles of sabotage, guerrilla, and open fighting against the Germans and substantially aided the Russian armies in their advance through Poland.

While the war lasted Poland's war effort was appreciated by her Allies and declarations of admiration and encouragement were lavished upon the Polish Nation. Poland was called "the inspiration of nations" and was repeatedly promised independence and support after the war. These words of encouragement were accepted at their face value by the Polish people. They firmly believed in the sincerity of the words spoken to them on behalf of America whom they had always trusted and admired.

How can one explain to these indomitable fighters for freedom and democracy that after the United Nations' victory, the principles in defense of which they fought would not be applied to them? How can one explain to the Polish Nation that their country is but a home on wheels to be pushed eastward or westward as may suit the imperialist aims of either of its mighty neighbors in defiance of the principle of self-determination of peoples for which they fought? Someday, answers to these questions will have to be found if justice is to survive.

Insidious propaganda has succeeded in making public opinion believe that the Polish people are always hostile to Russia. While this propaganda has been allowed to develop, the other side of the picture has been almost entirely suppressed. Public opinion still ignores the details of Russia's activities in Poland and of her treatment of the Poles during the war both in Poland and Russia. The fact that the Soviet Government has been steadfastly refusing to admit any Allied or neutral observers inside Poland is in itself ominous. As long as the war lasted, the Polish Government itself contributed to this regrettable blackout of true facts concerning Polish-Soviet relations for the sake of Allied unity so essential to the common victory. Moreover, it hoped that by avoiding friction, it might more easily reach an understanding with Russia which it sincerely desired.

Public opinion too easily forgets all the attempts made by the Polish Government and people to reach an understanding with Soviet Russia on normal lines and within the framework of international law. It forgets that these efforts were invariably rejected by Russia who then placed the blame and responsibility for failure to reach agreement upon the Polish Government, regardless of whether it was the government of General Sikorski, Mr. Mikolajczyk, or Mr. Arciszewski. Each of these truly democratic governments was accused of being composed of "fascists," "collaborationists," and "reactionaries." At any time during this war the problems requiring settlement between Poland and Soviet Russia could probably have been solved if Russia had admitted representatives of the legal Polish Government and Underground to sit down with her representatives and to tackle these problems in an atmosphere of mutual good will. But Russia preferred to present them—not as Soviet-Polish controversies, but as the quarrels of opposing factions of Poles between themselves.

Poland, represented by her legal Government, was never admitted to participate in discussions of Polish-Soviet relations. The conferences at Teheran and Yalta are examples in point. The decisions concerning Poland must therefore be regarded by the Polish Nation as verdicts "in absentia." No nation, no Government truly representative of its people, could ever accept decisions about their territory or system of government being taken without their participation.

The Polish people are deeply attached to their traditions of individual and national freedom. They will never cease to fight for these ideals. They will never sacrifice them as the price of agreement. They will never accept any system of government contrary to these principles and imposed upon them by any foreign power or group of Powers.

On June 29th Mr. Raczkiewicz, the constitutional President of the Polish Republic, issued from London an official Declaration to the Polish Nation, in the last paragraph of which he said:

. . . I remain at my post in accordance with both the provisions of the Constitution now in force, and, I think, in accordance with the will of an immense majority of the Polish people. I am confident that this decision of mine will be understood throughout the world by all those who hold freedom, justice, and law in higher esteem and regard than brute force or temporary victory of violence. It will be the duty of citizens of the Polish Republic, so grievously suffering under so many blows, to see to it that the great traditions of our national culture should not be lost, that

our links with our past should not be severed, that our ideals of freedom are not betrayed; it will be their duty to maintain their allegiance to the lawful authorities of the Polish Republic and not to weaken in their strivings for the restoration to the Polish Republic of its rights and for the place due to it among the free nations of the world. We are living through a period of great dangers and difficulties for our nation and our State, but I firmly believe that Almighty God will bless our efforts and will cause Poland to emerge from this new ordeal victorious, secure, and with her rights undiminished.

As Ambassador of Poland and personal Envoy of the President of Poland, on leaving my post of Ambassador to the United States, my conduct will be entirely guided by the directives given by the constitutional Head of the Polish State to all Polish people.